D1558712

THE PUBLIC LIFE OF
Aedanus Burke

Aedanus Burke
1743–1802

Courtesy of the Hibernian Society,
Charleston, South Carolina

THE PUBLIC LIFE OF
Aedanus Burke

REVOLUTIONARY REPUBLICAN IN POST-REVOLUTIONARY SOUTH CAROLINA

JOHN C. MELENEY

UNIVERSITY OF SOUTH CAROLINA PRESS

Library of Congress Cataloging-in-Publication Data

Meleney, John C., 1921–
   The public life of Aedanus Burke : revolutionary republican in
post-revolutionary South Carolina / by John C. Meleney.
     p.   cm.
   Bibliography: p.
   Index.
   ISBN 0-87249-610-4
   1. Burke, Aedanus, 1743–1802. 2. South Carolina—Politics and
government—1775–1865. 3. United States—Politics and
government—1783–1809. 4. Legislators—United States—Biography.
5. United States. Congress. House—Biography. 6. Judges—South
Carolina—Biography. I. Title
E302.6.B876M45   1989
328.73'092—dc20
  [B]   89-4863
                                           CIP

Published in Columbia, South Carolina, by the
University of South Carolina Press

Manufactured in the United States of America

First Edition

The University of South Carolina Press gratefully acknowledges
a grant from the Hibernian Society of Charleston, S.C.

Contents

Maps

Preface and Acknowledgments

This is the study of a public life, not a personal biography. Simply stated, the materials for a personal biography are not reasonably available for study. Those that are available, supplemented by the general historical record provided in governmental archives, newspapers, and the writings of contemporaries, are sufficient for the reconstruction of a public life.

The historian can trace the activities of historical figures, but the actors can be judged best on the basis of their own words when put in proper context. This is particularly true of Burke, who was the subject of few contemporary accounts other than those scattered through the newspapers of the period. Accordingly, quotations are extensive, and quoted passages are frequently connected by words that closely paraphrase the original text. Every effort has been made to assure that the quotations are accurate and that paraphrases fairly represent the words for which they have been substituted. For the convenience of the reader some abbreviations have been written out and some (but very few) obvious spelling or typographical errors corrected. The writer's punctuation and capitalization of words has been retained. There are no *"sics"* to interrupt the flow, and no emphasis has been added. Italicized and capitalized words and phrases appearing in quoted passages are all from the originals.

In his writings, Burke employed three distinct styles and appeared equally comfortable with each of them. One was the more or less formal style found in his surviving legal opinions and official communications where personality was subordinated to the purpose of the document and only occasionally appeared. Another was a style of simple eloquence, found particularly in his charges to grand juries and written to be spoken under circumstances where personality was permissible but restraint was required. Finally, there was the polemical style of his pamphlets, argumentative, colorful, full of imagery and the rhetorical devices characteristic of the time, occasionally strident and angry. This facility makes the identification of Burke's writings difficult and none has been ascribed to him without strong corroborating evidence. But there are some that he might have written, and a few have been identified as possibly his.

All statements as to lack of evidence for any stated proposition, such as "there is no evidence that" and other combinations of like tenor, should be taken to mean only that no such evidence was found. All errors are, of course, the sole responsibility of the author.

Robert M. Weir first introduced me to Aedanus Burke, and George C. Rogers, Jr. furthered the acquaintance by opening to me his extensive file of materials collected during years of research on the history of South Carolina and South Carolinians. As director of this study in its academic phase, Dr. Weir has been unfailingly helpful, appropriately skeptical, and extraordinarily patient. Even in retirement, Dr. Rogers has been always willing to take the time for discussion of an obscure point or to read another draft. I have words to acknowledge my debt to these eminent scholars but none to express adequately the depth of my gratitude for all that they have contributed.

I am of course also deeply indebted to many others. Constance B. Schulz, Herbert A. Johnson, and Charles B. Weasmer all ran the course with me and strove to keep me on the track with thoughtful comments, helpful suggestions, and timely questions. Kenneth Bowling read an early version of the chapters on Burke's service in the First Congress to my great benefit. If their efforts failed in any respect, the fault is mine.

Since there is no core collection of Burke manuscripts, access to various special collections was particularly valuable. Charlene Bangs Bickford and Helen E. Veit opened to me the files of the First Federal Congress Project at George Washington University. John P. Kaminski and Richard Leffler arranged for an examination of the files of the Ratification of the Constitution Project at the University of Wisconsin. David R. Chesnutt and the entire staff of the Laurens Papers Project at the University of South Carolina unfailingly offered guidance through and provided materials from that collection on request.

I have haunted the premises of the South Caroliniana Library, the South Carolina Department of Archives and History,

Preface and Acknowledgments

and the Charleston Library Society, burdened the staff of each with my requests, and benefited from assistance freely given, always with friendly courtesy. I am grateful to them all. Special thanks are due to Allen H. Stokes of the South Caroliniana Library who more than once has gone out of his way to locate and obtain relevant materials. Jerry Ulrey, of the Cartographic Laboratory in the University of South Carolina Department of Geography, prepared the maps for publication.

A generous grant from the Hibernian Society, Charleston, South Carolina, to the Press has materially contributed toward the cost of publication. I am grateful to the Society for this support. I am also grateful to the Institute for Southern Studies at the University of South Carolina, where I have been provided with the facilities necessary to complete the manuscript and prepare it for publication, and to Walter B. Edgar, the director of the Institute, for his encouragement and support.

Lastly, but by no means of the least importance, I acknowledge my debt of gratitude to Sue Thompson, practically perfect legal secretary and master of word processing thaumatology. She has typed every word, pursued typographical errors with diligent persistence, checked citations, and cheerfully managed the entire manuscript. Her assistance was invaluable.

John C. Meleney

Columbia, South Carolina

Abbreviations

Annals.	*The Debates and Proceedings in the Congress of the United States . . . March 3, 1789, to March 3, 1791, inclusive,* Joseph Gales, comp., 2 vols. (Washington: Gales and Seaton, 1834).
Bio. Directory.	*Biographical Directory of the South Carolina House of Representatives,* Vol. I, *Session Lists, 1692–1783,* Joan Schriever Reynolds Faunt, et al., comps. (Columbia: University of South Carolina Press, 1974); Vol. II *The Commons House of Assembly, 1692–1775,* Walter L. Edgar and N. Louise Bailey, eds. (Columbia: University of South Carolina Press, 1977); Vol. III. *1775–1790,* N. Louise Bailey and Elizabeth Ivey Cooper, eds. (Columbia: University of South Carolina Press, 1981); Vol. IV. *1791–1815,* N. Louise Bailey, ed. (Columbia: University of South Carolina Press, 1984).
Burke, *Address.*	"Cassius" [Aedanus Burke], *An Address to the Freemen of the State of South Carolina Containing Political Observations on the following Subjects, viz. On the Citizens making a temporary submission to the British Arms, after the reduction of this Country in 1780. On Governor Rutledge's Proclamation of the 27th of September, 1781. On the Mode of Conducting the Election for the Assembly at Jacksonborough.*

On the Exclusion Act, which cuts off the Citizen from the Rights of Election. The Confiscation Act. The Amercement Act. And concluding with Remarks to Prove the Necessity of an Amnesty or Act of Oblivion (Charleston: n.p., 1783; reprinted, Philadelphia: Robert Bell, 1783).

Burke, *Considerations*. "Cassius" [Aedanus Burke], *Considerations on the Society or Order of Cincinnati; lately instituted by the Major-Generals, Brigadier-Generals, and Other Officers of the American Army* (Charleston: A. Timothy, 1783).

Burke, *Salutary Hints*. [Aedanus Burke], *A Few Salutary Hints, Pointing out the Policy and Consequences of admitting British Subjects to Engross our trade and become our Citizens. Addressed to those who either risqued or lost their all in bringing about the Revolution* (Charleston: Burd and Haswell, 1785; reprinted, New York: S. Kollock, 1786).

CEG. *Charleston Evening Gazette* (1785–1786).

CGDA. *City Gazette and Daily Advertiser* (successor to *CMP* in 1787).

CH. *Columbian Herald* (1784–1796).

CMP. *Charleston Morning Post and Public Advertiser* (successor to *SCGPA* in 1786).

Elliot, *Debates*. *The Debates in the Several State Conventions on the Adoption of the Federal Constitution . . . ,* Jonathan Elliot ed., 2nd ed., 5 vols. (Philadelphia: J. B. Lippincott, 1836).

GSSC. *Gazette of the State of South Carolina* (1777–1800, 1783–1785).

Abbreviations

HSP.	Historical Society of Pennsylvania, Philadelphia.
JCC.	*Journal of the Convention of South Carolina which Ratified the Constitution of the United States, May 23, 1788,* indexed by A. S. Salley, Jr. (Atlanta: Foot & Davis Company, 1928).
JHR 1782.	*Journals of the House of Representatives of South Carolina, January 8, 1782–February 26, 1782,* A. S. Salley, ed. (Columbia: The State Company, 1916).
JHR 1783–1784.	*Journals of the House of Representatives, 1783–1784,* Theodora J. Thompson, et al., eds. (Columbia: University of South Carolina Press, 1977).
JHR 1785–1786.	*Journals of the House of Representatives, 1785–1786,* Lark Emerson Adams, et al., eds. (Columbia: University of South Carolina Press, 1979).
JHR 1787–1788.	*Journals of the House of Representatives, 1787–1788,* Michael E. Stevens, et al., eds. (Columbia: University of South Carolina Press, 1981).
JHR 1789–1790.	*Journals of the House of Representatives, 1789–1790,* Michael E. Stevens, et al., eds. (Columbia: University of South Carolina Press, 1984).
JHR 1791.	*Journals of the House of Representatives, 1791,* Michael E. Stevens, et al., eds. (Columbia: University of South Carolina Press, 1985).
JHR 1792–1794.	*Journals of the House of Representatives, 1792–1794,* Michael E. Stevens, ed. (Co-

---

	lumbia: University of South Carolina Press, 1988).
Journals of Congress.	*Journals of the Continental Congress*, Worthington Chauncey Ford, et al., eds., 34 vols. (Washington: United States Government Printing Office, 1904–1937).
Journals 1776–1780.	*Journals of the General Assembly and House of Representatives, 1776–1780*, William Edwin Hemphill, et al., eds. (Columbia: University of South Carolina Press, 1970).
JPC.	*Journals of the Privy Council, 1783–1789*, Adele Stanton Edwards, ed. (Columbia: University of South Carolina Press, 1971).
MHS.	Massachusetts Historical Society, Boston.
NYHS.	New York Historical Society, New York.
SCA.	South Carolina Department of Archives and History, Columbia.
SCAGG.	*South Carolina and American General Gazette* (pre–1780).
SCGGA.	*South Carolina Gazette and General Advertiser* (1783–1785, with minor name changes after October 1784).
SCGPA.	*South Carolina Gazette and Public Advertiser* (successor to *SCWG* in 1784).

Abbreviations

SCHM.	*South Carolina Historical Magazine* (formerly *South Carolina Historical and Geneological Magazine*).
SCHS.	South Carolina Historical Society, Charleston.
SCL.	South Caroliniana Library, Columbia.
SCSG.	*South Carolina State Gazette and Timothy and Mason's Daily Advertiser* (successor to *SGSC* in 1794).
SCWG.	*South Carolina Weekly Gazette* (1783–1784).
SGSC.	*State Gazette of South Carolina* (successor to *GSSC* in 1785).
Statutes at Large.	*The Statutes at Large of South Carolina,* Thomas Cooper and David McCord, eds., 10 vols. (Columbia: A. S. Johnston, 1836–1841).
WLCL.	William L. Clements Library, University of Michigan, Ann Arbor.
WMQ.	*William and Mary Quarterly,* 3rd Series.

The Public Life of
Aedanus Burke

Introduction

Generations of historians have studied the Revolutionary, Confederation, and Federalist eras in South Carolina, and each of them has known Aedanus Burke. His name appears and reappears in accounts of these periods with greater or lesser frequency depending on the individual historian's point of focus and selection of materials. In the panoramic views, he appears as a secondary figure, passing across the stage from time to time, and his presence is noted with a few good lines. Several incidental pieces, essentially unrelated to any larger context, assign him a more important role. But there has not as yet appeared any study of his career as a whole or any assessment of his historical significance that places him at center stage. Two plausible reasons may explain this simple fact, one essentially substantive and the other essentially methodological.

First, as a public figure, Burke variously appeared during the course of his career in South Carolina in the roles of soldier, legislator, judge, pamphleteer, Antifederalist, and pungent commentator on the local and national scene. Like the ubiquitous leading character in a popular historical novel, he turned up wherever and whenever important events occurred in the civil history of South Carolina between 1776 and 1800. On occasion, he was highly visible and remains so to the historian. But he was never a leader of the first rank, never on intimate terms of association with the Rutledges, Pinckneys, Laurens's, Middletons, and their establishment peers. Nor did he achieve any singular military distinction comparable to that of Marion, Pickens, Sumter, or even lesser partisans. On the bench, he was overshadowed initially by Thomas Heyward and Henry Pendleton and later by John Rutledge. No links have been found to active revolutionary leaders such as Christopher Gadsden and William Henry Drayton. Indeed, Burke's verifiable close personal associates were few. He was essentially a secondary figure, seldom a mover and shaker of events.

Second, the study of Burke's life presents serious practical problems to the researcher. Most importantly, there is no core of personal papers to serve as a point of departure. By his own direction his personal documents were destroyed soon after his death. His will was explicit in this regard.

> There is deposited by me in the new State Bank a small
> redish hair trunk containing some manuscripts of my own
> and many correspondences to and from my friends. If I
> lived I could make my own writings lucrative to me; but in
> case of my death, they may and would fall into hands, who
> thro' malice and self-interest, would not fail to make, not a
> good, but a very bad use of them, for this reason my will is,
> that my Executor will take all care, to have the trunk and all
> the papers in it, without unlocking or opening the said
> trunk, and without perusing any of the papers, destroyed
> by fire and reduced to ashes, and this burning to take place
> within three weeks (21 days) after my will shall have been
> proved in Charleston . . . it will take a very strong fire to
> consume some of these papers, there are three volumes in
> the trunk stitched and finished by a bookbinder. Neither
> wood nor coal alone will do, both these combustibles
> together make the hottest fire.[1]

His friend O'Brien Smith was his executor. "I have too much confidence in my Executor to doubt," Burke said, "but that he will duly execute the request I make."[2] Presumably his confidence was well placed; no corpus of documentary materials remotely resembling his own description of his accumulated papers has yet been discovered.

There are, however, three well known pamphlets, two published in 1783 and one in 1785. There are the journals and records of South Carolina's General Assembly, in which Burke served for most of the period 1778 to 1788, and of the First Congress of the United States, in which he served as a member of the House of Representatives between March 1789 and March 1791. Newspapers contain a wealth of data concerning Burke and illuminating

---

1. Aedanus Burke, Last Will and Testament, January 13, 1802, Charleston Will Transcripts, 28: 285–87, SCA.
2. Ibid.

Introduction

the events and circumstances of his life. Various published collections of documents contain relevant materials. Reports of early judicial decisions include a few of Burke's written opinions. Beyond these sources, the surviving Burke papers are scattered throughout a multitude of collections at a variety of widely separated locations. Even these consist principally of letters written by Burke unaccompanied by either the communication to which he was responding or the communication sent in reply. In one notable exception, a letterbook of Pierce Butler, there are a number of letters written to Burke in the mid-1790s, but none of those mentioned as having been received from him. Internal references in correspondence exchanged between contemporaries are even more elusive. Any full reconstruction of Burke's life would therefore involve an almost endless quest for isolated bits and pieces that might ultimately be assembled in a mosaic of innumerable small fragments. Nonetheless, there is enough to enable the story of his public life to be told with reasonable confidence that future discoveries will not materially alter it. That is the primary goal of this study and, as it has developed, the risk is that it underestimates his significance rather than the reverse.

Burke's very presence as a public figure in post-Revolutionary South Carolina sometimes challenges belief. Somewhat unpredictable and more than somewhat eccentric in the context of his time, Burke was also the subject of a rich anecdotal record that supplements the verifiable historical record of his life.[3] Most of the anecdotal tales exist in a variety of forms. They include incidents in court, chance encounters in the backcountry, fisticuffs with ferrymen and others, drinking bouts and their aftermath, and examples of sociability and humor. The im-

---

3. "Diary of Edward Hooker, 1805–1808," J. Franklin Jameson, ed., *Annual Report, American Historical Association, 1896* (Washington: United States Government Printing Office, 1897), 885–87; Alexander Garden, *Anecdotes of the Revolutionary War in America* (Charleston: A. Miller, 1822; reprint ed., Spartanburg: The Reprint Company, 1972), 192–97; E. S. Thomas, *Reminiscences of the Last Sixty-Five Years*, 2 vols. (Hartford: Case, Tiffany and Burnham, 1840), 1: 62–64; Joseph Johnson, *Traditions and Reminiscences Chiefly of the American Revolution in the South* (Charleston: Walker & James, 1851; reprint ed., Spartanburg: The Reprint Company, 1972), 429–37; John Belton O'Neall, *Biographical Sketches of the Bench and Bar of South Carolina*, 2 vols. (Charleston: S. G. Courtenay & Co., 1859), 1: 35–38; Benjamin F. Perry, *Reminiscences of Public Men*, Second Series (Greenville: Shannon & Co., 1889), 13–17; B. F. Perry, "Aedanus Burke," in U. R. Brooks, *South Carolina Bench and Bar* (Columbia: The State Company, 1908), 5–8.

3

portance of the anecdotal record lies not in whether the incidents related were in fact literally true but in that the stories were told and retold, even after Burke's death, and disclose something of his character and personality. No comparable anecdotal record exists for any of Burke's South Carolinian contemporaries.

Burke's public career in South Carolina covered a span of twenty-four years, from March 1778 to March 1802. Except for a two-year period of service in the First Congress of the United States, he was a judge in the highest courts of the state; and twenty of the twenty-two years of his judicial service were rendered in the crucially important civil and criminal common-law courts. In addition, he was one of three commissioners charged in the 1780s with responsibility to digest the state's laws and propose revisions appropriate to its newly won status as an independent polity, an undertaking of paramount importance that had its counterpart in all the states of the Confederation. The report of that commission has not survived, but its work was constructive and important to the state's legal history. In substantive terms, Burke's service on the bench was almost surely the most important part of his public career and, ironically, is the least visible to the historian.

Outside his judicial role, Burke's politics were largely reactive and oppositionist. In his legislative roles, he was seldom the persevering advocate of a defined goal and never an accomplished practitioner of parliamentary management. Most commonly, he responded to events as they occurred and then retired from the field. Similarly, in his pamphlets and other nonjudicial writings, he addressed issues of the moment that stimulated him sufficiently to produce an expression of his views. In substance, he applied the lawyer's arts in the realm of public affairs to identify problems and warn of consequences.

Burke's oppositionist turn of mind was admirably suited to the "paranoid style" of causal explanation common to the late eighteenth century. As Gordon Wood has pointed out, this explanatory paradigm was not pathological but the natural outgrowth of Enlightenment conviction that men could predict and control the course of human events and were therefore directly responsible for the consequences of their actions. Thus, events and combinations of related events could be explained as the product of the intentions or designs of the leading actors, and social processes could be analyzed as the manifestation of individual passions or interests. Being hidden in the mind of the actor, motive or intent could only be discovered indirectly by inference from subjectively observed effects or potential effects. By the late eighteenth century, Wood concluded, American secular thought was structured in such a way that conspiratorial explanations of complex events became normal, necessary, and rational. And a system of politics featuring circumspection, dissimulation, discretion, and good manners in turn encouraged a politics of opposition dedicated to the unmasking of hypocrisy.[4] In such an intellectual environment, there was little room for simple mistakes of fact, for errors of judgment, or for the concept of unintended or unexpected consequences in the conduct of political affairs. In the context of republican ideology, there was virtually none.

Republican thought evolved over time in the colonies, slowly through the middle years of the eighteenth century and more rapidly after 1763. Nevertheless, it remained amorphous, "vague and supple" in the words of Robert Shalhope. Only one thing was certain, Shalhope wrote in 1972. Americans rejected both monarchy and hereditary aristocracy as component elements of political and social organization. But that was the limit of consensus. There was no agreement on the form of republican government or the nature of republican society. The republican creed was therefore both deceptively simple and inherently ambiguous.[5] It clearly assumed that the new American polities

4. Gordon S. Wood, "Conspiracy and the Paranoid Style: Causality and Deceit in the Eighteenth Century," *WMQ*, 39 (1982): 401–41. James H. Hutson, "The Origins of "The Paranoid Style in American Politics': Public Jealousy from the Age of Walpole to the Age of Jackson," in David D. Hall, John M. Murrin, and Thad W. Tate, eds., *Saints and Revolutionaries: Essays on Early American History* (New York: W. W. Norton, 1984), 332–72, discusses the "paranoid style" in early American politics from a somewhat different perspective. Fear of aggressive power induced anxiety that was reflected in suspicion of all power, i.e., "jealousy."

5. Robert E. Shalhope, "Toward a Republican Synthesis: The Emergence of an Understanding of Republicanism in American Historiography," *WMQ*, 29 (1972): 49–80, quote at 72. Shalhope described the historiographic evolution of a republican "synthesis," which is articulated in its most fully developed form in Bernard Bailyn, *The Ideological Origins of the American Revolution* (Cambridge: Harvard University Press, 1967), and Gordon S. Wood, *The Creation of the American Republic, 1776–1787* (Chapel Hill: University of North Carolina Press, 1969). These and subsequent studies of republicanism in early America are followed in the ensuing discussion. Ten years later, Shalhope found the "synthesis" of 1972 no less vital but substantially more complex and problematic. See Robert

would be republics, polities in which the people would be constitutionally entitled to participate through an established electoral process. But it was neither consciously democratic in any modern sense of the term nor incompatible with the generally prevailing hierarchical structure of society in which men of learning, experience, and property were expected to lead.

Eighteenth-century republicanism incorporated elements drawn from the natural rights theories of the Enlightenment and from the ethical and millennial precepts embedded in Puritan thought. At its core, however, lay a comprehensive theory of politics that informed and guided both thought and action. Derived from ideas of the Commonwealthmen of seventeenth-century England, refined in the eighteenth century by "country" opponents of Robert Walpole's "court" party, and transmitted by them to the North American colonists, the theory postulated that all politics revolved around issues related to the disposition of power. Conceptually neutral and even a necessary attribute of government, power in action was aggressive, relentless, and pervasive. It throve on the innate weakness of human nature, man's susceptibility to corruption and lust for self-aggrandizement. Where power was the province of government, liberty was the right of the people. But liberty was fragile, always exposed to the aggressive expansion of power. Thus the republican creed assumed a continual struggle between power on the one hand and liberty on the other, with power always tending to encroach on liberty and liberty always on the defensive.[6]

A number of ancillary propositions evolved from the conceptualization of power as necessarily aggressive and corrupting. Since power would inevitably strive to encroach on liberty, the danger to liberty was all the greater should power be lodged in a few hands for long periods of time and the legislative, or popular, branch be reduced to servile dependence on the executive. Accordingly, the electoral process required protection against men in power lest wealth and patronage corrupt the guardians of popular rights. Elections should be frequent and rotation in office assured by limiting or foreclosing the ability of elected offi-

E. Shalhope, "Republicanism and Early American Historiography," *WMQ*, 39 (1982): 334–56.

6. Bailyn, *Ideological Origins*, 55–67. The evolution of South Carolina's particular version of country ideology is described in Robert M. Weir, *Colonial South Carolina: A History* (Millwood, N.Y.: KTO Press, 1983), 132–40, 344.

cials to succeed themselves. Property requirements for voting
and for office were appropriate to assure that those participating
in the political process and entrusted with authority would have
a sufficient stake in society to warrant confidence that they would
exercise independent judgment in the public interest. Parties and
factions were cabals organized to advance private interests. A
standing army, historically a mercenary force controlled by executive authority, was a potential instrument of oppression, particularly in time of peace. Good republicans deplored the very
concept of a standing army and endorsed the militia, citizens in
arms defending their liberty and property, as the acceptable institution for the defense of a republic and the maintenance of domestic order.

The stability of republican institutions depended on balance
and civic virtue, carefully guarded by constant vigilance. Once a
proper distribution of power was achieved, any change threatened to disrupt the delicate balance and expose liberty to risk.
The danger of disruption was always present. The threat might
be posed by designing men pursuing special privilege at the expense of the populace or abusing their trust for private purposes
unrelated to the public good. Conversely, lawlessness and extralegal political action on the part of the people against established
authority constituted licentiousness and threatened anarchy that
would inevitably end in despotism. Public virtue, conceptually
embodying the community's commitment to the common good,
supported the republican balance and was a necessary condition
to its preservation. Subject to corruption by extravagance, personal ambition, pursuit of private interests in preference to the
public good, the designs of encroaching power, or lawless disregard of civic responsibility, public virtue, like liberty, was always
at risk. In circumstances so fraught with danger, the security of a
republican polity, particularly when new born and experimental,
required unceasing watchfulness lest liberty be undermined by
aggressive power or popular licentiousness, by the conspiracies
of the few or the excesses of the many. Subject to seduction by
those seeking or abusing power, the people could only be
warned when threatened by the seducer's wiles; and survival required that warnings be frequent and timely.

In the hands of the American colonists, the republican theory of politics received from Britain, though never widely influential there, was admirably adaptable to their own stance in

opposition to the aggressive demands of British power. The precepts of republicanism, reinforced by a conspiratorial mode of causal analysis, coalesced into an ideological construct of related values and perceptions that ultimately shaped their response. As perceived by the colonists, corrupted and corrupting ministers of state and their agents appeared determined to challenge their constitutional rights as Englishmen, to undermine their independence, and thereby to reduce them to a dependent condition of slavery. Remote from the center of power, their appeals rejected, the only recourse of the colonists was to revolt.[7]

The locus of danger was simple enough to identify prior to the Revolution and through the ensuing years of war. Attention could easily be concentrated on British designs to subvert American freedom, and the ideology of republicanism was a unifying force during the years of conflict. With independence won, the political environment suddenly became more ambiguous and the sources of potential corruption both more numerous and less clearly identifiable as each of the newly independent states established its own institutions of civil government. Based as it was on a fundamental principle of human nature, the ideological frame of reference required that each of these new institutions of government be watched with jealous care. Since the republican creed taught nothing of the use of power, only that it was sure to be abused, some confusion and uncertainty was inevitable when rulers and ruled became interacting components in the same political community and the theoretical concepts of republican government encountered the realities of local interests and concerns. In the 1780s, the unity of the war years was diluted by sectional, cultural, and social differences and by variations in the weight attached to various strands of the ideological frame of reference.[8] The resulting conflicts were nowhere more evident than in South Carolina. "When some violent convulsion or revolution has been effected in the government of a country," a thoughtful South Carolinian observed in 1787, "some time must always intervene before new ideas can be received, new forms established, and the machine of government brought back to a regular motion." In the

---

7. Bailyn, *Ideological Origins*, pp. 94–143.
8. Bernard Bailyn, "The Central Themes of the American Revolution: An Interpretation," in Stephen G. Kurtz and James H. Hutson, eds., *Essays on the American Revolution* (Chapel Hill: University of North Carolina Press, 1973), 3–31, at 18–23.

Introduction

interim, political affairs would be unsettled. Defects in the new system would appear; changes would be required; and the government would fluctuate "between the two extremes of anarchy and slavery, until by improper measures it is suffered to fall into one or the other, or by skilful management at length rendered stationary at the proper point."[9] The post-war history of South Carolina featured precisely the tensions so graphically summarized.

Similar problems confronted all the new states, individually and collectively. To many observers, local popular excesses threatened republican values and the stability of republican institutions. The requisite civic virtue was not in evidence. Effective collective action in the Continental Congress was inhibited by its cumbersome structure, the irregular attendance of state delegates, and sectional differences. The period of the 1780s was truly a critical period, "not solely because members of the social and economic elite felt themselves and their world threatened, but because anyone who knew anything of eighteenth century political science could not help believing that the American republics were headed for destruction even as they were being created."[10] In response, the political structure of the new nation was fundamentally transformed. The concept of a constitution as a mere description of institutional arrangements was replaced by one that raised the constitution to the status of supreme law binding on both governors and governed and enforceable in the courts; and only the people were competent to enact the supreme law embodied in the constitution. Years of conceptual debate over the nature and locus of sovereignty were concluded when sovereignty was held to vest in the people themselves, leaving the people free to delegate authority as they chose to institutions of government established by them. Drawing their authority from the electorate, all government officials, not just those of the legislative branch, could be considered responsible agents of the people and therefore representative. The new Constitution drawn in 1787 vested unprecedented power in a centralized governmental structure. Constrained to doubt the

---

9. "Appius," *SGSC*, February 22, 1787. The quoted passage introduced a long discussion of debtor relief measures in which the author described the background of the issue in some detail and argued that the necessity that required legislative interposition in 1785 might no longer exist. The author is unknown but may have been Henry Pendleton.

10. Wood, *Creation*, 413–14.

9

regulatory force of civic virtue, the nationalist proponents of the new Constitution created an intricate series of institutional devices designed to enable the several departments of the national government to control each other and then justified the creation by asserting that a plurality of interests would preclude the appearance of a despotic majority.[11]

With ratification of the new Constitution in 1788, the frame of reference changed again. A latent British threat remained. The several state governments still required vigilant attention. But the primary point of focus inevitably became the new power center erected above the level of the states, a remote yet potentially threatening presence the future development of which could only be guessed. The political arena was significantly enlarged, and issues taken up at the remote center were necessarily examined from a wider range of local perspectives. New political alignments evolved as policy differences over current issues became the subject of extreme jealousy. Aggravating this condition, the new nation was caught almost immediately in the tangle of war between Great Britain and France and reduced to the role of pawn, powerless to protect its interests against those asserted by the contending powers. Consequently, any governmental action might be perceived as favoring one side or the other and hence as either Jacobin or monarchic. Foreign policy issues polarized the polity and stimulated the emergence of parties as no foreseeable domestic issue could have done.[12] This divisive condition continued throughout the remainder of Burke's life and strongly colored his perception of events during the 1790s.

Burke was not an assiduous student of the English Commonwealthmen and their eighteenth-century successors, at least on the face of his known writings. He endorsed the fundamental principles of the republican creed as received wisdom and promul-

---

11. Wood, *Creation*, Parts III–V, passim.
12. Lance Banning, *The Jeffersonian Persuasion: Evolution of a Party Ideology* (Ithaca: Cornell University Press, 1978), argues that the English opposition ideology that informed the leaders of the Revolution also shaped the early national experience and that, in opposition to Federalist centralizing measures, the Jeffersonians perfected a modified version of such ideology appropriate to the circumstances of the new nation. Given the established terms of political discourse, no other theme than that of endangered liberty would have served so well to rally opposition to Federalist policies and practices. Banning's theme is elaborated in Drew R. McCoy, *The Elusive Republic: Political Economy in Jeffersonian America* (Chapel Hill: University of North Carolina Press, 1980), 136–84.

gated them as definitive propositions applicable to the structure of political institutions and the conduct of political affairs. His intellectual tools were history and the law, including the classical writers on the law of nature and natural rights. Indeed, law and history were closely related, since the study of law in the eighteenth century was the study of its history. Both were relatively static and relied on precedent. Men believed that what had happened before would happen again, and historical precedent taught that political systems were born, matured, became corrupted, and declined. Occasionally, one reached the threshold of republican achievement only to fall back into despotism. Reflecting on the republican experiment in seventeenth-century England and the execution of Charles I in 1649, Burke wrote Ezra Stiles, president of Yale, in 1792:

> I consider the decisive heroic spirit of that day, which dared to bring kingly despotism to public justice, as nearly related to that spirit of kindred boldness, which lately in America animated our citizens to oppose regal oppression, and effected our independence. Nor do I think the less of the patriots of 1648, because they failed of success. The people of Britain went back to the flesh pots of Egypt, and relapsed into all the servitude of the old monarchy, because the world was not sufficiently enlightened to avail themselves of events. The principles of government, and the rights of man not being well understood, lay prostrate under the fatal prejudices of the times, and the superstitious idolatry for the name of a king.[13]

Burke's mission was to prevent, if he could, a recurrence in America of that sad relapse. Appropriating the rich imagery of John Milton's *Paradise Lost*, Burke saw himself the guardian of a modern republican paradise against the insidious devils of corrupting power. His model was Ithuriel, Milton's mythic angel who encountered Satan in Paradise in the form of a toad, waiting close at the ear of sleeping Eve to instill in her mind

> *Vain hopes, vain aimes, inordinate desires*
> *Blown up with high conceits ingendring pride.*

Touched with Ithuriel's spear, Satan started up, revealed in his own shape, and was promptly challenged

---

13. Burke to Ezra Stiles, September 17, 1792, published in *SGSC*, January 5, 1793.

Why satst thou like an enemy in wait
Here watching at the head of those who sleep?[14]

Burke believed in the capacity of the people's watchfulness to restrain ambitious leaders tempted to subvert their liberties. Like a latter day Ithuriel, he would aim the spear of his rhetoric at incipient despotism wherever he found it, so that, as anti-republican threats appeared, the people might be warned and grapple with the enemy before it was too late. But confidence in the ability of the people to respond to such warnings should not be confused with either democracy or egalitarianism as guiding principles of governance and social relations. Burke was no democrat and no egalitarian. Just as centralized executive power threatened an aggressive campaign of power against liberty, so abuse of power by the people threatened ultimate despotism. Both cases were historically supportable. A democratic or popular branch of government was necessary to achieve a proper balance, and support of the popular branch, in that context, did not make one a democrat. The appropriate role of the people when alerted to their danger was to present their grievances in an orderly manner to their elected leaders and to chose as leaders men of demonstrated wisdom and virtue. Burke had little sympathy for dissident demonstrators in the streets or for the lower orders unable or unwilling to recognize the requirements of the public interest. These he would refer to on occasion as "Yahoos" and characterize their excesses as "Yahooism."[15]

There was more to eighteenth century American republicanism than a set of political precepts. For many, it contributed "a moral dimension, a utopian depth to the political separation from England—a depth that involved the very character of their society." It carried "extraordinary hopes for the social and political transformation of America." More than commitment to a particular form of government, it was a vision drawn from the history of

---

14. John Milton, "Paradise Lost," Book 4, lines 789–826, *Milton's Poetical Works*, Douglas Bush, ed. (London: Oxford University Press, 1966), 293–94.
15. Burke often used the term "Yahoo", derived form Jonathan Swift's *Gulliver's Travels*, Part IV, "A Voyage to the Country of the Houyhnhnms" (1726). See Jonathan Swift, *Gulliver's Travels and Other Writings* (New York: Modern Library, 1958), 177–243. Swift portrayed Yahoos as humanoid creatures serving a race of horses endowed with reason. Swift's Yahoos were unteachable and incapable of rational thought. Over time, the term came to mean generically a rough, coarse, or uncouth person, a yokel, or a lout.

Introduction

both ancient and modern times.[16] Consequently, the rhetoric of republicanism ranged from near euphoria to deep despair, depending on whether the subject was the promise of republican government for the greater good or happiness of the people at large, or the danger that such promise might be undermined by a designing aristocracy or a putative despot hungry for power. Republican rhetoric thus had its bright side and its dark. The first expressed promise and hope; the second expressed exposure to danger and fear of failure. Burke's writings contain examples of both. And in describing his fears, he was quick to employ conspiratorial explanatory themes suggesting the machinations of a concert having as its purpose the enhancement of power at the expense of liberty.

Burke was well educated but not an intellectual. He was neither a political theorist nor an original thinker. He never articulated a theory of progress, a vision of the future other than a potentially apocalyptic one, an understanding of capitalist values, or a concept of republican political economy. His ideological cognitive structure was relatively simple and incorporated a limited inventory of the standard principles embraced by the republican creed. He had the vocabulary at his fingertips; but, in a sense, he was constrained by an ideological strait jacket that so featured fear of aggressive power and aristocratic pretensions as to impede constructive thought. He was a public figure of the middle range of importance and a republican of one time and place. But nearly all men of the time were republicans, and the words "republican" and "republicanism" were protean terms meaning different things to different people. The second purpose of this study, then, is to examine Burke's republicanism, in the context of his time and place, and his role as a middle range figure in the political spectrum of republicanism in South Carolina.

Some attention must be paid to the vocabulary of Burke's time. Words then in current use had well-understood meanings that are quite different from modern usage. Thus, "jealousy" meant suspicion tinged with apprehension. "Public virtue" concerned the basic relationship between citizen and state. The virtuous citizen practiced the private virtues of industry, temperance, and frugality, subordinated selfish ends to the common good, and served the common good in public office when

16. Wood, *Creation*, 47–48.

13

called upon to do so. "Corruption" was the opposite of virtue. The corrupt citizen pursued personal gain at the expense of common good and actively sought public office for private purposes. Similarly, elections were corrupted when improperly influenced; and the legislative branch was corrupted when packed with men made dependent upon others by patronage or promise of personal benefits. "Independence" meant the absence of external dominion or arbitrary control and was an essential quality for political leaders because only an independent man was capable of independent judgment in support of the public good. "Slavery" was the antithesis of independence, and chattel slavery was only the extreme form of subordinate dependence. Finally, "freedom" meant something more than independence, incorporating the security of each individual in his property and rights. The emphasis was thus on public and private responsibility, and the concept of freedom was perhaps more negative than positive, more freedom "from" than freedom "to."

Some terms were more ambiguous. "Equality," for example, might have more than one meaning. Nobody believed that equality of condition was realistic. Republican equality meant the elimination of all forms of subordination other than those naturally attributable to differences of capacity, disposition, or virtue. It also meant equality of legal rights and obligations, so that each man would stand on the same footing with all others. Similarly, "liberty" had more than one meaning. Liberty meant the right to participate in the political process and thus to be involved, directly or indirectly through representatives, in the enactment of laws to be binding on all. In another sense, liberty was akin to freedom "from," a negative and limited liberty to enjoy peaceable possession of property and to exercise individual rights protected by law. Finally, a more modern notion, conceptualizing liberty as the individual's right to pursue his own ends, was beginning to appear.[17]

Some attention must also be paid to the geographic and demographic characteristics of Burke's South Carolina. Eighteenth-century South Carolinians were experts in sectionalism. Lowcountry and backcountry were physically divided by an un-

---

17. Michael Kammen, *Spheres of Liberty: Changing Perceptions of Liberty in American Culture* (Madison: University of Wisconsin Press, 1986), 17–52, discusses the various meanings of "liberty" in the early republic.

productive sand hill region that served as a barrier to social and economic integration. Physical separation was reinforced by cultural differences. Most backcountry residents had migrated not through Charleston toward the western frontier but from the northern colonies, starting in Pennsylvania and working their way southward through western Virginia and North Carolina. They were small subsistence farmers, for the most part, who worked their land without slaves. They were Protestants, but mostly Presbyterians and Baptists, not Anglicans. Their ethnic origins were different. They were underrepresented in the legislature in relation to their numbers and chafed under lowcountry control, sharing with their coastal countrymen only their fierce personal pride and firm commitment to personal independence. Through the end of the century, these sectional differences remained strong, and conflicting sectional interests materially affected the course of political life.

In retrospect, the beginnings of sectional integration are perceptible, stimulated by growth in trade between the backcountry and the metropolis and by gradual expansion of commercial agriculture to inland regions. But commercial agriculture was in a time of transition during the late 1780s and the 1790s, recovering from the disruptive impact of the Revolution and facing an uncertain future. Although lowcountry rice remained the major staple crop, markets and patterns of trade were in a state of flux. The cotton kingdom of the nineteenth century was not yet discernible. The lowcountry landed establishment was hardly ready for major domestic political change.

The established political system was a hierarchical system in which property and prestige were inextricably linked. Only persons of property possessed the economic independence that was the essential precondition to virtuous behavior in the public interest. Only the ownership of property assured that those entrusted with power had a stake in the system sufficient to warrant confidence that its values would be upheld. Since land was the only significant resource for production, land and property were virtually synonymous terms. The landed interest was the predominant interest, and the landed gentry assumed a natural right to political leadership.

"In the eighteenth century world," Rhys Isaac has said, speaking of Virginia, "a man had to be either a master or a servant." Not every master was a gentleman, but no dependent servant could ever be one. In England, the rank of gentleman flowed from the ownership of land. In Virginia, where land was plentiful, the ownership of slaves was also essential. Successful merchants could aspire to recognition, but social convention required that those who accumulated wealth in trade should invest their wealth in land and slaves. Similarly, the learned professional could hope to achieve gentility, but recognition could only be secured by the accumulation of an estate.[18] So it was also in South Carolina, both socially and politically less developed than Virginia when independence was achieved and the new nation launched.

Burke was a professional man and therefore on the fringe. He yearned to be closer to the center than he ever was and for more recognition than he ever received. He yearned also for the independence and status that the ownership of property conferred. He did own property, and some slaves, but he never could claim to be a man of property in any significant sense. The extent of his disappointment in this respect will never be known. But the number of occasions when he went out of his way to say that he did not care what others thought, or whether others saw things as he did, suggest that he did care very much.

This is not a study of the life and times of Aedanus Burke. Given the nature of the available materials, however, it will be necessary to examine the times on occasion in search of influences shaping Burke's perceptions of his political environment and, from there, to attempt some reconstruction of the forces or motives underlying his responses to particular events. Thus, Burke will not always be at center stage, but in due course he will return to play his part.

---

18. Rhys Isaac, *The Transformation of Virginia, 1740–1790* (Chapel Hill: University of North Carolina Press, 1982), 132.

I

The Famous Judge Burke

1743–1802

Visiting Cambridge, South Carolina, in March 1806, four years after Burke's death in 1802, Edward Hooker found that people in the backcountry district of Ninety Six still spoke often of the famous Judge Burke. "He must by accounts have been a man of most singular humor: He was thought to be a good Judge of law, but so fond of fun, as to forget very often the awfulness of the place which he filled and turned the whole proceedings into a farce." To illustrate the point, Hooker described an occasion when Burke, pronouncing the sentence of death on a convicted criminal, added "but don't mind, my good fellow, it's only what we've all got to come to."[1]

Lawyers, judges, and courts were not universally admired in early America. Many judges were feared; and some were hated. A few were respected. How did it happen then that this judge, some years after his death, was still remembered as the famous Judge Burke?

Little is known of Burke's early life. On the record, he was born in Galway, Ireland, in 1743 and attended a Jesuit seminary at St. Omer in France.[2] He knew little of his family history "from a want of Spirit of inquiry into my Origins in my youth, which seems natural to a more advanced age." He knew that his grandfather came from Connaught, served as an officer in the Irish army of James II in the Jacobite war of 1689–1691, and settled in County Kilkenny when that army was disbanded after the Treaty

---

1. "Diary of Edward Hooker, 1805–1808," J. Franklin Jameson, ed., *Annual Report, American Historical Association, 1896* (Washington: United States Government Printing Office, 1897), 885. The same incident is described in Joseph Johnson, *Traditions and Reminiscences Chiefly of the American Revolution in the South* (Charleston: Walker & James, 1851; reprint ed., Spartanburg: The Reprint Company, 1972), 430.
2. *Bio. Directory*, 3: 105–107.

of Limerick in 1691. Of his father and mother, both left un-named, he mentioned only, and with pride, that they were par-tially of ancient Irish stock, being "ex materna parte, . . . of the old Milesian race."[3]

The Irish Burkes traced their ancestry to William de Burgh, Norman knight of noble lineage, who first went from Britain to Ireland circa 1185 and was soon thereafter made governor of Lim-erick. In the centuries that followed, the descendants of William, and perhaps other de Burghs or de Burghos from Britain, multi-plied and separated into numerous clans and branches, with sev-eral modernized versions of the name. Of these, Burk, Burke, and Bourke were the most common. By the seventeenth century, the most distinguished of the several lines was headed by the Earl of Clanricarde, whose title derived from Henry VIII of En-gland. Other lines carried other titles. In the army that fought for James II in Ireland in 1689 and 1690, the then current Earl of Clanricarde and three other Burkes (or Bourkes) served as colo-nels in command of infantry regiments. Moreover, the name ap-pears in the list of commissioned officers in twenty-nine other regiments.[4]

Even less is known of Burke's formal education. St. Omer, established by English Jesuits in 1593, was one of more than 150 Jesuit institutions founded in Western Europe between 1551 and 1650 to implement the educational reforms launched by the Council of Trent (1551–1563). Typically, these institutions com-bined a residential university for clerics and a secondary board-ing and day school for lay pupils. By attending St. Omer, Burke was not necessarily trained first for the priesthood as the stan-dard biographical accounts of his life have generally assumed. But there is no doubt that, if he stayed there long, he was edu-cated in the spirit of the Catholic reformation, emphasizing or-

---

3. Aedanus Burke to Dr. Thomas Burke, December 2, 1769, in Walter Clark, ed., *The State Records of North Carolina*, 16 vols. numbered consecutively with *The Colonial Records of North Carolina* as vols. 11–26 (Winston, Goldsboro, and Raleigh, North Carolina: The State of North Carolina, 1895–1914), 15: 676–80.
4. John D'Alton, *Illustrations Historical and Genealogical of King James Irish Army List, 1689*, 2nd ed., 2 vols. (Dublin: 1860), 2: 136. Eamonn Bourke, *Burke: People and Places* (Whitegate, County Clare, Ireland: Ballinakella Press, 1984), describes the Burke genealogical evolution in broad terms.

der, hierarchy, methodical organization, and a severe moral discipline supported by ardent piety.[5]

From these scattered facts, and the known facts of Burke's later life, some tentative conclusions may be drawn. He bore the name of a prominent Irish family of some substance, but was probably not in close proximate lineal relationship to the Irish peers of that name. Had the facts been otherwise, they would surely have been known and recorded by his contemporaries in South Carolina. He was educated, at least in part, in Catholic schools and was probably born to the Catholic faith. There is no evidence that he ever explicitly renounced Catholicism, or embraced Protestantism, or associated himself with any Protestant denomination. But, even after Anglican disestablishment in 1778, the constitution of South Carolina specifically provided that no person would be eligible to sit in the House of Representatives, as Burke did, "unless he be of the Protestant Religion, and hath been a Resident of this State for three years, previous to his Election."[6] Nominally, at least, Burke was a Protestant in South Carolina.

Burke was well educated by the standards of his time. He was presumably fluent in French. He knew history. He was well versed in the standard legal authorities. His library included a few works in Greek and Latin, among them the works of Aristotle in the original and in a Latin version.[7] Francisco de Miranda, a Spanish revolutionary committed to the cause of Latin American independence from Spain, met Burke on a visit to Charleston in mid-1783 and found him a man of intellect, ability, and good judgment. "It cannot be denied," de Miranda wrote in his journal, "that in the inclinations of individuals is discovered the anal-

5. T. J. Walsh, *The Irish Continental College Movement: The Colleges at Bourdeaux, Toulouse, and Lille* (Dublin: Golden Eagle Books, 1973), 50; Patrick J. Cornish, *The Catholic Community in the Seventeenth and Eighteenth Centuries* (Dublin: Helicon Limited, 1981), 25–26.
6. Constitution of 1778, Article XIII, *Statutes at Large*, 1: 140–41; David Duncan Wallace, *South Carolina: A Short History* (Columbia: University of South Carolina Press, 1951), 278–82. Burke's funeral service was held in St. Michael's church, and he was buried in an Anglican church yard in St. Bartholomew's Parish near Jacksonborough.
7. Aedanus Burke, Last Will and Testament, January 13, 1802, Charleston Will Transcripts, 28: 285–87, SCA. The books mentioned were given to the new library in Georgetown.

ogy of genius, talent, etc., because never before have I found a person so passionate an admirer of the excellence and good taste of our inimitable Miguel de Cervantes. I owe him particular friendship and esteem, having profited immensely from his conversation and knowledge during my entire residence in this city."[8]

Burke's first recorded appearance in America was in Marlborough, Stafford County, Virginia, in late 1769. From there he reported his activities to Dr. Thomas Burke, then practicing law in Norfolk. Like Aedanus, Thomas Burke was born in Galway. He emigrated to Virginia circa 1764 and later explained that he was "born in Ireland of a once affluent Family" but that "Family misfortunes reduced [him] to the alternative of Domestic Indolent Dependence, or an Enterprising Peregrination" to Virginia. Settling first in Accomac County, where he practiced medicine, he later took up the study of law, began practice in Norfolk, and moved to North Carolina in 1774. While in Virginia he wrote in opposition to the Stamp Act. In North Carolina, he assisted in the preparation of its first constitution, served in the provincial congress in 1776, represented the state in the Continental Congress between 1776 and 1781, and was elected governor in 1781.[9] On this record, Thomas Burke's credentials as a revolutionary patriot were impeccable.

Aedanus perhaps followed Thomas to colonial America. Referring in 1769 to the kindness with which Thomas had given instruction and advice and had "Engaged the influence of that distinction and character your merit both deserved and Acquired, to procure me Notice and Esteem among Your friends," Aedanus demonstrated friendship and high regard for his namesake but not, as has sometimes been suggested, any direct familial relationship between the two. He was in good health, he said, and leading a busy life. "I Read with the greatest application, but the common Law takes up the most of my time." In addition to English history and treatises on government and trade, "I have

---

8. John S. Ezell, ed., *The New Democracy in America: Travels of Francisco de Miranda in the United States, 1783–1784* (Norman: University of Oklahoma Press, 1963), 29.

9. William K. Boyd, "Thomas Burke," in *Dictionary of American Biography,* Allen Johnson, et al., eds., reprint ed., 10 vols. (New York: Charles Scribner's, 1957), 2: 282–83; Lyon Gardiner Tyler, ed., *Encyclopedia of Virginia Biography,* 5 vols. (New York: Lewis Historical Publishing Company, 1915), 2: 290; Thomas Burke, April 25, 1772, quoted in Kerby A. Miller, *Emigrants and Exiles: Ireland and the Irish Exodus to North America* (New York: Oxford University Press, 1985), 141.

lately read Dr. Keating's History of Ireland, which is very enter-taining and pleases me much in his accounts of the Antiquity, invincible bravery, benevolence and humanity which distin-guished the Native Irish whilst that unhappy Country was gov-erned by her own Laws and enjoyed freedom." He complained of "the Scandalous partiality of the English," who unjustly charac-terized the Irish "for Savageness, Cruelty and barbarism, a char-acter void of every foundation except that Instance of the rebellion in Car. I. Reign, which was dictated by a Spirit of free-dom and independence that inspired the unfortunate old nobility to reinstate themselves in their Ancient privileges and Liberty; and as to the circumstances of Cruelty that appeared, when we reflect on the resolution of the puritans, to give all the Papists to the Sword; just before the Rebellion, the tide of fanaticism and bigotry that overflowed the three kingdoms at that time, with many other reasons, laying aside Religion, the impartial will cease to wonder."[10] Since Keating's work appeared in 1629, Burke was here obviously expressing his personal understanding of some later events. And since his own youth in Ireland coincided with the penal law era that followed the Williamite victory over James II in the wars of 1689–1691, his Anglophobia and his re-publicanism must have derived at least in part from the Irish his-torical experience and his acute awareness of it.

Burke's letter from Marlborough in December 1769 is the only known record of his Virginia connection. Even so, that iso-lated scrap of evidence carries considerable significance. Marlbor-ough was located a day's ride northeast of Fredericksburg on a neck of land where Potomac Creek joined the Potomac River. It was originally established by the Virginia House of Burgesses to serve as Stafford County's official port city. The town never flour-ished, however, and in the 1760s was the private demesne of the distinguished Mercer family.[11] Accordingly, one such as Burke,

---

10. Aedanus Burke to Thomas Burke, December 2, 1769, in Clark, ed., *The State Records of North Carolina*, 15: 676–80. Keating's history of Ireland from earliest times to the English invasion, written circa 1629, was the first connected history of Ireland in the Irish language. A translation was published in London in 1723. "Geoffrey Keating," *Dictionary of National Biography* (Oxford: Oxford University Press, 1921–1922), 10: 1162–63. Burke's discussion of this work is the only re-corded reflection of his views on Irish history. He seldom referred to his Irish ancestry in his known writings.

11. C. Malcolm Watkins, *The Cultural History of Marlborough, Virginia* (Washington: Smithsonian Institute Press, 1968), 15–59.

obviously in residence at Marlborough, was necessarily associated with the Mercers in some direct fashion.

John Mercer, the head of the family until his death in October 1768, was born in Dublin in 1704 and emigrated to Virginia in 1720. He studied law, was admitted to practice in Virginia in 1728, and became one of Virginia's most successful lawyers and a large land owner. His first wife was Catherine Mason, aunt of the later famous George Mason. He published two editions of an abridgement of the laws of Virginia. Although no copy has survived, he is said to have written the first tract published in Virginia opposing the Stamp Act. His son James (1736–1793) was a well-known lawyer and later a judge in Virginia, a prominent patriot in the Revolutionary period, and a member of the Continental Congress.[12]

More importantly, Mercer accumulated over the years the largest law library and one of the largest general libraries in Virginia, and his library remained intact at least through 1770. The law library alone contained in 1770 some 284 titles of which 114 were probably not available elsewhere in Virginia. In addition, the Mercer library contained Rapin's *History of England*, occasionally cited by Burke, Keating's *History of Ireland*, specifically mentioned to Thomas Burke, and numerous other works on Greek, Roman, and English history. The classical Greek and Roman writers were well represented; and the works of literature included those of John Milton, William Shakespeare, Alexander Pope, and Ben Jonson. Among the works of Milton was an annotated edition of *Paradise Lost*.[13]

Burke's statement to Thomas Burke that "the common Law takes up the most of my time" clearly implies that he was reading law in Virginia, and there were few if any better places for such an enterprise than the Mercer family seat at Marlborough. There is no evidence from which to determine the length of his stay, but the normal time for a course of legal study would have

---

12. Watkins, *Cultural History of Marlborough,* 54–55; Tyler, ed., *Encyclopedia of Virginia Biography,* 1: 290; Richard L. Morton, "James Mercer," in *Dictionary of American Biography,* 6: 542.

13. Watkins, *Cultural History of Marlborough,* 61–62, 198–204 (inventory c. 1750); William Hamilton Bryson, *Census of Law Books in Colonial Virginia* (Charlottesville: University Press of Virginia, 1978), xii, xviii; "Library of John Mercer of Marlboro," Brock Manuscripts, Huntington Library, San Marino, California (inventory c. 1770, copy at Virginia State Library, Richmond).

been about four years, and a student's residence with his mentor was not at all unusual.[14] Consequently, Burke could have arrived at Marlborough as early as 1766. In all events, he remained in Virginia for more than a year after John Mercer's death. He finally left in early 1770, when he announced by notice published in the *Virginia Gazette* that he intended to leave soon for Europe.[15] He was out of sight thereafter until he reappeared in South Carolina in the mid-1770s.

Burke's association with the Mercer family in the late 1760s is important in another respect. The Virginian political culture highly valued individual autonomy, and he was there at a time when tensions in the commercial relationships of colonial planters and metropolitan merchants, particularly the increasing debt of the planters to the merchants, appeared to threaten loss of planter independence. Indeed, some perceived a merchant conspiracy to entangle the planters in debt, reduce them to dependent status, and then seize their lands and estates.[16] As planter fears mounted, oppositionist political ideas became more and more attractive; and through the Mercers, Burke was exposed to prominent Virginians who then and later resisted British assertions of sovereign authority that they perceived as incompatible with the rights of the colonists as free men. Thus, the ideological values initially shaped by Burke's Irish lineage must have been adapted and refined in colonial Virginia to incorporate the emerging American version of the republican creed. By the time he arrived in South Carolina, then, his personal version of that creed, heavily laden with antipathy to all things British, was fully formed and never changed thereafter.

The circumstances of Burke's decision to settle in South Carolina and the time of his arrival there remain unknown; and no records have been found to explain his ready acceptance by the existing establishment. David Ramsay, a prominent contemporary who should have known the facts if anyone did, described him as "an Irish gentleman, who, with the gallantry characteristic of his nation, came from the West Indies at the commence-

---

14. Alan McKinley Smith, "Virginia Lawyers, 1680–1776: The Birth of an American Profession" (Ph.D. dissertation, Johns Hopkins University, 1967), 181–204. Thomas Jefferson, for example, read law for five years with George Wythe.
15. *Virginia Gazette* (Rind), March 22, 1770.
16. T. H. Breen, *Tobacco Culture: The Mentality of the Great Tidewater Planters on the Eve of Revolution* (Princeton: Princeton University Press, 1985), 133–47, 156–59.

ment of the revolution as a volunteer to fight for American liberty."[17] On the scene, however, probably some time in 1775, his rise to positions of importance was truly remarkable. He was soon in military service. In April 1778, less than three weeks after the election of Rawlins Lowndes to succeed John Rutledge as President of South Carolina and the enactment of a new state constitution, he was elected one of four assistant judges on its highest common law court. Shortly thereafter, he was elected to the House of Representatives from the Charleston parishes of St. Philip and St. Michael.

Given prevailing social conventions, it is almost inconceivable that Burke did not reach South Carolina with letters of introduction to people of some importance in Charleston and other appropriate credentials. In particular, he must have had some credentials in the law. Thomas Burke, his early sponsor in Virginia and then in North Carolina, may have introduced him to any one of several prominent South Carolinians. James Parsons, Pierce Butler, and others of Irish nationality are among the possibilities. So is Henry Pendleton, a native of Virginia who preceded Burke to South Carolina in 1771. The earlier Mercer connection was no doubt useful. But there is not enough evidence to support even a tentative hypothesis. Nor is there evidence that Burke ever applied for admission to the practice of law in South Carolina. Indeed, he could not have complied with the applicable requirements even if he had completed a course of legal training elsewhere.[18]

Timothy Ford, a young lawyer from New Jersey practicing in Charleston with Henry W. Desaussure, has left the most extended, if not the most flattering, description of Burke's personality. Shortly after his arrival in South Carolina in 1785, Ford was invited to dinner with General Stephen Bull. Burke was present, and Ford described their meeting in his diary.

---

17. David Ramsay, *The History of South Carolina*, 2 vols. (Charleston: David Longworth, 1809), 1: 477–78.
18. Before the Revolution, admission to practice was governed by a rule of court. Five years of study in South Carolina, or three years in South Carolina and two at a law college abroad, were required. George C. Rogers, Jr., *Evolution of a Federalist: William Loughton Smith of Charleston (1758–1812)* (Columbia: University of South Carolina Press, 1962), 119, citing John Pringle to William Tilghman, November 1, 1774, Preston Davie Papers, SCHS.

I was politely treated and made an acquaintance with
Edanus Burk, Esq., the justice in Eyre. Chance seated me
near him at the table and a good deal of conversation
ensued between us and I found him a striking instance of
the difference men sometimes make in their appearance in
company and on paper. About 18 months ago I had read a
pamphlet of his on the Society of the Cincinnati; fraught
with solid learning and good sense; and dressed in a very
good stile. I had formed an idea of his being a very great
dignified and Learned judge. I found him an arrant
Irish man whose conversation though well enough aimed
never contained a sentence of good english but on the
contrary abounded with blunders vulgarisms and
Hibernianisms. The same was visible on the Bench—his
ideas seemed amazingly confused and he neither looked nor
spoke nor acted like a judge. In short he carries with him
less dignity than I have seen for a man of his learning and
station—I am told however that he is a Lawyer.[19]

Others took a more affirmative view of Burke's sociability.
"Your Brother Burke is become very pleasant—a Great Speaker,
and often entertains us with numerous strokes of fancy," William
Loughton Smith wrote John F. Grimke, one of Burke's judicial
colleagues, after a year with Burke in the First Congress of the
United States.[20] And the anecdotal record is in accord. E. S.
Thomas reported an occasion when Burke arrived home late one
evening and found forgotten dinner guests waiting. Burke proceeded immediately to the kitchen, gave appropriate instructions, and returned to entertain his guests "from his vast
resources of information and anecdote" until "a most excellent
dinner was smoking upon his table" some two hours later. In the
meantime, good wine circulated freely and "all forebodings of
disappointment were soon forgotten."[21]

One of Burke's most distinguishing personal characteristics
was surely his very Irishness. His speech was richly colloquial,

19. "Diary of Timothy Ford, 1785–1786," Joseph W. Barnwell, ed., *SCHM*, 13
(1912): 146. Burke evidently circulated in good company. Ford found him the
next evening dining with General John Barnwell.
20. William Loughton Smith to John F. Grimke, March 3, 1790, Emmet Collection, NYHS.
21. E. S. Thomas, *Reminiscences of the Last Sixty-Five Years*, 2 vols. (Hartford: Case,
Tiffany and Burnham, 1840), 1: 63–64.

and he often used earthy images to make a point. He was hot-tempered and often blunt. He enjoyed his wine and spirits. He could regard himself in humorous terms, but his humor had little of subtlety and was no doubt sometimes rough. On the bench, he was a judge with an occasional light touch, self-possessed and self-confident, unawed by the famous advocates who appeared in his court.

The anecdotal record fully supports Burke's reputation for occasional eccentricity in the performance of his judicial duties. "He always meant well, though he frequently took an awkward way of showing it," wrote Alexander Garden, "and secured confidence by his unremitting endeavors to deserve it." By Joseph Johnson's account, he was a "very liberal, enlightened and humane man; a delightful companion, full of humor and original wit, blended with much good sense; but from a heedless or hasty mode of expressing himself, he was often the subject of merriment among his friends, as he was the source of it." His "integrity and talents were unquestionable," Johnson continued. He "was a concise, close, and forcible reasoner," but "his actions were too often guided by the impulse of the moment." John Belton O'Neall later described him as "a pure, just judge" notwithstanding "his Irish rollicking character."[22]

Edward Hooker described an illuminating incident involving the eminent Charles Cotesworth Pinckney, leader of the Charleston bar. Becoming impatient one day with Pinckney's extended argument, Burke rose and left the bench. Pinckney stopped. "Go on, General Pinckney, go on," Burke said, "you love to hear yourself talk. Meanwhile, I'll go out, and take a ——— and a peep at the camel." There was indeed a camel on display in Charleston at the time and thereafter, so the story goes, "peeping at the camel became a bye word among the Carolina lawyers, for going out on any occasion."[23]

Court sessions were important occasions, featuring ceremony and solemnity. The judges wore robes of black silk and

---

22. Alexander Garden, *Anecdotes of the Revolutionary War in America* (Charleston: A. Miller, 1822; reprint ed., Spartanburg: The Reprint Company, 1972), 192; Johnson, *Traditions and Reminiscences*, 429–30, 432; John Belton O'Neall, *Biographical Sketches of the Bench and Bar of South Carolina*, 2 vols. (Charleston: S. G. Courtenay & Co., 1859), 1: 38.
23. "Diary of Edward Hooker," Jameson, ed., 885–86.

customarily entered and left the courtroom with their robes on. In Charleston, they sometimes left them overnight at the dry goods store of Madame Van Rhine near the courthouse. From this minor sequence arose one of the most enduring of the incidents included in the anecdotal record. Burke arrived late in court one morning carrying his robe under his arm. Struggling to get into it as he ascended the bench, he discovered to the amusement of all present that he had not his robe but a lady's black petticoat. "Before God," he remarked, "I have got on Van Rhine's petticoat."[24]

Many incidents of the anecdotal record were unquestionably based on fact. In February 1786, for example, Burke and Thomas Heyward sat in the Court of General Sessions on the trial of John Egan, charged with horse stealing. There was no question that Egan had taken the horse, but there was evidence suggesting that he "devoted himself to drinking, and in fits of intoxication frequently committed very foolish and extravagant actions." Burke told the jurors that they must determine the defendant's intention. "If nothing more was intended than a frolic," he said, "they would acquit the prisoner." Speaking for himself, "he thought there was a probability of the prisoner being more wantonly indiscreet than deliberately knavish." Heyward concurred, and pointed out to the jury that the prisoner was charged with a capital offense. The jury found him guilty but recommended mercy, virtually assuring a pardon.[25]

The trial of the drunken horse thief is a staple of the anecdotal record, usually embellished by Burke's express acknowledgment of personal experience with the unpredictable effects of excessive alcoholic consumption. In its most elaborate form, it is coupled with another incident of uncertain origin. After a convivial evening on circuit when corn whiskey was consumed in substantial amounts, a wag slipped two of the tavern keeper's spoons into Burke's pocket. The next morning, embarrassed, he arranged that the spoons be returned. Sitting later at the trial of the horse thief, and informed that the defendant was at the time drunk on corn whiskey, Burke allegedly advised the jury that he well knew how easily corn whiskey might lead a good man to

24. Thomas, *Reminiscences*, 1: 62–63; O'Neall, *Biographical Sketches*, 1: 37–38.
25. *CMP,* February 20, 1786.

appropriate the property of others. The prisoner was thereupon acquitted, so the story goes.[26]

Another famous incident is clearly based on fact. Burke made an extended trip to Philadelphia and New York in 1799. In September, while in New York, he acted as second to Aaron Burr in a duel with John B. Church, brother-in-law of Alexander Hamilton. Burr called out Church for remarks reflecting on his probity, which probably originated with Hamilton. On the dueling ground, Burr explained that the balls were cast too small for the pistols and that chamois leather, cut to the proper size, should be greased and wrapped around them so that they would seat properly. After Burr had taken his stand, he observed Burke hammering on the ramrod with a rock. When the pistol was handed to him, Burr drew the ramrod and pointed out that the ball was not yet home. "I forgot to grease the leather," Burke replied, "but you see he is ready, don't keep him waiting; just take a crack as it is, and I'll grease the next!"[27]

Burke was, of course, much more than a casual Irish bon vivant. He took seriously his legislative and judicial responsibilities. In his judicial role particularly, he was much more visible to the people of the state than were most other political leaders. The court to which Burke was elected in 1778 was an itinerant court, headquartered in Charleston and serving six outlying or "country" districts. Twice a year, in spring and fall, traveling on horseback or by chaise, two of the sitting judges departed Charleston, one proceeding to Georgetown, Cheraw, and Camden, the other to Beaufort, Orangeburgh, and Ninety Six, and both then returning to Charleston. The circuit might take six to eight weeks to complete. In the course of each circuit, the presid-

---

26. Thomas, *Reminiscences*, 1: 64; Johnson, *Traditions and Reminiscences*, 430; B. F. Perry, "Aedanus Burke," in U. R. Brooks, *South Carolina Bench and Bar* (Columbia: The State Company, 1908), 7.

27. Matthew L. Davis, *Memoirs of Aaron Burr*, 2 vols. (New York: Harper & Brothers, 1836), 1: 417–18; James Parton, *The Life of Aaron Burr*, 2 vols. (Boston: Houghton Mifflin and Company, 1892), 1: 240; Thomas, *Reminiscences*, 1: 62; O'Neall, *Biographical Sketches*, 1: 35–36. No serious damage was done to either party. The duel and Burke's appearance as Burr's second were reported in the *CGDA*, September 18, 1799. The pistols used were those later used in the duel between Burr and Alexander Hamilton in which Hamilton was killed. The problem was not that the balls were too small but that the bore of the pistols was larger than the .50 caliber or less acceptable under the conventions of proper dueling practice. *The Church Pistols* (New York: The Chase Manhattan Bank, N.A. Archives, n.d.). The balls therefore had to be wrapped to seat properly.

ing judged stayed in each community where the court convened until the work of the session was finished or the time fixed for the sitting expired. While there, he met the leading citizens of the district sitting as grand or petit jurors and mingled with the public at large.

Traveling on circuit throughout the state, the judges thus had more direct contact with the people than most other public officials. Judicial office entitled the holder, prima facie, to respect and deference, which might be enhanced or lost on the basis of performance, but which conferred on the sitting judge both authority and influence. His charge to the grand jury at the beginning of each session customarily included a brief lecture on the major issues of the day as well as instruction on pending legal issues. The judges were more than teachers of law. They also spoke directly to the people on the principles of governance, standards of political behavior, and the requirements of civic virtue. They received from the grand juries statements setting forth local grievances and needs and transmitted such statements to political leaders in the metropolis for appropriate action. They were thus, for better or worse, channels of communication between the people on the one hand and the state's legislative and executive branches on the other, particularly in the outlying districts where few such channels existed; and their charges to the grand juries were frequently set out in full in the public press to spread and reinforce their messages throughout the entire community.

Although stern on occasion, Burke was a compassionate judge. In early 1789, just as he was preparing to leave for New York and the First Congress of the United States, the inhabitants of Ninety Six District delivered an address complimenting his administration of justice, his firmness, and his understanding.[28] Edmond Genet, meeting Burke in Camden in 1793 on his way from Charleston to Philadelphia, observed that "he is loved by these people and possessing their entire trust."[29] To the extent of their respective capacities to relate with sympathetic understanding to the mood and temper of the people from district to district, the judges were in a unique position to speak for the backcountry when the occasion arose. Where Burke was respected and trusted in the backcountry, John F. Grimke, Burke's contempo-

---

28. *SGSC*, March 9, 1789.
29. Report, c. 1795, Genet Papers, Library of Congress.

rary on the bench, trained at the English Inns of Court, was considered "a stern, unbending Judge in a Court of Law," inflexible and uncompromising, and was heartily disliked.[30] They represented the poles to the backcountry folk. Burke had a reputation for fairness and compassion in the application of the law, reinforced by earthy humanity, and he understood more perceptively than most the problems and concerns of the backcountry people. In this sense, at least, Burke is believable as a spokesman for backcountry interests, as some historians have seen him, notwithstanding that he lived in Charleston.

The state was his "country," but Charleston was his home. He lived there continuously from the time of his arrival in South Carolina, probably taking rooms at first but in his own house in the later years. He purchased property in Charleston from the Commissioners of Forfeited Estates in June 1783, making the initial payment with indents originally issued to him and giving a mortgage for the balance, which he satisfied in 1787. He obtained a grant in 1784 covering 640 acres near the Saluda River in Ninety Six District. He also acquired a tract of unknown size on the Wateree River.[31]

Little is known of Burke's financial resources, but he was not a man of great property. In his will, he complained that his "own stupidity in being security for others" prevented him from making adequate provision for his primary legatee, Miss Ruth Savage, or leaving to valued friends "even a trifling memorial of me." He left to Miss Savage £300, together with a small set of china and his gold watch, and the monetary bequest was to have priority of payment. "I have been for some years back engaged to Miss Savage by ties of great esteem," he said, and just before he was taken ill they had "engaged to be married." He left a brace of pistols to Aaron Burr and small items of personal property to

---

30. O'Neall, *Biographical Sketches*, 1: 40–41.
31. Account of Purchasers of Confiscated Property on which Indents have been received by the Commissioners for Forfeited Estates and Paid into the Treasury, April 10, 1784, SCA (Charleston house and lot); Mortgage and Satisfaction, October 12, 1787, Records of the General Assembly, SCA (satisfaction of mortgage on Charleston house and lot); Deed, October 15, 1784, State Grants, 3: 170, SCA (Saluda River tract adjoining land of Henry Pendleton and William Wood). Burke's will confirmed the ownership of a Charleston house and lot and the Wateree River tract at the time of his death. The Saluda River tract, for which a stated consideration of £64 sterling was paid, was not mentioned in the will and was presumably disposed of prior to Burke's death.

other friends. He left a specific bequest of £250 to Isabella Murphy, 7 Cedar Street, New York, in trust for the boy George Burke, "which legacy I give to be in full acquittance of every sort of claim and demand which Mrs. Murphy has already or may make against me, for the boarding schooling and cloathing of that boy, for my wish is to have him bound to the sea, about October next 1802." Finally, he directed that the Charleston house and lot and the Wateree River tract be sold and that the proceeds of the sale be held and applied "for the sole purpose of giving a little aid to such poor Irish immigrants and their successors as shall arrive in this Country."[32]

The bequest for the benefit of "poor Irish immigrants" was not as strange as it might at first seem. There was a steady stream of emigration from Ireland to America both before and after the Revolutionary War. That stream accelerated following the abortive Irish revolt against England in 1798 and supplied part of the impetus to organization of the Hibernian Society in Charleston in 1799. Burke does not appear as a member of the Society in its records, but he was undoubtedly aware of its existence and purposes. In all events, the Society succeeded to the trust in 1818 and received as trustee the sum of $12,786.[33] Burke's portrait hangs in Charleston's handsome Hibernian Hall today.

Laudatory obituaries are not generally regarded as solid sources of hard historical data but may be indicative of the reputation of the deceased in his community. Judge Burke, his obituarist wrote when Burke died in 1802, "united a heart full of justice and philanthropy" with "a mind strictly independent and scrupulously impartial." His eccentricities "were of an agreeable cast, generally harmless, always variable, and appeared but as the corruscations of elevated and uncommon endowments." On the bench, his "perception was prompt; his attention strong and vigilant; his judgment accurate; his reasoning sound, yet perspicacious. . . . To the accused, his countenance seemed always rather lighted up with the complacent smiles of a father, than

---

32. Aedanus Burke, Last Will and Testament. A few items of furniture, glassware, and other personal property were valued at $250.41 in an appraisal filed years later. Charleston County, Inventory of Estates, 1810–1818, 239, SCA. This amount cannot represent a full valuation of Burke's property at the time of his death.
33. Arthur Mitchell, *The History of the Hibernian Society of Charleston, South Carolina, 1799–1981* (Charleston: n.p., 1981), 22–23.

exhibiting the severity of a judge. To the innocent, he was a protector; to the unfortunate, a benefactor; to the poor and fatherless, a friend."[34] Nothing was said of his service in the General Assembly and the First Congress beyond mention of the bare facts.

Burke clearly considered himself a gentleman, with all that term implied in South Carolina in the late eighteenth cen-, and was no doubt accepted as such. He was active beyond tics in the affairs of his city and country. He was a member of the Charleston Library Society[35] and an incorporator and one of e first directors of the Santee Canal Company.[36] He was a ber of the Mount Sion Society, dedicated to the advancement learning, and was elected to a three year term as one of the first trustees of the new academy authorized to be established under its auspices at Winnsboro in 1785.[37] He was also a member of the Palmetto Society, described by Richard Walsh as one of two mechanic clubs that "added the weight of their influence to the Marine Anti-Britannic Society" in the early 1780s, and was elected senior warden in 1786.[38] He has never been identified, however, as a member of the Marine Anti-Britannic Society and was later highly critical of its extralegal tactics. Nor has he ever been identified as a member of any of the several republican or democratic-republican societies organized in South Carolina in the 1790s.

Gentleman though he was, Burke was never part of the inner circle of South Carolina's influential establishment. Although he no doubt wished to be, he was too independent to conform his own views and values to those of others. Such deference as he received was that due him as a judge of the superior court of the state and that earned by his performance on the bench and in

---

34. *CGDA*, April 2, 1802; "Marriage and Death Notices from the City Gazette," Jeannie Heyward Register, comp., *SCHM*, 27 (1926): 45–48.

35. Charleston Library Society, *Journal, 1759–1790*, 186, 228.

36. *CMP*, March 25, 1786. Charles Cotesworth Pinckney, John F. Grimke, Thomas Sumter, Alexander Gillon, and Henry Laurens, Jr. were also on the board.

37. *Charleston Yearbook 1887* (Charleston: Lucas, Richardson & Co., n.d.), 340; *SCGPA*, July 16, 1785; *Statutes at Large*, 4: 674–78.

38. *CMP*, June 29, 1786; Richard Walsh, *Charleston's Sons of Liberty: A Study of the Artisans, 1763–1789* (Columbia: University of South Carolina Press, 1959), 116. The meeting at which the election occurred commemorated the Society's tenth anniversary. Edward Weyman, active leader of the Charleston mechanics during the pre-Revolutionary and Revolutionary years, was president. On Weyman, see Walsh, *Charleston's Sons of Liberty*, 68–69, 111, 113, 116.

the legislature. Beyond that, he was best known for the sometimes eccentric behavior that appeared to his obituarist as merely "the corruscations of elevated and uncommon endowments." The impact was more complex. "During his administration he perpetuated many an Irish bull for his own amusement and the people around him," John Belton O'Neall wrote in 1859.[39] Burke's "Irish bulls" may have served a functional purpose—some no doubt did—but they colored his image in his own time and for years thereafter.

39. John Belton O'Neall, *The Annals of Newberry, Historical, Biographical and Anecdotal* (Charleston: S. G. Courtenay and Co., 1859), 285.

II

The Politics of Independence

1775–1778

Burke arrived in South Carolina to support the cause of liberty, as David Ramsay put it, sometime during the course of 1775.[1] Three years later, in early 1778, he entered the public life of his new country as an assistant judge on the bench of the Court of Common Pleas and General Sessions, the state's highest common-law court. His election to that office coincided with, and perhaps was also one result of, the state's first great political crisis, when moderate hopes for ultimate reconciliation with Great Britain gave way to the imperatives of independence. Burke was not a visible figure in the crisis, either as it developed or as it was resolved, but he was a close observer of events as were all the politically aware citizens of Charleston.

Although the precise date of Burke's arrival in South Carolina is uncertain, the direction and the gathering momentum of events were not. As the year 1775 progressed, the American colonies moved inexorably toward the ultimate break with England. Before the year was out, the contending positions of colonies and mother country became manifestly irreconcilable. Britain might offer to conciliate, but she would not surrender the principle of sovereignty. The Americans were equally determined to control their own affairs. At the end of the year, the atmosphere in Charleston, the colonial South's great hub of trade, was more martial than commercial.[2]

---

1. Burke served with the Second South Carolina Regiment, which became part of the Continental Line in September 1776. He resigned in February 1778. His service in the Continental forces was "a few months" short of the three years of service required for membership in the Cincinnati. Assuming that "a few" is not more than six, and counting back from February 1778, Burke's service would have begun in August 1775.
2. Thomas Tudor Tucker to St. George Tucker, December 27, 1775, Tucker-Coleman Papers, Department of Manuscripts and Rare Books, Swem Library, College of William and Mary.

South Carolina proceeded toward revolution by committee, building on precedents established during the Stamp Act crisis of 1765–1766 and the nonimportation movement of 1769–1770. As opposition to the so-called Intolerable Acts spread through the colonies in 1774, mass meetings of the citizenry in Charleston created a general committee, which thereupon issued a call for an assembly of citizens drawn from all parts of the colony to meet in Charleston on July 6. Extralegal though it was, that assembly constituted the most broadly based representative body in the history of South Carolina to that time. Some 104 representatives of the more remote sections joined with those of the lowcountry establishment in Charleston to adopt resolutions condemning the new round of oppressive British measures, to authorize participation in the First Continental Congress in 1774, and to select representatives to attend that Congress for South Carolina. It also established a new general committee authorized to act on behalf of the general meeting, thereby creating a de facto temporary government for the colony until another general meeting convened. Membership consisted of fifteen merchants and fifteen mechanics representing Charleston and sixty-nine planters representing the rest of the province, assuring that participation in these extralegal proceedings would reflect geographic and demographic differences. Vacancies were to be filled locally.[3]

The First Continental Congress met from September 5 to October 26, 1774, adopted a program to embargo trade between the colonies and Great Britain, and set the stage for a Second Continental Congress to meet in May 1775. When the South Carolina delegation returned home, the general committee called for an election of delegates to a general meeting to assemble in Charleston in January 1775. Again, a representative participation was desired, and numbers were assigned for election from the established parishes and from otherwise unorganized election districts defined on the basis of identifiable geographic boundaries. In the confused circumstances of the time, however, little

---

3. The most recent description of the coming of the Revolution to South Carolina is in Robert M. Weir, *Colonial South Carolina: A History* (Millwood, N.Y.: KTO Press, 1983), which is unannotated but includes an extensive bibliography. The evolution of the de facto governmental structure that replaced the Royal Government in 1775 is described in Eva B. Poythress, "Revolution by Committee: An Administrative History of the Extra-Legal Committees in South Carolina, 1774–1776" (Ph. D. dissertation, University of North Carolina, 1975).

attention was paid to the matter of apportionment. The primary political objective was unity in time of danger. "The question," Joseph Alston said in 1807, "was not how many members ought to be *allowed* to attend from the several districts, but how many could be *induced* to attend." The committee members from Charleston, according to Alston, announced that the city would send thirty members and that the rest of the country might send "as many as they please." Country members "happened to observe that they did not believe it would be *convenient* for more than six to attend from their respective parishes, and *six* was immediately fixed as the number."[4] There was no recorded objection at the time, but the apportionment of representation so casually effected in late 1774 would ultimately give rise to bitter controversy between backcountry and lowcountry that simmered in the 1780s, flared to a heated pitch of intensity in the 1790s, and was not resolved until 1808.

The general meeting in January 1775 promptly denominated itself a Provincial Congress. After extended debate, the embargo proposed by the First Continental Congress was approved subject to an exception for rice, which had been exacted by the South Carolina delegation. A new general committee was established. The Provincial Congress then adjourned, subject to recall by the general committee.

The outbreak of hostilities in Massachusetts in April 1775 further charged the political atmosphere throughout the colonies and particularly in South Carolina. The news reached Charleston in May.[5] The Provincial Congress reconvened on June 1. Two regiments of infantry and one of rangers were established, and various measures for the defense of Charleston were adopted. An issue of paper money was authorized to provide for payment of the costs incurred. A Council of Safety was created to serve as an interim executive body. A call was issued for the election of a new Provincial Congress to meet December 1 and to continue for a stated term of one year. In addition, the members adopted an "association" declaring their readiness to sacrifice their lives and fortunes to secure freedom and safety against every foe, such

---

4. *Speech of Joseph Alston . . .* (Georgetown, S.C.: Francis M. Baxter, 1808), 21–22. Not all the districts outside the consolidated Charleston district of St. Philip and St. Michael were limited to six delegates.

5. *South Carolina Gazette and Country Journal*, May 16, 1775; *Crouch's South Carolina Gazette Extraordinary*, May 19, 1775.

commitment to continue in full force until a reconciliation should take place "upon Conciliatory Principles, an Event which we most ardently desire." The association was put out for public subscription and those unwilling to subscribe would be held "inimical to the Liberty of the Colonies." A committee was appointed to circulate the association among the inhabitants of Charleston and to return the names of nonsigners to the general committee.[6]

As the crisis deepened, the goal of unity became all the more critical. To a degree, the political leaders of the province shared the "country" ideology propelling the colonies toward independence and featuring jealousy of power and exquisite concern to resist the least prospective threat to liberty. Nonetheless, most of the elite establishment were moderates, reluctant to take any irrevocable step, anxious to contain such firebrands as Christopher Gadsden and William Henry Drayton, and concerned to protect their own power and status. In the circumstances, the long-standing cleavage between lowcountry and backcountry, only partially ameliorated by the recent measures designed to include the backcountrymen in the evolving political system, was an immediate problem.[7]

To all outward appearences, South Carolina was Charleston in 1775 and vice versa. Charleston was the center of trade and commerce and the point of connection between colonial South Carolina and the larger world beyond. For the limited area of Charleston and its immediately surrounding parishes, to a radius of some sixty miles to the north, west, and south of the city, "the harmony we were famous for" lamented by Christopher Gadsden in 1784 may have indeed prevailed for most of the notables for most of the time.[8] But it hardly represented reality for the province as a whole after the influx of immigrants from the northward into the backcountry beginning in the 1760s and continuing into the 1770s.

On the eve of the Revolution, the lowcountry region surrounding Charleston was essentially self-contained and self-

---

6. *South Carolina Gazette and Country Journal,* June 6, 1775.
7. Weir, *Colonial South Carolina,* 131–40.
8. "A Steady and Open Republican" [Christopher Gadsden], *GSSC,* July 17, 1784, in *The Writings of Christopher Gadsden,* Richard Walsh, ed. (Columbia: University of South Carolina Press, 1966), 206–28, quote at 207.

centered, secure in its stability, rectitude, and assumed right and capacity to govern. The larger backcountry was essentially insecure, still lacking many of the basic institutions of local government and linked to the lowcountry only by the most tenuous of ties. Cultural differences reinforced geographic barriers dividing the state. Neither bonds of kinship nor of common experience linked the two areas. In contrast to lowcountry homogeneity, the backcountry was still largely fragmented, the processes of political and social integration barely begun. Backcountry communities were islands of unity bound together by local leaders and local circumstances. "Shared resentment against the central administration in Charleston," Rachel Klein has said, "acted as an important bond among backsettlers."[9] Lowcountry leaders were thus viewed with suspicion in the backcountry. Those leaders, in turn, largely disregarded the backcountry folk except in times of such crises in their attenuated relationship that the immediate problems of governance could no longer be ignored. Equally important, serious tensions existed within the backcountry, many reflecting the conflicts that produced the Regulator movement of the late 1760s and thereafter only partially resolved.[10]

Relations between lowcountry and backcountry in South Carolina were thus of paramount concern to lowcountry political leaders in the mid-1770s. There was potential for both dangerous discord and added strength in the approaching confrontation. Clearly, the course of events had legitimized and institutionalized backcountry participation in the political process, so that the principle of backcountry representation in the legislature was solidly established in the two Provincial Congresses that preceded the adoption of a formal constitution of government. Even so, the relationship was fragile. The well-known expedition of William Henry Drayton and William Tennent to the backcountry produced only a vague commitment to neutrality. Subsequent hostilities around Ninety Six were concluded with a new

---

9. Rachel Klein, "The Rise of the Planters in the South Carolina Backcountry, 1767–1808" (Ph.D. dissertation, Yale University, 1979), 34.

10. Richard Maxwell Brown, *The South Carolina Regulators* (Cambridge: Harvard University Press, 1963) describes the Regulator movement as a whole. Robert Stansbury Lambert, *South Carolina Loyalists in the American Revolution* (Columbia: University of South Carolina Press, 1987), 28, points out that "the animosities generated between individual families and neighbors very probably carried over into the civil war that raged through the backcountry during the Revolution."

understanding, equally uncertain. The Revolution may have "unequivocally made backcountrymen part of the political community," as Robert Weir has said.[11] But their commitment was hardly firm, and, until the British tipped the scale after the fall of Charleston, the backcountry remained, as it was in 1774 and 1775, "much more concerned with its own problems than with the constitutional strife between the coastal residents and the mother country."[12]

In September 1775 the royal government of South Carolina collapsed when Governor Campbell moved from Charleston to a British ship anchored in the harbor. The second Provincial Congress convened on November 1, a month ahead of schedule, sat until November 29, and reconvened for its second session on February 1, 1776. Stimulated by a recommendation of the Continental Congress, work began almost immediately on a formal constitution. The work was entrusted to a committee of eleven dominated by lowcountry establishment leaders but reflecting opinions ranging from conservative to moderately radical. Although a new constitution was drafted and approved, the radicals significantly failed to achieve a declaration of independence despite Gadsden's dramatic arrival in mid-February with a copy of Thomas Paine's *Common Sense* in hand. The conservative wing was not impressed.[13]

South Carolina's Constitution of 1776 was adopted as much out of necessity as conviction. Reciting an extended list of grievances to justify the action taken, it was nonetheless expressly designed only to serve "during the present situation of American Affairs, and until an accommodation of the unhappy differences between Great Britain and America can be obtained (an event which, though traduced and treated as rebels, we still earnestly desire)." Consequently, changes in the operating structure of the established government were as few as possible. There was no change in the membership of the existing de facto legislative body, in which the newly created backcountry constituencies were represented. The second Provincial Congress simply became the first General Assembly. A Legislative Council of thir-

---

11. Weir, *Colonial South Carolina*, 333.
12. Poythress, "Revolution by Committee," 45.
13. Weir, *Colonial South Carolina*, 325–28; Carl J. Vipperman, *The Rise of Rawlins Lowndes, 1721–1800* (Columbia: University of South Carolina Press, 1978), 189–92.

teen members was established, to be elected by the General Assembly out of its own membership, and constituting the functional equivalent of an upper house of the legislature. A president, to be elected by the General Assembly and the Legislative Council, replaced the royal governor. A Privy Council was created, consisting of the vice-president, three members chosen by the General Assembly, and three chosen by the Legislative Council. The president was granted power to veto legislation and was eligible for reelection. Judges were granted tenure during good behavior, but the constitutional structure of the judicial system was otherwise unchanged. The obligatory oath of office only required that the new constitution be supported and defended "until an accommodation of the differences between Great Britain and America shall take place."[14]

The new constitution was approved on March 26, 1776, marking the end of a painful transition from royal government to home rule. The second Provincial Congress adjourned and reconvened the same day as the first General Assembly. As Henry Laurens described the event, "Congress metamorphosed in the twinkling of an eye into a General Assembly."[15] Its term of office would be less than one year, since a new General Assembly would be elected on the last Monday in October and biannually thereafter. John Rutledge was elected president and commander in chief.[16]

The expectations of those hoping for reconciliation with Britain were soon dashed. The spirit of independence was spreading rapidly, stimulated particularly by William Henry Drayton, the new chief justice, and Christopher Gadsden. In April, no doubt influenced by Thomas Paine, Drayton delivered a ringing charge to the grand jury in Charleston in the form of a history lesson contrasting the advantages of the new constitution to the disad-

---

14. The formal proceedings are reported in William Edwin Hemphill, et al., eds., *Extracts from the Journals of the Provincial Congresses of South Carolina, 1775–1776* (Columbia: South Carolina Archives Department, 1960), 182, 184–85, 227–30, 232–44, 252, and 254–55. The text of the Constitution of 1776 appears in Hemphill, et al., *Extracts from the Journals*, 256–63, and in *Statutes at Large*, 1: 128–34. The long preamble was written at the last minute by John Rutledge. John Drayton, *Memoirs of the Revolution*, 2 vols. (Charleston: A. E. Miller, 1821), 2: 179–80.
15. Henry Laurens to John Laurens, March 28, 1776, Laurens Papers, Yale University.
16. *Journals 1776–1780*, 3. Rutledge won on the second ballot. Nobody had a majority on the first.

vantages of British rule. Politely acknowledging the constitution's expressed hope for reconciliation, he then blew the point away. Britain's conduct and intransigence toward the American colonies, he concluded, "demonstrate to a mind in the least given to reflection upon the rise and fall of empires, that true reconcilement can never exist between Britain and America, the latter being in subjection to the former—The Almighty created America to be independent of Britain; let us beware of the impropriety of being backward to act as instruments in the Almighty Hand, now extended to accomplish His purpose; and by the completion of which alone America, in the nature of human affairs, can be secure against the craft and insidious designs of *her enemies who think her property and power* ALREADY BY FAR TOO GREAT."[17]

The British cooperated by launching an attack on Charleston in June, which was repulsed in the famous defense of Sullivan's Island behind breastworks of palmetto logs. An Indian uprising on the western frontier, put down in July and August, was widely attributed to British machinations. In July, the Declaration of Independence issued from Philadelphia, signed by all the South Carolina delegates to the Continental Congress. In August, the independence of the United States was celebrated in Charleston; and the Declaration was enthusiastically endorsed at a special session of the General Assembly in September. As this pattern of events developed, Henry Laurens in Charleston concluded that "there were few Men here who had not lost all inclination for renewing our former connection with Great Britain." For Laurens, the great point was settled.[18]

Almost immediately, work began on a new constitution to establish a permanent frame of government appropriate to the sovereign status of an independent state. When a new constitution was finally completed and adopted in March 1778, substantial changes in political structure were effected, but some pressing issues were passed over.[19] A bicameral General Assembly was created, consisting of a Senate and a House of Representatives, both to be elected by the people. The Legislative Council

---

17. Drayton, *Memoirs of the Revolution*, 2: 259–74, quote at 274.
18. Henry Laurens to John Laurens, August 14, 1776, Berol Collection, Columbia University.
19. Constitution of 1778, *Statutes at Large*, 1: 137–46. The most important of the deferred issues was that involving the apportionment of representation.

was abolished and the Privy Council retained. The president was redesignated as governor, shorn of the veto power, and denied the right to succeed himself during a period of four full years following completion of his term in office. Neither the father, a brother, nor a son of the sitting governor was eligible for membership on the Privy Council. The existing constituencies were virtually unchanged. In two instances, new constituencies were carved out of existing ones; but in each case, the representation of the old districts was subdivided among the new. Property qualifications for office holders and voters were retained. More importantly, express provision was made for reapportionment of representation seven years after enactment, and every fourteen years thereafter, "in the most equal and just manner, according to the particular and comparative Strength and taxable Property, of the different Parts of the [State]; Regard being always had to the number of white Inhabitants and such taxable Property." The problem of malapportionment was thus recognized, but not resolved. Writing of the new constitution to Thomas Bee in October, Christopher Gadsden observed:

> I hardly know of any material fault in it but the great
> disproportion of members in a few Parishes with respect to
> others, a matter which tho' generally seen and admitted,
> having got a footing from necessity could not from want of
> proper data at its framing be then better regulated and
> which the Constitution . . . has provided shall be set to
> rights at a future period, in the interim trusting to the
> virtue common prudence and true policy of such parts as
> glaringly have the greatest superiority both with regard to
> situation and number of representatives that no
> inconveniences or disturbances would arise on their part by
> their ungenerously and unwise assuming too much on their
> present advantages.[20]

In addition, the Constitution of 1778 disestablished the Anglican Church and granted full religious liberty to all Protestant denominations. Because ministers of the gospel were "by their Profession, dedicated to the Service of God, and ought not to be diverted from the Great duties of their function," they were ineligible for election to high executive or legislative office. The elec-

---

20. Gadsden to Thomas Bee, October 5, 1778, in *The Writings of Christopher Gadsden*, Walsh, ed., 154–58.

tion of most state officers was committed to the General Assembly. The principle of rotation in office was applied to Privy Councilors and even to sheriffs. Provision was made for impeachment proceedings against state officers charged with corrupt conduct in their respective offices. As soon as proper laws could be passed, the state would be divided into districts and counties and county courts established. The state's harsh penal laws would be reformed, "and Punishments made, in some cases, less sanguinary, and, in general, more proportionate to the Crime." Freemen were protected in their freeholds, liberties, and privileges and could not be deprived of life, liberty, or property but by the judgment of their peers or by the law of the land. The military would be subordinate to the civil power of the state, and liberty of the press inviolably preserved. There was thus something for everybody.

Progress from the Constitution of 1776 to the Constitution of 1778 was neither quick nor easy. It began in October 1776 toward the end of the second session of the first General Assembly. In mid-October, on the motion of Christopher Gadsden, a committee headed by Rawlins Lowndes, consisting entirely of lowcountry establishment figures, was appointed to consider and report on revision of the Constitution of 1776.[21] The committee reported promptly, declared that all political connections with Great Britain were dissolved, and recommended a number of specific changes. In particular, the Legislative Council should be either popularly elected or elected by the General Assembly from the public at large, no future president should serve more than one two-year term within any eight year period, and representation should be reduced and apportioned as soon as practicable on the dual basis of population and property. The report was debated for two days. By the end of the first day, the decision was made that the Legislative Council should be popularly elected from the several parishes and election districts. "By this means," William Tennent observed, "one avenue of family intrigue seems to be obstructed." The next day, the Assembly unanimously endorsed the principle of rotation in the governor's office. "This is hardly digested by our ambitious people," Tennent said, 'but none

---

21. Rawlins Lowndes, John Mathews, Christopher Gadsden, Thomas Bee, Thomas Heyward, Charles Pinckney, Paul Trapier, Alexander Moultrie, and John Edwards, all representing lowcountry parishes.

dared to oppose it openly." The committee's recommendation that ministers be barred from the legislature, which Tennent thought was aimed at him, was rejected by a substantial majority. Only the proposal on representation encountered serious difficulty, and in Tennent's view was the only proposal "against the privileges of the people" that succeeded. "Advantage was taken of the disproportion and the excessive number for Charleston," Tennent said, and the vote to endorse that proposal was carried only by the casting vote of the Speaker, James Parsons.[22]

On completion of the debate, the same committee was directed to bring in a bill to effect the agreed-upon changes. But it was by then too late, because, by the express terms of the existing constitution, the legislative term could not extend beyond October 21. Nonetheless, the first General Assembly left to the second a clear set of recommendations for constitutional revision. When the elections were held, everyone understood that the incoming General Assembly intended to adopt a new constitution.[23]

At this point the historian confronts a sadly deficient public record of events. The legislative journals for all of 1777, all of 1778, and 1779 to August 31 have been lost. Moreover, a major fire devastated Charleston in mid-January 1778. More than 250 houses were lost. Peter Timothy's printing establishment was destroyed, and his *Gazette of the State of South Carolina* did not resume publication until June 24. John Wells's establishment was less seriously damaged, and his *South Carolina and American General Gazette* was back in business by January 29. But Wells was at best a cautious patriot. He was highly selective in his reporting of developments prior to the British occupation of Charleston and openly supported the British after they arrived. The se-

---

22. The proceedings in the second session of the first General Assembly can be followed in *Journals 1776–1780*, 143, 148–49, 150, and 159–63, supplemented by William Tennent, "Historic Remarks on the Session of Assembly began to be holden Tuesday, September 17, 1776," in "Writings of the Reverend William Tennent, 1740–1777," Newton B. Jones, ed., *SCHM*, 61 (1960): 189–93.

23. Gervais to Henry Laurens, March 16, 1778, in "Letters from John Lewis Gervais to Henry Laurens," Raymond Starr, ed. (hereinafter Gervais-Laurens Letters), *SCHM*, 66 (1965): 27–31; David Ramsay, *The History of the Revolution of South Carolina . . .* (Trenton: Isaac Collins, 1785), 1: 128–29. The elections in every part of the state, Ramsay said, were conducted on the idea that the members chosen, over and above the ordinary power of legislators, "should have the power to frame a new constitution suitable to the declared independence of the state."

quence of events, then, must be pieced together from a variety of sources without the central core of an official or quasi-official record.[24]

The second General Assembly took up the legacy left by the first and constitutional revision was before the House early in January 1777. On January 11, Tennent delivered a long speech calling for disestablishment of the Anglican Church, a specific constitutional prohibition against any future establishment "of any one religious denomination or sect of Protestant Christians in this state by way of preference to another," and provisions granting all Protestants "free and equal civil privileges." Tennent argued basically from principles of justice and natural rights. Mere toleration would not suffice. But he emphasized also the importance of unity in the people. "Grant this petition and the foundation of religious discord is eternally removed," he said. "It is inequality that excites jealousy and dissatisfaction. . . . If all your people are equally free and happy, it will not matter who is *in* or, who is *out*, i.e. in respect to denomination."[25]

By the end of the month, a proposed new constitution was completed by the General Assembly and forwarded to the Legislative Council. Presumably persuaded by Tennent's argument, the bill incorporated all he had sought in a long provision that ultimately carried over to the completed Constitution of 1778. In most other respects it followed the outline approved in October 1776. It contemplated an elective Legislative Council and General Assembly. The veto power was eliminated and the governor could not succeed himself, but no other state official was similarly barred. Relatives of the governor were barred from the Privy Council. Complementing the grant of religious freedom, ministers were barred from election to the legislature. Nothing was said about the organization of counties, reform of the penal code, freedom of the press, and protection of due process of law. These were all provisions that found their way into the final ver-

24. The great fire of January 15, 1778, is described in detail in John Wells to Henry Laurens, January 23, 1778, William Gilmore Simms collection of Laurens papers, formerly in the Long Island Historical Society and now in the Kendall Whaling Museum, Salem, Massachusetts (hereinafter Kendall Collection), and in Gervais to Henry Laurens, February 16, 1778, held in private collection.
25. William Tennent, "Petition of the Dissenters" and "Speech . . . Delivered in the House of Assembly, Charleston, January 11, 1777," in "Writings of Tennent," Jones, ed., *SCHM*, 61 (1960): 194–209.

sion a year later. As initially recommended, however, reapportionment was contemplated "when proper information can be had of the particular and comparative strength and taxable property of the different parts of the state."[26]

The new constitution lay before the public for nearly a year. Work was resumed by the General Assembly, the popularly elected house of the legislature under the Constitution of 1776, in January 1778 and continued into early February. By then, the General Assembly and the Legislative Council were engaged in a direct and fundamental confrontation. The Assembly apparently denied the right of the Council to participate in the making of the constitution, asserting "that this is the prerogative of the people alone, and is to be done by themselves or their representatives, without the intervention of any other body whatever," while the Council refused to surrender its power to reject acts approved by the Assembly. As late as February 16, the Assembly and the Council were still far apart on a number of material issues, and President Rutledge did not expect that the conflict would be resolved. Ultimately, the two houses agreed to meet in conference, while the Assembly backed its claim to preeminence by insisting that no other public business would be done until the new constitution was finished.[27] In the final stage of the proceedings, an unsuccessful effort was made to reduce the size of the House of Representatives by cutting the number of delegates from each constituency in half; the provision barring relatives of the governor from the Privy Council was in and out and in again, obviously the subject of some disagreement; the open-ended provision on reapportionment was tightened to require revision within seven years; and the governor's veto was clearly a

---

26. *Bill for Establishing the Constitution of the State of South Carolina* (Charleston: Peter Timothy, 1777). The bill was ordered published by the Legislative Council on February 4.

27. "A View of Coastal Carolina in 1778: The Journal of Ebenezer Hazard," H. Roy Merrens, ed., *SCHM*, 73 (1972): 177–93; John Rutledge to Henry Laurens, February 16, 1778, Gratz Collection, HSP; Gervais to Henry Laurens, February 16, 1778, held in private collection. The hard line positions of the General Assembly are described in the Hazard journal, *SCHM*, 73 (1972): 186 (February 9) and 190 (February 25). Hazard was on a tour of the South in his official capacity as a surveyor of the post roads to investigate and improve postal communications. In that capacity he had access to and met with influential people in and out of government while he was in South Carolina.

matter of contention.[28] But differences were resolved by March 5, when a new constitution was engrossed and presented to Rutledge for his signature.

To the consternation of all in attendance, Rutledge vetoed it, precipitating the state's first major political crisis. He could not assent to the new constitution without violating his oath of office, Rutledge said, and it was "otherwise not meeting with his approbation." He argued that the General Assembly was obligated to adhere to the Constitution of 1776, "not admitting any innovation of it." In particular, "the legislative authority, being fixed and limited, cannot change or destroy itself without subverting the constitution from which it is derived." In violation of that principle, the presidential veto had been removed and one branch of government (the Legislative Council) had been eliminated. The people preferred to retain the Legislative Council, he asserted, since it was elected out of the General Assembly and would therefore consist of men of the greatest integrity and ability. Moreover, in a statement clearly broad enough to encompass the commitment to reapportion representation in the new House of Representatives, he complained that the new system tended to enlarge the democratic power, which experience had shown to be "arbitrary, severe, and destructive." Finally, he was unwilling to abandon the prospect of reconciliation with Britain, proclaiming that it was "as desirable now as it ever was." But he assumed that his remarks would not "influence your minds in a matter which has been so lately the subject of debate," and he accordingly submitted his resignation. John Lewis Gervais called the sequence of events "an unexpected Revolution."[29]

---

28. Draft Constitution of South Carolina, Constitutional Documents, 1776–1808, SCA. There is no way to determine whether this heavily interlined manuscript originated in the General Assembly or in the Legislative Council. It is a fair assumption, however, that the Council supported reduction of the number of representatives to sit in the House, opposed the provision barring relatives of the governor from the Privy Council, and opposed elimination of the governor's veto. The seven year period provided for the reapportionment of representation was probably a compromise. No time was specified in the provision proposed by the General Assembly, and the Legislative Council presumably opposed reapportionment.
29. *SCAGG*, March 12, 1778; Gervais to Henry Laurens, March 16, 1778, in the Gervais-Laurens Letters, *SCHM*, 66 (1965): 27–31. Rutledge's remarks are set forth in full in Ramsay, *Revolution of South Carolina*, 1: 132–38.

Modern commentators have found Rutledge's arguments specious and have suspected a power play "designed to throw the government into confusion and to force alterations in the new constitution that would prevent the limited diffusion of political power it proposed."[30] Rutledge's views and intentions had been closely guarded. After all, the proposed constitution had been before the public for some time; and Rutledge had nothing whatever to say of it when he delivered his first message to the General Assembly in January.[31] He may indeed have been so confident in his office and public reputation as to expect that his abrupt rejection of the new constitution and immediate resignation would force the legislature to reconsider and revise those provisions of the document that he did not approve. If so, he was disappointed.

Rutledge's unexpected action surprised and immobilized the legislature until Lowndes took charge. On the motion of Lowndes, seconded by Gadsden, a joint committee of the Legislative Council and the General Assembly was appointed to consider appropriate action. After apparently warm debate, the committee reported that Rutledge was entitled to resign, that his resignation should be accepted, and that a new president should thereupon be chosen. According to Gervais, the committee was evenly divided on the question whether Rutledge "could not pass it consistent with his oath," and Lowndes "gave the Casting vote" against that proposition on which Rutledge had so heavily relied. At the ensuing election on March 7, Arthur Middleton declined the post on grounds similar to those pronounced by Rutledge, and the choice then fell on Lowndes. The proposed constitution was brought in again, re-enacted without alteration, and then signed by the new president on March 19. The election of Lowndes was reported in John Wells's *South Carolina and American General Gazette* in the same issue that reported Rutledge's resignation, but enactment of the new constitution was never mentioned.[32] Late in the session, Gadsden was elected vice-president "by the plenitude of the Wanton power of a bare

---

30. Edward McCrady, *South Carolina in the Revolution, 1775–1780* (New York: The Macmillan Company, 1901), 242–43; Vipperman, *Rawlins Lowndes*, 204–5. The quoted passage is from Vipperman, *Rawlins Lowndes*, 205.
31. *SCAGG*, January 29, 1778. The message was delivered on January 9.
32. Gervais to Henry Laurens, March 16, 1778, in the Gervais-Laurens Letters, *SCHM*, 66 (1965): 27–31; *SCAGG*, March 19 and 26 and April 2, 1778.

house." Parsons was excused for reasons of health, Gadsden told William Henry Drayton, "and I saw plainly their Views, but could not avoid accepting without throwing the State into Confusion. But this I did not do without letting them know I plainly perceived their Motive—To get rid of me at the next meeting and to make me ineligible at next Election."[33]

The controversy over the Constitution of 1778 represented the first clear breach in the facade of harmony at the top. Whether or not Rutledge had sought to pressure the legislature for a constitution more to his liking, the Rutledge faction never forgave Lowndes for his attachment to Gadsden and his acceptance of the succession to Rutledge.[34] Partly as a result of that faction's political enmity, but also partly as a result of his own cautious and conservative style of executive leadership, Lowndes struggled through a brief term as president and left office in January 1779 with his political career in temporary ruins.[35]

The most deeply divisive controversy arose in connection with a new loyalty oath enacted by the legislature in late March, just after Lowndes took office. The law required every free white male inhabitant of the state not only to swear allegiance to the state but also to promise that he would "without Delay, discover to the Executive Authority, or some one Justice of the Peace of this State, all Plots and Conspiracies that shall come to my knowledge against the State, or any other of the United States of America." Penalties for failure to comply included loss of rights to hold office, to vote, to serve on juries, to sue in the courts, to hold, buy, or sell property, or to exercise any profession or trade. Those who preferred to leave the state would be exposed to trial for treason and would be subject to the death penalty should they subsequently return. Compliance was required within thirty days in certain cases and within sixty days in all others.[36]

The 1778 "test act" was the first of that nature of general application; and controversy was inevitable. Disaffection was wide-

---

33. Gadsden to William Henry Drayton, June 1, 1778, in *The Writings of Christopher Gadsden*, Walsh, ed., 126–29.
34. John Wells to Henry Laurens, September 6, 1778, Kendall Collection.
35. Vipperman, *Rawlins Lowndes*, 207–21.
36. *Statutes at Large*, 1: 147–51. The act became effective on March 28 and was published in full text by the *SCAGG* on April 2. The related proclamation implementing it was published in a supplement to the same journal on the same date.

spread. Many loyalist sympathizers, including some valuable mechanics and some prominent citizens, announced their intended departure.[37] By May, "two vessels full of Tories unwilling to take the oath were preparing to sail from Charleston."[38] Apprehensions were somewhat eased when news of the treaty with France arrived in late May. "The tide was fairly turned," David Ramsay wrote. "Instead of that hankering after Great Britain, which had made a separation painful, the current of popular opinions and prejudices ran strong in the opposite direction."[39] Thereafter, a "number of reluctant Whigs headed by the Rutledge men found their resolution stiffened and their ambitions whetted by the encouraging news."[40]

Lowndes had had trouble enough with the problems initially presented by the oath. His problems were compounded when the Continental Congress recommended that the time for taking the oath be extended and that a general pardon and amnesty be offered to those who had not yet complied with the law.[41] Gadsden took the lead in urging Lowndes and the Privy Council to adopt the recommendation, and on June 5, with the consent of the Privy Council, Lowndes issued a proclamation extending the deadline to June 10 and promising to apply to the General Assembly for confirmation of his actions.[42]

A new storm of patriotic sentiment promptly erupted. The best description of the outburst was provided by Lowndes himself, writing to Henry Laurens.

> Will you not be surprised Sir to hear that before the
> Proclamation could pass through the formality of a
> publication the Bells of St. Michaels were set ringing, the
> people collected and my Conduct reprehended in the
> severest terms as Contravening an Express Law, and
> superceding the Legislative Authority: a deputation was
> immediately sent to me, with Intimations that the People

---

37. Wells to Henry Laurens, April 20, 1778, Kendall Collection; Vipperman, *Rawlins Lowndes*, 210.
38. Gervais to Henry Laurens, April 20, 1778, in private collection.
39. Ramsay, *Revolution of South Carolina*, 1: 179–80.
40. Vipperman, *Rawlins Lowndes*, 211.
41. *Journals of Congress*, 10: 381–82.
42. Gadsden to William Henry Drayton, June 15, 1778, in *The Writings of Christopher Gadsden*, Walsh, ed., 131–33.

were in such a ferment that fatal Consequences were to be apprehended if I did not recall the Proclamation; this I absolutely refusing to do, all the printers were prohibited to print the proclamation, and the Acting Magistrates from administering the Oath, so that I was reduced to the Single means of declaring that I would in despite of all personal danger, administer the Oath to all who would apply to me within the limited time; and the Vice President made the same declaration; some accordingly have taken the Oath, but the menaces of the populace have deterred many and frustrated the best plan that could be devised for Conciliating Peace and Union amongst us.[43]

Gadsden described the event in somewhat more colorful terms. The proclamation, he said, "was hardly got into the Sheriff's Hands before some Myrmidons Alarm'd the Town, Setting up a Proclamation against the Law; we were going to ruin their Liberties and What not!" And he observed that, in his opinion, even if the populace were not incited by the disaffected Rutledge faction, "the old Leven was at least not sorry for it, as it was echoed amongst the people, I am told, that had Mr. R. been president Nothing of this Sort would have happened."[44] The proclamation was not published, and on June 10, "at a meeting of a great number of respectable inhabitants of Charleston," a resolution was unanimously adopted to the effect that the March act "ought and shall be strictly carried into execution" and that the penalties imposed thereby would be "assuredly inflicted upon all defaulters."[45] Gadsden understood that the resolution was drawn by Edward Rutledge.[46]

Wells reported these events to Laurens on the day of the public meeting. The proclamation created "unspeakable uneasiness" among the people, he said, and he declined to print it because "the consequences would be very disagreeable." Gadsden had offered him support and protection, but Wells "had not the

---

43. Lowndes to Henry Laurens, June 17, 1778, Kendall Collection.
44. Gadsden to William Henry Drayton, June 15, 1778, in *The Writings of Christopher Gadsden*, Walsh, ed., 131–33.
45. *SCAGG*, June 11, 1778. The proclamation was not published until it appeared in Timothy's *Gazette of the State of South Carolina* on June 24, the first publication of that paper after the January fire.
46. Gadsden to William Henry Drayton, June 15, 1778, in *The Writings of Christopher Gadsden*, Walsh, ed., 131–33.

smallest idea of being a *Scape Goat.*" Lowndes was by no means a popular president, Wells continued, and "Mr. Gadsden, by averring himself the proposer of the offensive Proclamation, has given great offense to many." Popular meetings were bad for new governments, he added, resulting in loss of respect.[47]

The proclamation brouhaha was not Lowndes's only problem in 1778. Violence was continuing in the backcountry. The British were moving against Georgia and backcountry loyalists were moving to support them. The western Indians were threatening, and all the intractable problems of preparation for defense demanded attention. In September, the peace of Charleston was disrupted by a violent riot between French and American sailors in which shots were exchanged and several killed. When the General Assembly convened in September, Lowndes found his issuance of the June proclamation under investigation and the legislature slow to respond to his request for support. Gervais put the state of affairs in reasonable perspective. The June affair had made Lowndes unpopular, he conceded, but Lowndes had another great fault. "He is very difficult in giving orders for money and will know every particular what it is for—Depend upon it, he has already saved many thousands." Nonetheless, the dissatisfied always had friends to support them, and "a good Steward of the public will have a great number of Enemies."[48]

Wells was more critical. Lowndes was "very unpopular," he told Henry Laurens in September. His association with Gadsden and his acceptance of the presidency "when vacated by Mr. Rutledge, it is generally said, have gained him the ill will of that powerful family, which by their opponents is stiled 'The Family Compact.' " In addition, the proclamation issued in June "occasioned his being called a Friend to Tories, and some former parts of his conduct, not according with the ideas of the violent Party made many of them class him among those obnoxious People." Finally, agreeing with Gervais, Wells observed that Lowndes's frugality and economy, his strict investigation of all public accounts, and "his dealing out the public money with a very sparing hand" had given some offense. Wells had been called, he said, to testify before the committee investigating the June distur-

47. John Wells to Henry Laurens, June 10, 1778, Kendall Collection.
48. Gervais to Henry Laurens, July 2, 1778, in private collection.

bance. "From the Complexion of a majority of the Committee," he observed, "I apprehend that the Enquiry will end *in fume*."[49]

And so it did. Gadsden was distressed and complained of "artful opposers and disturbers of our peace" who, he thought, were taking advantage of "the weakest part of the Constitution, the present allowed disproportion of numbers, in order to throw all into confusion and when an Opportunity serves get the whole new modeled more to their gout." Looking back on the events of June, he complained also of the state of affairs in which executive action authorized by the Privy Council had been "counteracted and defeated by a managed misinformed part of the Town dextrously practiced on . . . by the bellowing tools of a few ill-intending, restless, disappointed, self-important men behind the scenes."[50] Thus, the General Assembly never vindicated Lowndes. It did, however, extend the time within which the oath of allegiance might be taken and simplified the administration of it.[51] When the new General Assembly convened in January under the Constitution of 1778, President Lowndes stepped away with dignity and John Rutledge was elected to serve as the first governor under the instrument of government he had previously rejected. "Nothing but the critical situation of our public affairs would have induced me to accept" the office of governor in 1779, Rutledge later told Laurens. He could not refuse "the general wish of my Country."[52] Years later, Lowndes said much the same thing with regard to his acceptance of the Constitution of 1778. He assented to it, he said, because it had been approved by the people.[53]

Such was the background to Burke's entry into the public life of South Carolina. In March 1778, shortly after Lowndes took office and signed the new constitution, Burke was elected to sit on

49. John Wells to Henry Laurens, September 6, 1778, Kendall Collection.
50. Gadsden to Thomas Bee, October 15, 1778, in *The Writings of Christopher Gadsden*, Walsh, ed., 154–58. Gervais also commented on the reluctance of the General Assembly to vindicate Lowndes. Gervais to Henry Laurens, September 9, 1778, in the Gervais-Laurens Letters, *SCHM*, 66 (1965): 32–34. See McCrady, *South Carolina in the Revolution, 1775–1780*, 267–77.
51. *Statutes at Large*, 4: 450–52.
52. John Rutledge to Henry Laurens, April 24, 1779, Gratz Collection, HSP.
53. Elliot, *Debates*, 4: 297. Lowndes observed that he had also opposed the Declaration of Independence, but that his duty as a citizen was to promote its due observance when it received the approbation of the people. Elliot, *Debates*, 4: 274.

the Court of Common Pleas and General Sessions. Lowndes signed his commission on April 1.[54] The records of the General Assembly for that period have been lost as previously described, and the available supplementary record tells nothing of the circumstances of Burke's selection. But a persuasive hypothesis may be constructed to fill the evidentiary gap.

Concurrently with adoption of the Constitution of 1776, the departed provincial judges, all British placemen, were replaced by William Henry Drayton as chief justice and by Thomas Bee, John Mathews, Joshua Ward, and Henry Pendleton as assistant judges. Ward declined to serve, and no replacement was named.[55] Drayton and Mathews left for the Continental Congress in mid-March, 1778, and Drayton died in Philadelphia in 1779. Only Bee and Pendleton remained in South Carolina to serve as active, sitting judges.

The reconstituted court was thus seriously shorthanded when Lowndes assumed office in 1778. Many of the qualified lawyers, an eminent but small group of leading men, were otherwise occupied on state business or in preparation for its defense. Some may have been divided in their loyalty. Some were undoubtedly adherents to the Rutledge interest; and those could hardly have expected elevation to the bench after the controversy over the new constitution or have been willing to serve if selected. Others may have been simply unwilling to undertake a burdensome and relatively unrenumerative assignment. Burke was qualified in the law but presumably too recent an arrival to qualify for legal practice. In short, he may simply have been the best available candidate who was willing to serve in time of need; and it is entirely possible that he was not the first choice.

Burke immediately left Charleston to ride the southern circuit. He must have held court at Beaufort in early April and at Orangeburgh some ten days later. Sitting in Ninety Six on April 25, he greeted the grand jury with a charge appropriate to the occasion. He explained the new constitution and other major enactments of the just completed legislative session including the

54. Commission, Rawlins Lowndes to Aedanus Burke, April 1, 1778, Miscellaneous Records of the Secretary of State A, 61, SCA. Burke's election was not mentioned in the *SCAGG*, which was apparently ignoring Lowndes as much as possible. Nor was it mentioned by any of those in Charleston regularly corresponding with Henry Laurens.
55. *Journals 1776–1780*, 4, 5, 26, 28.

controversial "test act." He compared the benefits of the new form of government to the deficiencies of British rule. "The liberty of the people is no longer exposed to the baneful influence or arbitrary exertions of monarchical prerogatives," he said. "Our government being founded on the virtue and equality of the people . . . the unnatural distinctions of noblemen and commons are justly exploded from amongst us, and every citizen is, by the spirit of our government, supposed to hold a certain personal nobility and independence, by his obedience to the laws, or services to his country." The offices of government, he continued, "formerly conferred on the underling tools and minions of a British ministry," were open to all citizens. The powers of the constitution were vested in the people at large and were returned to them at short and fixed intervals, so that, "by this regular circulation, the free spirit of our government will be preserved." The grand jury respectfully thanked the judge for his illuminating remarks and asked that the charge be duly published.[56]

Burke's remarks were unexceptionable. His endorsement of the new constitution was unequivocal and emphasized fundamental tenets of the republican creed—escape from the exercise of "monarchical prerogatives," escape from the "unnatural distinctions" of an hereditary aristocracy, faith in the virtue of the citizenry, the good sense of the people, and rotation in office. But he could not have been unaware that there were those who had opposed it as tending "to enlarge the democratic power" and that Rutledge was the leader and principal public spokesman for that interest. There is no direct evidence that a faction led by Rutledge actively sought to undermine Lowndes. But that perception was in circulation, and perceptions color both action and opinion. Surely the Rutledge men had not been supportive of the Lowndes administration; and the widely held belief that Rutledge represented a conservative or aristocratic faction opposed to extensions of popular participation in the affairs of government, and hence potentially despotic, must have remained with Burke and colored his own response when he came to consider Rutledge's actions at a later time.

The words, concerns, and ideas of others may not be imputed to Burke, and Burke himself is not on record. But he entered public life in the midst of a political crisis, "an unexpected

---

56. *SCAGG*, May 21, 1778.

Revolution." By accepting office, he necessarily aligned himself with Lowndes and the legislative majority that enacted the liberalizing Constitution of 1778 over the opposition of Rutledge, Middleton, and other conservative Carolinians. Intellectually, he occupied the middle ground of moderate radicalism, committed to independence but also to the law and orderly processes of political action, as compared to the conservative restraint of the establishment elite to his right and the radical enthusiasm for extralegal pressure to his left. He entered the legislature shortly thereafter, while the crisis of the new constitution was fresh in the minds of everyone; and he was entitled to question the role that Rutledge had played.

That role was at best ambiguous. Rutledge was within his constitutional powers when he vetoed the bill presented to him for signature. He was entitled to express his substantive objection to it, although he might have spoken sooner. But he was not required to resign. He could have sent it back with a statement of the reasons for his action and then held his ground. His theory of the source of constitution-making authority was somewhat in advance of his time,[57] and there is no evidence that it was shared by a majority of South Carolinians. Ten years later, all might have agreed, and Laurens agreed at the time. Rutledge's resignation gave him inexpressible concern, Laurens said, and all Rutledge's friends in the Continental Congress "agree your principle was good, but many say, and among these be pleased to number me and forgive my candour, you ought to have done everything you did, the last act excepted." Rutledge acknowledged without comment.[58] Nevertheless, the view that Rutledge rejected the new constitution for substantive reasons and attempted to pressure the legislature by his resignation, while advancing technical legal grounds for public consumption, is circumstantially persuasive.

---

57. The theory was spelled out in John Rutledge to Henry Laurens, March 8, 1778, Draper Collection, Wisconsin Historical Society, Madison, Wisconsin. Rutledge argued that the legislature had no lawful power to establish another legislative body, that power residing "only in the people, on a Dissolution of Government, or Subversion of the Constitution." Therefore, consistent with his oath, he could not consent "to the Establishment of a Different Legislature." This was a tenable technical position, even though undermined by the circumstances of the particular case. Nothing was said in this letter about Rutledge's substantive objections.
58. Henry Laurens to John Rutledge, May 4, 1778, Laurens Papers, SCHS; John Rutledge to Henry Laurens, June 15, 1778, Library of Congress.

The situation of South Carolina public affairs was as critical in March 1778 when Rutledge rejected the new constitution as it was in February 1779 when he took office under it, perhaps more so. Unity was imperative, and the proposed constitution contained many new features designed to promote it. The people and their representatives had been expecting, and debating, constitutional revisions since October 1776. Rutledge could have accepted the Constitution of 1778 without risking public disapprobation. Rutledge indeed raised a delicate point, which Henry Laurens identified precisely. Writing to his son John, Laurens called Rutledge's resignation "an act which involves very momentous considerations." He accepted Rutledge's view of the demands of the presidential oath of office; but he understood the underlying issue. "I am not ignorant," he said, "that this may be called a moot point, the question admitting much debate, and of very refined argumentation, to be determined, or perhaps more properly, undecided by nice Casuistry."[59] In the circumstances, Burke had reasonable grounds to determine for himself who was the casuist and who the man of principle.

---

59. Henry Laurens to John Laurens, March 29, 1778, Laurens Papers, SCHS.

III

Disruption and Restoration

1778–1782

The Revolutionary War was fought largely in the south after 1778, first in Georgia and thereafter in South Carolina. Savannah was taken by the British in late December 1778. Throughout 1779, South Carolina was under mounting pressure. Violence erupted in the backcountry, and Charleston was continually threatened. By January 1780, Charleston was under siege. British forces finally occupied the city in the spring of 1780 and fanned out from there to dominate the entire state. Gradually driven back in 1781, they remained in control of Charleston until December 1782, more than a year after the Franco-American victory at Yorktown. For most of 1780 and all of 1781, civil government throughout South Carolina was virtually suspended, although order was maintained in Charleston by British military government and John Rutledge continued to direct military operations from various locations.

The conflict in the outlying areas of South Carolina pitted British regulars against troops of the Continental Line and local loyalists against state militia and partisan irregulars. The struggle, in many respects a genuine civil war, was bitter, bloody, and destructive. Plunder was taken on both sides, farms and plantations ravaged, stock and equipment appropriated or destroyed. Many slaves either escaped or were taken by the British, some estimates of the number lost ranging as high as 20,000 to 25,000. The "disorders of war" shattered both the polity and the economy of South Carolina.[1]

---

1. Jerome J. Nadelhaft, *The Disorders of War: The Revolution in South Carolina* (Orono: The University of Maine at Orono Press, 1981), 27–43; Robert M. Weir, " 'The Violent Spirit': The Reestablishment of Order, and the Continuity of Leadership in Post-Revolutionary South Carolina," in Ronald Hoffman, Thad W. Tate, and Peter J. Albert, eds., *An Uncivil War: The Southern Backcountry during the American Revolution* (Charlottesville: University Press of Virginia, 1985),

The first General Assembly elected to serve under the Constitution of 1778 thus gathered in an atmosphere of crisis. Indeed, although called to convene on January 5, 1779, so many members of the House of Representatives were absent on military duties that no quorum could be assembled until January 19.[2] Various measures were taken to strengthen the state's defenses. John Rutledge was elected governor, returned as chief executive less than a year after his controversial resignation. The time within which the oath of fidelity and allegiance might be taken was further extended to June 1 and the procedures for administering it simplified.[3] An ordinance was enacted declaring any person withdrawing from the defense of the state or joining its enemies guilty of treason. Upon conviction, the penalty was death and confiscation of all property. The families of those convicted could be banished should their continued presence in the state be found "dangerous to the safety of the community," and the same provision was specifically made applicable to the families of those leaving the state because of refusal or failure to take the required oath of fidelity and allegiance.[4] Moreover, the new governor was authorized to direct the judges to hold special courts of sessions at locations other than those where the criminal activity occurred, purportedly against the possibility that circumstances might inhibit the ability of the courts to try cases at the usual places.[5]

Burke was not a member of the House of Representatives when it convened in January 1779. He was on hand, however, when the second session met in July, representing the combined parishes of St. Philip and St. Michael.[6] In that session and the

---

70–98; Robert Stansbury Lambert, *South Carolina Loyalists in the American Revolution* (Columbia: University of South Carolina Press, 1987), 198–215.

2. *GSSC*, January 20, 1779.

3. *Statutes at Large*, 4: 468–69.

4. *Statutes at Large*, 4: 479–80.

5. *Statutes at Large*, 4: 500–502. Such courts would have concurrent jurisdiction with the Court of General Sessions to try cases prosecuted under the ordinance cited in note 4 above. John Mathews and Thomas Heyward were subsequently commissioned to conduct a special court for the trial of persons charged with sedition and desertion. Miscellaneous Records of the Secretary of State A, 115–16, SCA. Lambert, *South Carolina Loyalists*, 83–85, describes the ensuing proceedings.

6. *Bio. Directory*, 1: 179–86; *Journals 1776–1780*, 317–23. The surviving journal begins in mid-session, on August 31, 1779. Burke appears on that date as a participating member of the House. Necessarily, then, he had previously taken the

next, he performed a variety of ministerial functions but was not, on the limited record available, involved in any major legislative project. In August, he served on a committee to consider a bill, which was ultimately rejected, granting amnesty to those who took an oath of allegiance to Britain during the British foray into South Carolina after the fall of Savannah.[7] In February 1780, he presented a petition of backcountrymen complaining of the high price of salt, asserting that the per diem allowance to militiamen was insufficient and not regularly paid, and requesting that the militia law be amended to permit exchange if captured.[8] The matter was referred to a committee that never reported.

The most startling events of the period relating to Burke concerned his judicial office. During the first session, when he was probably not yet a member of the House, Peter Timothy's *State Gazette* reported that the General Assembly had elected Burke and Thomas Heyward as assistant judges.[9] There is no mystery in Heyward's case. But Burke already held the office. The objective may have been to confirm Burke's tenure under the Constitution of 1778, although no similar election was held for the other judges. Or some technical defect may have been found in the prior proceedings involving Burke. In all events, Governor Rutledge issued him a new commission in due course.[10]

A year later, in January 1780, Burke abruptly presented his resignation to the House, asserting that the holding of his commission as assistant judge had been for some time past attended with many inconveniences to him. "When I am conscious that I possess every warm wish and inclination to serve this State and support the independence of it on all occasions," he said, "it is not without concern, I own, that I find myself under an absolute necessity of resigning."[11] The matter ended there. The resigna-

---

requisite qualifying oath, representing that he was "of the Protestant Religion, and hath been a Resident of this State for three Years, previous to his Election." Constitution of 1778, Article XIII, *Statutes at Large*, 1: 140–41. The ordinance establishing the form of qualifying oath, which was not set forth in the Constitution, was adopted in October 1778, at the last session of the second General Assembly. *Statutes at Large*, 4: 457–58.

7. *Journals 1776–1780*, 186, 190–91, 208.

8. Ibid., 275.

9. *GSSC*, February 24, 1779. The date of the election was not stated.

10. Commission, John Rutledge to Aedanus Burke, February 15, 1779, Miscellaneous Records of the Secretary of State A, 101, SCA.

11. *Journals 1776–1780*, 261.

tion was either withdrawn or ignored. On his later record, Burke might have objected to the special courts of sessions established in 1779 as subjecting persons to trial outside the areas of their residence. But if he was unhappy with the course of events in 1779 and early 1780, there is no other recorded evidence of his displeasure.

Like most of his contemporaries, Burke also served in the military forces of the state. He was a lieutenant in a regiment of the Continental Line in 1778, resigning just prior to his appointment to the bench.[12] He thereafter joined a Charleston militia regiment commanded by Colonel Maurice Simons[13] and was captured with the defending force when the British occupied Charleston in May 1780. There is no record of his experience while in British hands except for a statement, written years later, that he had been "a prisoner of war in the hands of the British for Sixteen months, captured with the Garrison in Charleston."[14] His name does not appear on the lists of those incarcerated in the prison ships in Charleston harbor. He was not among those sent to St. Augustine, but he was one of the larger group released and shipped away for exchange in mid-1781.[15] Reaching Philadelphia, he became sufficiently well acquainted with Arthur Middleton, then representing South Carolina in the Continental Congress, to begin a regular correspondence with him that continued over the next several months.

Burke's itinerary en route back to South Carolina can be traced through his letters to Middleton. On October 9, he was in Baltimore and suggested to Middleton that "our Carolina friends" traveling south should take another route unless well supplied with funds. On October 16, he was with the Continen-

---

12. Bobby Gilmer Moss, *Roster of South Carolina Patriots in the American Revolution* (Baltimore: Genealogical Publishing Company, Inc., 1983), 124 and sources cited. The Second Regiment of South Carolina, in which Burke served until February 1778, was heavily involved in the successful defense of Charleston in June, 1776. If Burke was in service at that time, as he may well have been, he probably saw his share of action. The South Carolina forces were not transferred to the Continental Line until September 1776.
13. "Regimental Order Book of Captain James Bentham, 1778–1780," Robert B. Simons, ed., *SCHM*, 53 (1952): 15, 111.
14. Burke to Madison, September 13, 1801, in Gaillard Hunt, "Office Getting During Jefferson's Administration," *American Historical Review*, 3 (1897–1898): 278–79.
15. "Josiah Smith's Diary, 1780–1781," Mabel L. Webber, ed., *SCHM*, 34 (1933): 78–84, at 79.

tal and French forces before Yorktown, and on October 19 watched the British force march out to lay down its arms. Although he detested the British army, "and despise from my soul the mass of unfeeling men which compose its officers," he could, he said, understand their feelings in defeat. He remained with the army near Yorktown for nearly a month, delayed by an injury to his horse and staying with the family of General St. Clair. By November 18, he was in Petersburg, preparing to accompany St. Clair's division on the march south.[16]

Meanwhile the state was being governed by John Rutledge under emergency powers covering "all matters and things which may be judged expedient and necessary to secure the liberty, safety and happiness of this State, except taking the life of a citizen without trial," granted in February 1780.[17] Despite Burke's later charges against him, Rutledge exercised the dictatorial powers conferred upon him with reasonable restraint and as much efficiency as the circumstances and his peripatetic existence would allow. He directed his attention primarily to military matters and, lacking other advisors, to consultation with the state's delegates to the Continental Congress. As early as November 1780, he was looking toward the time when the British might be driven back upon Charleston. Then civil government might be reestablished in some part of the country, the legislature reconstituted, and laws made and enforced.[18]

By the summer of 1781, the hope of 1780 seemed to be nearing realization. "I wish most anxiously," Rutledge told the delegates in Philadelphia, "to have an assembly elected, and sitting as soon as possible." But action was deferred because "it would be ungenerous to exclude our worthy friends lately Prisoners

16. Burke to Middleton, October 9, October 16, and November 18, 1781, in "Correspondence of Arthur Middleton, Signer of the Declaration of Independence," annotated by Joseph W. Barnwell (hereinafter Middleton Correspondence), *SCHM*, 26 (1925): 184–90. Burke to General Arthur St. Clair, October 13, 1781, St. Clair Papers, Library of Congress, bears St. Clair's note "Judge Burke was one of my aids."
17. *Statutes at Large*, 4: 504–506. Burke was serving in the House of Representatives when these extensive powers were granted to Rutledge.
18. Rutledge to the Delegates of South Carolina in the Continental Congress, November 20, 1780, in "Letters of John Rutledge," Joseph W. Barnwell, ed., *SCHM*, 17 (1916): 142–45.

in St. Augustine and Charles Town from a share in the Legislature . . . and injurious to the public to deprive it of their Abilities and Services."[19]

In September 1781, while Burke was either still in or just leaving Philadelphia, Rutledge was finally ready to act. On September 27 he issued a proclamation offering amnesty to certain British supporters, including those who had voluntarily accepted British protection while under British control, upon appearance within thirty days to take an oath of loyalty to the state and agreement to serve six months in the militia. There were exceptions, specifically those holding military or civil commissions under the British, those who had previously refused pardons, and those guilty of conduct so "infamous" as to be undeserving of the privileges of American liberty. Those Charlestonians who had affirmatively welcomed the British in 1780 were similarly excepted.[20]

In November, Rutledge called for the election of a new General Assembly to convene at Camden (later changed to Jacksonborough) on January 8, 1782. The writs of election were on a printed form, datelined "at the High Hills of Santee this Twentieth Day of November, 1781," and called for the election to be held on December 17 and 18. By the terms of the writ, those designated to conduct the election were instructed to observe the requirements of the existing election law and the state constitution with one important exception. "Inasmuch as it is inconsistent with, and repugnant to the Spirit, Intent, and Meaning of the said Constitution, that Persons who have withdrawn their Allegiance to the State, and borne Arms with, or received Protection from the Enemy, should be admitted to vote for, or be eligible as Members of the Legislature," the writs expressly directed, "you are not to receive the Vote of any Person under the Description abovementioned or return any such Person as a Member of the [General Assembly] unless he shall have returned

19. Rutledge to the Delegates of South Carolina in the Continental Congress, August 6, 1781, in "Letters of John Rutledge," Barnwell, ed., *SCHM*, 18 (1917): 136–37.
20. John Rutledge, Proclamation, September 27, 1781, in R. W. Gibbes, ed., *Documentary History of the American Revolution*, 3 vols. (Columbia: Banner Steam-Roller Press, 1853; reprint ed., Spartanburg: The Reprint Company, 1972), 3: 175–78.

to his Allegiance" and manifested that return in the manner specified in the amnesty proclamation issued in September.[21]

For those parishes still in British hands, essentially those in and around Charleston, the election was to be held as near as possible to the normal polling places to encourage the maximum possible participation. Even so, the elections were sparsely attended. Tories and "protection men" who had not complied with the amnesty offer, or could not qualify under it, were excluded as directed. Many voters were still in service elsewhere. Voting had to be conducted outside the city for residents of Charleston. Many potential voters were still no doubt reluctant to commit themselves. Jerome Nadelhaft, in a recent study of the period, found that fifteen Charleston voters, "who ventured out of the city or returned from other parts of the state," elected thirty representatives and two senators for St. Philip and St. Michael.[22] One of the representatives so elected was Burke.

The Jacksonborough Assembly convened on January 8 as scheduled, and Rutledge delivered his opening address ten days later. The state was still at war, and tensions remained high. Castigating the British as a cruel and unrelenting foe, and congratulating the Assembly on the pleasing change of affairs, Rutledge called for measures to frustrate any attempt by the British to reinforce Charleston or again to subjugate the state by raising and equipping, with all possible expedition, a respectable permanent force. The conduct of loyalist citizens also called for deliberation. "It is with you to determine," he said, "whether the Forfeiture and Appropriation of their Property should now take Place." Finally, he asked for repeal of the laws making paper money legal tender, recently suspended by proclamation pursuant to his emergency powers. In a suggestive juxtaposition of ideas, he concluded by observing that "it would be difficult if not impractica-

---

21. Writ of Election issued to Lewis Golson, James Taylor, and John Harrisperger for election to Senate in St. Matthews and Orange Parishes on December 17 and 18, 1781, dated at the High Hills of Santee, November 20, 1781, with return attached, John Rutledge Papers, SCL. The writ is in printed form with blanks. An identical document, completed by hand for use in a different election district, is in John Rutledge Papers, NYHS. A standard form is assumed. No evidence has been found that separate lists of preferred candidates were circulated, as Burke later charged. On issuance of the writs, see Rutledge to the Delegates of South Carolina in the Continental Congress, November 22, 1781, in "Letters of John Rutledge," Barnwell, ed., *SCHM*, 18 (1917): 163–66.
22. Nadelhaft, *Disorders of War*, 73.

ble to levy a Tax in any considerable amount, towards sinking the Publick Debt, nor will the Creditors of the State expect that such a Tax should at this time be imposed; but it is just and reasonable that all unsettled demands should be liquidated, and satisfactory Assurances of Payment given, to the public Creditors."[23]

Although Rutledge never specifically recommended confiscation of loyalist property or punitive action against loyalists of any kind, his address, delivered in the context of a bitter continuing conflict, clearly played to anti-loyalist passions and invited anti-loyalist response. "Since the last meeting of a General Assembly," he began, "the good People of this State have not only felt the common calamities of War, but, from the wanton and savage Manner in which it has been prosecuted, they have experienced such Severities as are unpracticed, and will scarcely be credited by civilized Nations." Disregarding "the sacred Ties of Honor, destitute of the Feelings of Humanity, and determined to extinguish, if possible, every spark of Freedom in this Country," the British, "with insolent Pride of Conquerors, gave unbounded scope to the Exercise of their Tyrannical disposition, infringed their public Engagements, and violated the most solemn Capitulations." Prisoners of war were killed in cold blood, he said, and others were delivered over to savages and tortured. Even women and children were victims "to the inveterate Malice" of the relentless enemy. "They have tarnished the Glory of the British Arms, disgraced the Profession of a British Soldier, and fixed indelible Stigmas of Rapine, Cruelty, Perfidy, and Profaneness, on the British name."[24]

Rutledge's address set the tone for the session. After John Mathews was elected governor to succeed Rutledge, the Assembly settled down to legislative business. Sixteen significant measures were enacted. Among other things, the emergency powers previously granted to the governor were extended. The Continental Congress was authorized to impose a 5 percent impost on imports, subject to the granting of such authority by the other states. The statute of limitations on civil actions was suspended, so that actions not barred on January 1, 1775, could be brought until February 1, 1783. The Court of Special Sessions was directed to resume operations and to prepare new jury lists from

23. *JHR 1782*, 9–13.
24. Ibid.

names shown on specified schedules, "and no other person." The most important of the Jacksonborough enactments, however, were a confiscation act, a punitive amercement act, a more conciliatory act of conditional amnesty, and an exclusion act that continued, for elections to the next General Assembly, the exceptions specified in the writs of election issued on Rutledge's authority in November 1781.[25] With the usual lowcountry control diluted by absenteeism, these measures bore with particular weight on Charlestonians and their immediate lowcountry neighbors, although many of the estates affected were in other parts of the state.[26]

The confiscation act recited that, in view of the seizures of American property and the authorization of retaliation by the Continental Congress, it was "inconsistent with public justice and policy to afford protection any longer to the property of British subjects, and just and reasonable to apply the same towards alleviating and lessening the burdens and expenses of the war, which must otherwise fall very heavy on the distressed inhabitants of this state." Six categories of loyalists were established, ranging from known subjects of the king who had taken up arms against the Americans to persons who had voluntarily avowed their allegiance to the king and who, by the tenor of their conduct, showed attachment to the British government. Lists were attached and the real and personal properties of all listed persons were to be confiscated and sold at auction. The lives of those listed in certain categories were also to be forfeited, although execution could be avoided by acceptance of banishment upon penalty of death should the exile return to the state. Some 238 persons were specifically named, and the total number of estates initially affected has been estimated at 377.[27]

The amercement act supplemented the confiscation act by providing that 47 named persons be taxed 12 percent of the appraised value of their respective estates. In addition, a 30 percent

25. *Statutes at Large*, 4: 510–11 (exclusion act), 4: 516–23 (confiscation act), 4: 523–25 (amercement act), and 4: 526–28 (conditional amnesty act).

26. Jerome J. Nadelhaft, " 'The Snarls of Invidious Animals': The Democratization of Revolutionary South Carolina," in Ronald Hoffman and Peter J. Albert, eds., *Sovereign States in an Age of Uncertainty* (Charlottesville: University Press of Virginia, 1981), 62–94, at 72–73; Lambert, *South Carolina Loyalists*, 237–38.

27. Nadelhaft, *Disorders of War*, 81–85; Nadelhaft, "Snarls of Invidious Animals," 73.

tax was laid on all those persons who contributed financially toward raising troops of cavalry for service with the British forces. The conditional amnesty act granted pardons to lesser offenders who failed to comply with Rutledge's amnesty proclamation of September 1781 but later performed military service for the state upon payment in specie or in slaves of 10 percent of the value of their real and personal property. Thus, the total number affected by the measures adopted at Jacksonborough was significantly greater than the 285 persons specifically named, and a majority of those affected were from Charleston.[28]

Burke had an active but not a leading role at Jacksonborough. He performed a variety of minor functions, such as examining credentials and administering the requisite oath to members as they arrived. He presented bills terminating the status of paper money as legal tender and providing for the reopening of the Court of General Sessions.[29] He opposed, as did others, the confiscation and amercement acts. But there is no evidence, on the official record or otherwise, that he opposed the exclusion act disenfranchising suspected British sympathizers; and the committee appointed to prepare new jury lists, of which he was a member, was directed to exclude from such lists those disenfranchised by its terms.[30]

The flavor and temper of the Jacksonborough Assembly is lost in the bare outline of the official journal, although occasionally found in the preambles to the several enactments. The informal record of events is more revealing. Writing to Arthur Middleton from Jacksonborough on January 25, Burke described the distressed situation of the country and the prevailing public spirit of vengeance aimed at the British and their loyalist supporters. The Assembly, he said, was "composed of very respectable good men and we are happily extricated from that Tory dead weight which used to embarrass our Councils in Charles Town." Burke approved exclusion of "the Tory Interest" and commented that "Governor Rutledge conducted the business with good policy in excluding from voting all such persons who had not borne arms antecedent to 27th September." Although the number ex-

---

28. Ibid.
29. *JHR 1782*, 8, 24.
30. Ibid., 15.

cluded was enough to produce grumbling in some parishes, "I would think it madness to allow men to influence our Elections, who had borne arms against us without giving some Test of their attachment to us—for ought we know it would be giving away our Country, and the resources of it." But the question of confiscation was more troublesome. "This will make a great noise and will bring so many families and their children to beggary and ruin, that I would devoutly detest it, although I think the men who are the objects of it should never be received into the bosom of this Country." Moreover, confiscation established a potentially dangerous precedent. "I will ask you one political question," he said. "Can Property be secure under a numerous democratic Assembly which undertakes to dispose of the property of a Citizen? The men of property in our house join heartily in this measure, but they do not reflect the time may come when the Precedent may be execrated by their posterity." In the construction of the lists, he observed, "everyone gives in a list of his own and the State's enemies and the Enquiry is not so much what he has done, as what Estate he has."[31]

Burke's last point was confirmed by others. The identification and listing of those to be subjected to penalty was hardly consistent or wholly disinterested. Some insignificant and seemingly innocent persons were included, and others who actively and openly supported British interests were omitted. Not everyone directly tied to specified actions was listed. Edward Rutledge told Arthur Middleton that he did all he could "to restrain the tempers of the tempestuous." He was not opposed to confiscation in principle, because "we can't raise troops without it;" but he worked hard to eliminate from the lists those for whom something could be said. Alexander Garden recalled one session engaged in the making of the lists when the cry went up "A fat sheep. Prick him. Prick him."[32]

Burke remained with the army near Jacksonborough at least through May 1782, when he again wrote at length to Middleton. Although there were many who justly deserved punishment, he

---

31. Burke to Middleton, January 25, 1782, Middleton Correspondence, *SCHM*, 26 (1925): 190–95.
32. Rutledge to Middleton, January 28 and February 26, 1782, Middleton Correspondence, *SCHM*, 26 (1925): 211–13, 27 (1926): 6–10; Alexander Garden, *Anecdotes of the Revolutionary War in America* (Charleston: A. Miller, 1822; reprint ed., Spartanburg: The Reprint Company, 1972), 196.

said, he had opposed confiscation. On further reflection, "I am not sorry for it," he continued. It was bad precedent to condemn without hearing or even provision for hearing. Although bills of attainder were not uncommon in Britain, they were universally condemned; and it was simply unrealistic to cast blame on those who accepted British protection when they had no reasonable alternative. "However," he added, "I would have my throat cut for saying this in publick." Internal enemies, he thought, should be either banished or pardoned, and he had hoped for an act of oblivion (that is, the erasure from the record of past defections), "with some exceptions to satisfy publick justice, and as you would throw a Tub to a whale to satisfy the vengeance of those who had suffered." Moreover, the public mood was for strict enforcement of the penal laws and the burden on the courts after years of unrestrained violence would have been severe. Many subject to penalty or punishment, deprived of hope for reconciliation, were ravaging the country in small armed parties. In these circumstances, Burke "had a difficult card to play, with regard to holding Courts." He was then the only judge available to sit, he said, and saw himself exposed as a tool to gratify revenge. The governor and the Privy Council "wanted to drive me on a business that would bring dishonor on the Country and infamy on myself." Strict enforcement of the law in the still disrupted civil society of South Carolina "would disgrace us with posterity."[33]

These views were elaborated in a further letter to Middleton in July. "Considering the state of the country," Burke said, "it was clear to me that opening the Court of Sessions would be highly improper." No line could be drawn to limit the range or grounds of public condemnation. "Several members and others of the Back Country warned me against permitting lawyers to plead for the Tories, and as to myself, that I should be cautious how I adjudged any point in their favor." He replied "that there

---

33. Burke to Middleton, May 14, 1782, Middleton Correspondence, *SCHM*, 26 (1925): 197–202. The parable of throwing a tub to a whale is referred to in the preface to Jonathan Swift's *Tale of a Tub* (1704). "Sea-men," Swift said, "have a Custom when they meet a *Whale*, to fling him out an empty *Tub*, by way of Amusement, to divert him from laying violent Hands upon the Ship." According to Swift, the whale was "mythologized" as Hobbes's Leviathan and the ship as the Commonwealth. His *Tale of a Tub* was a diversion. See Jonathan Swift, *Gulliver's Travels and Other Writings* (New York: Modern Library, 1958), 269.

would be one spot of neutral ground in Court, where I sat, where no distinction of Whig or Tory should be admitted." He was shocked, he said, "at the very idea of trying and condemning to death after so singular, so complicated, and so suspicious a revolution."[34]

Middleton was clearly a trusted and sympathetic correspondent, and Burke occasionally turned from current events to larger subjects. In one such passage, he disclosed his traditionally republican interest in popular education. "Before many years," he told Middleton, "I hope to see a beautiful and elegant Seat of Learning erected in our own Country." Such an institution would bring honor and benefit to the state. "The spreading of knowledge and learning through the Land would have this good effect," he concluded, "the Youth of our Back Country would become valuable and useful men, instead of being, as they are at present, brought up deer hunters and horse thieves, for want of Education."[35]

Burke's concern about the reopening of the courts should not be confused with his reservations about the legislative determination to punish loyalist sympathizers by confiscation and banishment or by amercement. Lawlessness and violence were rampant, and a judge might have concluded that the duty of the courts was to restrain the prevailing lawlessness and thus to restore public regard for the rule of law. The very presence of the court, after being so long closed, would have helped to some extent, and Burke was never one to shirk his duty. Nonetheless, he decided otherwise. "In order to settle the peace of the State then," he told Middleton, "you will see the necessity there was to quiet the minds of the people, to prevent their being horrified by the apprehension of continued prosecutions, and to give them some assurance that no after game, or future measures could hang over their heads to disturb them." He made a policy decision, on his own motion so to speak, and he was censured for it by some. "Let what would come of it," he said, "until the Assembly meet again."[36]

34. Burke to Middleton, July 6, 1782, Middleton Correspondence, *SCHM*, 26 (1925): 202–206.
35. Ibid.
36. Burke to Middleton, May 14 and July 6, 1782, Middleton Correspondence, *SCHM*, 26 (1925): 197–206.

In part, Burke's problem was a practical one. Only two judges were available, Pendleton and Burke, and Pendleton was soon captured by the British. But Burke had good substantive grounds for his position. The war was not over. Partisan bands on both sides were involved. The public interest in law and order could not be denied. But the fair and impartial administration of justice represented a value at least as high, and therein lay the responsibility of the judge. Burke knew all about the violence that had disrupted the backcountry between 1776 and 1779. In September 1778, for example, after Burke had taken the bench, "desperate Villains were committing cruel ravages at and about Orangeburgh," assaulting, robbing, burning and killing, and that part of the country was in such a panic, and so intimidated, that none dared to protect their own security lest, "by so doing, they should bring upon themselves the resentment of these banditti and share the fate of them who have so dearly paid for their displeasure." Rawlins Lowndes sent a company of troops into the area to help the militia maintain order, and directed them to deal summarily with disturbances of the peace, settling "the point of Law on the spot for the Decision of the Courts does not seem to be an adequate remedy at this time."[37] The situation was much the same throughout the backcountry in 1782. In such circumstances, Burke simply decided that he would not take the court to the backcountry in its existing state of confusion, that after "so singular, so complicated, and so suspicious a revolution" the legal process could not function in an environment where provocation, motive, and intent would be so ambiguous.

Burke understood well the problems of judicial administration in a disrupted polity, but he apparently never understood the policy of confiscation, amercement and exclusion as a necessary exercise in statecraft.[38] Even he had recognized the propriety of those measures up to a point. The issue was more of degree than of principle. Some action was required to cool the public temper and to demonstrate the capacity of the incumbent leadership to act effectively in the public interest. Acknowledging that objective, the confiscation act expressly declared that the peace and safety of the state would be served by the exemplary punish-

---

37. Rawlins Lowndes to Henry Laurens, September 22, 1778, Kendall Collection.
38. Weir, "The Violent Spirit," 80–84, 89–91.

ment of serious offenders. These measures accordingly constituted, in part, a symbolic assertion of governmental authority designed to quiet public clamor as hostilities wound down.

The legislature never intended or expected that enforcement would be left to the courts. No responsibility for enforcement was assigned specifically to the courts. Indeed, the problem was largely removed from the courts except to the extent that judicial intervention might be required to protect the property rights of third parties. As the source of policy, the legislature could exercise discretion in individual cases to a degree wholly inappropriate for the courts; and, almost immediately, the legislature was recognized as the proper body to which application should be made for relief. Opposed to the indiscriminate range of confiscation and amercement on both policy and legal grounds, Burke later condemned that practice as degrading to citizens forced to plead for legislative relief. But it was not inconsistent with traditional views of the proper role of the legislative body, as compared to that of the courts, in the administration of justice.

Between May and July 1782, Burke traveled south to Georgia to buy property near Savannah for Thomas Burke, his early sponsor in Virginia.[39] The two had been reunited when Thomas Burke was captured by the British and brought to Charleston while his former protege was also being held there. The incident is of no great importance but of some passing interest because Burke seems to have been acting more or less on his own. There is no surviving correspondence on the subject directly between the two. Thomas Burke was informed of the transaction by others. But he was far from certain that he would ever move to Georgia. "I have written largely on the Subject in Several letters to our friend Judge Burke," he replied to one correspondent, "who, I fear has been carried too far by his regard for me."[40] He died shortly thereafter, in 1783, and there is no record that he ever acquired property in Georgia.

---

39. Burke to Middleton, July 6, 1782, Middleton Correspondence, *SCHM*, 26 (1925): 202–206. Burke may have had a larger public purpose for the trip to Georgia. If so, it remains undetected.
40. Andrew Armstrong to Thomas Burke, July 10, 1782; James Armstrong to Thomas Burke, August 25, 1782; Thomas Burke to Thomas Bourke, October 12, 1782, in Walter Clark, ed., *The State Records of North Carolina*, 16 vols. numbered consecutively with *The Colonial Records of North Carolina* as vols. 11–26 (Winston, Goldsboro, and Raleigh, North Carolina: The State of North Carolina, 1895–1914), 16: 629–30, 646–47, 657–58.

Disruption and Restoration, 1778–1782

Burke returned from Georgia to spend four months with the Charleston militia guarding Georgetown, the principal port of entry and supply depot for South Carolina while Charleston remained in British hands. While languishing there, he was elected chief justice of Georgia by its House of Assembly.[41] He declined the office. He was the only available Carolina judge when the offer was made, he wrote an unidentified correspondent (probably General Lachlan McIntosh) in November. "When the Carolinians chose me their judge," he said, "I was almost as great a stranger to them, as I am to the Georgians; and I was resolved I should give them no reason to be sorry or repent of their reliance on me in any circumstance."[42]

A functioning judicial system was finally restored in early 1783. In June, Burke presided at the first Court of General Sessions to convene in Charleston after the war and delivered the customary charge to the grand jury. "It is going on four years since we enjoyed the privilege of meeting each other in the court of sessions," he said, "and we now offer you our warmest congratulations, that the bitter calamities through which you passed during that period, are, by the blessings of heaven at an end; that happy peace is once more returned; our country in its independence, and holding dignity among nations. Our objective now must be to restore harmony under the protection of law." Commenting on the prevalence of violence in the country, he was concerned that the citizenry, "from the habit of putting their enemies to death, have reconciled their minds to the killing of each other; and it is too true, I fear, that man by custom may be so brutalized as to relish human blood, the more he has shed of it." If union and harmony were to be restored, the spirit of vengeance had to be suppressed. "Whoever considers how fatally, after civil troubles, the spirit of private revenge directs the conduct of men, and that this has a direct tendency to create disorder and anarchy, he, I say, will not think my remarks on the subject foreign to my duty. *Private revenge* may be truly called *the demon of discord* and should be banished the land as if it were a pestilence."[43]

---

41. Allen D. Candler, ed., *The Revolutionary Records of the State of Georgia*, 3 vols. (Atlanta: The Franken Turner Company, 1908), 3: 184–8.
42. Burke to ———, November 15, 1782, Gratz Collection, HSP.
43. SCGGA, June 10, 1783.

Burke's plea was persuasive, restrained, eloquent. No blame was assessed. No faction was charged with pursuit of personal aggrandizement. From the vantage point of the bench, Burke played the role of instructor to the public at large, issuing a call for unity and statement of hope for the future. "A felicity so glorious as this is, hath not been hitherto found," he said, "but in the fine descriptions which poets and philosophers have pourtrayed in their fond zeal and wishes for the happiness of human nature. Our new republic is beginning the world, and launching into the immense ocean of future time, blessed with peace and security; our own happiness, and that of generations unborn given in charge to us; a distinction, a trust this, awfully great; and which must excite in every human creature who interests his heart in the welfare of his kind, a reverential concern mixed with glowing pious wishes for our welfare."[44]

Burke was surely too much the realist to expect that the power of words would bring the millenium to pass. He knew that human nature was not so perfectible as to be free of high regard for self interest, personal advantage, or aggrandizement of power. But the spirit of republicanism was in the air, and this address was a powerful articulation of its utopian or bright side. The launching of the new republic was the beginning of a new world; harmony was to be restored under the protection of law; a trust had been established for the benefit of generations unborn.

Five months later, charging the grand jury in Ninety Six District, Burke returned to this theme, but with a warning. Peace to the country was absolutely necessary, he urged, lest advantage be taken of the people while turmoil prevailed. "This reflection," he continued, "brings to mind another which every republican should engrave in his heart and teach his children. . . . The government of South Carolina is a government of the people, and there ever was, in every such country, and ever will be, men whose schemes and interest are very foreign to the true interests of the people. If we have no such men amongst us at present, we shall have plenty of them by and by. These are people of cunning heads and cool tempers, who, without being in a passion themselves, would behold with pleasure the people disgrace themselves by violent passions, violent measures, by disorder

44. Ibid.

and licentiousness; nay such would think it their interest to encourage it."[45]

Although phrased in general terms, Burke's warning reflected his growing concern that actual and potential antirepublican forces were already gathering strength in South Carolina, both from a putative aristocracy on the right and unruly groups among the populace on the left. That perception was more fully developed in his two famous pamphlets published in 1783, one in January and one in October. The regenerative elements of republican ideology were not rejected, but the fragility of republican government when exposed to the insidious threat of corruption could never be ignored. The pamphlets took up its defense, but in terms quite different from the affirmative voice of the charges. To the public at large, the Burke of the charges and the Burke of the pamphlets, all written by the same pen in the same year, must have seemed two quite different men.

---

45. *SCGGA*, December 18, 1783. The same charge was probably delivered at Beaufort and Orangeburgh.

IV

Ithuriel's Spear

1783

Many leaders in addition to Burke had advocated a lenient policy toward the loyalists in South Carolina. Some, such as Greene, Marion, and other military leaders, perhaps feared that the retaliatory measures enacted at Jacksonborough would stimulate further resistance by those proscribed and accordingly expose their limited defense forces to unnecessary burdens. Others were troubled by the legal strictures imposed on the essentially passive segments of the population caught in the ebb and flow of military operations, particularly under British control in Charleston. Some were troubled also by the casualness of the selection process—the "fat sheep" approach—which colored the identification of those to be most severely punished. A few were troubled further by the total lack of any of the elements of due process of law. Christopher Gadsden, after describing to Francis Marion the proceedings at Jacksonborough, and claiming personal credit for provisions designed to limit the ability of speculators and land jobbers to acquire confiscated property on advantageous terms to the detriment of the general public, concluded "but 'tis now a law and we must patiently wait 'till the next Assembly to endeavor to have its severities at least mitigated where there is room; and I am sure, if I am on the floor, it shall not want my utmost endeavors to bring it about; and happy shall I be if they are attended with any success."[1]

One of the important decisions taken at Jacksonborough limited the term of that Assembly and of the officials elected by it to one year, notwithstanding that the Constitution of 1778 provided for two year terms of office. Accordingly, new elections were held

---

1. Gadsden to Francis Marion, November 17, 1782, in *The Writings of Christopher Gadsden*, Richard Walsh, ed. (Columbia: University of South Carolina Press, 1966), 193–98, quote at 196.

on November 25 and 26, 1782, before the British evacuation of Charleston. The same restrictions on voting participation and eligibility for office applied in the election of 1781 remained in effect under the exclusion act adopted by the Jacksonborough Assembly.

The new General Assembly convened in Charleston on January 6, 1783, barely four weeks after British evacuation of the city, and was shortly greeted with Burke's *An Address to the Freemen of South Carolina*, published in Charleston under date of January 14, 1783.[2] Writing as "Cassius," Burke attacked not only the excesses of confiscation and amercement policy but the propriety and legitimacy of the Jacksonborough proceedings as a whole.[3] "The people at large in whom the sovereignty of the State *should be vested*," he said, "ought to be informed whether public measures be right or wrong; and it therefore becomes the duty of every citizen to present the subject in as open and public a light as opportunity or knowledge may enable him." Submission to a conqueror was no crime, he argued. "As the Republick could not give the citizen protection, which is the equivalent he receives for allegiance, he owed none." When the government was restored, those citizens who had accepted protection were "as fully entitled to all the rights and freedom of citizenship, as those who were detained prisoners of war, or took refuge to the northward." When a select few presumed to determine who should be restored to the rights of citizenship and who should be excluded, an arbitrary government of those few was thereby established, the people were deprived of their liberties, and the constitution overthrown. "The laws of nations as well as the rights of nature therefore dictate, that when a country oppressed by a foreign power regains its liberty, the citizens should be restored to all the rights and liberties they before enjoyed." And when men in power arbitrarily asserted that citizens were guilty of crime and dishonor when neither crime nor dishonor was involved, their

---

2. Burke's *Address* appeared before any of the Charleston newspapers resumed publication after the British evacuation in December 1782. Consequently, he had no other way to present his views to the public and his first foray as pamphleteer may have been wholly fortuitous.
3. After Gaius Cassius (died 42 B.C.), one of the three principal leaders of the conspiracy to assassinate Julius Caesar in 44 B.C. At the time of his death, Caesar was a monarch in all but name. In the republican political culture of ancient Rome, the unwritten constitution required resistance to tyranny, by tyrannicide if necessary, as a civic duty ranking above any oath of allegiance.

actions had "the same pernicious effects on the multitude, that private scandal and defamation, has on an innocent individual. It breaks that spirit, and generous pride, which is the best guardian of public liberty and private honour. It overwhelms the public as well as the private mind, with conscious inferiority; degrades men in their own opinion, and renders them fit tools for the ambitious designs, and arbitrary disposition of haughty aspiring superiors."[4]

The root of the issue lay, in Burke's view, with the restrictions imposed by Governor John Rutledge in calling the Jacksonborough Assembly and subsequently perpetuated in the disenfranchising provisions of the exclusion act. And such restrictions derived from the proclamation of September 27, 1781, which had offered amnesty on conditions virtually impossible for many to satisfy. "The privilege of voting," Burke said, "is a right so inherent in every citizen of our State, that the Governor or Legislature, who pretends under any condition or limitation to deprive him of it, and then return it as a matter of favor, actually plays the tyrant by so doing: It is *at once vesting the government in the few independent of the whole"* and *"high treason against the sovereignty and liberties of the people."* At law, the trustee's authority would be abrogated when he betrayed the faith conferred on him by his principal. By analogy, the governor effectively destroyed the basis of the authority entrusted to him by the people when he acted in contravention of their proper interests. It was the act of a usurper employing the form of law "to rivet his usurpation." Moreover, with Yorktown taken and the Pennsylvania Line on the march South, the measure could not be justified on grounds of military expediency.[5]

The Jacksonborough exclusion act was predicated, Burke continued, on the proposition that all those who failed to comply with the preceding offer of amnesty, whatever the reason or circumstances, had forfeited their liberty and that those who did comply were entitled to be restored to their lost freedom. But the war was fought for the liberties and happiness of all. Now, when peace and happiness should prevail, "this wretched country" was split into two factions, a set of "mongrel freemen" begat by

---

4. Burke, *Address*, 2–3, 5, 9, 11–12, 43. Burke claimed seven years of public service in South Carolina, which would date his presence in South Carolina back at least to 1775.

5. Burke, *Address*, 3, 16, 19–21.

Rutledge and his party and a set of aliens "divested of every privilege we have been contending for these seven years past."[6]

The constitution conferred on every citizen a participation in the sovereignty of the state, which neither governor nor Assembly could "take away without establishing a tyrannical government on the ruins of our Liberties." The right of the citizen to vote was personal, could not be surrendered or resigned, and could be forfeited only upon "conviction of some notorious crime, on a fair tryal by his peers." The extraordinary power conferred on the governor in the crisis of 1780 only authorized him to support "the charter of our liberties" and "the fundamental laws of the State." By this precedent, he had "exposed us in future to all the mischiefs of arbitrary power." So singular a measure "must be produced by some uncommon motive." Burke thought the motive clear enough. It was "calculated for no other end but to sow the poisonous seeds of faction and party, to disgrace the middling and lower class of our citizens, and to throw the whole weight and powers of government out of the people into a few families." Unless undone by a future legislature, the plan carried at Jacksonborough would "fasten at one blow in this country, a fierce and jealous aristocracy which has been gaining ground for seven years past."[7]

Burke attacked the confiscation and amercement acts as bills of attainder and ex post facto laws, lacking even the rudiments of compliance with "the law of the land," the contemporary equivalent of the modern concept of due process of law and explicitly embodied in the Constitution of 1778, by failing to provide for notice, hearing and confrontation of accusers. "An *ex post facto law*," he said, "is such a law as is made *today*, to punish the action of *yesterday*, tho' yesterday's action was innocent," a succinct statement at once clear to the layman and sufficiently precise to satisfy the most particular lawyer. Republics, he continued, must be particularly careful not to transgress the law by arbitrary measures. The extravagant tyranny of monarchs was well known. But a popular assembly combining the functions of legislators and judges in the same body and ignoring fundamental law was even more dangerous. Such a body, establishing the law and then applying it, as the General Assembly was doing under the confisca-

---

6. Ibid., 24–25.
7. Ibid., 14, 19–21.

tion and amercements acts, would "give more loose to malice, avarice, or revenge; commit more injustice and glaring partiality; and differ in outrage from one tyrant, as one firebrand is inferior to many hundreds lighted together, and blown up by a fierce gale. Such deviations from justice, moderation, and temper, would fix disgrace on the very name of a republic."[8]

Moreover, one arbitrary exercise of power opened the way to others. "There is hardly an instance in history of a law made to be revenged on enemies, but that very law was brought in as a precedent to destroy friends; and the thing is quite natural," he said. If the legislature could arbitrarily appropriate the property or banish the person of one, they could do so again. Factions and revolutions have been the lot of every republic, and the new republican government would no doubt have its share of them. "Time which changes all things, may bring matters about so as to turn the tables against the very men who were foremost in driving down those laws; for after this precedent I see nothing they have to depend on, but factions, cabals, or influence in the legislature: And the sheets on which those laws are written, may wrap in winding sheets some of their descendants."[9]

The amercement act, in particular, was "the most impolitic that could be devised." If unrepealed, it would do more lasting damage than the war had done. The misfortunes of the war would soon be outgrown "by a young country, so fertile and full of resources as ours." But the bitterness and divisiveness created by amercement would remain "as an inheritance to our children," irritating one half of the people against the other and disgracing both, by the injustice done to one side and the reproach fixed on the other. Many worthy citizens, "of as good families as any we have," were "being handed down on the journals of both houses as traitors and enemies to their country." This law alone "would be sufficient to disturb the peace of the country, and alarm every thinking man in it; and he who thinks otherwise has but little knowledge of human nature."[10]

The exclusion, confiscation, and amercement acts should be repealed, Burke concluded, and an act of amnesty and oblivion

---

8. Ibid., 28–30, 37–39.
9. Ibid., 40.
10. Ibid., 42–43.

adopted, wiping the slate clean with as few exceptions as possible and with appropriate procedural safeguards. "It is a maxim of politics," he said, "that if a breach be made in the constitution of a government, and it be not healed, it will prove as fatal to its freedom, as a wound that is neglected and suffered to mortify, would to the life of a man." Those deserving of punishment should be brought to trial in accordance with the law of the land. The present Assembly should be dissolved and a new one elected by all the citizens of the state. Only such measures could "reconcile us to the friendship of each other;" put an end to factions; and "leave us at liberty to shake hands as brethren, whose fate it is to live together."[11]

Burke's public exhortation obviously differed sharply in tone and substance from the more moderate views expressed in his letters to Arthur Middleton a few months before, particularly with regard to the exclusion act. He had then approved exclusion of "the Tory Interest" from the right to vote. He had acknowledged, at least implicitly, the propriety of banishment for some. As implemented, however, confiscation and amercement policy cut too broadly and too deeply to permit an early return to harmony and suppression of the spirit of vengeance. Burke's case in the *Address* was made in support of due process for all, but primarily on behalf of the essentially passive portion of the population which had submitted to British power for lack of any realistic alternative. He never abandoned the principle that internal enemies should be either banished or pardoned, but he insisted that punishment could be inflicted only on the basis of proceedings conducted with due regard for the traditional rights of prior notice, hearing, and proof.

The General Assembly was convening in Charleston just as the *Address* appeared, and it can be interpreted simply as a broadly based argument, no more extravagantly polemical than others of the Revolutionary era, designed to persuade the new Assembly to reexamine the matter on the basis of fundamental principles following removal of the disruptive presence of the British army. Although there is no reason to doubt the sincerity of Burke's views, there is a possible alternative explanation for his decision to take his case directly to the public.

11. Ibid., 54–55.

The substance and particularly the timing of the *Address* may also have been an expression of personal political disappointment. The elections for the new Assembly were held in November 1782. The election returns for St. Philip and St. Michael have been lost, but Burke was not included in the first contingent to qualify from the Charleston parishes, when the House of Representatives convened in January 1783. After the numerous vacancies were sorted out, a writ of election for seven additional members was issued on January 29; the election was held on February 10–11; and Burke was one of seven who qualified on February 13.[12] Had he been elected in November, Burke might well have been prepared, as Gadsden proposed, to address the problems of exclusion, confiscation, and amercement from the floor of the House. Apparently denied that opportunity, the hortatory *Address* was the only alternative means by which he could give weight to his views. It is thus a fair inference that the *Address* was written after the election in November and was rushed into print to greet the new General Assembly. In addition, Burke's objections to the exclusion act and perception of incipient aristocratic control may have been sharpened by belief that disenfranchisement of those Charlestonians who had passively accepted British occupation somehow operated against him in the election. That could have been the case if his views were generally known in November by those antipathetic to "the Tory interest." In all events, his bruised feelings, if bruised they were, were presumably assuaged by his election in February. But it is noteworthy that, as a political tract, Burke's argument would appeal neither to the conservative establishment nor to patriotic supporters of punishment for loyalists. The moderate center was a narrow constituency indeed in early 1783.

The impact of the *Address* is difficult to assess. At least one North Carolinian liked it. "I am wonderfully pleased with the plain good sense of Judge Burke's pamphlet," he wrote to George Hooper, a Charleston merchant, "and I ardently wish we could have a cargo of them distributed in this State; particularly in the back country. It seems to be a hasty, and, as to the style and diction, an unfinished piece but the humanity, good policy and sound reason with which it abounds amply make amends for these trivial defects, which will not even be observed by the peo-

---

12. *JHR 1783–1784*, 642–43.

ple in general." If the General Assembly of South Carolina should be persuaded to adopt maxims of sound and moderate policy, he continued, "it must add to the soreness which Mr. R——— must have felt from the Judge's lash. Considering him a man of understanding and a lawyer, he has got a most damnable flagellation."[13]

The reaction of Rutledge and his supporters is unknown, but they could not have been pleased. Burke expressly disclaimed any dislike of Rutledge and asserted that he criticized the measures, not the man. But he immediately went on to suggest that Rutledge would not have been the first of men to subvert liberty in the guise of preserving it and that aggrandizement of family and perpetuation of power were often more important to the ambitious man than public freedom.[14]

Nothing occurred at the session of the General Assembly in 1783 to ease Burke's concerns. Although minor amendments to the confiscation and amercement acts were adopted, all proposals for a general amnesty were stoutly resisted. Some names were added to the lists. More than 250 petitions for relief were submitted to the General Assembly, and the slow process of sifting through them in committee began. Many claimed error, others extenuating circumstances, and some special circumstances resulting in unintended consequences. Ignoring the principle of separation of powers, designated committees of the General Assembly performed essentially judicial functions, holding hearings and taking evidence in individual cases. In the aggregate, 137 confiscation cases were processed during the first session in 1783, and in most of them total or partial relief was recommended. Moreover, the General Assembly eased the harshness of the original acts by suspending sales of property confiscated from those whose petitions for relief were pending. Amercement cases were, for the most part, deferred.[15] In response to the evident trend toward relief of all but the most aggravated cases, ultra-patriots protested and demanded strict enforcement. And when

---

13. A. Maclaine to George Hooper, February 9, 1783, in Walter Clark, ed., *The State Records of North Carolina*, 16 vols. numbered consecutively with *The Colonial Records of North Carolina* as vols. 11–26 (Winston, Goldsboro, and Raleigh, North Carolina: The State of North Carolina, 1895–1914), 16: 932–36.
14. Burke, *Address*, 26.
15. Robert Stansbury Lambert, *South Carolina Loyalists In the American Revolution* (Columbia: University of South Carolina Press, 1987), 286–91.

the judges went on circuit after the session was over, they found lawlessness and conflict rampant throughout the backcountry. This was the context in which Burke discovered the Society of the Cincinnati.

The Society was organized in Newburgh, New York, in May 1783, shortly before the Continental Army disbanded. Its structure and purposes were embodied in an "Institution," drafted by General Henry Knox. It was to be a national organization with subsidiary chapters in each state. Regular national meetings would be held at which the several state chapters would be represented by delegates. It was in part a fraternal organization and in part an incipient political pressure group. Neither officers nor men had been paid for their service, and Minor Myers, the Society's most recent historian, has described it as a "constructive alternative to an ultimatum from an army refusing to lay down its arms until paid." Officers of the Continental forces with three years service were eligible for membership, and each member was to contribute one month's pay into a permanent charitable fund. Membership would pass to the eldest male descendants of the founders. An elaborate medal in the form of a gold eagle was adopted as the badge of membership.[16] As the organization evolved, Forrest McDonald has said, it "quickly hardened into an informed, influential, and durable pressure group, interested both emotionally and financially in strengthening the Union— and virtually the only national organization except for Congress itself."[17]

The first national officers were elected by the founders in June 1783. Washington, who had had no part in the founding, was elected president-general. The organization of state chapters began promptly thereafter, and General William Moultrie, the senior Continental officer in South Carolina, was informed of the plan in July. At a meeting called by Moultrie and held in Charleston on August 29, the South Carolina chapter was formed and the Institution adopted, subject to a declaration disclaiming "all Intention of Interfering in any degree with the Constitutional powers of Congress or the Civil Authority of the State." Generals

---

16. Minor Myers, *Liberty Without Anarchy: A History of the Society of the Cincinnati* (Charlottesville: University Press of Virginia, 1981), 1–47, quote at 24.
17. Forrest McDonald, *E Pluribus Unum* (Boston: Houghton, Mifflin & Co., 1965), 33.

Moultrie and Huger were elected president and vice-president, respectively. No person "who has joined the Enemy or taken protection from them since the Declaration of Independence" would be eligible for membership.[18]

Burke learned of the Society in August when Moultrie described the plan to organize a South Carolina chapter at the Corner Club in Charleston. Within moments, he later said, he determined to oppose it. The result was his *Considerations on the Society or Order of the Cincinnati*, first published in Charleston under date of October 10, 1783.[19]

Again writing as "Cassius," Burke denounced the Society as a dire threat to the future of the fragile new republic. "I have often thought," he said, "that the revolution in America would reduce it to a certainty, whether mankind was destined by nature for liberty or slavery; for a republican government never before has had, what we call fair play, in any part of the globe." The Society was intended to establish, and in time would establish, an impregnable hereditary peerage, reducing the mass of the people to subservience before the experiment was fairly begun. It had been planted "in a fiery, hot ambition, and thirst for power, and its branches will end in tyranny." However apparently innocuous its purposes, it would inevitably produce discord, not union, dividing the country into two ranks of men, "the patricians or nobles and the rabble." Such would be the "natural result of an establishment, whose departure is so sudden from our open professions of Republicanism, that it must give a thinking mind most melancholy forebodings." Indeed, the creation of a noble class, "just as we were setting out in the world, is making that liberty which the Almighty has given us, a means for feeding our pride, and turning the blessings of Providence into a curse upon us." Should the Society prevail, it "would give a fatal wound to civil liberty through the world" and prove that the

---

18. Myers, *Liberty Without Anarchy*, 40; Proceedings of the Society of the Cincinnati in South Carolina from August 29, 1783 to April 15, 1784, photostatic copies at SCL from originals in NYHS.

19. The circumstances under which Burke learned of the Society and determined to oppose it are set out in "Cassius" [Aedanus Burke], "To the Public," *SCGPA*, May 15, 1784. Burke angrily denied a circulating report to the effect that he had been motivated by distress because his own term of service in the Continental army, "wanting but a few months of three years," did not qualify him for membership. The author of the report, Burke said, was propagating a falsehood, "and I make no ceremony to tell the Public he is a Liar."

teachings of philosophers from Plato to Locke on the subject of human happiness, "though appearing well on paper, yet are no more than ideal pictures of a fine imagination."[20]

Burke then brought the argument home to South Carolina, where the impact of the Society "will be sooner and more severely felt." Conceived as a democracy under the Constitution of 1778, he said, the government of South Carolina "naturally ran into an aristocracy." The nature of the climate, the unequal distribution of property, the retention of control by the gentry through the war, and the want of men of knowledge and capacity for business, all combined "to establish the dominion and authority of a *few* below," that is, the establishment elite residing in the lowcountry. South Carolina had become a pure, simple aristocracy of those few, in which the bulk of the citizenry "are excluded from any share or interference in the government; although most of them are natives; capital settlers of old families; good whigs; and the descendants too of men, who first planted this country, and helped to raise it to its present flourishing greatness." This "revolution" was effected by law at the Jacksonborough Assembly. The power vested in the few by the exclusion act disenfranchising suspected loyalists was augmented by the confiscation and amercement acts that broke up or weakened and debased important families who might otherwise have challenged the action taken. Instead of redressing these calamities, the current General Assembly "degraded the citizens, by forcing them on the humiliating necessity of petitioning, and cringing, to get off the lists." While the gentry had since Jacksonborough indicated a tendency toward compassion, "the democratic part of our Assembly are eyed, as unfeeling and inconsiderate, and making no scruple to abuse their power, even to the trampling on the laws and rights of their fellow citizens, for the glorious exploit of hunting down a Tory." These observations "may appear trivial," but they "serve to show that the freedom of a country may be overturned by causes imperceptible to the multitude; and that when popular assemblies are carried away by violent passions, and strike at persons instead of things, they are then closely working for the aggrandizement of others; and while they avenge party injuries on petty enemies, only lay a snare for that liberty

20. Burke, *Considerations*, 7–8, 14–15.

which should be held most dear to them and their posterity." And the Society in South Carolina, by excluding from its membership those who had accepted British protection, would complete what the Jacksonborough policies had left undone.[21]

The legislature should immediately adopt resolutions against the Order, Burke concluded. "Let them tell the Order, and the world, that however pious or patriotic the pretence, yet any political combination of military commanders, is, in a Republican government, extremely hazardous, and highly censurable." The institution of exclusive honors and privileges in an organization having hereditary membership "is a daring usurpation on the sovereignty of the republic, a dangerous insult to the rights and liberties of the people, and a fatal stab to that principle of equality, which forms the basis of our government."[22]

Burke had no illusions that the Society would be dissolved. The leading gentry "will find their interest in supporting a distinction, that will gratify their ambition, by removing them far above their fellow citizens." And they would be supported by a party of those who sought to link their own ambitions to the interest of the gentry. The middling order of gentry and land holders "may see its tendency, but they can take no step to oppose it; having little to do with the government." The lower class, including the city population, "will never reason on it, till they feel the smart, and then they will have neither the power nor the capacity for a reformation." But a resolution of condemnation would nonetheless serve a valuable public purpose. "It would, like Ithuriel's spear in Milton, touch the Order; and however plausible the external appearance, under which it now sits transformed, the resolution would oblige it, as the fallen angel in paradise, to start up in its own true hideous shape and likeness; and then we should know how to grapple with it."[23]

Public opposition to the Cincinnati began almost as soon as the public became aware of the Society's existence. Its intensity was fueled by the evident relationship between the organization of the Society and other subjects of current public concern. In March 1783, the Continental Congress, over intense opposition,

---

21. Ibid., 25–29.
22. Ibid., 30–31.
23. Ibid.

granted the officers of the army five years of full pay in government securities, with six percent interest, in commutation of a
prior award of half pay for life. That action was taken in response
to demands from the army for back pay prior to disbanding from
the camp at Newburgh, reflecting in part concern of the officers
that they would never receive the promised pensions. Nationalist
politicians, frustrated in their efforts to centralize control over finance and establish a national source of revenue, seized the opportunity to renew their efforts to persuade the states to
authorize a national impost. Virginia had recently withdrawn its
consent to a national impost, and Rhode Island had never acqui-
esced. Payment of the claims would require new sources of
funds; and, to the nationalists, the impost was the only viable
source. Commutation was thus designed to join the army's interests to the interests of other public creditors. The Society appeared on the national scene, then, at a time of controversy
featuring traditional republican views on standing armies, wide
opposition to military pensions in general and commutation in
particular, and a continuing debate over a national impost.[24] In
the circumstances, public perception of the Society as a powerful
upper class political interest group was not irrational.

Burke was not by any means alone in condemning the Society. Opposition was strongest in New England and was strong
also in Virginia and North Carolina. John Adams, John Jay, Elbridge Gerry, and many others were highly critical.[25] But Burke's
spear ignited a full dress debate, and his *Considerations* became its
centerpiece. It was reprinted in pamphlet form in Philadelphia,
Hartford, New York, and Newport, was published in complete
text in newspapers in Massachusetts and Connecticut, and was
widely quoted elsewhere.[26] As opposition spread from New England southward, Governor Guerard delivered an extended cri-
tique of the Society in his annual message to the South Carolina
General Assembly in February 1784, concurring in Burke's analy-

---

24. Richard H. Kohn, "The Inside History of the Newburgh Conspiracy: America
and the Coup d'Etat," *WMQ*, 27 (1970): 187–220; E. James Ferguson, *The Power
of the Purse: A History of American Public Finance, 1776–1790* (Chapel Hill: University of North Carolina Press, 1961), 146–76; Myers, *Liberty Without Anarchy*,
1–22.

25. Wallace Evan Davies, "The Society of the Cincinnati in New England 1783–
1800," *WMQ*, 5 (1948): 3–25; Myers, *Liberty Without Anarchy*, 48–49.

26. Myers, *Liberty Without Anarchy*, 49–50; Davies, "Society of the Cincinnati in
New England," 5–6.

sis in all material respects. When men set themselves apart from the mass of the people and presumed superior rank, Guerard said, their action implied that those excluded were "their inferiors, which . . . will most certainly be generative of Suspicion, Jealousy, division and domestic discord." The army was entitled to gratitude and honor, he concluded, but should reconsider this "alarming institution" and "weigh well" the arguments advanced against it.[27]

In the spring of 1784, the Society was on the defensive. In April, Washington sought Jefferson's advice. "The Pamphlet ascribed to Mr. Burke," he said "had its effect. People are alarmed, especially in the Eastern States." He requested Jefferson's opinion of the Society and suggestions as to measures that might be presented for consideration at its national meeting to be held later in the year.[28] Jefferson's reply was duly deferential but his observations clearly implied his own negative view of the organization and suggested that Washington would be well-advised to disassociate himself from it.[29]

The *Considerations* was not universally admired in 1783, nor has it been since. An anonymous contemporary observer published an undistinguished point-by-point reply, denying categorically any ulterior purposes.[30] Another anonymous commentator, writing in 1853, characterized the early critics of the Society as men "who had not forgotten or forgiven the manner in which the army had resisted the attempt to whistle it down the wind, a prey to fortune," or whose busy imaginations perceived the threat of a privileged class growing in the midst of a free republic like "a noxious weed in a bed of flowers." He dismissed Burke as "one of those men who are born to disappoint every expectation of their friends." After all, what sense could be expected of one who made a joke of his duties as Burr's second in a duel, appeared on the bench in a lady's black petticoat, and excused horse thieves who happened to be drunk? His pen was specious,

27. *JHR 1783–1784*, 403–404.
28. Washington to Jefferson, April 8, 1784, in *General Washington's Correspondence Concerning The Society of the Cincinnati*, Edgar Erskine Hume, ed. (Baltimore: Johns Hopkins Press, 1941), 130–31.
29. Jefferson to Washington, April 16, 1784, in *General Washington's Correspondence*, Hume, ed., 135–39.
30. "An Obscure Individual," *Observations on a Late Pamphlet entitled Considerations Upon the Society or Order of the Cincinnati* (Philadelphia: Robert Bell, 1783).

his reasoning absurd. Having recently attacked "Governor Rutledge and the dominant faction of the day" in a pamphlet addressed to local affairs, his mind was fired against the Society by their support of it. But his "language made a considerable impression at the time, all over the country."[31] A recent historian of the Society in North Carolina dismissed Burke as "a radical Irish immigrant" who later led the South Carolina backcountry in opposition to the Constitution.[32]

Benjamin Franklin was as much amused as concerned when his daughter sent him a copy of the *Considerations*. He replied that an hereditary society was an "absurdity." With passing generations, he suggested, the latter day knight's share of the bloodline of his ancestral Continental officer would be so diluted that no citizen would willingly hazard the envy of his countrymen to claim it. Better the practice of the Chinese mandarins. The Cincinnati should give their badges to their parents and through them to their more remote predecessors. "I hope, therefore," he concluded, "the order will drop this part of their project, and content themselves . . . with a life enjoyment of their little badge and riband, and let the distinction die with those who have merited it."[33]

Franklin contributed more to Burke's reputation by giving a copy of the *Considerations* to Honoré Gabriel de Riquetti, le Comte de Mirabeau, who promptly took up Burke's case to launch his own career as a polemicist. In July 1784, Mirabeau showed his own draft to Franklin who approved and suggested additional arguments.[34] Forced to leave France by family legal conflicts, Mirabeau completed the project in London, and his *Considerations sur l'Ordre de Cincinnatus* was published there, in French, in September.[35] To make a book of it, Mirabeau included a translation of Richard Price's well known pamphlet of advice to the new

---

31. *North American Review*, 77 (October 1853): 290–92.
32. Curtis Carroll Davis, *Revolution's Godchild: The Birth & Death, and Regeneration of the Society of the Cincinnati in North Carolina* (Chapel Hill: University of North Carolina Press, for the North Carolina Society of the Society of the Cincinnati, 1976), 28.
33. Benjamin Franklin to Sarah Bache, January 26, 1784, cited and quoted in Myers, *Liberty Without Anarchy*, 54.
34. Myers, *Liberty Without Anarchy*, 146–50, 154. An affiliated Society had been organized in France under the leadership of Rochambeau, with the approval of the king, in January 1784.
35. Honoré Gabriel Riquetti, Comte de Mirabeau, *Considerations sur l'Ordre de Cincinnatus* (London: Johnson, 1784).

nation.[36] The major part of Mirabeau's work, that relating directly to the Cincinnati, was then translated into English on Mirabeau's authorization by Sir Samuel Romilly and ultimately found its way into print in the United States.[37]

Neither Mirabeau nor Romilly blatantly appropriated Burke's work. Specific credit was given for both idea and substance. Moreover, although many paragraphs were lifted almost verbatim, the presentation was substantially reorganized, some arguments expanded, others omitted. In particular, virtually all references to the relation between the incipient threat of the Society and the existing state of politics in South Carolina were eliminated. For all its variations from the original, however, the Mirabeau-Romilly exposition upheld Burke's basic theme of antipathy to an hereditary order of putative elitists.

Burke was not pleased. In an open letter addressed to Mirabeau, published in late 1785, he complained that "you seized this offspring of mine, and after stripping it of the plain homespun in which the hands of its parent had arrayed it, you with the spoils dressed out a publication of your own, named it after mine," and "sent it into the world as your own production." Burke conceded that Mirabeau had acknowledged the source of his ideas. But the book consisted "of little else but whole pages, paragraphs, and sentences which you took out of mine," and those parts that were Burke's were not identified for the reader. "With respect to me," Burke said, "who want talents, inclination, and leisure to write, stripping my book . . . was like robbing the poor, and taking from it the little covering it had to wear."[38]

In the end, the wide-spread opposition to the Society had only limited effect. Washington, to be sure, led the national organization to amend the national Institution in response to the popular outcry and to recommend to the state branches that all political activity be renounced, that their funds be surrendered to

36. Richard Price, *Observations on the Importance of the American Revolution and the Means of Making it a Benefit to the World* (London: T. Codell, 1784). A second London edition was published in 1785. The pamphlet was intended for circulation in the United States and was reprinted in Boston (1784), in Philadelphia, New Haven, and Trenton (1785), and in Charleston (1786). Bernard Peach, ed., *Richard Price and the Ethical Foundations of the American Revolution* (Durham: Duke University Press, 1979), 10. Burke could well have agreed with much of Price's advice to the new nation, but he is nowhere on record to that effect.
37. Samuel Romilly, *Considerations on the Order of Cincinnatus* (Philadelphia: Seddon and Spottswood, 1786).
38. *SCGPA*, December 21, 1785.

state control, and that the principle of hereditary descent be abandoned. Some state societies, with the New York society and Alexander Hamilton in the lead, resisted these changes, and the principle of hereditary succession to membership was retained in most of the states.[39] But the Society never became an effective political organization, as Hamilton had hoped it would, and by the time Charles Cotesworth Pinckney succeeded Hamilton as president-general in 1805, it was in decline and nearly defunct. Like other perceived threats to the virtue of the new republic, the threat of the Society evaporated with the passage of time. Nonetheless, Burke deserves credit for his contribution to that result. He was the first to put the Cincinnati under close scrutiny, the most comprehensive in describing its threatening potential in the idiom of the republican creed, and one of the first, if not the first, to apply the conspiratorial mode of explanatory analysis to a private group acting outside the established structure of government. For the rest of his life, and to succeeding generations, he was best known to the public at large as the author of the leading attack on the Society of the Cincinnati; and his perception of its potential dangers never weakened.[40]

Nor was Jefferson ever satisfied. Initially lulled by the amendments to the national Institution adopted in 1784, he told Washington in 1786 that he viewed the Society as a potential danger. Based on his observations in Europe, he said, he believed "that tho' the day may be at some distance, beyond the reach of our lives perhaps, yet it will certainly come, when a single fibre of this institution will produce an hereditary aristocracy which will change the form of our governments from the best to the worst in the world."[41] And in 1794, criticizing Washington's denunciation of the recently organized democratic-republican societies, he wondered what line their detractors could draw to distinguish such societies, "whose avowed object is the nourish-

---

39. Myers, *Liberty Without Anarchy*, 56–65, 76–79.
40. For example, as described in Chapter VII, Burke assiduously searched for the Society's tracks in the proceedings leading to the creation and ratification of the new federal Constitution in 1787 and 1788. In 1793, "A Humble Republican," possibly Burke, submitted for publication an extract from a European history of the United States describing the Society and its anti-republican tendency and praising Burke for his role in disclosing the danger it threatened. *CH*, December 28, 1793.
41. Jefferson to Washington, November 14, 1786, in *General Washington's Correspondence*, Hume, ed., 270–71.

ment of the republican principles of our constitution," from the self-created Society of the Cincinnati, "carving out for itself hereditary distinctions, lowering over our constitution eternally, meeting together in all parts of the Union, periodically, with closed doors, accumulating a capital in their separate treasury, corresponding secretly and regularly, of which society the very persons denouncing the democrats are themselves the fathers, founders, and high officers."[42] Thus, jealousy of the Cincinnati was one thread of linkage among those gathering under Jefferson's leadership as the first parties in the new nation were being formed.

Historians have generally treated the *Considerations* for what it purports to be, an attack on a private organization in which membership would be elitist and hereditary and whose very existence threatened fundamental principles of republicanism. But Burke's attention never strayed far from his own "country." Distressed by the failure of the General Assembly to effect the changes he thought essential, he seized the occasion to restate and reinforce the argument of the earlier *Address*. The two pamphlets are thus two parts of the same piece. Together they tell much of Burke's learning and intellectual orientation.

The *Address* was essentially a legal argument, buttressed by historical precedent, set out in the familiar rhetoric of republican ideology, and adopting the conspiratorial mode of explanatory analysis. Burke drew basically from writers on public law and natural rights, particularly Pufendorf, Grotius, Vattel, and Thomas Hobbes, to demonstrate that those who passively submitted to British dominion and control committed no crime.[43] Pufendorf

---

42. Jefferson to Madison, December 28, 1794, in *General Washington's Correspondence*, Hume, ed., 384–85.
43. Samuel Pufendorf (1632–1694), German jurist and writer; Hugo Grotius (1583–1645), Dutch statesman and jurist; Emerich de Vattel (1714–1767), Swiss philosopher and jurist; Thomas Hobbes (1588–1679), English political theorist. Where specific citations were given that can be traced into the work of the cited writer, the quotations were accurate in all material respects, with only minor differences presumably attributable to differences in editions and translation. Compare, for example, (a) Burke, *Address*, 5–6, with Pufendorf, *De Jure Naturae et Gentium Libri Octo* (1688), James Brown Scott, ed., 2 vols. (Oxford: Clarendon Press of Oxford University Press for the Carnegie Endowment for International Peace, 1934), 2: 1114–16 and 1358, (b) Burke, *Address*, 7–9, with Hobbes, *Leviathan* (1651), Michael Oakeshott, ed., (Oxford: Basil Blackwell, 1957), 145, 218, 461–62, and (c) Burke, *Address*, 7, with Vattel, *The Law of Nations* (Philadelphia: Abraham Small, 1817), 97.

also supported the proposition that, when the enemy withdrew, the once-conquered people immediately recovered their "liberty and ancient state."[44] Burke called on Blackstone for the principle that elections must be free and that manipulation of the electorate by the magistrates constituted a breach of public trust.[45] On confiscation, Beccaria was cited and quoted as follows:

> The law which ordains confiscation, sets a price on the head of the subject; with the guilty punishes the innocent; and by reducing them to indigence and despair, tempts them to become criminal. Can there be a more melancholy spectacle, than a whole family, overwhelmed with infamy and misery, from the crime of their chief? A crime, which if it had been possible, they were restrained from preventing, by that submission which the laws themselves have ordained.[46]

Burke called on Blackstone again for the principle that bills of attainder were never intended for application to the people at large, but were designed to be applied only to high officials guilty of a breach of public trust.[47] David Hume provided examples of the unprincipled use of bills of attainder as instruments of tyranny.[48] The whole was illustratively supported by examples from Greek, Roman, and English history. Burke's argument may not have been conclusive, but it was well constructed and solidly based on respectable authority.

In the *Considerations*, the propositions of the *Address* were essentially taken as given. It was a polemic addressed to a per-

44. Burke, *Address*, 12–13; Pufendorf, *De Jure Naturae et Gentium*, 2: 1314–15.
45. William Blackstone (1723–1780), English jurist. Compare *Address*, 20, with Blackstone, *Commentaries on the Laws of England*, reprint of 1783 ed., 4 vols. (New York: Garland Publishing, Inc., 1978), 1: 178.
46. Cesare Beccaria (1738–1794), Italian lawyer and writer on the reform of criminal justice. Compare Burke, *Address*, 28, with Beccaria, *An Essay on Crimes and Punishments* (London: F. Newberry, 1775), 91-92. Beccaria's *Essay* was published in Philadelphia in 1776, in Charleston in 1777, and again in Philadelphia in 1778. Adolph Caso, *America's Italian Founding Fathers* (Boston: Branden Press, 1975), 41–42.
47. Burke, *Address*, 33. The quoted passage does not appear at the page cited in the 1783 edition of Blackstone's *Commentaries*.
48. David Hume (1711–1776), Scottish philosopher and historian. Compare Burke, *Address*, 35–37, with Hume, *The History of England from the Invasion of Julius Caesar to the Revolution of 1688*, 8 vols. (London: A. Strahan, 1802), 4: 197–98, 207–208.

ceived threat to republican liberty, not a legal argument. Antici-pating the subornation of the polity at the hands of the Cincin-nati, Burke reacted accordingly.

> Could I for a moment view this Order with indifference, it would be impossible not to smile, to behold the populace of America, in their town committees and town meetings, so keenly bent on petty mischiefs; in full chase and cry after a few insignificant Tories, and running on regardless of an establishment, which ere long must strip the posterity of the middling and lower classes of every influence or authority, and leave them nothing but insignificance, contempt, and the wretched privilege of murmuring when it is too late. So thoughtless are the multitude![49]

The Society assumed a distinction among men, Burke ar-gued, the existence of a higher order "which looks down, as from a high mountain, on all beneath them." It would lay in ruins "that fine, plain, level state of civil equality, over which the sight of the beholder passed with pleasure, which God laid out for our use and happiness, and which our Laws and the nature of a Re-publican government promised us." Could "any man in his senses believe that the remaining rights of the people which are yet left untouched, will not be invaded and violated, by men, who disdaining the condition of private citizens, as below them, left it, and mounted up to the elevated and exclusive dignity of hereditary title?" Independence was won by gallant men "who fought for themselves, and not for masters; and whose spirit was not trammeled or broken down by the oppression of an insolent nobility." The Society threatened to nullify their achievement, and independence would then have been gained "not for the good of the people, but for a few families to aggrandize them-selves, and monopolize the power of the continent, and enjoy the fruits of it."[50]

Teaching by example, historical experience confirmed the danger. In the ancient Greek and Roman republics, and in the early European republics, honored military leaders soon turned to despotism. In America, the risk was much greater. Because the toils and sufferings of the American patriot officers were

---

49. Burke, *Considerations*, 5.
50. Ibid., 9–11.

crowned with ultimate success, they were "the most renowned band of men, that this day walk on the face of the globe." In the aggregate, they constituted "a very broad and respectable foundation for raising a hereditary nobility in America;" and they were much more likely to produce it than were the first founders of the ancient and modern nobility in the old world. The origins of that nobility were simple and limited, like "a small spring which forms the head of a great river." The Cincinnati and its prospective honorary members "is *that river* pretty nearly formed, already broad, deep, and forceable, and swoln to such a height, that rolling on in *direct lines*, and *collateral meanders*, it would in a short time rise into such a *fresh*, as to over flow its banks, and lay the country round it in one dismal scene of ruin."[51]

The *Address* and the *Considerations* both feature the conspiratorial mode of explanation in which men were assumed to intend the actual or prospective consequences of their actions. Both reflect the classical pattern of thought about government, the pattern of growth, perfection, and decay, as taught by history. The *Considerations*, in particular, is a near classic example of the anticipatory intellectual paranoia frequently encountered in the late eighteenth century. The division of society into orders was "a deep-laid contrivance" designed to establish a hereditary aristocracy which would "terminate at last in monarchical tyranny."[52] In the case before him, already clear in South Carolina and threatened in the other American republics, Burke saw decay commencing at birth, with no chance to achieve perfection.

Given Burke's intellectual orientation and cognitive structure, the question whether the Jacksonborough measures in fact threatened the dire consequences that he foresaw, or were designed to achieve any such end, is largely irrelevant. Burke's perception of Rutledge was shaped and colored in 1777 and 1778 when Rutledge opposed the Constitution of 1778 and particularly those features of it implementing the republican creed. These included such provisions as those extending the range of popular participation in the political system, legislative supremacy over the executive, rotation in office, and appropriate apportionment of representation. Burke was no egalitarian democrat. But he was clearly to the left of Rutledge's restricted, hierarchical concept of

51. Ibid., 19, 21–23.
52. Ibid., 29.

the appropriate political structure for South Carolina. Moreover, in the events of 1778, Rutledge and his supporters had demonstrated to the satisfaction of many a willingness to employ manipulative tactics to achieve desired goals. Burke was an observer of that scene and, on the evidence before him in 1783, had no difficulty in reaching the conclusion that "anti-republican" designs underlay the Jacksonborough measures which limited the vote, banished or improverished former leaders who might have challenged the establishment, reduced a substantial segment of the citizenry to a slavish dependency on legislative indulgence, and riveted in place "a fierce and jealous aristocracy, which has been gaining ground for seven years past."[53] In a footnote to the *Address*, he observed:

> I have been told that certain gentlemen frequently make it their business in company, to propagate a notion, that the people of this State are not capable to govern themselves, and that the constitution should be changed into an aristocracy, or the government of certain potent families. Does not this let the cat out of the bag, and account for late proceedings.[54]

For Burke, it was the same old game played once before, in which tyranny was obliged, "like the original tempter in Paradise, to assume a shape which may conceal its subtilty," and in which ambition would "assume all shapes and colors, and humble itself to the very dust to accomplish its purpose!"[55] Christopher Gadsden, another veteran of 1778, held similar views in 1783, complaining of "secret aristocrats" and "aristocratical shoots . . . slily thrust in" the state's constitution.[56]

In the heat of his argument, Burke probably overplayed his hand to some extent. Although he had good legal and historical grounds for his objections to the breadth and generality of the confiscation and amercement measures, he never acknowledged the larger public purposes those measures were intended to advance. In principle, if not in detail, they were supportable on policy grounds, particularly at a time when the war was still in

---

53. Burke, *Address*, 14.
54. Ibid., 22.
55. Burke, *Address*, 22; Burke, *Considerations*, 17.
56. Gadsden to Francis Marion, November 3, 1782, in *The Writings of Christopher Gadsden*, Walsh, ed., 189–90.

progress, and they were never applied as harshly as they were written. Those subject to their strictures were apparently content to leave well enough alone and to petition for relief in the General Assembly. Neither purchasers of confiscated property nor anti-loyalist segments of the populace were interested in repeal. Accordingly, few South Carolinians rallied to his call; and none who petitioned for relief called upon Burke to support his cause.

Most South Carolinians were similarly calm in the face of his attack on the Cincinnati, notwithstanding that many throughout the new republic shared his fears of the Society. The General Assembly never responded to Guerard's call in January 1784, and elected General Moultrie lieutenant governor in February.[57] There was no outcry in the press. What Burke did achieve with the *Address* and the *Considerations* was to introduce to public awareness in the new republic a brand of anti-aristocratic rhetoric which others more radical than he picked up, improved upon, and applied to their own ends within the polity. For the most part, those ends, and the means employed to pursue them, were not ends or means that Burke could countenance.

---

57. *JHR 1783–1784*, 453–54.

V

Publicist and Legislator

1783–1786

" 'The times that tried men's souls,' are over—and the greatest and completest revolution the world ever knew, gloriously and happily accomplished." So Thomas Paine proclaimed in April 1783, commemorating the eighth anniversary of the battle of Lexington. But he added words of caution. The transition from war to peace, from dependence to independence, would require "a gradual composure of the senses to receive it." Given peace, independence, and the benefits of free commerce, the states, individually and collectively, would have leisure and opportunity to regulate and establish their domestic concerns "and put it beyond the power of calumny to throw the least reflection on their honor." Nonetheless, America's great national character depended on the union of the states. The division of the American empire into states "is for our own convenience, but abroad this distinction ceases." The affairs of the states were local. Not even the richest of them could sustain itself in the world at large. "In short, we have no other national sovereignty than as United States."[1] Much of the decade of the 1780s was spent in contemplation of these simply stated propositions.

The reality of the situation confronting the American states in 1783 was somewhat more complex. The fighting war was over but neither sovereign independence nor the terms of peace was yet confirmed by treaty. Since 1781, the Continental Congress had sought to establish a direct source of revenue by urging that the states authorize a national impost. That effort never succeeded and Congress was left with the uncertain device of requisition on the states to satisfy its operating needs and to provide for a heavy load of national debt. Moreover, before the end of 1783, the an-

---

1. Thomas Paine, "The Crisis, No. 13," in *The Writings of Thomas Paine*, Moncure Daniel Conway, ed., 4 vols. (New York: G. P. Putnam's Sons, 1894–1896), 1: 370–76.

ticipated benefits of free commerce evaporated as the British withdrew from negotiations on favorable terms of trade with their former colonies and reconfirmed the major components of their pre-war mercantilist policy with the Americans, for the most part, on the outside looking in. Early in 1784, the substance of Lord Sheffield's famous pamphlet on British trade policy was known in the American states, including South Carolina.[2] In substance, Sheffield argued that, despite military defeat, Britain might yet retain her dominance by full employment of her economic resources. Britain had only to maintain and reinforce her mercantilist navigation system to retain the American market. The Americans had no manufacturing establishment to compete with British goods. Neither the French nor the Dutch could compete effectively. British goods were cheaper, and only British merchants could extend the liberal lines of credit American purchasers would require. Many Americans perhaps sensed that he was right, and for them, at least, Britain remained the preeminent threat to their hard won independence. Concrete evidence confirming this perception was provided when, in mid-1783, a British order in council closed trade with her West Indian colonies to American shipping.[3]

A gradual composure of the senses in the aftermath of war was nowhere more difficult than in South Carolina. Restoration of the civil institutions of government, begun at Jacksonborough in early 1782, was essentially complete in 1783. But the polity remained seriously divided, and the essential goal of political leadership in the 1780s was to reconcile differences and to establish an appropriate framework of political community. That goal was only partially achieved, and the obstacles to be overcome were particularly intractable. One was the depressed state of a ravaged economy and the loss of a substantial part of the state's slave labor force, which could only be replaced at a high cost in debt to a system of agricultural production traditionally short of liquid assets. Another was the prevailing disorder throughout the back-

2. John Baker Holroyd (Lord Sheffield), *Observations on the Commerce of the American States with Europe and the West Indies* (London: J. Debrett, 1783).
3. Charles Gregg Singer, *South Carolina in the Confederation* (Ph.D. dissertation, University of Pennsylvania, privately printed, 1941; reprint ed., Philadelphia: Porcupine Press, 1976), 88; Charles R. Ritcheson, *Aftermath of Revolution: British Policy Toward the United States, 1783–1795* (Dallas: Southern Methodist University Press, 1969), 6.

country, stimulated by civil strife during the war years and continuing thereafter in an ambiguous admixture of simple predatory lawlessness and war-related conflict that the governmental forces of law and order centered in Charleston were unable to contain. A third was a substantial reservoir of Anglophobia, the most pervasive intangible legacy of the British conquest of the state, which was reflected initially in the debate over confiscation and amercement and related policies. Very shortly, controversy concerning British merchants who remained behind when Charleston was evacuated further inflamed anti-British sentiment. Aggravated by the loss of slaves and the failure to receive compensation for the loss, and aggravated further by jealousy of Britain's evident intent to reassert economic dominion over American commerce, no people in America were more wary of British designs than were the South Carolinians. Moreover, as the Continental Congress sought to obtain powers commensurate with its responsibilities and untried institutions of local government sought to establish both authority and legitimacy, new targets of opportunity inevitably appeared to those most sensitive to the potential threats inherent in the age-old confrontation between power and freedom. Charleston was awash in controversy during the years 1783–1785, and Burke was in the midst of it, first with the *Address,* the *Considerations,* and the charges to the grand juries in 1783, later with another provocative pamphlet and in other less highly visible ways.

The British evacuated Charleston on December 14, 1782, and the waiting Americans moved in as the British embarked. Scheduled to convene on January 6, 1783, the General Assembly finally achieved a quorum on January 20. Governor Mathews delivered his initial address on January 24, outlining an agenda of matters for legislative consideration appropriate to the times. Most importantly, he reported on the Anglo-American negotiations proceeding in Paris and advised that, as of September, "nothing was then determined thereon." In the circumstances, his agenda was heavily weighted toward the security of the state and its immediate financial requirements. In addition, a range of issues involving former loyalists was submitted. Prominent among them was an agreement made with British merchants doing business in Charleston during the years of British occupation.[4]

---

4. *JHR 1783–1784,* 31–34.

Prior to the evacuation, the British commanding general protested the confiscation and amercement policy established at Jacksonborough and threatened retaliation. Concurrently, British merchants petitioned state authorities for leave to remain behind when British military forces withdrew for a period of time sufficient to enable them to liquidate their stocks and collect their accounts. Agreements dealing with both these matters were ultimately reached. Slaves under British control, except those who had rendered themselves obnoxious by their actions, were to be returned to their masters. Debts owing to British citizens would not be interfered with by executive officials of the state, and the legislature would not enact measures to seize such debts in the future. British citizens would be allowed the same rights in the courts as citizens of the state. None of the returned slaves would be punished by state authority. Neither the persons nor the property of families that departed with the British would be subjected to harassment or violence. Those merchants who wished to do so could remain for a period of six months, a period substantially less than the eighteen months requested.[5]

Issues involving loyalists, loyalty, and the status of British citizens remaining in South Carolina were thus at the forefront of public consciousness from the outset of the legislative session in early 1783. Almost immediately, the General Assembly was inundated with petitions for relief from the stringent penalties of the confiscation and amercement acts and, as the session progressed, the procedures adopted to deal with the petitions and the decisions announced as they were processed evidenced a legislative inclination toward leniency except in the most aggravated cases.[6] As the trend became clear, the proponents of strict enforcement began to stir.

Their concerns were aggravated by the continued presence of the British merchants, widely perceived as blatant profiteers. Such merchants were the only ones with stock to sell when the Americans returned to Charleston, and prices were promptly advanced. Contrary to the spirit of their agreement, William Logan

---

5. Jerome J. Nadelhaft, *The Disorders of War: The Revolution in South Carolina* (Orono: The University of Maine at Orono Press, 1981), 91–93; Paul A. Horne, "The Governorship of John Mathews, 1782–1783" (Master's thesis, University of South Carolina, Columbia, 1982).
6. Robert Stansbury Lambert, *South Carolina Loyalists in the American Revolution* (Columbia: University of South Carolina Press, 1987), 286–88.

alleged on behalf of himself and other citizens in early February, they "refused their goods then on hand at the prices they sold at while under the British government and decline to take produce in payment, by which means they collect a great part of the circulating Specie in this State." A number of them were "purchasing at Public and private Sale quantities of useful articles which they sell out to consumers at an exorbitant advance." In addition, other British subjects were "distressing the good inhabitants of this Country" by purchasing goods from the contracting British merchants and by importing goods on their own, and then reselling such goods "at an enormous advance, thereby making artificial Scarcities of the most necessary articles." To counteract the practices of these "Extortioners, Speculators and Monopolizers, so prejudicial to the Circumstances and real Interests of the Good people of this Country," the petitioners proposed what amounted to a cooperative merchandising venture and requested that the General Assembly endorse and support it.[7]

The precise practices of individual British merchants and their allies cannot be determined, but there is no doubt that they enjoyed access to sources of credit not available to prospective domestic competitors and acted to maximize their advantages. Undeterred by local resentment, with business booming, and with stocks replenished from England, these merchants applied for an extension of time in March 1783, and an extension was granted to March 1784. Some conditions were imposed. A new agreement would be required by June 14, 1783, with those who elected to remain. They would not be allowed to add to their existing stock of goods for sale, although they could purchase produce for export. They would be subject to local parochial and poor rates, and they would be subject to immediate expulsion and confiscation of goods for any action "injurious to the Interest of this State, the United States, or their Allies."[8]

New agreements were never made. In April, the Continental Congress issued a proclamation announcing the end of the war and ratified the provisional treaty agreed upon in Paris the pre-

---

7. *JHR 1783–1784*, 86–89.
8. Ibid., 153–54, 171, 186–87, 192–93, 206–207. The motion to extend the permitted stay was carried in the House of Representatives 57 to 41. Several days later, a motion to rescind the prior motion was defeated 41 to 53.

ceding November. After the news reached Charleston, the Privy Council, over objections by Alexander Gillon and Benjamin Waring, determined to postpone the matter until the next meeting of the General Assembly, previously called to convene in special session on July 7.[9] When the legislature met, Guerard duly reported the postponement and the General Assembly responded by declaring that, with ratification of the preliminary articles of peace, no further compact with the British merchants would be necessary.[10] The merchants were accordingly allowed to remain and became eligible for citizenship.

All this was too much for the mechanics, artisans, and seamen of Charleston, the heirs of the pre-war Sons of Liberty, and a series of tumultuous proceedings began that continued intermittently through 1784 and into 1785. Disorder erupted in early July 1783 when Thomas Barron, a British subject, "imprudently and grossly insulted a citizen" on Broad Street in Charleston.[11] A riot ensued and general disorder prevailed for at least the next two days, featuring assaults, pumping, and various other forms of corporal indignity visited on suspected friends of Britain. Guerard promptly issued a proclamation calling for order and threatening vigorous prosecution of offenders.[12] In response, general meetings were held to draw resolutions protesting the continued presence of British merchants in Charleston and tacitly threatening further disagreeable consequences.[13]

These events precipitated the first major newspaper debate of the post-war years, which continued through the summer of 1783. Meanwhile, in the most important substantive action taken during the short legislative session in mid-1783, the General Assembly incorporated Charleston, provided a separate governmental structure for the city, and incidentally created a new arena for

---

9. *JPC*, 64–65. The *SCGGA* reported the provisional treaty on March 15, 1783, outlined its terms on April 9, and published the proclamation of the Continental Congress on April 20. The definitive treaty signed September 3, 1783 was reported in the *SCGGA* on December 18.

10. *JHR 1783–1784*, 322, 330, 340, 349.

11. *SCGGA*, July 8 and 12, 1783. Commenting on these events some months later, John Lewis Gervais observed that the disorder was occasioned "by the Lenity shown to the Tories and by their own imprudence." Gervais to Henry Laurens, February 12, 1784, Lafayette Manuscripts, Manuscripts Department, Lilly Library, Indiana University.

12. *JPC*, 70–71; *SCGGA*, July 12, 1783.

13. *SCWG*, July 12, 19, and 26, 1783; *SCGGA*, July 12, 15, 19, and 22, 1783.

political controversy. Charleston's small merchants, mechanics, and artisans, whose participatory role in the political system was established and confirmed in the years immediately preceding the Revolution, already active and highly vocal in the early 1780s, promptly became equally active and vocal in the affairs of the city.

By the incorporating act, the General Assembly transferred to municipal officers all responsibility for the day-to-day management of the rambunctious city's affairs. It was divided into thirteen wards and would be governed by a board of thirteen wardens, one elected from each ward. After the election of wardens, a city-wide election would select one of them as intendant. The intendant and wardens would together constitute the City Council, vested with broad general authority to govern the city. Among other things, it was empowered "in case of tumult or riot, or appearance or probability of tumult or riot," to adopt such measures "as shall appear most advisable for preventing or suppressing such tumult or riot." Any inhabitant refusing to obey the orders of the intendant, for purposes of suppressing any riot or tumult, was subject to fine.[14]

The turmoil of mid-1783 was largely spontaneous and unorganized, and the people of Charleston had no particular quarrels with the proposed structure of city government. Accordingly, the first municipal elections in Charleston passed calmly enough.[15] By the end of the year, however, pockets of organized political opposition to the establishment were clearly in evidence. In November, Alexander Gillon and James Fallon in effect took over

---

14. *Statutes at Large*, 7: 97–101. Wardens would be elected within a month after passage of the act and annually thereafter, beginning in 1784. In practice the elections were held early in September. An amendment of the act in 1784 authorized the wardens to act as a court for the enforcement of city ordinances and by-laws. The court of wardens could commit violators to "close prison" and was granted the powers of the judges of the Court of Common Pleas "touching all matters within the limits of their jurisdiction, and which do not exceed in value twenty pounds." *Statutes at Large*, 7: 101–102. The controversial history of the court of wardens is described in James W. Ely, "Charleston's Court of Wardens, 1783–1800: A Post Revolutionary Experiment in Municipal Justice," *South Carolina Law Review*, 27 (1975): 645–60. The incorporation of Charleston is sometimes described as a direct response to the turbulence experienced in the city during the spring of 1783. Some provisions of the incorporating act were no doubt drawn with that experience in mind, but the subject was first considered and approved in principle at the January session. *JHR 1783–1784*, 215–16, 289–90.

15. *SCGGA*, August 26, September 2, 6, 13, and 20, 1783.

the Smoking Society, an existing organization of mechanics and artisans, renamed it the Marine Anti-Britannic Society, and scheduled its anniversary date on December 14 of each year to commemorate the date of the British evacuation of Charleston.[16] Throughout 1784, and into 1785, the Society was in the forefront of public protest against returning loyalists and the activities of British merchants.

The first major confrontation was precipitated in March 1784 when John Rutledge invoked legislative privilege against Captain William Thompson, proprietor of the City Tavern and a member of the Marine Anti-Britannic Society. Thompson was summoned before the General Assembly to answer for an alleged insult to Rutledge, refused to apologize personally to Rutledge, and was jailed for the remainder of the legislative session, a period of approximately one week.[17] Promptly following his release, the Marine Anti-Britannic Society adopted a resolution of thanks to Thompson "for his *spirited, manly,* and patriotic conduct" in defending the rights and privileges of his fellow citizens, violated in his own person, "when *Aristocratical principles* endeavoured to subvert and destroy every *genuine idea of real republicanism.*"[18] John Miller, the state printer, refused to publish the resolution in his *South Carolina Gazette and General Advertiser,* and members of the Society countered by resolving to cancel their subscriptions and deny him any further advertising.[19] After his release, Thompson published a vitriolic account of the incident, attacking the establishment elite as "the NABOBS of this State, their servile *Toad-eaters,* the BOBS,—and the servilely-servile tools and lick-spittles of Power to *both,* the BOBBETTS." For Thompson, the fundamental issue was whether the people or the pro-British aristocracy would control the state, not merely technical questions concerning the doctrine of legislative privilege. The objective of the proceeding, as he saw it, was to humiliate "a *Publican,* a *stranger,* a wretch of no higher rank in the Commonwealth than that of a *Common-Citizen:* for having dared to dispute with *a John*

---

16. *GSSC,* November 20 and 27, 1783.
17. Michael E. Stevens, "Legislative Privilege in Post-Revolutionary South Carolina," *WMQ,* 46 (January 1989): 71–92. Rutledge took his seat in the House on January 30, 1784. In a nice touch by someone, Burke was designated to swear him in. *JHR 1783–1784,* 392.
18. *GSSC,* April 1, 1784.
19. *SCGPA,* April 3–7, 1784; *GSSC,* April 8, 1784.

Rutledge, or any of the NABOB Tribe." Privilege resided in the people, he said, and he defended his refusal to submit as a defense of the people, because submission "would be an insult on the people's majesty, and on the privileges of every citizen within the land, had I administered to them *so odious a precedent.*"[20]

Unrest continued through the spring months of 1784, stimulated principally by the General Assembly's lenient treatment of those initially subjected to the penalties of confiscation and amercement.[21] James Cook, one of those relieved, was burned in effigy; lists were posted warning thirteen named persons to leave the state within ten days or face the consequences of public wrath; and Governor Guerard offered a reward for those responsible for the lists and charged them with presumptuously assuming legislative, executive, and judicial powers.[22] Turbulence became tumult in early July. For several days, street disturbances in Charleston appeared beyond the control of city authorities, and a special force of trusted citizens was recruited to reestablish order. While Fallon led the demonstrators in the streets, Gillon met with the Privy Council, of which he was a member, to consider means by which the public peace might be restored.[23]

The disorder was put down, but a new wave of angry attacks on the "arrogant aristocracy" erupted and found a forum in a spirited contest for office in the municipal election of 1784, when small merchants, mechanics, artisans, and other dissidents led by Gillon challenged the establishment for control. One of the prin-

---

20. *GSSC*, April 29, 1784.
21. *Statutes at Large*, 4: 624–26 and 6: 634–35; Gervais to Henry Laurens, April 15, 1784, Laurens Papers, SCL; Gervais to Henry Laurens, May 5, 1784, Charles Francis Jenkins Collection, HSP. Lists of those relieved by the General Assembly were published in the *SCGGA*, March 30, 1784.
22. *SCGGA*, April 27, 1784; Nadelhaft, *Disorders of War*, 109–110. Lambert, *South Carolina Loyalists*, 293, and Kathy Rowe Coker, "The Punishment of Revolutionary War Loyalists in South Carolina" (Ph.D. dissertation, University of South Carolina, 1987), 82–87, describe the Cook case and its aftermath. Cook was relieved of banishment but his estate was amerced and he never returned to South Carolina.
23. *JPC*, 115–22 (July 8, 9, and 12, 1784); *GSSC*, July 8, 1784; William Washington to Nathanael Greene, July 8, 1784, Greene Papers, WLCL. Washington described the demonstrating crowd as "contemptible in number and quality" but made clear that force was used to disband the demonstrators. He recruited "about 30 volunteer Horse" to support the city authorities.

cipal issues was the propriety of the conduct of the city administration in suppressing the July disorders. Inevitably, the issues expanded to include the City Council's management of the city's affairs generally, and the act of incorporation was attacked as an unlawful delegation of authority to a subordinate body in which executive, legislative, and judicial functions were combined. Throughout the summer, conservatives and moderates complained of lawlessness, disorder, and party, and dissidents denounced Tories, British citizens, and the aristocracy. The challenge failed. When the vote was counted in September, the Gillon forces were decisively defeated, and Richard Hutson was elected intendant.[24] A second strident challenge in 1785 similarly failed, even more decisively, and Arnoldus Vanderhorst was elected intendant to succeed Hutson.[25]

The excitement of 1783 and 1784 should not be overweighted by historians as evidence of deep-seated class conflict and democratic beginnings. Socio-economic factors were not irrelevant, but the tension and the issues were essentially war-related, part of the aftermath of a long and bitter struggle, in which one thing led to another until the underlying resentment of Whig against Tory was either spent or redirected. Particularly in 1783, before news of the definitive treaty of peace arrived, the circumstances of crowd action were similar to those that precipitated the demonstrations against British authority before the war and the amnesty proclaimed by Rawlins Lowndes in 1778. Moreover, the number involved was relatively small, and the motives of the leaders were all suspect. Gillon, for example, was a leading speculator in the purchase of confiscated property, particularly in Charleston, and had no interest in relief for former loyalist owners.[26] James Fallon was a known rabble-rouser, in trouble with authority wherever he settled.[27] Henry Perroneau, identified by William Washington as one of the most respectable participants in the July crowd, was perhaps more interested in demonstrating the loyalty of his family, who had been subjected to confiscation and banishment and were then seeking relief.[28]

24. *GSSC*, September 2, 4, 7, and 14, 1784; Nadelhaft, *Disorders of War*, 118–19.
25. *SCGPA*, September 6, 10, and 13, 1785; Nadelhaft, *Disorders of War*, 119–20.
26. Lambert, *South Carolina Loyalists*, 293.
27. John Carl Parish, "The Intrigues of Doctor James O'Fallon," *Mississippi Valley Historical Review*, 17 (1930): 230–63.
28. William Washington to Nathanael Greene, July 8, 1784, Greene Papers, WLCL; Lambert, *South Carolina Loyalists*, 293. Coker, "Punishment of Revolu-

William Thompson was probably encouraged by Fallon.[29] In all events, the dissident leaders were promptly isolated and either effectively banished or coopted. Gillon survived, but after the general election of 1786, in which he barely won a seat from the Charleston parishes, he elected to sit in the General Assembly from Saxe Gotha.[30] Thompson lost his lease on the City Tavern and left town in early 1785.[31] Fallon also left town in early 1785 and, when his name appeared in 1787 on a petition from the backcountry for permission to incorporate a new Irish social organization, the Friendly Hibernian Society, the petition was overwhelmingly rejected.[32] Finally, despite claims of support by a secret Whig Club of 600, the Marine Anti-Britannic Society never had as many as three hundred members and the active membership was substantially less. In May 1784, "Another Patriot" reported that only 39, not 600, had appeared at a recent meeting and observed that "most have at last seen through the cheat."[33]

Moderates were as appalled by the course of events as conservatives. When the disturbances first erupted in 1783, "A Patriot" entered an eloquent plea for moderation on traditional republican grounds. "Law should be the basis of political liberty," he said, "and whatever exceeds this is licentiousness in the garb of it." Faction and tumult, "where there is no oppression, can only spring from a contempt for government, or views of ambition." Public disorder was destructive of the public interest, the Patriot continued, and particularly of commerce. Wise policy would promote commerce by promoting competition among merchants and would not exclude good men, who offered to become citizens, merely because they once were British citizens. Mobs were a reproach to free governments, "not tolerable but in cases of oppression, and where redress cannot be obtained through the legal channel." When mobs appeared in a free government,

---

tionary War Loyalists in South Carolina," 358–63, describes the problems of Henry Perroneau, Sr., who was relieved of banishment but whose estate was amerced. He never returned to South Carolina.
29. Thompson's representative in his exchange of correspondence with Rutledge was one "Major Phelon." *JHR 1783–1784*, 579–80. The Marine Anti-Britannic Society roster listed no member by that name.
30. *CMP*, December 5, 1786; *JHR 1787–1788*, 637–38.
31. Stevens, "Legislative Privilege in South Carolina."
32. *SCGGA*, February 26, 1785; *JHR 1787–1788*, 80, 127–28.
33. "Another Patriot," *SCGGA*, May 11, 1784. See also *Rules of the Marine Anti-Britannic Society* (Charleston: A. Timothy, 1784), with attached list of 245 members. The Charleston imprint of the Rules is at WLCL.

they originated "in licentiousness and not in oppression, excited by ambitious or unfriendly views, and the people should be on guard against both."[34]

The Patriot returned to this theme a few days later and asked those "deluded" into a licentious promotion of their views "to consider well how far their advisers are connected with the happiness of the country, and whether their views are not to bring the government into ruin or contempt, or to answer some private views, or whether some person, utterly unfitted for the advantages of social life, and an outcast from every community in which he may have ever attempted to live before, is not employed here to fan into a flame the sparks of commotion and riot."[35] Later, viciously attacked by "Brutus," the Patriot dismissed him as like death, sparing none. Brutus played the patriot, "but if he had a touch of Ithuriel's spear, he would appear in his true character."[36]

Christopher Gadsden, writing as "A Steady and Open Republican," proclaimed similar views in a series of communications to the public in 1784 initially stimulated by the extralegal tactics of the Marine Anti-Britannic Society in March, which he called "Retail Tyranny," and later evolving into an extended exchange with Gillon and his supporters as the municipal campaign in Charleston proceeded toward election day in September.[37] In July, "Aristides" noted that the tone of public affairs had changed with the achievement of peace and indepen-

---

34. "A Patriot," *SCGGA*, July 15, 1783. There were four letters of the "Patriot" in July and August 1783, the first of which was initially issued as a broadside and then reprinted. The style, substance, and timing suggest that Burke might have been the author. The reference to Ithuriel's spear in the August 12 letter, mentioned below, is suggestive but not conclusive. The style of the letters is quite similar to the style of Burke's two charges to grand juries described in Chapter III and the letters appeared after the first and before the second, and thus at a time when Burke was not occupied with judicial duties. Note also the warning in the second charge against designing men who take advantage of unrest to advance personal objectives. At least the first two, and probably all, the "Patriot" letters were written before Burke learned of the Society of the Cincinnati as described in Chapter IV.
35. "A Patriot," *SCGGA*, July 19, 1783. The reference is probably to Fallon.
36. "A Patriot," *SCGGA*, August 12, 1783.
37. May 6, July 17, and August 5, 1784, in *The Writings of Christopher Gadsden*, Richard Walsh, ed. (Columbia: University of South Carolina Press, 1966), 200–38. Gadsden charged Gillon with either authorizing or editing many of the antiestablishment diatribes published during the period. Gillon, whose responses were reasonably restrained in the circumstances, denied the charge. Fallon was perhaps the better candidate.

dence. Some, he said, "with a fickleness natural to the mind of man, and others with ill designs now spurn the blessings Heaven gave them," condemning the constitution, insulting the executive and the legislature "in the grossest manner," and forming unconstitutional voting blocs committed to secrecy.[38] At the end of the year, Thomas Tudor Tucker, urging the necessity for an early convention to revise the state constitution, carefully and explicitly disassociated himself from the demonstrating dissidents, deprecated both "faction and party spirit," and denounced secret combinations as "insidious and treacherous attempts of a minority to rule a majority; which is the very definition of an aristocratical government, so loudly and so justly condemned."[39]

Burke's position was less explicit but nevertheless reasonably clear. As a man of law and a judge, he was never on the side of riot, tumult, or lawlessness. In the *Address*, notwithstanding a ringing denunciation of South Carolina's putative aristocracy, he advocated legal solutions to the problems he perceived, not direct action. In the *Considerations*, he disparaged the thoughtless multitude who aggressively pursued a few insignificant Tories while ignoring the more serious threat of the Cincinnati. A staunch defender of legal rights and civil liberty, Burke was never one to incite the populace, or any part of it, to direct action against established authority serving under republican institutions of government. Like the Patriot and Gadsden, Burke believed that the path of opposition to perceived wrongs lay through channels. Direct action was licentiousness and concealed private ambitions for personal preferment or advantage. Yet, in the tumults of 1783 and 1784, he found the rhetoric of opposition, which he had employed to identify latent dangers and to propose corrective measures within a framework of law and order, adopted by a dissident faction, reduced to a vulgar level of vitriolic abuse, and turned first to extralegal purposes and then to influence the electoral process.[40]

---

38. "Aristides," *SCGPA*, July 21–24, and 24–28, 1784.
39. "Philodemus" [Thomas Tudor Tucker], *Conciliatory Hints. . . .* (Charleston: A. Timothy, 1784), 6, 19.
40. "Democratic Gentletouch" [William Hornby], *GSSC*, May 13, 1784, is one clear example. Defending the Marine Anti-Britannic Society against Gadsden's first attack, Hornby echoed Burke's *Address* in criticizing the acts of the Jacksonborough Assembly.

Years later, with all the benefits and limitations of hindsight to be sure, Burke described the tumults of 1784 and Fallon's role in those proceedings. Fallon, he said, was a man of intelligence and ability who nevertheless involved himself and the public in "perpetual broils," proclaiming to the people that liberty was dead, "smothered, as he said, by the aristocrats and tories," and calling for direct action by the people "to right themselves." According to Burke, Fallon conducted nightly meetings in March 1784 "of what he called a committee of 600." One morning printed handbills were posted ordering named British merchants to quit the state by a specified day. The governor, deeming the action an insult to public authority, issued a proclamation against any such proceedings. The next day a counter proclamation appeared doubling the number required to depart. Several nights later "a multitude of men . . . burst forth from the City Tavern, formed an array in the street and marched with colours flying, towards the square of St. Michael." In response, "the peaceable part of the citizens flew to their arms and met in the square, some on foot, some on horseback and all of us in consternation, not knowing the nature or direction of this singular appearance." The mob was dispersed by a force that included Thomas Pinckney, William Washington, and John Blake. "Fallon kept behind the curtain," Burke said, "as if he had no hand in it; and still continued to give dissertation upon *democracy*, whose high priest he still affected to be." His real purpose, "which he kept out of sight, while he held out to the people a pretext, as a shewman does *cups* and *balls*," was to take over political leadership and reform the government. Able though he was, Fallon "had received from the hand of nature a crook or bend to mischief; and as there existed at the time in our community some little ferment floating on the disputes of whig and tory, and some short live'd differences which the enthusiasm of the war had created," he sought to take advantage of that situation to advance his own opportunistic goals.[41]

Moreover, the noise of the crowd concealed much slow but steady progress in political affairs. Almost as soon as the General

---

41. *SCSG*, March 5, 1796. The occasion was an attack by Burke on Robert Goodloe Harper's opportunism in supporting reapportionment in South Carolina in the mid-1790s, described in Chapter IX. Burke compared Harper to Fallon and, in the process, identified himself as on the law and order side in 1784.

Assembly convened in January 1783, serious work began on a variety of measures of major importance. Taking up the provisions of the Constitution of 1778 that called for a division of the state into counties and the creation of a system of subordinate county courts, Henry Pendleton brought in bills to achieve those objectives and was instrumental in carrying them through to enactment in early 1785.[42] Christopher Gadsden began early to press for constitutional revision and his initiative was picked up by Pendleton and others, including Thomas Tudor Tucker, in the ensuing years.[43] The exclusion act adopted at Jacksonborough, so strenuously objected to by Burke in the *Address*, expired by its terms.[44] Proceedings under the confiscation and amercement acts in the General Assembly produced almost exactly the results that the original opponents of the policy had sought. In effect, the legislative branch performed the functions of a court in reviewing and deciding individual cases on the basis of evidence submitted by the parties affected. The most reprehensible offenders were punished and lesser offenders were relieved in whole or in part depending on the degree of their guilt.[45] Work was begun on a project to revise and publish the laws of the state, and in 1785 Pendleton, Burke, and Grimke were appointed as commissioners to complete that important task.[46] Tax reform was enacted in 1784, and an independent Court of Chancery was established to replace the Privy Council as the forum having jurisdiction in eq-

---

42. *Statutes at Large*, 4: 561 (appointing commissioners on division of state into counties, 1783); 4: 661–66 (establishing counties, 1785); 7: 211–42 (establishing county courts, 1785). Pendleton's instrumental role in the creation of South Carolina's county court system in 1785 is described in David Ramsay, *The History of South Carolina*, 2 vols. (Charleston: David Longworth, 1809), 2: 127–28, and in S. R. Matchett, "Unanimity, Order and Regularity: The Political Culture of South Carolina in the Era of the Revolution" (Ph.D. dissertation, University of Sydney, Australia, 1980), 312–15.
43. *JHR 1783–1784*, 70 (January 30, 1783), 327 (August 5, 1783), 407 (February 2, 1784), 529 (March 8, 1784). Tucker, *Conciliatory Hints*, gave reasons for the failure to achieve constitutional revision in 1784 and proposed procedures to advance that project.
44. The act adopted by the Jacksonborough Assembly applied only to "the next General Assembly," that is, the General Assembly elected in November, 1782.
45. Lambert, *South Carolina Loyalists*, 286–96; Coker, "Punishment of Revolutionary War Loyalists in South Carolina," 39–51.
46. *JHR 1783–1784*, 139; *JHR 1785–1786*, 35, 227. Creation of the commission was authorized by statute. *Statutes at Large*, 4: 659–60. The commissioners were directed "to form a complete and accurate digest of the statute laws of this State, with such additions, alterations, and amendments, as to them shall seem just,

uity cases. A variety of internal improvements were under way, and the Santee Canal Company was established in 1785. A new academy was founded in Winnsboro in 1785. Burke was one of the first directors of the canal company and on the first board of trustees of the new academy.[47]

In addition, the state was generally supportive of measures proposed by the Continental Congress in the years 1783–1785. A 5 percent national impost was authorized by the Jacksonborough Assembly in 1782. When support was not forthcoming from all the other states, that authority was rescinded in 1783, only to be regranted in 1784.[48] The Continental Congress was also authorized to adopt limited retaliatory measures in response to the closing of trade with the British West Indies.[49] The proposal of Congress requesting broad authority to regulate commerce with foreign nations was also before the General Assembly in mid-1785, strongly endorsed by the Charleston Chamber of Commerce and others. There was opposition, however, from some who feared any further grant of general power to a central government and from others who feared equally the perceived commercial avarice of the eastern states.[50]

By then, other issues were more pressing. The economy was in tatters. Virtually no specie was to be had. Pre-war debts remained unpaid. Post-war debts were mounting, reflecting the purchase of slaves to replace those lost during the war, other costs incurred for reconstruction of the agricultural economy, some loss of markets and bounties, and some conspicuous consumption after years of deprivation. Pre-war debts, deferred in 1782 and again in 1784, were beginning to come due in 1785. Compounding the problem, bad weather and other factors seriously affected agricultural production in 1784 and 1785. The balance of trade remained heavily unfavorable.

In these circumstances, creditors became increasingly insistent in pursuit of their claims. British merchants in Charleston,

---

right and expedient." Each commissioner was granted the sum of £ 300 to cover his expenses.

47. *Statutes at Large*, 4: 627–38 (ad valorem tax on land and certain other property in lieu of prior flat tax); 7: 208–11 (Court of Chancery). Burke's involvement with the Santee Canal Company and, through the Mt. Sion Society, with the Winnsboro Academy are described in Chapter I.

48. *Statutes at Large*, 4: 594–96.

49. *Statutes at Large*, 4: 596; Singer, *South Carolina in the Confederation*, 90–92.

50. *JHR 1785–1786*, 312–13; Singer, *South Carolina in the Confederation*, 93–96.

many of whom had become naturalized citizens, were among the largest of the creditors demanding payment. Naturally enough, they bore with the courts the burden of public displeasure. In April 1785, planters, farmers, and others, faced with suits on outstanding debts and with execution of judgments entered in prior suits, blocked Judge Grimke's attempt to convene the circuit court in Camden and effectively forestalled the conduct of any judicial business.[51] In August 1785, a correspondent to the *Columbian Herald* reported that the courts of the state were virtually suspended everywhere but Charleston and that few sheriffs dared serve civil process outside Charleston's city limits.[52] Some action was clearly required lest the entire judicial system fall into total disarray and the public peace be shattered, and Governor William Moultrie responded to the immediate pressure of events by calling the General Assembly into special session in September. On September 26, its first working day, he declared that he had no desire to interfere in the private concerns of individuals but that, for lack of circulating specie, even the most well inclined debtors, anxious to satisfy all proper claims, were in danger "of falling a pray to aliens." In conclusion, he suggested that the Assembly call on the judges "for more particular information of the causes that had occasioned the suspension of the laws."[53]

Burke was intimately familiar with the dangers threatening the judicial system and public peace and order, and he had his own distinctive opinion as to the underlying cause. Accordingly, in advance of the special session, he elected to press for a national navigation act designed to counter Britain's oppressive mercantilist policy although he knew, as everyone did, that the goal of the session was to enact measures promising immediate relief for distressed debtors. *A Few Salutary Hints*, his third famous pamphlet, appeared on September 27, just after the special session met but before its work was fairly begun.[54]

---

51. "John F. Grimke's Eyewitness Account of the Camden Court Riot, April 27–28, 1785," Robert A. Becker, ed., *SCHM*, 83 (1982): 209–13.
52. "Americanus," *CH*, August 22, 1785. The consequences were particularly prejudicial to residents of Charleston, since they could be sued but could not recover debts due them from outside the city.
53. *JHR 1785–1786*, 313–14.
54. Burke's *Salutary Hints* was first published by Burd and Haswell in Charleston in September 1785, just a week after the special session of the General Assembly convened. *SCGPA*, September 24 and 27, 1785. It was reprinted by S. Kollock in New York in 1786. No copy of the Charleston imprint has been found.

The policy of permitting British merchants to remain after the evacuation of Charleston and ultimately permitting them to become citizens had proven ruinous, Burke argued. "I was one," he said, "whose opinion it was, that they would soon incorporate with us, make good citizens, and that after the war was over, our enmities should be forgotten; but I am sorry that I fell into such an error; for the conduct of Great Britain since the peace—the mercantile war she now wages against us—the disposition and sentiments held forth by her subjects here, even after they became our citizens, now convince me, that I did not know them." Amnesty was sound in principle, but "not for those who seek to rule as masters." In a ringing denunciation of British arrogance, he charged that "they let loose upon us, as from Pandora's box, a ruinous luxury, speculation, and extravagance," plunged the state into debt, and now "the whole country, one estate after another, is to be set up to sale by sheriffs and constables, for cash too, after they themselves raked together and sent off all the circulating coin." The legislature would for a time interpose its authority to execution sales, he predicted. The result would be injustice and calamity to creditors, but the question was who should possess the soil and control the administration of the country. "Such is the anarchy they have thrown us into, that our government at this moment cannot enforce obedience to the Court of Common Pleas, above 20 miles beyond the gates of our city; perhaps not so far; and so peculiarly deplorable is the state of our affairs altogether, that the very best and only remedy to save us, will turn out a public misfortune."[55]

Burke reacted to Lord Sheffield's strictures with patriotic fervor. Let any man read Sheffield's pamphlet, he said, "and if he be a friend to America, it must rouse his indignation to see, that we are estimated by those people only as consumers. . . . Such contempt for ourselves, our government and policy; such confidence that we are a rope of sand; that Congress will have no power to bind us together, or regulate our trade. We have nothing to do but wear their manufactures, consume their productions, promote their trade, starve the New-England men, make our Negroes work, buy more as we can get credit, live luxuriously, and spend our days as consumers of British good things.

---

55. Burke, *Salutary Hints*, 4, 11, 14.

This is the plan laid down for us by that dignified scribbler, now pursued by his nation, and fatally adopted by ourselves." In short, still full of animosity "against us and our republic," the British goal was to reduce America to commercial servitude.[56]

The General Assembly should repeal the alien law and thereby exclude Britons from citizenship except by special acts of naturalization. It should also invest Congress with power to regulate foreign trade and to adopt navigation laws forbidding the produce of America from being carried except by American vessels or the vessels of nations that allowed Americans reciprocal benefits. Such navigation acts would benefit both North and South. A foundation would thus be laid for an American maritime establishment. With the growth of a shipbuilding industry, "the numbers and industry of the northern states, would give security, strength, and splendor to the South; and the wealth of the South, instead of going into British coffers . . . to answer British purposes against us, would then enrich ourselves, and reward the laborious inhabitants of the North; and thus would the resources of each part, contribute to add to the strength and glory of the whole empire." The northern and southern states would then be cemented together, "as one people, united in friendship, harmony, and mutual interest."[57]

No author was named in the *Salutary Hints*. Burke admitted authorship, however, in a letter written to General Greene in November 1785. He credited Greene with many of the ideas expressed and suggested that "in some sense you ought to father the whole of it." The writing was hastily done, he said, but "the pain it cost me to write it, was a trifle, compared with the difficulty I had to get it printed: so much afraid was every creature of offending the British. It put me in mind of a conspiracy whenever I spoke of it to anyone."[58] Burke was always alert to suspect conspiracy, and this one is somewhat suspect, perhaps embellished for Greene's benefit. There was not that much new in the *Salutary Hints*, except that Burke, for the first time, seemed to be

---

56. Ibid., 7–10.
57. Ibid., 15.
58. Burke to Nathanael Greene, November 27, 1785, Greene Papers, WLCL. Greene may have solicited Burke to speak on his behalf to avoid a repetition of the controversy occasioned when he "interfered" in local politics in 1783. See Edward McCrady, *The History of South Carolina in the Revolution, 1780–1783* (New York: The Macmillan Company, 1902), 688–93.

taking the side of the dissident artisans, mechanics, and small merchants of Charleston and diverting attention from the immediate problem at hand.

The *Salutary Hints* was thus a political tract aimed at the General Assembly and designed to elicit support for the regulatory authority requested by the Continental Congress. In addition, elements of private interest were involved. At the time, Burke was attempting, without notable success, to assist Generals Greene and Wayne in dealing with their pressing creditors in South Carolina and Georgia.[59] Greene apparently urged a nationalist approach that Burke accepted. British mercantilist policy, particularly as described in Sheffield's pamphlet, provided a convenient target. To a mind so conditioned to suspicion as Burke's, British anti-republican objectives were perfectly clear. Even so, Greene evidently urged him on.

In all fairness to Burke, legislative interposition in the private relationship between debtor and creditor was no easy choice for a lawyer and judge. In the eighteenth century, a debt was a moral obligation; and failure to pay was virtually a species of fraud. Modern legal doctrine recognizing that default is not necessarily the equivalent of personal dishonor did not evolve until some years later. The conservative Timothy Ford reflected the prevailing legal culture when he called the relief acts of 1785 "impolitic" and "iniquitous" and observed: "Such is the nature of republican government! And it is hard to decide which is most blamable, the premeditated fraud of the debtor; or the weak and unsuspecting confidence of the creditor."[60] Thus, Burke was never an enthusiastic supporter of debtor relief, perceiving, as he said in the *Salutary Hints*, that legislative interposition would produce injustice and calamity to creditors and that "the very best and only remedy to save us, will turn out a public misfortune." He must have foreseen that the controversy could be resolved only if rights of private property were subordinated to interests of state, and he would accept the remedial measures on that ground. But the choice was difficult, even for the most committed republican.

59. George C. Rogers, Jr., "Aedanus Burke, Nathanael Greene, Anthony Wayne, and the British Merchants of Charleston," *SCHM*, 67 (1966): 75–83.
60. "Diary of Timothy Ford, 1785–1786," Joseph W. Barnwell, ed., *SCHM*, 13 (1912): 194–95.

The General Assembly was far more concerned with the immediate domestic problem than with retaliation against British economic policy or the niceties of legal theory. In a brief session, it enacted two extraordinary measures designed to provide temporary relief for distressed debtors and deferred consideration of authority to regulate trade and commerce for further study. An act relating to sales of property on execution of judgment, soon better known as the "pine barren act," permitted a debtor to offer property in payment of his debt at 75 percent of its appraised value. The creditor could either accept the property in payment or extend the debt. It applied to debts incurred both prior to and after 1782 but would expire at the end of the next session of the General Assembly. In addition, to increase currency in circulation, the General Assembly authorized up to £100,000 of new paper money for issuance in the form of loans secured by property. The new paper money was not legal tender. It could be used to pay taxes, but private debtors could decline to accept it. The execution sales act, however, made refusal dangerous. In substance, the legislature subordinated private rights of property to the immediate requirements of public peace and order.[61]

Henry Pendleton dominated the proceedings of the special session almost from the outset, advocating that imports of slaves be prohibited for three years to improve the unfavorable balance of trade and personally presenting the execution sales and paper money proposals. When the slave import restriction was defeated, he pressed the other measures. The present distress, he said, "proved us the most inconsistent people under the sun." The debate was centering on "what we would have, instead of the necessary question what we should not have." Later, after a period of inconclusive debate, he observed bluntly that "he did not wish to argue with gentlemen that were determined not to be convinced; to reason with such was to fight a spectre. . . . If gentlemen were determined to oppose every scheme, and no relief could be given, we should go from bad to worse; every man would be a sovereign, until at last the whole would end in our being ruled by a dictator." The opposition then broke down. Ed-

61. *Statutes at Large*, 4: 710–12 (execution sales act), 712–16 (paper money). See Robert A. Becker, "Salus Populi Suprema Lex: Public Peace and South Carolina Debtor Relief Laws, 1783–1788," *SCHM*, 80 (1979): 65–75, and Nadelhaft, *Disorders of War*, 155–172, on the issue of debtor relief generally.

ward Rutledge, opposed in principle to paper money, endorsed Pendleton's plan. "It was laid down with so much judgment—had been supported by such clear comprehensive arguments," that it would have his support. Within a few days, the bills were prepared, debated further, and enacted.[62]

Although before the House, the question whether the Continental Congress should be empowered to regulate trade with foreign nations was considered only in passing. Edward Rutledge favored the idea, arguing that the superior advantage of Britain's position entitled the American states to seek an off-setting advantage to relieve the distress of the eastern states. "He did not say we should sacrifice everything, but it becomes us to give a little, and sacrifice something for the good of the whole."[63] Although various members spoke to the issue, Burke was apparently silent. In the rush to adjourn when the valuation and paper money bills were completed, the question fell by the wayside, referred to a committee of thirteen for study prior to the regular session in January 1786.[64]

A year later Pendleton explained to the grand juries in the Georgetown, Cheraw, and Camden judicial districts the rationale underlying the execution sales and paper money acts adopted in 1785 and his personal assessment of the state of the republic. Frugality, economy, and obedience to law were essential if Americans hoped to remain a free people. The "pine barren act" was only the least exceptionable of the several measures proposed to contain the consequences of post-war folly and extravagance, and was appropriate in the circumstances. But measures for debtor relief were only temporary expedients. Unless all government was to be relinquished, the laws would ultimately have to be voluntarily obeyed or executed by force.[65]

Pendleton refused to blame the British. It was ridiculous, he said, "to abuse one nation for profiting from the follies of another." The solution lay with the citizenry. The country must

---

62. The proceedings of the special session are described in detail in *CEG*, September 27, 28, 29, 30, October 1, 5, 6, 7, 10, 13, and 18, 1785. The formal proceedings are covered in *JHR 1785–1786*, 311–57.
63. *CEG*, October 5, 1785.
64. *JHR 1785–1786*, 349. John Rutledge was the chairman. Burke was a member. Edward Rutledge and C. C. Pinckney were also members. See Singer, *South Carolina in the Confederation*, 97–98.
65. Charge to the Grand Juries of Georgetown, Cheraw, and Camden Districts, November 1786, *CMP*, December 13, 1786.

learn to live within its income and seek to establish a favorable balance of trade. The people must exert themselves, and support themselves as free citizens, acknowledging no master but the law, which they themselves had made for the common good. "No society ever long endured the miseries of anarchy, disorder, and licentiousness," Pendleton observed. Without a change of conduct, and unity among the good men of the state, "we are an undone people, the government will soon tumble about our heads, and become a prey to the first bold ruffian who shall associate a few bold adventurers, and seize upon it."[66]

Pendleton's purposes were in part explanatory and in part hortatory to be sure, and Burke would probably have concurred in much of his argument, but the differences in their respective presentations is nonetheless dramatic. Both sensed a danger to the fragile new republic. But Pendleton appealed to republican virtue, calling for frugality, moderation, and mutual regard for property and civil order. Burke virtually ignored the moral component of the republican creed, attacked British mercantile policy as a subversive plot against American independence, and called for retaliatory measures. Pendleton's measures were limited in time and purpose; success or failure would ultimately depend on character and unity. In contrast, apparently lacking confidence in virtue, and perhaps recalling the conspiratorial concerns of the debt-ridden tobacco planters in pre-Revolutionary Virginia, Burke appealed to a rising public temper that had been steadily building for more than three years. His proposed navigation act, already supported by a substantial body of opinion, was long range, problematic at best, and presented with strident rhetoric that must have offended at least some who believed as he did. Responding to criticism from "Horatio" toward the end of the special session, Burke took the time to deliver a sharp reply. "Horatio they tell me is a British subject lately admitted a Citizen," Burke said. "He proves, that he who is in his heart an enemy, is, by an oath of allegiance, turned into a friend—pretty nearly as much as a strumpet is made an honest woman of, by the matrimonial ceremony." Evading the argument submitted, but greedy to attack it, Horatio was "like a monkey, who seeing a chestnut in the fire wishes to devour it, yet has sense enough to

---

66. Ibid.

know the risk he runs in burning his fingers in the attempt." The pamphlet had "no other passport to recommend it, but truth," and would answer for itself.[67]

One other probable product of Burke's pen appeared in the public debate during the special session of 1785. On September 27, 1785, the date on which the *Salutary Hints* appeared, "The Spear of Ithuriel" addressed a letter to the "impartial public" that was published on October 1.[68] Its timing, its substance, and its style all strongly suggest that it was Burke's.

Ithuriel addressed two subjects—freedom of the press and British trade policy. The first arose out of the municipal election campaign during the summer of 1785 in which the conduct of the incumbent city administration during the street disturbances of July 1784 had been strongly criticized. In August, "Old Homespun," one of the anti-administration faction, had promised to provide a full account of that affray but changed his mind in September on receipt of advice that he might be charged with seditious libel.[69] Ithuriel damned the advice and the lawyers who gave it. "Should this *wicked* doctrine be established among us, and that *some* would wish to have it established is with me indubitable, what else would it tend to but to abolish the sacred freedom of the press, that *palladium* of our liberties; to sap the glorious fabrick of democracy; to rivet upon our necks those galling chains of *passive obedience* and non-resistance, which we have lately broken and thrown off, and to fashion us, *once more*, into *pliant tools*, for the most debasing species of despotism to work with!"[70]

The discussion of British trade policy responded to a letter of "Caroliniensis" published on September 23.[71] Caroliniensis ar-

---

67. "To the Public" from "The Author of SALUTARY HINTS," *CEG*, October 11, 1785.
68. "The Spear of Ithuriel," *SCGPA*, October 1, 1785.
69. "Old Homespun," *SGSC*, September 22, 1785. At common law in the eighteenth century, freedom of the press meant only freedom from prior censorship, and the writer (or publisher) remained responsible for his words. In broad terms, any attack on the government or governmental officials that tended to lower it or them in public esteem or threatened to disturb the public peace might be construed as seditious libel. The doctrine was clear but enforcement was relatively rare. Prosecution tended to be selective and exemplary. Leonard W. Levy, *Emergence of a Free Press* (New York: Oxford University Press, 1985), 7–9.
70. "The Spear of Ithuriel."
71. "Caroliniensis," *CH*, September 23, 1785.

gued that neither exclusion of foreign shipping from the American carrying trade nor restraint on British transport of American produce to the British West Indies would solve the state's pressing economic problems. In particular, northern shipowners, "who will naturally take every advantage," would be the primary beneficiaries and southern planters would be adversely affected. Moreover, established American markets would be threatened. "Commerce, like a coy mistress, *must be courted,* not treated with insolence and contempt if we wish to retain her favour." Nor would paper money offer an acceptable remedy, since to declare it legal tender in payment of pre-existing debts would be dishonorable and the system of credit on which the agricultural interest depended would be seriously impaired. Accordingly, Caroliniensis concluded that the closing of the courts for a limited time would be the least dangerous of the available expedients and the least oppressive to South Carolinians.

These arguments were not, of course, conclusive, and Ithuriel responded to them with an argument that was in all substantive respects a replay of the just published *Salutary Hints.* But his language was extreme, whether or not he knew the author. Caroliniensis was castigated as "some BRITON, or *degenerate* AMERICAN, a wretch principled to betray the land of his nativity," and as a *"pretended* patriot," dressing his argument in smooth language with intent to deceive. That worthy, Ithuriel pronounced, would have the Americans "turn TURKS" by abandoning themselves to British economic domination. "Let the TRUE *American* judge whether he is not in reality a BRITISH patriot in disguise," he concluded, playing to the outermost limits of propriety Ithuriel's role as Burke conceived it.[72]

Burke's tangential involvement, in the role of publicist, with the issues of 1783–1786 seems clear enough. His performance as legislator, however, is more difficult to assess. Although he sat in the House of Representatives of the fifth, sixth, and seventh General Assemblies (1783–1788), his tenure was never secure. He was not returned in the general election held in November 1782, notwithstanding his service in the Jacksonborough Assembly, but won a seat from the Charleston parishes of St. Philip and St. Michael in a subsequent special election to replace a delegate

---

72. "The Spear of Ithuriel."

who chose to serve from another parish.[73] He won a seat in the general election of 1784 but lost again in 1786 and was seated only after another special election.[74]

Legislative proceedings were reported in the newspapers, but the reports rarely included detailed accounts of debates on the floor or in a committee of the whole house until the *Charleston Evening Gazette* commenced publication in mid-1785. Thereafter, for a time, more comprehensive reports were provided, and Burke's involvement in the business of the House can be observed during the special session in mid-1785 and the regular session in early 1786 more closely than at any other period of his service in the General Assembly. In general, he was reasonably active and visible but not ranked with the elite leadership in terms of prestige. He served on a number of committees, but never reported for any major committee.[75] His most important assignment was to the commission to revise and digest the state's laws, of which Pendleton was first named and therefore the senior in rank. With Pendleton, he formulated a revision of the rules governing the admission of attorneys to the practice of law.[76] But he never initiated any major legislation and never demonstrated the kind of sustained effort that Pendleton, for example, devoted to establishing the county court system between 1783 and 1785, to the measures for debtor relief adopted in 1785, to reapportionment of the legislature, and to constitutional revision. Since individual votes were not recorded in the official journals until 1787, Burke's voting record on the many important issues before the fifth and sixth General Assemblies cannot be determined, but there is no collateral evidence indicating that he made significant contributions to the legislative action taken on any of them.

When the General Assembly convened in January 1786, Governor Moultrie called for action on the proposal to grant regulatory authority over trade and commerce to the Continental Congress, and observed that, "although such power may be attended with some disadvantage to ourselves, as a State, yet I

---

73. *JHR 1783–1784*, 642–43.
74. *JHR 1785–1786*, 607; *JHR 1787–1788*, 637.
75. Burke served on nineteen committees in the fifth General Assembly and thirty-five in the sixth. Data derived from indices and references in *JHR 1783–1784* and *JHR 1785–1786*.
76. *JHR 1783–1784*, 204; *Statutes at Large*, 4: 668–69.

trust We shall not be so wanting in our Attachment to Our Sister States in the Union, but that we will Sacrifice some local advantages for the general good." The measure was promptly enacted, without a division in the House of Representatives and with little discussion in the press.[77] Burke was not in evidence on the pages of the official journals or in the contemporaneous newspaper accounts, although he served under the leadership of John Rutledge on the committee that brought in the bill. The balance of the session, however, faced more controversial issues.

Early in February, Pendleton raised again the questions of reapportionment and constitutional revision. He referred specifically to the measure adopted in 1785 dividing the state into counties and called for reapportionment in order that representation in the House "might be composed of gentlemen from every part of the state." Patrick Calhoun opposed, foreseeing infinite debate and recommending postponement. Calhoun acknowledged that many parts of the constitution required alteration but contended that "the general mass of the people were so much bent for a democratical government that . . . a convention at this time would do more harm than good." Charles Cotesworth Pinckney and Jacob Read also recommended postponement. Dr. John Budd, one-time Marine Anti-Britannic, opposed the proposal, fearing innovation detrimental to "our present free constitution" and the "despotic sway" that appeared to exist in Charleston. Burke "considered the proposition as a matter of the greatest importance and wished that the constitution was firmly settled, by a convention of the people." But he "wished that the business might be put off until a future day, when . . . the honorable mover would be better furnished with ideas on the subject."[78] Ultimately, the House voted to call a constitutional convention, but its bill died in the Senate. A concession to backcountry interests was made, however, when both houses agreed to remove the capital from Charleston to the interior and created a commission to establish Columbia as the state's new capital city.[79]

Debtor relief remained a pressing issue. An additional issue of paper money was proposed and rejected. In the course of the

---

77. *JHR 1785–1786*, 365, 382–83, 395, 396. See Singer, *South Carolina in the Confederation*, 98–101.

78. *CEG*, February 3, 1786; *CMP*, February 4, 1786.

79. *Statutes at Large*, 4: 751–52.

debate, Burke commented that the distress of debtors was serious, particularly in the case of merchants who had judgments outstanding for duties "which the want of circulating specie, put it out of their power to discharge."[80] The debate then turned to the act regulating execution sales, which, by its terms, would expire after the "next session" of the General Assembly. There was some sentiment for repeal, and a lively dispute arose as to whether the "next session" meant the sitting session of the sixth General Assembly or the entire term of the seventh, which would sit into 1788. Burke contributed little, but he said enough to indicate his general views on debtor relief. Debts contracted since 1782 were "amazingly great," he said, "and the law suits commenced since 1784, were truly alarming." Property was selling at execution sales for only one fourth of its value, occasioning "alarming opposition to the Executive Power of the Courts of Law." If suits were to continue, "he would not say what might be the consequence." He lamented the necessity for the law, but, should it be repealed, "five thousand of the best troops in the world would not be enabled to enforce the process of the courts of law, for our people were spirited, and would not suffer their property to be taken from them." Hugh Rutledge disagreed. The people understood the law would be continued, and whatever damage it would do to the honor and welfare of the state was already done. When the question was put, the House agreed that the act should be revised. But it was neither repealed nor revised, and the ambiguity as to the term of its effectiveness remained to confront the seventh General Assembly in 1787.[81]

Finally, the alien act was repealed, as Burke had recommended in the *Salutary Hints*, and one more limiting adopted to replace it. Under the act adopted in 1784, all free white persons were eligible for citizenship after one year of residence by taking an oath of allegiance to the state. Two years later, they would become eligible to vote, but could not hold office without a special act of the legislature conferring that privilege. The 1786 act

---

80. *CEG*, February 7, 1786. The paper money authorized in 1785 was not issued until mid-1786.
81. *CEG*, February 21, 1786. A House bill amending the execution sales act was rejected by the Senate. *JHR 1785–1786*, 589–90, 593–94. Senate opposition was reported in the *CEG*, February 18, 1786.

was substantially the same, except that the right to vote and jury service were made subject to a prior special act.[82]

Burke presumably supported the new alien act and delivered several distinctive views in the course of debate. First, he suggested that clergymen coming into the state from foreign parts should be obliged to take the oath of allegiance "as their doctrines having great influence placed it in their power to do much mischief to the state." Second, he elaborated on the British threat. British immigration must be checked, he said, "to prevent their flocking here, and by their riches and address, overrun the country, and turn out those who fought and conquered, and gained the independence of America." He acknowledged that there were some "good" British citizens in South Carolina, but caution was essential. In his firm opinion, "it was the intention of the British to embrace the first favorable opportunity of commencing hostilities against us." After all, "the English papers had already told us, that large reinforcements of troops, with Sir Guy Carleton at their head, were destined for Canada." Third, when Edward Rutledge asked why the proposed oath of clergymen was required only for those who arrived after 1782, Burke replied "that several disciples of John Wesley, had since that time gone around the country, to preach up their doctrines, and had told the country people that the King of Great Britain was one of the best of Kings, and that those who had taken up arms against him would have a great deal to answer for at the day of Judgment." This observation, the reporter recorded, "caused a hearty laugh in the house."[83]

Burke's basic constituency is uncertain, but the results of the election of delegates to represent St. Philip and St. Michael in 1784 and 1786 suggest that it was limited. In 1784, the election followed the highly charged municipal election of that year, and there was much talk in the press of the importance of the forthcoming general election. One correspondent submitted the names of sixty-three persons whom he considered suitable candi-

---

82. *Statutes at Large*, 4: 600–601, 746–47. In addition, the jury law was amended in 1786 to eliminate provisions facilitating actions by transient suitors. *Statutes at Large*, 4: 754. Edward Rutledge and others opposed, arguing that the law as it stood encouraged foreign trade. The House vote was a tie and the outcome determined by the casting vote of the speaker. *CEG*, February 16, 1786.
83. *CEG*, February 11 and 16, 1786.

dates for election from the Charleston parishes, listing all the familiar establishment figures and including Burke.[84] When the results were announced, Henry Laurens headed the list of those elected with 446 votes and Burke was returned with 244.[85] In 1786, David Ramsay and Edward Rutledge headed the list of winners with 426 votes each. William Johnson with 425 and Charles Cotesworth Pinckney with 422 followed. Rawlins Lowndes, Alexander Gillon, William Somersall, and Michael Kalteisen, with 207, 203, 202, and 201 votes, respectively, were the low winners.[86] Burke, therefore, received no more than 200 votes, less than half the high winning number. As in prior elections, a number of the elected delegates either declined to serve or chose to sit for other parishes. Five members to represent St. Philip and St. Michael were chosen in subsequent special elections to fill vacancies in the delegation and qualified after the session opened. One was Burke, and he qualified in the House on February 8, 1787.[87]

The election of 1786 was clearly more competitive than the election of 1784.[88] Burke blamed his 1786 defeat on "improper influence" exerted by the Charleston intendant, John F. Grimke, his colleague on the bench, and a "cabal formed and composed of foreign merchants, combined with a party of our own citizens, to bring it about." The citizen, he said in a memorial to the House of Representatives, could render no more important service "than to assist in preventing measures that would spread a general corruption over the state, by debauching our citizens into

---

84. "An American," *GSSC*, November 24, 1784. Twenty of the thirty representatives elected were on the list. Twenty-one members of the Marine Anti-Britannic Society were listed, of whom four and one other member of the Society were elected.
85. *CH*, December 7, 1784.
86. *CMP*, December 5, 1786.
87. *JHR 1787–1788*, 69–70, 637. The special election was held on February 6. *CMP*, February 7, 1787.
88. *CMP*, November 21 and 29, 1786. The managers of the election in the Lower District between the Broad and Saluda Rivers reported that a mob destroyed the box containing the votes when it appeared that former loyalists would win. *JHR 1787–1788*, 11. Thomas Tudor Tucker challenged Ralph Izard to a duel after Izard delivered a "public harangue" in opposition to Tucker's election, even though Tucker conceded that Izard "confined himself entirely to my Political Opinions." Thomas Tudor Tucker to St. George Tucker, April 8, 1787, Tucker-Coleman Papers, Department of Manuscripts and Rare Books, Swem Library, College of William and Mary.

the infamous practice of bartering their suffrages, and making the country a theatre for the endless feuds of contending parties. The liberty, peace, and safety of this country depend solely on the freedom of elections, and to allow British subjects, whether they be of that class of them called citizens, or not, to form combinations, or to be employed by any party among ourselves to manage our elections; to allow this I say, would be wretched policy, if we judge the temper of the British nation since the peace; the ruinous schemes they are driving at against this country, and the incurable animosities which their subjects too plainly discover—the man must be infatuated who hopes for any other consequence from their interfering in our elections and public councils, than perpetual cabals and machinations on their side, and inevitable confusion and misfortune on ours."[89]

Burke was not contesting the election of any one of the successful candidates. Voters simply cast their votes for whom they chose and the thirty leaders were returned to represent the Charleston parishes. His complaint was more general. Specifically, he alleged that the intendant employed his official authority to influence the outcome of the election, "in making out chosen lists of candidates, distributing those lists among some of the Wardens, and other officers from the Corporation, who busily dispersed them through the city, and in recommending in some instances to the managers of the election, what manner of persons ought, and ought not to vote, some of whom, although unqualified voted accordingly." The principle of free elections was therefore violated, notwithstanding that the members elected to represent the city were all fully qualified.[90]

The memorial was referred to the House Committee on Privileges and Elections. Extended hearings were held which took up much of Burke's time and the time of others. The evidence was predictably inconclusive, although it did appear that some lists were in circulation. Before the session ended, legislation proposed to establish procedures for dealing with controverted elec-

---

89. "Memorial of Aedanus Burke," *JHR 1787–1788*, 46–47; *CMP*, February 7, 1787. In substance, Burke's announced purpose was to protect the integrity of the electoral process, a subject he had dealt with earlier in the *Address*. Among other things, he complained that the electorate had been packed with unqualified voters.

90. "Memorial of Aedanus Burke," *JHR 1787–1788*, 46–47; *CMP*, February 7, 1787.

tions was rejected by the Senate.[91] By then, Burke had already returned to the House.

Return to the General Assembly probably soothed Burke's feelings to some extent. But he may also have recognized that his sudden entry into the debate on trade policy, and his related and apparently effective attack on the naturalization process, had not served him well. In the *Address*, he had spoken for fundamental rights, due process of law, and measures he believed would promote order and unity. In the *Considerations*, he had spoken for fundamental principles of republicanism, opposing the Cincinnati as a self-established higher order in society. Whether men agreed with him or not, he was on the side of the angels. His established reputation as a publicist was then put to service in a more ambiguous and divisive context where important issues of public policy were under debate, where reasonable men might differ on both measures and priorities, and where the individual rights of naturalized citizens were first questioned and then limited.

On the surface, the *Salutary Hints* was an exercise in advocacy. Greene may have provided the stimulus, as Burke suggested he did, but the style and content were Burke's and appealed more to passion than to reason. He added nothing new to the debate, either as to facts or perspective. He demonstrated no awareness of the complexities inherent in the administration of a national policy on foreign trade and commerce. At a deeper level, the *Salutary Hints* may be interpreted as an extended lament. Nothing was working as it should. The domestic economy was in shambles; the judicial system was undermanned, in disrepute, and possibly facing a temporary suspension of business; traditional concepts of law and property were threatened; individual citizens were challenging out-of-doors their own republican institutions of government and thereby opening the way to anarchy and potential despotism; the young republic was threatened with neocolonial subservience to the economic power of Great Britain; and friends of Britain were actively subverting the

---

91. *JHR 1787–1788*, 47; *CMP*, February 5, 1787. At the committee's hearings, Burke requested that testimony be given under oath, but the committee refused. Most of the witnesses proved singularly deficient in their recollection of relevant events. *CMP*, March 9, 1787. An ordinance authorizing the committee on privileges and elections to administer oaths to witnesses in contested election cases was approved by the House but rejected by the Senate. *JHR 1787–1788*, 190, 204, 238, 240.

domestic electoral process. After the war, "laws and government soon triumphed throughout the State, over the intemperance of individuals and parties." But now, as demonstrated particularly by the disruption of the court in Camden and the circumstances that precipitated it, "the present state of our government" in South Carolina was "truly critical." Peace of mind, personal independence, and public harmony all were at risk.[92] What was the matter or, in the analytical format that Burke often favored when examining political affairs, who was to blame? Burke might have appealed more to virtue, as Pendleton did, but virtue was nowhere in evidence. Instead, he chose to blame the British and their domestic "agents" in an attack that reflected more undiluted Anglophobia than commitment to republican principles or sound political judgment. In the process, he must have offended some Charleston merchants and their friends even though the bulk of the merchant community supported national authority to regulate foreign trade and commerce in principle. He must also have offended those who opposed any grant of such authority as well as those who recognized his implicit reservations with respect to measures for debtor relief and perceived his argument as an extravagant diversionary tactic against the purposes of the special session called specifically to consider such measures. His style and timing prejudiced a basically sound position, and the loss of forty-four votes in the 1786 election is hardly surprising.

By the end of 1786, Burke was clearly distressed, surely by his defeat at the polls and probably also by the negative response to his well-meant rhetoric. His distress was suggested in late 1785 when he told Greene, in the same letter in which he acknowledged his authorship of the *Salutary Hints,* that he was thinking of moving his estate from the Wateree to Georgia.[93] In February 1786, he was more specific. He was considering the purchase of property in Georgia, he told Greene, where property of good quality was cheaper than he could find in Carolina. "Nor do I care a farthing," he said, "what effect the removal of my little property may have as to my *political standing* here. . . . Independence is my wish, and a little would amply content me."[94] No significant improvement was perceptible at the end of the year.

92. Burke, *Salutary Hints,* 3–4.
93. Burke to Nathanael Greene, November 27, 1785, Greene Papers, WLCL.
94. Burke to Nathanael Greene, February 7, 1786, Greene Papers, WLCL.

Notwithstanding his return to the House in early 1787, he was ready for a change of direction, and the occasion for it arose in 1787 when the movement for reform of the governmental structure established under the Articles of Confederation produced the Philadelphia convention and a new national Constitution.

VI

Legislator and AntiFederalist
1787–1789

By the end of 1786, many thoughtful men, with good reason, were questioning the viability of the governmental structure established by the Articles of Confederation. Moreover, they could reasonably conclude that no measures of reform would be forthcoming from the Continental Congress. Two intractable problems demanded attention and solution. First, a reliable source of revenue was required to fund the war debt and to support a functioning establishment at the federal level. Second, centralized authority to establish and direct a common policy on trade and commerce was essential before free access to international markets, the perceived sine qua non of national independence since 1775, could be effectively pursued. A general sense of insecurity and apprehension developed as the confederated states appeared to lack that sense of national identity and purpose essential to support coherent pursuit of national interests and to confront an indifferent world of monarchical great powers.[1] Within the year, a proposed new federal Constitution offered solutions to these problems, only to be vigorously opposed by many leaders of the Revolution whose study of history taught that a republican polity was a vulnerable polity and whose republican ideology taught that centralized power was peculiarly susceptible to corruption and therefore invited despotism. Burke was not a major figure in the initial stage of the ensuing confrontation, but he embodied the conflict in microcosm. Arguing the crucial importance of a common commercial policy in the *Salutary Hints*, he had articulated a vision of the American republic as an interdependent and harmonious community of freemen, one people united in friend-

---

1. Frederick W. Marks, *Independence on Trial: Foreign Affairs and the Making of the Constitution* (Baton Rouge: Louisiana State University Press, 1973), 96–141, describes the "national mood" contributing to the movement toward reformation of the national government.

ship and mutual interest. But when the vision was reduced to operational form, he could not accept the terms.

Frustrated by the failure of piecemeal attempts to strengthen the federal establishment, proponents of reform sought means to escape the constraints and jealousies inhibiting the Continental Congress. The first step was the Annapolis Convention, called on the initiative of Virginia, with James Madison its leading advocate, to consider means to achieve a common commercial policy for the several sovereign states. On the surface, the attempt appeared a failure. Nine states elected delegates but only five were represented when the assembly gathered in September 1786. Action was accordingly postponed, and the proceedings adjourned after only three days of discussion. But the participants issued a report, ostensibly written for the legislatures of their respective states but distributed to the Continental Congress and to the governors of all the other states, which opened the road to the Philadelphia convention in 1787.[2]

Unwilling to proceed on the basis of so partial a representation, the men of Annapolis urged "speedy measures" to organize a general convention of the states. The authority of the delegates should not be limited to matters directly related to commerce. The power to regulate trade and commerce, the report observed, "is of such comprehensive extent, and will enter so far into the general system of the Federal Government, that to give it efficacy, and to obviate questions and doubts concerning its precise nature and limits, may require a correspondent adjustment of other parts of the Federal system." Important defects in the existing system were acknowledged in the acts of the states concurring in the Annapolis meeting. Moreover, closer examination would probably disclose that such defects were greater and more numerous than those acts implied. Accordingly, the United States confronted a situation both delicate and critical, which required "an exertion of the United virtue and wisdom of all the members

---

2. Marks, *Independence on Trial*, 91–95; Jack N. Rakove, *The Beginnings of National Politics: An Interpretive History of the Continental Congress* (New York: Alfred A. Knopf, 1979), 368–70, 372–75. South Carolina sent no delegates to the Annapolis Convention because the General Assembly had previously voted to grant regulatory powers to the Continental Congress and believed participation in the Convention "would be inconsistent, and have an appearance of either revoking or infringing on those powers." Pierce Butler to _____ , May 30, 1786, Miscellaneous Manuscripts, Series II, SCHS.

of the Confederacy." The delegates thereupon urged their respective states to initiate action for a convention to meet in Philadelphia on the second Monday in May 1787.[3] When news of the report reached Charleston, one commentator was sufficiently encouraged to suggest that "we may hope to see the federal union of these states established on principles which will serve the dignity, harmony, and felicity of these confederated republics, and not only rescue them from their present difficulties, but from that insolent *hateur* and contemptuous neglect which they have experienced as a nation" since they achieved their independence.[4] Although the Continental Congress sat on the report from September 1786 until late February 1787,[5] a number of the states began to move.

When the first session of South Carolina's seventh General Assembly met in Charleston in January 1787, Governor William Moultrie presented the report of the Annapolis Convention and observed that "the appointment of a Convention of the States appears to be indispensable."[6] Within a few days, a House committee concurred. A bill authorizing the appointment of delegates was brought in on February 24; it passed through both House and Senate by March 8 without a division at any stage of the proceedings; and John Rutledge, Henry Laurens, Charles Cotesworth Pinckney, Charles Pinckney, and Pierce Butler were named delegates on that same day. Laurens declined to serve for reasons of health and no replacement was designated.[7]

The sequence of events is illuminating. By February 21, 1787, when the Continental Congress finally endorsed the plan, Virginia, New York, Delaware, New Jersey, North Carolina, Pennsylvania, and Massachusetts had already elected to participate in the Philadelphia convention and the process was already far ad-

---

3. John Dickinson, Chairman of the Convention, to the President of Congress, September 14, 1786, *Journals of Congress*, 31: 677–80 (September 20, 1786).
4. *CMP*, October 23, 1786.
5. Congress did not resolve to endorse the proposed convention until February 21, 1787. *Journals of Congress*, 32: 71–74.
6. *JHR 1787–1788*, 14–15.
7. Ibid., 23, 73, 136, 140, 143, 161, 184–85, 193–94, 223, 261–62, 282; *Statutes at Large*, 5: 4–5. The act recited that the purpose of the convention was to vest "more ample" power in the national government because the powers vested in the Continental Congress by the Articles of Confederation "are found by experience greatly inadequate to the weighty purposes they were originally intended to answer."

vanced in South Carolina. The remaining states, except Rhode Island, promptly followed, thus confirming a broad consensus in support of at least some revision and strengthening of the federal structure wholly unrelated to any impetus generated by the Continental Congress. In addition, South Carolina carefully selected its most knowledgeable and experienced men to serve on its behalf, "cosmopolitans" as compared to "localists" in the well-known dichotomy formulated by Jackson Turner Main,[8] all experienced in the affairs of government, all drawn from the low-country establishment and sharing its outward looking, commercially oriented world view. All might reasonably be expected to support a significant strengthening of the central governmental structure if it could be accomplished in a manner consistent with the interests of their own country.[9]

The balance of the first session (January 1–March 28, 1787) was devoted largely to the intractable problem of debtor relief, which remained serious despite the short term measures of 1785. In late January, Pendleton advised the House that he and Burke considered the act regulating execution sales "null and void," having expired by its terms.[10] The ambiguity recognized but unresolved in 1786 was thus determined. There was no strong sen-

8. Jackson Turner Main, *Political Parties before the Constitution* (Chapel Hill: University of North Carolina Press, 1973), 15. As used by Main, these terms "refer to opposing *world views* that are based on the contrasting experience of men. At one pole is the man of broad outlook, usually urban, urbane, and well educated, who has traveled widely and has had extensive contacts with the world because of his occupation, the offices he has held, or his interests. . . . At the opposite pole stands the man of narrow horizons—most often rural and sparsely educated—whose experience is limited to his own neighborhood: he is provincial, parochial." Main concedes that the difference is subjective even though the identification is necessarily based on objective data indicating the probability that a given individual holds one or the other of the contending world views. The terminology is useful whether or not one agrees with Main's classification in a given case because the terms themselves are sufficiently specific to be clearly understandable. Main's analysis of South Carolina and his listing of South Carolinian cosmopolitans and localists are at 268–95 and 448–55, respectively. Burke is not named in either category.
9. Laurens, Rutledge, Butler, and Charles Pinckney had all served in the Continental Congress and were thoroughly indoctrinated to the frustrations of such service. Pinckney was a member of the South Carolina delegation to the Continental Congress in 1786 and was instrumental in pressing for extensive reform. Merrill Jensen, *The New Nation: A History of the United States during the Confederation, 1781–1789* (New York: Alfred A. Knopf, 1950), 419–20; Rakove, *Beginnings of National Politics*, 370–71; *Journals of Congress*, 31: 494–98.
10. *CMP,* January 30, 1787. Burke was not then sitting in the House.

timent for reenactment, and a proposal to issue a modest amount of additional paper money was overwhelmed 135 to 2.[11] But some legislative action was imperative. Prior legislation had extended the obligation to pay debts incurred before January 1, 1782, and the measures of 1785 had provided some protection against proceedings to collect the first installment of such debts due in 1786. The installment payment concept represented the least radical solution to a still pressing problem, and a new installment payment act, covering all debts incurred before January 1, 1787, provided for payment of such debts in three annual installments beginning in March 1788. Debtors were required to pay interest on deferred installments and to provide security if demanded by their creditors. To control the level of additional debt, and incidentally to calm the fears of distressed creditors, the importation of slaves was banned for three years. Finally, to deter violent self-help by distressed debtors, additional penalties were prescribed for any mistreatment of public officials.[12]

Burke took no significant part in these proceedings. He was not seated until February 8. He voted with the majority against the issuance of additional paper money, but did not vote on the slave import restriction or the installment payment bill. He entered the debate briefly on February 22 when a proposal to except small debts from the protective provisions of the installment payment bill was before the House. Exceptions of £5 and £20 were suggested. Burke opposed a general exception because, he argued, most of the debts outstanding had been incurred by speculators. He wanted a limited exception to relieve mechanics and artificers, some of whom were laboring under great distress. One of his constituents, Burke said, asked for help in selling a negro carpenter in order to obtain funds for the common necessities of life. He accordingly moved for an exception covering debts due handicraft tradesmen for services performed after October 1785. Gillon objected. Burke "had lately been so much engaged in electioneering business," Gillon said, "that his head was still full of it;" and Gillon feared "that his honorable friend was swayed by the great number of voters among the mechanics." The House would surely not agree to this exception, Gillon concluded. "What, give the mechanics full power

11. *JHR 1787–1788*, 150–51.
12. *Statutes at Large*, 5: 36–38.

to receive all money due to them from us, and leave it optional in them, whether they will pay us what they owe? This was partiality with a witness."[13] The motion was lost and Burke retired from the field.

Other important issues were raised in the first session. In mid-March, the House took up the question of constitutional revision. Ramsay unsuccessfully sought to defer the matter until after the forthcoming convention in Philadelphia. The House then voted to call a convention to be held in Charleston, conceding the propriety of constitutional revision, but the measure died in the Senate once again. A proposal to repeal the confiscation and amercement acts was soundly defeated after extended debate. A committee was appointed to consider revision of the act incorporating Charleston to limit the broad and allegedly unconstitutional authority of the board of wardens, but the matter progressed no further.[14] Burke voted for the constitutional convention, but was not otherwise much in evidence on the available record with respect to any of these matters.

Between the General Assembly's first and second sessions, the Philadelphia convention completed its work, and the South Carolina delegation played a major part in the complicated bargaining that preceded agreement on the terms of a new federal Constitution to replace the Articles of Confederation. The convention delivered the proposed Constitution to the Continental Congress, which on September 28 resolved to transmit it to the several states for submission to ratifying conventions. Its terms were published in Charleston on October 2.[15] Thereafter, through South Carolina's ratifying convention in May 1788, the public press reported debate and progress in other states on a regular basis, and provided a forum for the expression of local opinion.

The proposed Constitution came under attack even before it left the Philadelphia convention when, in the convention's closing days, Elbridge Gerry of Massachusetts and Edmund Ran-

---

13. *CMP*, February 23, 1787. The "electioneering business" referred to must have been the proceedings described in Chapter V that followed Burke's defeat in the general election of 1786.

14. *JHR 1787–1788*, 216–19, 224–27 (constitutional convention), 124–26 (repeal of confiscation and amercement acts), 79, 208 (Charleston charter revision). *CMP*, March 15 and 16, 1787, reported on the proposed constitutional convention. The final House vote for the convention was close, 71 to 69.

15. *CH*, Extraordinary Issue, October 2, 1787; *SGSC*, October 4, 1787.

dolph of Virginia urged that the states be permitted to propose amendments for consideration by a second general convention before it could become effective.[16] The campaign for amendments was taken up in the Continental Congress by Richard Henry Lee of Virginia, who sought to include proposed amendments in the submission to the states.[17] It was continued by Samuel Bryan of Pennsylvania in his early "Centinel" essays and, after the turbulent ratification proceedings in Pennsylvania where the opportunity to propose amendments was denied, in a ringing denunciation of those proceedings by the dissenting minority.[18] Thus, by the end of 1787, a reasonably coherent and rational campaign of opposition was developing. Its initial impetus originated in Virginia and early support was offered from Pennsylvania. Other states, particularly Massachusetts, New Hampshire, and New York, adhered as ratification proceedings moved forward. It involved three major elements: first, general agreement on essential amendments; second, generally concurrent conventions, postponing those already called if necessary, so that all would be acting together and could coordinate their objectives; and, third, a second general convention to consider all proposed amendments prior to ratification of any new instrument of national government.[19]

South Carolina was one of the last of the states to call a ratifying convention. The proposed Constitution was debated first

---

16. Max Farrand, ed., *The Records of the Federal Convention of 1787*, rev. ed., 4 vols. (New Haven: Yale University Press, 1937), 2: 479, 563–64, 631–32, 633, 634. Gerry, Randolph, and George Mason of Virginia also refused to sign the completed document after their proposed changes were rejected.
17. Richard Henry Lee to George Mason, October 1, 1787, in James Curtis Ballagh, ed., *The Letters of Richard Henry Lee*, 2 vols. (New York: The Macmillan Company, 1914), 2: 438–40.
18. Samuel Bryan, "Centinel No. 1" and "Centinel No. 2," in John P. Kaminski and Gaspare J. Saladino, eds., *The Documentary History of the Ratification of the Constitution: Commentaries on the Constitution Public and Private*, 4 vols. to date (Madison: State Historical Society of Wisconsin, 1981–1986), 1: 328–36, 457–68; "The Address and Reasons of Dissent of the Minority of the Convention of the State of Pennsylvania to their Constituents," in Kaminski and Saladino, eds., *Documentary History of Ratification: Commentaries*, 3: 13–34. "Centinel No. 1" and "Centinel No. 2" were first published on October 5 and October 24, 1787, respectively. The "Dissent" was first published on December 18, 1787. All were reprinted in South Carolina.
19. The evolution and progress of the campaign through the first federal elections is described in Stephen R. Boyd, *The Politics of Opposition: Antifederalists and the Acceptance of the Constitution* (Millwood, N.Y.: KTO Press, 1979).

in the House of Representatives on January 16–19, 1788. The only issues to be resolved were whether to call a convention to consider it, an issue that was never in doubt, and where and when the convention would be held. Nonetheless, the Federalist leadership carefully orchestrated the proceedings to present the Constitution in a favorable context, to inform the backcountry representatives on its principles and benefits, and to counteract oppositionist propaganda circulating in the backcountry.[20] Charles Pinckney, Charles Cotesworth Pinckney, John Rutledge, and Pierce Butler, all present at the creation, led the argument in support. The veteran Rawlins Lowndes carried the burden of the argument in opposition, virtually alone.

Charles Pinckney delivered the keynote address, emphasizing the origins of the Philadelphia convention in the actions of the states outside the Continental Congress, the deficiencies and weaknesses of the existing federal system, and the benefits of the system designed to replace it. In the course of the address, he anticipated many of the objections then and later raised by the opposition. He thus set the tone and, when he finished, a proposal to read the Constitution by paragraphs was defeated, assuring that the debate would proceed primarily on the basis of broad principles.[21]

Lowndes spoke in opposition for himself and for a constituency of backcountry representatives less experienced than he in legislative debate. Although not wholly ignoring structural questions and recommending that a second convention be held to meet all objections on "fair grounds," he based his major argument on the politics of state self-interest. The security of a state, he said, was jealousy; and he was profoundly suspicious of the intent and apparent good will of the northern states. In substance, he argued that the proposed Constitution so heavily favored the interests of the northern states that the southern states would ultimately be reduced to a subservient neocolonial status in relation to them; that northern interests would be aggressively

20. David Ramsay to John Eliot, January 19, 1788, and David Ramsay to Benjamin Lincoln, January 29, 1788, in "David Ramsay, 1749–1815: Selections From His Writings," Robert L. Brunhouse, ed., *Transactions of the American Philosophical Society*, Vol. 55, Part 4 (Philadelphia: American Philosophical Society, 1965), 118–19.
21. Elliot, *Debates*, 4: 253–63.

pursued at southern expense; and that the southern states would soon be shorn of all pretension to independence. He sincerely believed, he said, that "when this new Constitution should be adopted, the sun of the southern states would set, never to rise again." To this, Edward Rutledge tartly replied that he thought the "Confederation so very weak, so very inadequate to the purposes of the Union, that, unless it was materially altered, the sun of American independence would indeed soon set—never to rise again."[22]

Insofar as the available record discloses, Burke had nothing significant to say during the entire course of the debate in the House. He did, however, cast one vitally important vote. On the general question of calling the convention, the House was unanimously in favor. On the specific question of calling the convention to meet in Charleston, the question was carried by a vote of 76 to 75, the issue being whether to hold the convention in Charleston, considered a Federalist stronghold, or at some other location. Burke voted for Charleston, as did the entire delegation from the parishes of St. Philip and St. Michael.[23] Since delegates would be elected on the same basis of apportionment established for the General Assembly, the lowcountry establishment would be firmly in control. Elections were held on April 11 and 12, and Burke was elected from the Lower District between the Broad and Catawba Rivers.[24] It was the first time that he represented any constituency other than the Charleston parishes of St. Philip and St. Michael and presumably reflected his conclusion that a known critic of the Constitution could not expect to be elected from Charleston.

Burke emerged as a recognized opponent to ratification during the period between the House session and the convention. No record of his views or of the progression of his thought has been found, but by April he was identified abroad as a leader of

22. Elliot, *Debates*, 4: 271–72, 273–74, 287–91, 307–11. Lowndes's part in the House debate is described in Carl J. Vipperman, *The Rise of Rawlins Lowndes, 1721–1800* (Columbia: University of South Carolina Press, 1978), 241–51.

23. *JHR 1787–1788*, 330–32. The proceedings were reported in the *CH*, January 14, 17, and 21, 1788, and in greater detail in the *CGDA*, January 15–21, 24–26, 28–31, and February 1, 1788.

24. *CH*, April 17, 1788; *CGDA*, April 22, 1788.

the opposition in Charleston.[25] Possibly, perhaps probably, he was influenced by the report of the dissenters at the Pennsylvania convention, which was reprinted in Charleston just after the General Assembly acted to call South Carolina's convention.[26] Surely, their account of the proceedings in Philadelphia, and the overbearing determination of the Constitution's proponents to override all attempts at opposition, was well calculated to catch the attention and stimulate the concern of one so attuned to fear the excesses of men made arrogant by power. In all events, at South Carolina's convention in May, he was clearly opposed to ratification of the Constitution as presented. He was a staunch federalist, he told the convention, clearly using that term in its literal sense and not in the sense appropriated to themselves by committed adherents of the Constitution. He "wished as heartily as any member on this floor to have a strong government." But that disposition would not induce him to accept any plan that was offered. Arguments based on fear that rejection would result in civil war "did not appear very formidable to him; anarchy was not so dangerous as despotism, for a war must be succeeded by a peace, but despotism was a monster very difficult to get rid of."[27]

After a long introductory address by Charles Pinckney, the convention took up the proposed Constitution paragraph by paragraph. When the debate reached the subject of the Senate and the senatorial term of office, Burke rose to speak for the principle of rotation in office. He agreed that, in South Carolina, "we had carried our patriotic jealousy too far, by limiting the period of state officers continuing in their places." In the proposed national government, however, "the senate are in fact the executive body, and as they are under the influence of the prince, or president, and distant from us 900 miles . . . we might be in the dark as to their conduct for six years." During that time, "they might lose sight of their country's welfare, and consult only the dictates of inordinate ambition." They might be relied upon with safety if under close inspection, "but so far removed from us they

---

25. "Extract of a letter from Charleston (S.C.)," April 9, 1788, Philadelphia *Independent Gazeteer*, April 19, 1788. The statement is almost surely correct, but the basis for it is unclear. None of the local writings on the merits of the Constitution is either clearly or tentatively attributable to Burke. He was no doubt vocal, and his views probably spread by word of mouth.
26. *SGSC*, January 21, 24, 28, 31, and February 4, 1788.
27. *CGDA*, May 20, 1788.

will be no more within our power than the dey of Algiers," the archetypical villain of the day as leader of the marauding Algerine pirates against whose depredations the Continental Congress was helpless. In such circumstances, the only security the people had for their liberties was to rotate their officers of government regularly and frequently; history abounded with instances of tyranny and corruption in officers continued for an unlimited time.[28] Turning to the authority of the Senate to sit as a court of impeachment, he observed that "the president was a prince under a republican cloak, and wondered it was not possible to find other judges to try him for crimes, than his accomplices." Voltaire, he said, compared a prince to a highwayman. The situation here should be compared to that of two highwaymen who have committed an act of villainy and then one is deputed to sit in judgment on the other.[29]

These were Burke's only recorded remarks to the convention. When Sumter moved several days later to adjourn to October 20, obviously hoping to stall the proceedings, Burke supported the motion. It was defeated by a substantial majority, and the contest was all but over.[30] Nonetheless, after defeat of Sumter's motion, Edward Rutledge proposed a committee to consider amendments and was supported by John Julius Pringle, "who thought a few points were liable to objection." A committee was duly appointed, headed by Edward Rutledge but including none of the active critics of the Constitution.[31] It reported the next day and identified four substantive deficiencies for correction. First, the right reserved to the states to control the mechan-

---

28. *CGDA*, May 20, 1788. The anecdotal record embellishes this account. According to Joseph Johnson, Burke observed that he opposed all concealment from the people, which would "always be resorted to by those who wish to screen themselves from public censure." He was reminded, he said, of a certain domestic animal, "who, having been at dirty work, resorts to concealment by covering it over." Joseph Johnson, *Traditions and Reminiscences Chiefly of the American Revolution in the South* (Charleston: Walker and James, 1851; reprint ed., Spartanburg: The Reprint Company, 1972), 430–31.
29. *CGDA*, May 21, 1788.
30. *JCC*, 13–23. The vote was 89 to 135 and is probably the best evidence of the actual division of sentiment.
31. The committee members in addition to Rutledge were Thomas Bee and John Julius Pringle of St. Philip and St. Michael (Charleston), Henry Pendleton of Saxe Gotha, John Huger of St. Thomas and St. Dennis, William Wilson of Prince Frederick, John Hunter of Little River, and Francis Cummings and William Hill of the New Acquisition. *CGDA*, May 22 and 23, 1788; *JCC*, 24.

ics of elections to national offices should be "forever inseparably annexed to the Sovereignty of the Several States" and should never be subject to interference from the general government, "except in cases where the Legislatures of the States shall refuse or neglect to perform and fulfill the same." Second, nothing contained in the Constitution would warrant a contention that the states did not retain every power not expressly relinquished. Third, the general government ought never to impose direct taxes except when monies arising from duties and excise taxes were insufficient for "public exigencies," and then only if Congress had assessed the states and the states had failed or refused to pay. Fourth, in the last clause of Article VI, providing that public officers of the federal and state governments should be bound by oath or affirmation to support the Constitution, but that "no religious Test shall ever be required as a qualification to any office or public Trust under the United States," the word "other" should be inserted between "no" and "religious."[32]

The committee report was approved but various individual efforts to submit proposed amendments failed. Burke, an avowed opponent of ratification, moved to limit the term of the presidential office. The eligibility of the president after the expiration of four years was dangerous to the liberties of the people, his motion stated, and would perpetuate in one person for life the high authority and influence of that magistracy and ultimately terminate in a hereditary monarchy. Benjamin Cudworth, also an avowed opponent, moved to expunge the words "without the Consent of the Congress," from the section in Article I limiting the right of federal officials to accept any present, emolument or title from any foreign state. John Lewis Gervais, who voted against ratification, moved that the state militia should not be subject to the rules of Congress or marched out of any state without the consent of the executive of such state. John Bowman, another avowed opponent of ratification, moved that a committee be appointed to draw up a bill of rights. All were rejected.[33]

---

32. *JCC*, 37–38; *CGDA*, May 23, 1788. The fourth recommendation was clearly added to placate Cummings, a minister, who argued that the change was essential to preserve the sacred character of an oath. Cummings's statement in support of this position was published in the *CGDA*, May 23, 1788.
33. *JCC*, 25–36, 38–39. Burke's motion was defeated 68 to 139. The other motions were rejected without a division.

Legislator and Antifederalist, 1787–1789

The Constitution was ratified 149 to 73 on May 23. The vote confirmed the recommendations of the committee on amendments and directed the representatives of the state to exert their utmost abilities and influence to effect an alteration of the Constitution "conformably to the foregoing Resolutions." Thereafter, the leaders of the opposition, including specifically Sumter, Burke, Cudworth, Patrick Dollard, and Peter Fayssoux, "in a liberal and candid manner, expressed their intention, as so large a majority appeared in favor of the constitution, that they would exert themselves to the utmost of their abilities to induce the people quietly to receive, and peaceably to live under the new government."[34] They were all no doubt sincere. But such assurances were not incompatible with a reservation of intent to work within the system for change.

South Carolina was not the first state to propose specific alterations in the Constitution by action of its ratifying convention. The precedent was set by Massachusetts in February 1788, and a record of the Massachusetts proceedings was presented to the South Carolina convention in May.[35] New Hampshire, Virginia, and New York followed in June and July.[36] The circumstances in these other states were different than South Carolina's, however, because in each of them the concession was an essential condition precedent to ratification. Nonetheless, although clearly not required to induce a favorable vote in South Carolina, the gesture was important. Gabriel Manigault, for example, thought that the convention's willingness to consider amendments "insures the Ratification of the Constitution by a great majority."[37] More significantly, South Carolina's explicit endorsement of amendments was at least broadly compatible with the goals of the ongoing Antifederalist campaign.

Among those most active in organizing the Antifederalist opposition was a group of New Yorkers in which General John Lamb was a prominent leader. In May, while the convention in South Carolina was in progress, Lamb sent to Rawlins Lowndes, and through Lowndes to Burke and Sumter, a plan of concerted

---

34. JCC, 39–53; CGDA, May 24, 1788.
35. JCC, 3.
36. Boyd, *Politics of Opposition*, 124–35.
37. Gabriel Manigault to Margaret Izard Manigault, May 22, 1788, Manigault Papers, SCHS.

opposition to ratification without prior amendments.[38] Lowndes received Lamb's letter in mid-June, promptly delivered those enclosed for Burke and Sumter, and replied to Lamb on June 21. "Had your plan been proposed in time," he said, "I doubt not it might have produced very good effect in this country. A strong systematic opposition, wherein the opinions and sentiments of the different States were concentrated, and directed to the same specific objects, would have had a weight, which the advocates of the Constitution must have submitted to; and have removed the force of an objection, strongly insisted upon, arising from the diversity and dissimilarity of the several amendments contended for."[39]

Two days later, Burke submitted his own account of the proceedings. The Constitution was carried in South Carolina, he said, "notwithstanding four-fifths of the people do, from their souls detest it." The opposition was inactive and unorganized, while "its friends and abettors left no expedient untried to push it forward." With few exceptions, all the lowcountry was for it. Former Tories and British adherents were for it. "From the British Consul (who is the most violent man I know for it) down to the British scavenger, all are boisterous to drive it down." The whole weight of the Charleston press was in support, and there was no press outside Charleston. "The printers are, in general, British journeymen, or poor citizens, who are afraid to offend the great men, or merchants, who could work their ruin. Thus, with us, the press is in the hands of a junto, and the printers, with most servile insolence discouraged opposition, and pushed forward publications in its favor, for no one voted against it." The principal factor, he continued, was the holding of the convention in Charleston, where the populace was for it and kept continuous open house for the backcountry and lowcountry members. When news of Maryland's ratification arrived on the sixth day of

---

38. The substance of Lamb's letter was reprinted in *SGSC*, June 26, 1788. The courier between Lamb and the South Carolina dissidents, at least as far as Virginia, was probably Colonel Eleazar Oswald, publisher of the Philadelphia *Independent Gazeteer* and a long time friend and colleague of Lamb's. Oswald's trip to Virginia was made in connection with an effort by Virginia and New York Antifederalists to coordinate the campaign for amendments and a second convention in their respective states. Lamb must have known that the South Carolina convention was sitting when he wrote. But his view was longer term. Lamb's plan of campaign is described in Boyd, *Politics of Opposition*, 127–28.
39. Lowndes to Lamb, June 21, 1788, Lamb Papers, NYHS.

the convention, Peter Fayssoux, "one of our best speakers in the opposition . . . gave notice that he would quit the ground, as Maryland had acceded to it." Thereafter, the opposition continued to lose support. But "notwithstanding these misfortunes, the few of us who spoke, General Sumter, Mr. John Bowman, a gentleman of fortune and fine talents, from the lowcountry; myself and a few of the backcountry men, found it necessary, in supporting the opposition, to exert the greater spirit and resolution, as our difficulties increased."[40]

The minority at the convention represented a far greater number of the citizens than the majority, Burke claimed. "The minority are chiefly from the backcountry where the strength and numbers of our republick lie—and although the vote of the Convention has carried it, that has not changed the great body of the people respecting its evil tendency. In the interior country, all is disgust, sorrow and vindictive reproaches against the system and those who voted for it. . . . You may rely on it if a fair opportunity offers itself to our backcountry men they will join heart and hand to bring ruin on the new plan unless it be materially altered." Nobody saw the matter as he saw it, he continued, "or if any one did, he must be crazy, if he told his mind. The true, open, rising ground, no one has dared to take, or will dare to do it, 'till the business is all over. If you live two or three years, you will find the world will ascribe to the right author, this whole affair, and put the saddle on the right horse, as we say. I find myself approaching too near to forbidden ground, and must desist." When it is finally put in motion, he concluded, "then you and I, and all of us, will be obliged to take it, as we take our wives, 'for better or for worse.' " But then, implicitly indicating awareness that perhaps all was not lost, he suggested that the system would "fall to pieces" if either Virginia or New York rejected it. In that event, "or in any other that may give us an occasion to serve the Republic your communication will be duly attended to by me."[41]

40. Burke to Lamb, June 23, 1788, Lamb Papers, NYHS. Burke's description of Fayssoux's change of heart is accurate. His objections to the Constitution were principled, Fayssoux said, but Maryland's decision was decisive. "I will sacrifice my own feelings to the peace and tranquility of my country," as continued opposition "would only tend to irritate men's minds" and "would be criminal." *CGDA*, May 24, 1788.
41. Burke to Lamb, June 23, 1788, Lamb Papers, NYHS.

This was a remarkable letter as much for what it omitted as for what it said. It explained, subject to some reservations, how the ratification process was orchestrated by proponents of the Constitution. It did not explain why the backcountry opposed it. Nor did it explain why Burke opposed it, although it suggests that he was strongly influenced by Anglophile support. He surely overstated his case when he said that no opposing views were carried in the public press.[42] He was characteristically opaque when he observed that nobody saw the matter as he saw it, that no one dared to take the "true, open, rising ground," and that he found himself "approaching too near to forbidden ground, and must desist." And who was the mysterious figure behind the scene that he feared to name, the "right author" of the whole affair on whom the saddle would ultimately be put?

The "right author" was probably meant to be Washington.[43] Although Burke would later be much more critical of Washington, he had reason enough to be wary. He never lost his suspicion of the Cincinnati; and he knew, as everyone did, the importance of Washington's role in the Philadelphia convention. If he needed a reminder, it was provided locally. Just prior to the final vote in the South Carolina convention, the Reverend Cummings announced that, in his considered judgment, the prospective benefits of the proposed Constitution outweighed its defects. He was impressed, he said, by those who labored to produce it,

---

42. The coverage in the press of Charleston was reasonably balanced. The proceedings in Pennsylvania and Massachusetts, including the several amendments recommended by the Massachusetts convention, were adequately covered. Several of Bryan's "Centinel" essays were reprinted. As previously noted, the dissent of the Pennsylvania minority was reprinted. So was Luther Martin's "Genuine Information." Most of the supporting essays were either local or unattributed. None of the "Publius" essays published in New York (collectively *The Federalist* papers), at least through Number 75, were reprinted in Charleston. In addition, Antifederalist literature was widely circulated in the backcountry. C. C. Pinckney to Rufus King, May 24, 1788, King Papers, NYHS; Boyd, *Politics of Opposition*, 115.

43. George C. Rogers, Jr., *Evolution of a Federalist: William Loughton Smith of Charleston (1758–1812)* (Columbia: University of South Carolina Press, 1962), 157. Hypothetical cases can be made for others, however, particularly Hamilton on the national scene and either John Rutledge or Charles Pinckney in South Carolina. The question ultimately turns on whether Burke intended to refer to the national or the local scene. If the former, Washington remains the best choice. If the latter, Rutledge (or a Rutledge-Pinckney faction) is perhaps the better choice. Either might conceivably be construed as "forbidden ground."

particularly General Washington, "whose unsullied and patriotic character, is equal if not superior to any in this world," who had put his name to it, and "who would not suffer a blot to his reputation or wink at the ruin of his country."[44]

Was it really true, as Burke informed Lamb, that four-fifths of the people of South Carolina detested the new Constitution "from their souls" and would refuse to support it? Burke perhaps believed it. Alexander Garden reported an anecdote, which he attributed directly to Burke. According to Garden, Burke was returning from the circuit when he fell in with a wagon train conveying produce from North Carolina to Charleston. In the course of the journey, he inquired of the wagonmen whether they thought the new Constitution "would prove useful and acceptable to the People." The reply was unanimous. "By no means. We abominate it, and to such a degree, that should the President think proper, on any emergency, to call us into the field, we would refuse obedience to a man." When Burke remonstrated on their duty to their country, they forced him to ride alone at the end of the line.[45]

The wagonmen may as well have been North Carolinians setting out for Charleston as South Carolinians on a return trip. But the underlying sentiment may be accurately reflected. More likely, Burke relied on the population differential between seacoast and backcountry and assumed substantial backcountry unanimity. The assumption was probably warranted. Contemporary opinion was to the same effect, and the vote by election district on both Sumter's motion to adjourn and final ratification tends to support that view. Nevertheless, there were pockets of contrary opinion in both the lowcountry and the backcountry. St. Bartholomew's Parish in Charleston District was opposed, for example, and a correspondent from Camden, Thomas Sumter's po-

---

44. *CGDA*, May 26, 1788.

45. Alexander Garden, *Anecdotes of the Revolutionary War in America* (Charleston: A. Miller, 1822; reprint ed., Spartanburg: The Reprint Company, 1972), 195–96. Patrick Dollard, at the ratifying convention, delivered the only public statement of such extreme opposition. His constituents, Dollard proclaimed, "say they will resist against it; that they will not accept it except by force of arms, which this new constitution plainly threatens; and then, they say, your standing army, like Turkish janizaries enforcing despotic laws, must ram it down their throats with the points of bayonetts." Dollard's basic complaint was the absence of a bill of rights, and he was the only speaker on the record of the convention who emphasized that point above all others. Elliot, *Debates*, 4: 336–38.

litical demesne, reported a celebration of ratification and claimed that there were many staunch Federalists in the Camden District despite the backwardness of support there.[46]

Carl Vipperman, in his biography of Rawlins Lowndes, observed that the people of the backcountry, "like their counterparts elsewhere, possessed faith in government in direct proportion to their influence upon it, highest in their immediate vicinity and diminishing with distance from home."[47] The principle is essentially sound. James Lincoln argued it to the House of Representatives in January to good effect,[48] and Burke reiterated it to the convention in May. But backcountry concerns in South Carolina focused primarily on Charleston and the lowcountry elite. Demands for constitutional revision in South Carolina were as yet unfulfilled. Relocation of the capital to Columbia was not yet effective. Debtor relief was still unresolved. These local problems were problems enough. The backcountry yeomen had neither interest in nor liking for a new superpower with which to contend while still unsatisfied with the political structure of their home country. In this respect, at least, the relationship between lowcountry and backcountry was still much as it had been in 1774–1775, and most of the backcountry folk were "localists," not "cosmopolitans."

David Ramsay, ardent Federalist, had a quite different view of the situation in South Carolina than that expressed to Lamb by Lowndes and Burke. The objectives of South Carolina's Antifederalists, he told Benjamin Rush in April, "are almost peculiar to the State." He identified three major objections: first, the importation of slaves was a matter of domestic policy, and the northern states had no business to interfere; second, agricultural products would be subjected to higher freight charges if British shippers were excluded or highly taxed; and, third, debtor relief measures would be eliminated or impaired.[49] On another occasion, Ramsay

---

46. CGDA, June 11, 1788.
47. Vipperman, *Rawlins Lowndes*, 242.
48. Elliot, *Debates*, 4: 312–14. Liberty is "the power of governing yourselves," Lincoln told the House of Representatives. "If you adopt this Constitution, have you this power? No: you give it into the hands of a set of men who live one thousand miles distant from you. Let the people but once trust their liberties out of their own hands, and what will be the consequence? First, a haughty, imperious aristocracy; and ultimately, a tyrannical monarchy."
49. Ramsay to Benjamin Rush, April 21, 1788, in "David Ramsay: Selections from his Writings," Brunhouse, ed., 120.

called upon his Carolinian countrymen to examine carefully both the provisions of the Constitution relating to paper money and ex post facto laws and the character and circumstances of those who opposed its ratification. "Perhaps you will find," he said, "the real ground of the opposition of some of them, though they may artfully cover it with a splendid profession of zeal for state privilege and general liberty."[50] Lowndes raised the issue before the House in January, observing that the treaty power and the supremacy clause "entirely did away the instalment law; for, when this Constitution came to be established, the treaty of peace might be pleaded against the relief which the law afforded."[51] Charles Cotesworth Pinckney also pointed specifically to the debtor relief issue. Most of the delegates who voted against the Constitution at the convention "have declared that they will exert themselves in its support," he told Rufus King in June, "and some districts that were very averse to it, are altogether reconciled to its adoption. Indeed if we were allowed to pass installment and valuation laws as heretofore, an antifederalist would be a rare avis in this State."[52]

Whatever the contribution of the debtor relief issue to Antifederalism in South Carolina, that issue was not central to Burke's response. As in 1787, the General Assembly in January 1788 turned from national to local questions and took up the growing clamor for further debtor relief. There was no strong inclination to break new ground. Alexander Gillon's motion to stay all judgments was defeated 97 to 48, with Burke voting against it. Gillon's further motion for a seven year installment payment bill was defeated 119 to 18, with Burke not voting. Pierce Butler's proposal for a new valuation bill was rejected 92 to 53, with Burke again not voting. Sumter's proposal for a substantial additional issue of paper money was rejected without a division, and an elaborate plan for the creation of a new state bank submitted by Chancellor John Mathews was deferred for further study. Finally, a proposal to remove the ban on slave imports was defeated 93 to

---

50. "Civis" [David Ramsay], *An Address to the Freemen of South Carolina on the Subject of the Federal Constitution, Proposed by the Convention, which met in Philadelphia, May 1787* (Charleston: Bowen and Co., n.d.); *CH*, February 4, 1788. The connection is discussed at some length in *JHR 1787–1788*, xviii–xx.
51. Elliot, *Debates*, 4: 266.
52. C. C. Pinckney to Rufus King, June 21, 1788, King Papers, NYHS.

40. On this question Burke was with the minority, opposing the ban as he had before and would again.[53]

The effect was therefore to maintain the status quo established in 1787, and the issue was still open, politically troublesome, and unresolved when the ratifying convention met in May. At the special session in October, convened primarily to provide for the election of national officers under the new Constitution, debtor relief was again forced on the attention of the General Assembly. Burke described the mounting pressure in late September. The country was "in a rage" for a seven-year installment act, he told General Wayne, with petitions to the General Assembly from "every quarter." The whole state was divided into two powerful factions—debtors and creditors. "We have not one political Doctor, I believe, who sees the nature or extent of the disorder; I for my own part, have all along believed that the evil lay very deep in the body; and like a Cancer, mixing with the flesh, blood and sinews, required a sharp corrosive remedy to apply which requires decisive Counsel and such a decisive execution neither of which are to be hoped for, from the jarring interests, and yahooism of a popular Assembly. Year after year, patch upon patch—'tis disgraceful . . . to our form of Government. 'Tis Racoonism, and will keep our Country in hot water (as we say) for a long time."[54] In the General Assembly, a committee report submitted to the House by Hugh Rutledge found that further legislative interposition was "indispensably necessary" and was approved 95 to 37 with Burke voting aye. Butler's reintroduced valuation bill was rejected 89 to 43, with Burke voting no. A seven-year installment payment bill was rejected in favor of one limited to five years, an extension of the three year bill enacted in 1787. Burke did not vote on either measure, but he was present and voted against an extension of the slave import ban.[55]

53. *JHR 1787–1788*, 412–14 (Gillon stay motion rejected), 469–71 (seven-year installment payment bill rejected), 474–76 (valuation bill rejected), 480–82 (state bank deferred), 482 (additional paper money rejected). Removal of the ban on slave imports was proposed earlier in the session and rejected; *JHR 1787–1788*, 344–45.

54. Burke to Wayne, September 22, 1788, Wayne Papers, WLCL.

55. *JHR 1787–1788*, 583 (committee report approved), 588–89, (valuation bill rejected), 614–16 (seven-year installment payment proposal rejected, five-year installment payment bill approved, and extension of slave import ban rejected). See *JHR 1787–1788*, xv–xx, for a general discussion of the intensity of demand

This record leaves Burke's views even more ambiguous than usual. He decried the problem but advanced no remedy. He at least acknowledged, as he had reluctantly in 1785, that some form of legislative action was required in the public interest. He opposed an additional emission of paper money in 1787 and probably did again in January 1788. Whether or not he approved the regulation of execution sales in 1785, he opposed Butler's comparable valuation act in 1788. He did not vote on any of the installment payment bills proposed. He consistently opposed the ban on slave imports, perhaps because he owned undeveloped land in the backcountry that he hoped some day to cultivate. But if he shared this backcountry view he accepted debtor relief measures only from necessity and not by conviction; and his Antifederalism cannot be explained as resistance to constitutional restraints that might inhibit the retention or extension of measures for debtor relief. He was a structural Antifederalist, consistently focusing on the traditional conflict between governmental power and political liberty and vigilant to expose any structural feature the holders of power might exploit to their advantage. There is no evidence whatever that he was motivated by personal interest of any kind.[56]

When further debtor relief was finally assured in October 1788, the General Assembly turned to the business for which the special session was called and adopted an election law providing for the election of representatives to the new federal Congress. The principal issue was whether representatives to the national House of Representatives should be elected at large, which could have produced five Antifederalist representatives if opposition to

for further measures of debtor relief in 1788. The General Assembly apparently held off action on an election law until the debtor relief issue was resolved. Report of proceedings in House of Representatives on November 4, 1788, *CGDA*, November 11, 1788.

56. The impact of the Constitution on the measures proposed in October 1788 was the subject of debate in the General Assembly. One question was when the Constitution would be effective, immediately or only when the new national government began to function. Some argued that all debtor relief measures were prohibited, others that they were not. *CGDA*, October 18, 27, 28, 29, and 31, 1788, and November 13, 15, 17, and 21, 1788. Burke was not among those named as speaking to the issue. Since the new act contained the same provisions as the 1787 act requiring that interest be paid on deferred installments and that the debtor provide security if demanded by the creditor, the argument might have been made that the act operated only on the time of payment and did not impair the underlying obligation. The act is in *Statutes at Large*, 5: 88–92.

the Constitution outside the lowcountry was as solid as many believed, or by districts, which could be expected to produce at least one Federalist from the lowcountry establishment. With only 113 of 203 members voting, the House rejected the recommendation of its committee and approved election by districts. Burke voted with the majority and therefore not in accord with a strictly partisan Antifederalist stance. Five districts were specified, based on the existing judicial districts: Charleston, Beaufort and Orangeburgh combined, Georgetown and Cheraw combined, Camden, and Ninety Six. The election was scheduled to be held on November 24 and 25.[57] A list of candidates was published in the *City Gazette* on November 8. Burke was listed among those standing for election in the combined Beaufort-Orangeburgh District, where John Bull, John Barnwell, and John Kean were also named as candidates, and he won the election there with 422 votes, notwithstanding that the representatives of the several constituencies in that District voted heavily in favor of ratification at the convention in May.[58]

Predictably, the reaction to Burke's nomination and election was mixed. On November 21, just before the election, William Thomson wrote Richard Hampton, saying "I never knew that Judge Burke would serve in the new Congress until Monday last . . . which I am exceedingly happy to hear. And if you think as I do there is no doubt of his being elected." Early in January 1789, John F. Grimke referred to the state's elected representatives as "a black list." At about the same time, Timothy Ford informed Robert Morris of the election and commented that "we do not anticipate as much respectability on the floor of the Con-

57. *JHR 1787–1788*, xii; *Statutes at Large*, 5: 84–86; Merrill Jensen and Gordon Den-Boer, eds., *The Documentary History of the First Federal Elections, 1788–1790*, 3 vols. to date (Madison: University of Wisconsin Press, 1976–1987), 1: 154–69. The House declined to elect the state's senators at the special session. Pierce Butler and Ralph Izard were elected in January after Lowndes declined to be a candidate and Charles Pinckney stood aside to accept election to the governor's chair. *JHR 1787–1788*, xi, 624–25; *JHR 1789–1790*, xvii–xviii, 56, 59.
58. *CGDA*, November 8, 1788. One constituency failed to submit a proper return but reported 199 votes for Burke, 2 for Bull, and 1 for Barnwell. The Privy Council declined to count these votes, but Burke's margin was surely higher than the official returns indicated. Jensen, et al., eds., *Documentary History of First Federal Elections*, 1: 198–99. The combined vote of those representing the several constituencies comprising the Beaufort-Orangeburgh District on ratification of the constitution was 30 for ratification and 14 against.

gress as this state could have entitled herself to by a different election. Our men of first abilities uniformly declined and the people most straitened in their choice resorted to those who offered themselves as candidates."[59]

Burke requested and received leave of absence from his judicial position to attend the new Congress. A question arose, however, as to whether he should continue to receive any part of his compensation. In January 1789, the General Assembly agreed that his salary should cease so long as he remained a member of the Congress. The House attempted to revise this determination so that pay would be stopped only when he was absent from the state. The Senate refused and a conference committee was unable to compromise the issue.[60]

As the General Assembly completed its work in late 1788 and Burke prepared to depart for New York and service in the First Congress, one major assignment remained open—the digest and revision of the laws commissioned in 1785. Pendleton died in late 1788, and responsibility for presentation of the commission's completed work then fell to Burke. The report was finally ready in January 1789. Consisting of a digest of existing statutes and proposals for major substantive revisions, it was necessarily of substantial size. Burke first delivered it to the House in person and was shocked to receive a negative reaction. He could not have foreseen, he wrote Jacob Read, Speaker of the House, "that the nature and design of it could have been so much misunderstood, or such opposition made against it." Apparently, the House had not expected so comprehensive a production and suspected that the judges, in drafting comprehensive new laws on a number of important subjects, were advancing their own "new hints and schemes" and thereby exceeding their authority and impinging on that of the legislature.[61] Thus forewarned, Burke

---

59. Jensen, et al., eds., *Documentary History of First Federal Elections*, 1: 173, 205–206.

60. *JHR 1789–1790*, 59, 71–72, 75, 127, 153, 162, 164.

61. Burke to Jacob Read, January 24, 1789, General Assembly Papers, Miscellaneous Communications 1776–1861, SCA. Timothy Ford had anticipated the problem. The authority granted the commission, he observed, "has laid the foundation for greater evils" by "making these men law givers." "Diary of Timothy Ford, 1785–1786," Joseph W. Barnwell, ed., *SCHM*, 13 (1912): 198.

was careful to spell out the purposes of the commissioners in a long letter transmitting the report to the Senate.[62]

One great subject of concern to the commissioners was the structure of the judicial system. Under the system inherited from the British, established in 1769 and still essentially unchanged, all judicial proceedings were centered in Charleston. The court in Charleston was the only court of record. All writs and other process were issued only in Charleston and were returnable only to Charleston. Consequently, the practicing bar was concentrated in Charleston and, with the records of the proceedings to be heard, traveled the circuits just as the judges did. Burke graphically described the operation of the system as established in 1769 and conducted thereafter.

> All writs then were, and now are, made to issue from the clerk's office in Charleston, and there returnable; for if a man residing as far back as the mountains be served with a writ, he must enter an appearance in town, or judgment, right or wrong, goes against him. The writ being returned, the pleadings are conducted and the issue made up in town; then the whole proceedings are sent to the district court, for the trial of the issue; then returned to Charleston, where judgment on the verdict is entered, from whence execution is to issue, and then again be returned to town.

In such circumstances, the services of the judicial system could hardly be efficiently delivered to the public.

The commissioners accordingly recommended a reorganization of the circuit court system in which each of the "country courts" would constitute a separate court of record and, "in order to preserve a uniformity of decision and practice throughout all of the courts," the creation of a court of errors and motions to sit in Columbia at the end of each circuit. They also recommended that the jurisdictions of law and equity be combined in the same court. Finally, they urged that the burdensome jury system be reformed to provide for compensation of jurors and that fees for judges be abolished altogether as repugnant

---

62. Burke to Daniel Desaussure, January 26, 1789, General Assembly Papers, Miscellaneous Communications, 1776–1861, SCA. No copy of the report has survived. Burke's letter of transmittal contains the only known summary of its contents and is the source of the quoted passages in the following five paragraphs. It was published by order of the Senate in the *CGDA*, February 3, 1789.

to the nature and dignity of judicial office. The judges should be allowed "moderate but sufficient salaries to assure their independence."

In the course of his comments on the report, Burke acknowledged the deficiencies of the county court system established in 1785, which was functioning in the backcountry but not in the lowcountry, and suggested that the General Assembly address the problem. If the backcountry would not relinquish the system, and the lowcountry would not embrace it, "if it be not so organized as to answer alike in all parts of the state," then the resulting legal division of backcountry and lowcountry might "prevent the country from cementing together into that close union of all its parts which to bring about should be the wish of every good man among us." But he denied that the report's recommendations were so closely tied to the defective county court system as to be useless. The substance of the report would still be the same, he said, whether county courts be rejected or the system modified.

With respect to the substance of the law, Burke pointed out that many of the laws nominally in effect "are grown obsolete or out of use by length of time, the alteration of circumstances, and numberless acts, by the emancipation of the country from the regal government." Many had expired or had been repealed "by subsequent acts, crossing and contradicting each other." Some were duplicated, "whilst those that are in force, are featured up and down our code, without order or connection, and intermingled with those others that are expired, repealed or become obsolete." A number of English statutes were incorporated "only by their titles and sections, and only to be found scattered here and there in the English statute books." Thus, "the laws on which depend the lives and properties of the people, now lie concealed from the eyes of the citizens, mingled in confused chaos, under a stupendous pile of old and new law rubbish, past all possibility of being known, only to the law professors."

The decision of the Assembly to commission a digest of the laws, he continued, "does great honour to the people; and will, I trust, convey to future time a noble testimony, that their next first care was, to form their laws into a regular system, in order that their posterity might participate in the blessings earned by the toils and dangers which they had passed through." Out of the confused mass of the substantive law, the commissioners had assembled "one compact plain uniform act; cutting off the fatiguing preambles and shameful tautologies . . . and we retained as much as it was possible from the identical words and sentences of the laws from which we made the selection, for it was apprehended that if different words and phrases were substituted, new interpretations and uncertainties would of course ensue." Applicable British laws were adapted "to the local circumstances and situation of our country, having always in view the operation and [policy] of the common law, and strictly attending to the spirit and principles of our popular government." Primogeniture was eliminated "with sundry other decayed branches of antiquated feudal policy." A simplified criminal code was proposed, following Blackstone. The project was complete except for a few digests on which Judge Pendleton was working at the time of his death. These would be digested anew and submitted to the House. There may be some want of connection of the parts, Burke said, "chiefly owing to the frequent intervals of Mr. Pendleton's absence on account of his health; for the work was pretty evenly divided between the three commissioners." As for himself, Burke concluded, "whatever may be the fate of this production of our labor, it shall, during my life, be the most ardent wish of my heart, that my fellow citizens, and their generations, may forever enjoy, under equal laws and liberty, every public and private happiness."

Although the code of law prepared by Burke, Pendleton, and Grimke was never enacted in its entirety, many of its substantive and procedural recommendations were reflected in the Constitution of 1790 and related legislation. And one important byproduct of their labor was preserved when Grimke, in 1790, published his *Public Laws of the State of South Carolina*.[63] Grimke's compilation was the first of its kind and was widely distributed as a standard work of reference. No credit or acknowledgement was extended to Pendleton and Burke. Even so, Burke's work on the commission was his most enduring contribution as servant to the public interest in the decade of the 1780s.

Apart from this major achievement, Burke's performance in the seventh General Assembly was generally undistinguished. Perhaps he was overburdened by his judicial duties, work on the

---

63. John F. Grimke, *Public Laws of the State of South Carolina* (Philadelphia: R. Aitken & Son, 1790).

digest of laws, or other unknown concerns. But in the first session, he voted on only eight of the nineteen issues on which individual votes were recorded after he qualified in February. In the second session, he voted on only three of sixteen. He was granted leave of absence for ten days and was penalized for ten days of unauthorized absence. In the third session, he participated in four of ten recorded votes. He made no identifiable contribution to the work of the General Assembly on any of the important state issues before it.[64]

This record suggests a waning of Burke's interest in local affairs, perhaps partially reflecting the adverse public reaction to the *Salutary Hints* and his subsequent problems at the polls. At least, his enthusiasm for further polemics was somewhat cooled, and in November 1788 he backed away from a project apparently begun at General Wayne's behest. "I went to work on the subject you proposed, and made progress on it," he told Wayne. But he was reluctant, he said, to step forward on a partisan issue on behalf of an interest "whose aim (in the opinion of the other powerful party, the Creditors) was to level law and justice and civil contracts with the dust." Such an undertaking "would undoubtedly bring down on my head the evacuations of a thousand Yahoos at least."[65] The subject was not more clearly identified, but it must have involved the issue of debtor relief. On the record, that was not a subject Burke wanted to confront. For once, prudence perhaps overcame a desire to accommodate a prominent contemporary.

By the end of 1788, then, Burke's attention was redirected, as he turned away from local issues and became increasingly preoccupied with national affairs and the larger problems posed by the new Constitution. A second general convention of the states was not a realistic possibility. Although the major objectives of the Antifederalist campaign as originally conceived in New York and Virginia had failed,[66] the campaign for amendments was by no

---

64. Data derived from *JHR 1787–1788*, index and references.
65. Burke to Anthony Wayne, November 21, 1788, Wayne Papers, WLCL. Burke continued to advise Wayne, however, on Wayne's problems with his creditors, as he had from 1786. Paul David Nelson, *Anthony Wayne: Soldier of the Early Republic* (Bloomington: Indiana University Press, 1985), 186–227.
66. The campaign failed in the sense that neither Virginia nor New York insisted on amendments prior to ratification. After Virginia ratified, the pressure on New York was simply too great. Boyd, *Politics of Opposition*, 130–32.

means dead. The burden was shifted to the First Congress, and a broad agenda of recommended changes was on hand from the conventions of Massachusetts, New Hampshire, Virginia, and New York as well as South Carolina. By the time New York ratified in July 1788, some seventy-seven specific proposals were on the table. Many, of course, were duplicative, as each state convention took care to express itself in its own language.[67]

Madison later classified these various proposals in three categories: first, those addressed to the theory of the governmental structure; second, those addressed to the substance of governmental powers; and, third, those addressed to the omission of safeguards for basic rights and liberties.[68] The first two categories may be conveniently combined into one general class of "structural" amendments, most of which proposed some affirmative change in the provisions of the Constitution relating to the organization and powers of the government, while a few were simply clarifying or declaratory. The third, which Madison considered the most strongly urged and the most easily resolved, may be conveniently referred to as a separate class of "protective" or "rights" amendments. Though these terms are not elegant, they do convey the essential difference between the two classes without elaboration or qualification.

The first three of the recommendations endorsed by the South Carolina convention—limitation on national authority to impose direct taxes, limitation on national authority to interfere with electoral procedures in the states, and express confirmation that powers not delegated to the national government were reserved to the states—were similarly endorsed, in one form or another, by all the other states proposing amendments. Moreover, the proposals of Burke, Cudworth, and Gervais, respectively calling for rotation in the presidential office, absolutely prohibiting receipt of emoluments or titles from foreign governments, and

---

67. The amendments submitted by Massachusetts (9), South Carolina (4), New Hampshire (12), Virginia (20), and New York (32) are set out in *The Documentary History of the First Federal Congress of the United States of America, March 4, 1789–March 3, 1791*, Vols. 4–6, *Legislative Histories*, Charlene Bangs Bickford and Helen E. Veit, eds. (Baltimore: Johns Hopkins University Press, 1986), 4: 12–26.
68. *The Papers of James Madison*, William T. Hutchinson, et al., eds., 14 vols. to date (Chicago: University of Chicago Press, 1962–1977, vols. 1–10; Charlottesville: University Press of Virginia, 1977–1983, vols. 11–14), 12: 193–95.

restricting the power of the national government to direct state militias, were all covered and elaborated upon in the recommendations of New Hampshire, Virginia, and New York. Finally, all the other states, with varying degrees of specificity, included proposals for protective or rights amendments such as those that Bowman presumably had in mind when he unsuccessfully sought at South Carolina's convention to establish a committee to draw up a bill of rights.

The collective agenda included much more than these basic points. New Hampshire, Virginia, and New York proposed restrictions on the creation of a standing army and on the scope of the jurisdiction conferred on the federal courts. Those three states and Massachusetts proposed prohibition of grants of monopoly power. Virginia proposed limits on the exercise of the treaty power and a two-thirds vote in Congress on navigation laws. New York proposed restrictions on excise taxes and the borrowing of money. Not all these proposals were of the same order of significance, to be sure, but all were congenial to those such as Burke who were concerned with the aggregation of unrestrained authority at a distant power center.

In January 1789, Governor Thomas Pinckney submitted to the General Assembly a circular letter from the Virginia legislature calling for a second constitutional convention. The House voted to consider the question, together with the proposed amendments of Massachusetts, Virginia, and New York. Rawlins Lowndes reportedly observed that he would give the House "very little trouble" over amendments, and Edward Rutledge reportedly replied that he hoped Lowndes "would decline giving any at all."[69] The matter ended there, however, as nothing further was recorded in the journals of the House or mentioned in the newspapers.

Clearly, the South Carolinians had done all they intended to do, at least for the moment. But the recommendations of their convention suggested a consensus in support of specified amendments, and the state's representatives were directed to press for them in the First Congress. With that directive from his own state, and the prospect of support from others, Burke could reasonably hope that his views, and the views of those who saw the

---

69. *JHR 1789-1790*, 12-13, 15; *CGDA*, January 16, 1789.

same dangers in the new Constitution that he did, might yet prevail. Massachusetts, New Hampshire, Virginia, and New York were on record. Support could also be expected from Pennsylvania and Maryland.[70] In addition, he could rationally look upon the political scene in South Carolina and conclude that he was as well qualified as any other to pursue that goal. Some such motive must have stimulated his decision to seek election to the First Congress and abandon, even temporarily, his seat on the bench. In the circumstances, he could consider it his duty to his "country" and as the opportunity to serve the republic of which he had written to Lamb.

Burke's position and role in the contest over the Constitution were almost unique. Fragmentary as the record is, his position was more fully articulated than that of any other South Carolinian Antifederalist except Lowndes. Burke embodied all the attributes of cosmopolitanism. His announced grounds of opposition were relatively narrow and principally addressed structural issues concerning executive power and the subordination of the sovereign states to the new central government in matters of critical importance. He had no evident prejudice against the eastern states and never endorsed the neocolonial arguments advanced by Lowndes. As recently as 1785, he had argued in the *Salutary Hints* for a nationally centered navigation system, which the Constitution authorized. But in the historically verified contest between power and liberty, all threats to liberty were of the same magnitude and each had to be confronted, pari passu. Accordingly, he could contemplate service in the First Congress not only as an opportunity for service, but also as a mission; and he could reasonably expect that he would not stand there a lone voice in the wilderness. Unaware that the voters in other states were turning away from Antifederalism in the first federal elections and increasingly inclined to give the new Constitution a "fair trial,"[71] he would be disappointed; but his purpose was consistent with his deep commitment to republican principles.

---

70. The Maryland convention was prepared to propose amendments and appointed a committee to submit recommendations. Thirteen proposed amendments were approved, but the plan collapsed when a minority of the committee insisted on offering amendments rejected by the majority and the committee thereupon resolved not to recommend any. Boyd, *Politics of Opposition*, 121–22. These proceedings were reported at length in the *CGDA*, June 2, 1788.
71. Boyd, *Politics of Opposition*, 161–63.

VII

Congressman Burke

1789

As the First Congress convened in New York on March 4, 1789, eleven of the thirteen states of the old confederation were represented. Only North Carolina and Rhode Island, having failed to ratify the new Constitution, would be absent. The task before the assembly was formidable. The country as a whole was just beginning to recover from the effects of the post-war economic depression. A heavy burden of national and state debt threatened to oppress government and people alike. The new Constitution was a skeleton without flesh, particularly in the executive and judicial branches, and a governmental structure was required to implement the broad outline provided by the Constitution. An entirely new system of national revenue was essential. The regulation of foreign and domestic commerce in the national interest was nearly as important. In the states, the people were watchful, expecting with varying levels of insistence that amendments to the new Constitution would be forthcoming. In the world beyond, where monarchy was generally accepted as the form of government best suited to the human condition, the parvenu republic was still on trial. The larger responsibility of the First Congress, then, was to demonstrate that a functioning governmental establishment could be constructed on republican principles and ideals.[1]

---

1. The *Annals* remain the best available source of information on the proceedings of the First Congress. The *Documentary History of the First Federal Congress of the United States of America, March 4, 1789–March 3, 1791*, 6 vols. to date, Linda Grant DePauw (vols. 1–3) and Charlene Bangs Bickford and Helen E. Veit (vols. 4–6), eds. (Baltimore: Johns Hopkins University Press, 1972–1986), is invaluable and will become even more so as future volumes are published. Kenneth R. Bowling, "Politics in the First Congress, 1789–1791" (Ph.D. dissertation, University of Wisconsin, 1968) analyzes the work of the First Congress in detail and has been relied upon below for its general history.

The First Congress was a Federalist body, committed to support of the new Constitution and the creation of an effectively functioning system of government. Only ten members on hand for the first session of the House of Representatives had actively opposed ratification of the Constitution, and each of them was prepared, after his own fashion, to permit the new system a fair trial notwithstanding his personal reservations. Only the South Carolina delegation had a majority of Antifederalists,[2] and its history, particularly after the first session, featured the rise of William Loughton Smith to a position of eminence and leadership as a supporter of the administration and a confidant of Alexander Hamilton.[3] After an active beginning, Burke was no more than a supporting player, somewhat erratic, on occasion disruptive. Thomas Tudor Tucker was visible and reasonably consistent but never a force. Thomas Sumter offered occasional pungent comment but generally remained in the background. Daniel Huger was a cipher. Due largely to poor health, he was seldom in evidence. Smith and Huger were Federalists, Burke, Sumter, and Tucker Antifederalists. Of the five, only Burke failed to return for a second term in 1791.

When the first session of the House of Representatives officially opened, less than half the elected members were there, and the House adjourned from day to day until a quorum finally appeared on April 1. Tucker, one of South Carolina's delegates to the Continental Congress in 1788, was the only member of the Carolinian delegation present from the outset. Burke, Smith, and Huger arrived on April 13. Burke, Tucker, and Huger took lodgings at Michael Huck's boarding house at the corner of Wall and Smith Streets, where they were joined by Thomas Scott of Pennsylvania. Sumter, when he finally appeared on May 25, took rooms at 40 Wall Street, a block or so away. Smith lived around the corner, on Broadway, next to the Spanish minister. And Isabella Murphy, a mantua maker later named a legatee under Burke's will, lived nearby at 23 Little Queen Street.[4]

2. Bowling, "Politics in the First Congress," 14–51, deals with the composition of the House. Two additional Antifederalist members entered with the North Carolina delegation in 1790. By then, most issues dividing the House on Federalist-Antifederalist lines had been resolved.
3. George C. Rogers, Jr., *Evolution of a Federalist: William Loughton Smith of Charleston (1758–1812)* (Columbia: University of South Carolina Press, 1962), 167–225.
4. *Annals*, 1: 95, 121; New York City Directories, 1789 and 1790, NYHS.

Recognizing that no governmental establishment could function without revenue, the House took up the matter of finance as its first order of substantive business. The debate was already in progress when Burke arrived on April 13. As presented by Madison, a leader in the House of Representatives from the outset of its proceedings, the revenue measure contemplated both tariff and tonnage duties that inevitably conflicted with important sectional interests. The tariff proposal was trouble enough, with support centered in northern manufacturing and shipping interests and opposition from southern agricultural interests. The tonnage proposal was even more controversial. In effect, Madison presented an American navigation system, favoring American ships over foreign vessels in American ports, reserving coastwise trade to American vessels, and assessing materially higher charges on ships of foreign nations who were not party to commercial treaties with the United States. His clear immediate target was Great Britain. More broadly, he sought to reinforce union by stimulating a community of interest between North and South based on mutual concessions in support of the national interest.[5] His concept was thus broadly consistent with Burke's argument in the *Salutary Hints*.

The southerners, and particularly the South Carolinians, were quick to realize that most of the concessions would come from them. But they were not recalcitrant. Tucker, for example, discussing the impost on imported steel, called attention to the burden it would impose on agriculture and the melancholy condition of the agricultural interest in South Carolina. He thought five percent ad valorem sufficient and acceptable. Conversely, Burke supported the imposition of a modest duty on imported hemp, necessary for the production of cordage. South Carolina's staple products "were hardly worth cultivation," he observed, and "the planters are, therefore, disposed to pursue some other." Hemp would be suitable; and cotton was "likewise in contemplation among them." Burke, Tucker, and Smith opposed any duty on salt, required in the feeding of farm animals, as burdensome to South Carolinians. Burke observed that the cost was already

---

5. Irving Brant, *James Madison, Father of the Constitution, 1787–1800* (Indianapolis: Bobbs-Merrill Company, 1950), 251–54; Drew R. McCoy, *The Elusive Republic: Political Economy in Jeffersonian America* (Chapel Hill: University of North Carolina Press, 1980), 136–44.

oppressive, particularly for those required to ship long distances from seacoast to backcountry. Smith emphasized the point by mentioning the opposition of the South Carolina backcountry to the new government. "It would be a melancholy circumstance," he said, "to entangle ourselves, at this time, among the shoals of discontent." But no stronger impulse could be given for opposition than the proposed tax on salt.[6]

The debate on the tariff schedule was completed without undue rancor, and acceptable compromises were ultimately reached. The tonnage issue was more difficult and southern concerns more clear cut. Even so, the opposition was restrained. Admirably containing his antipathy to all things British, Burke spoke for South Carolina in familiar terms. His constituents were not jealous of the northern states, he said, and they looked forward to a future time when northern shipping would be adequate to transport southern produce. Until then a high tonnage rate on British shipping would be prejudicial. Accordingly, Burke would favor higher rates only if payable at some distant future time.[7] Smith and Tucker were more broadly negative. Tucker asserted that discrimination would increase freight costs to the level of the highest tonnage duty payable. Smith declared that South Carolina was dependent on British shipping, and that a high duty on navigation aimed specifically at the British would force the planters to reduce prices of their agricultural commodities. The high rates proposed should at least be substantially reduced to avoid injury to the trade of the southern states generally. South Carolina, struggling to recover from post-war economic distress and a severe shortage of specie, was particularly vulnerable and could ill afford any risk of damage to its trade. Should the government prevent recovery by a heavy tonnage duty, then the government should be answerable for the consequences.[8]

Madison's proposal on tonnage passed the House of Representatives over southern and some northern opposition. But the Senate rejected the concept of discriminatory rates, and a conference committee accepted the Senate's position. As the measure was enacted, American-owned ships paid a tonnage duty of

---

6. *Annals*, 1: 148, 155, 158–60.
7. Ibid., 1: 256–57.
8. Ibid., 1: 259–61, 263–64.

six cents per ton and all foreign-owned ships a standard duty of fifty cents per ton.[9] The outcome was thus a partial stand-off, but the duty on foreign shipping was higher than the Carolinians had been prepared to support.

Debate on the revenue and navigation acts continued into May and overlapped the beginning of discussion on the formation of the requisite executive departments. On May 21, Burke was appointed one of a committee of eleven to prepare bills creating the first major departments of the executive branch, Foreign Affairs, Treasury, and War.[10] From the outset, the locus of power to remove department heads appointed by the President with the advice and consent of the Senate was the issue of primary concern. One body of opinion held that the power of removal was an executive prerogative exercisable by the President alone. The opposition, to which Smith, Tucker, and Sumter adhered, held that concurrence of the Senate should be required. The issue came to a vote in late June on a compromise proposal that was silent on the question of the President's power of removal, thus avoiding both an explicit restraint and a specific grant and bypassing the sensitive question of congressional authority to construe the Constitution in cases where it was silent or ambiguous. Just prior to the vote, in one of his few appearances on record, Sumter condemned the bill as "so subversive of the Constitution, and in its consequences so destructive to the liberties of the people, that I cannot consent to let it pass, without expressing my detestation of the principle it contains." Smith, Tucker, and Sumter voted against the bill; Burke voted for it; and the measure passed by seven votes.[11]

Burke's affirmative vote appears anomalous. Given his frequently stated fears concerning prospective abuse of executive power, a contrary position would not have been surprising and would have aligned him with his Carolinian colleagues. Although present, he never spoke to the issue during the course of the debate. The committee report was submitted by Abraham Baldwin of Georgia.[12] Burke's views in committee were nowhere disclosed. Reticence on matters perceived as presenting questions

9. Burke, Smith, and Tucker concurred in the final vote. *Annals*, 1: 618–19.
10. *Annals*, 1: 396.
11. Ibid., 1: 591.
12. Ibid., 1: 417.

of principle was not a notable feature of Burke's personality. If he was reluctant to challenge the distinguished sitting President, no comparable inhibition was apparent before or after the event. The result is an unexplained inconsistency in Burke's usually predictable patterns of response.

As the debate on the governmental departments overlapped that on the revenue, so the debate on constitutional amendments overlapped both. Madison, passed over for election to the Senate from Virginia and committed to action on amendments in his campaign for a seat in the House,[13] pressed the issue as soon as he reasonably could. Early in May, he gave notice that he intended to offer amendments before the end of the month, and Theodorick Bland presented an application from the Virginia legislature calling for a new convention to consider amendments.[14]

When Madison's proposals were finally presented in June, many of his colleagues were singularly reluctant to proceed. James Jackson of Georgia set the tone in colorful terms. "If I agree to alterations in the mode of administering this Government," he said, "I shall like to stand on the sure ground of experience, and not be treading air." The Constitution was like a vessel awaiting her maiden voyage and should not be altered until its defects were known.[15] Benjamin Goodhue of Massachusetts pointed out that Jackson opposed any amendments. His constituents, Goodhue said, expected amendments "to secure in a stronger manner their liberties from the inroads of power." Yet the time was premature "inasmuch as we have other business before us, which is incomplete, but essential to the public interest." Burke concurred. He thought amendments necessary, "but this was not the proper time to bring them forward." The organization of the government should be completed. Moreover, consideration of amendments "might interrupt the harmony of the House, which was necessary to be preserved in order to dispatch the great objects of legislation."[16]

Madison wanted to proceed, wanted the subject before the House, "that our constituents may see we pay a proper attention

13. Brant, *Madison, Father of the Constitution*, 235–42.
14. *Annals*, 1: 247–49.
15. Ibid., 1: 425–26.
16. Ibid., 1: 426.

to a subject they have much at heart." Continued delay "may occasion suspicions, which, though not well founded, may tend to inflame or prejudice the public mind against our decisions." The people "may think that we are not sincere in our desire to incorporate such amendments in the Constitution as will secure those rights, which they consider as not sufficiently guarded." Smith replied that "the important and pressing business of the Government" should be dealt with first. Elbridge Gerry of Massachusetts wanted amendments taken up promptly in order to forestall any movement of the states to call a new convention, to gain the confidence of absent North Carolina and Rhode Island, and finally to gain the confidence of the people so that the full powers of the government might be exercised with energy and dispatch. Sumter thought the matter of such importance to the union that he would be glad to see it taken up at any time. He was prepared to accept postponement "to a future day, when we shall have more leisure," and assumed that at the proper time the applications of the state conventions would be considered. Failure to do so, he said, "will give fresh cause for jealousy; it will rouse the alarm which is now suspended, and the people will become clamorous for amendments."[17]

Madison had his way to the extent that his proposed amendments were presented to the House. Further consideration was thereupon deferred in favor of other pending business. The preliminary skirmishing was nonetheless instructive. Some members were satisfied with the Constitution as it stood. Others hoped to effect structural change, particularly to clarify and reinforce the position of the states. For Antifederalists, such as Burke, Sumter, and Tucker, the tactics of delay were tactics of weakness. Too few to carry structural change, they could only attempt to build a record and await events that might shift the balance of opinion in their direction. Madison was prepared to sponsor and adopt amendments confirming basic civil liberties, but he would not support amendments diminishing the authority of the national government or threatening its efficient operation. His was a policy of expediency, and his problem was to distinguish from among his adherents those who were well-meaning supporters of

17. Ibid., 1: 426–27, 429, 444–45, 448–49.

his goal and those who intended to pursue more fundamental alterations.[18]

Weeks later, on July 21, Madison "begged the House to indulge him in the further consideration of amendments to the Constitution." After desultory debate, Madison's proposed amendments were referred to a committee consisting of one member from each state "with instruction to take the subject of amendments generally into their consideration and to report thereupon to the House." Burke was appointed to that committee as the representative of South Carolina.[19]

The committee reported a week later, proposing eighteen substantive amendments to be incorporated in the body of the Constitution. None was incompatible with Madison's stated objective, and none dealt with those structural matters of primary concern to the state conventions in Massachusetts, South Carolina, New Hampshire, Virginia, and New York, such as state control of electoral procedures, limitations on the authority of the national government to impose direct taxes, rotation in the presidential office, and the power of the president and senate, acting together, to make treaties that would become part of the supreme law of the land. Traditional political and civil liberties were carefully protected by provisions that, refined and combined, were ultimately included in the ten amendments constituting the Bill of Rights. Indeed, a provision later deleted by the Senate expressly prohibited state infringement of rights of conscience, freedom of speech and press, and the right of trial by jury in criminal cases.[20] Since there was no dissent or minority report, Burke's part in the work of the committee cannot be determined except by inference from his subsequent remarks.

Following Madison's lead, the House began working its way through the amendments proposed in the committee's report. Burke was initially quiet. But he finally announced his displeasure in the course of debate on Tucker's proposal that the provi-

---

18. Madison's position was developed in the course of an extended debate on June 8, 1789. *Annals*, 1: 431–42.
19. *Annals*, 1: 660–65.
20. The legislative history of the amendments, including the text of the amendments proposed in the ratifying conventions of Massachusetts, South Carolina, New Hampshire, Virginia, and New York, appears in the *Documentary History of the First Congress*, Bickford and Veit, eds., 4: 1–48. The committee report referred to in the text is at 4: 27–31.

sion on speech, assembly, and petition be expanded to confer upon the people the right to instruct their representatives. He did not propose to insist on Tucker's amendment, he said, but the amendments reported by the committee and likely to be adopted in the House were not "those solid and substantial amendments which the people expect." They were "little better than whipsyllabub, frothy and full of wind, formed only to please the palate," or "like a tub thrown out to a whale, to secure the freight of the ship and its peaceable voyage." The people would not be gratified. "Upon the whole," he concluded, "I think it will be found that we have done nothing but lose our time, and that it will be better to drop the subject now, and proceed to the organization of the government."[21]

Madison responded in his own defense and in defense of the committee. The people had been told that their rights would be protected, he said, and the committee's amendments were designed to achieve that objective. But he would oppose any amendments "likely to change the principles of the Government, or that are of a doubtful nature." They would not be approved by the House or ratified by the states. "Therefore, as a friend to what is attainable, I would limit it to the plain, simple, and important security that has been required."[22] Madison's response was skillful, even disingenuous. He contemplated more than a mere tub for the whale, but not much more. In response, Burke denied charging anyone with want of candor. But "he would appeal to any man of sense and candor, whether the amendments contained in the report were anything like the amendments required by the States of New York, Virginia, New Hampshire, and Carolina; and having these amendments in his hand, he turned to them to show the difference, concluding that all the important amendments were omitted in the report."[23]

Gerry, Burke, and Tucker did their best, but Madison continued to have his way. Gerry's motion to the effect that those amendments proposed by the states but not included in the committee's report be taken up concurrently, strongly supported by

---

21. *Annals*, 1: 745–46.
22. Ibid., 1: 746–47.
23. Ibid., 1: 747. Immediately following Burke's statement, Tucker's proposal was rejected 10 to 46. Burke never explicitly supported it, and the individual vote was not officially recorded.

Tucker, was soundly defeated.[24] A series of amendments offered by Tucker was rejected without a division.[25] Burke sought to restrict the creation of a standing army by amendment to the provision on the militia and confirming the right of the people to bear arms. "A standing army of regular troops in time of peace is dangerous to public liberty," his proposed amendment declared, "and such shall not be raised or kept in time of peace, but from necessity, and for the security of the people, nor then without the consent of two-thirds of the members present in both Houses; and in all cases the military shall be subordinate to the civil authority." The proposal was defeated by thirteen votes without debate.[26] Burke was also defeated on a proposal to insert language expressly prohibiting national interference in the conduct of state elections to national office. Madison opposed it. He "was willing to make every amendment that was required by the States, which did not tend to destroy the principles and the efficacy of the Constitution." But "he conceived that the proposed amendment would have that tendency." Burke knew there was a majority against him, he said, but he would "do his duty, and propose such amendments as he conceived essential to secure the rights and liberties of his constituents." He denied assertions that "this revolution, or adoption of the new Constitution, was agreeable to the public mind" and that "those who opposed it at first are now satisfied with it." Many who agreed to ratification without amendments, he continued, "did it from principles of patriotism, but they knew at the time that they parted with their liberties; yet they had such reliance on the virtue of a future Congress, that they did not hesitate, expecting that they would be restored to them unimpaired, as soon as the Government commenced its operations conformably to what was mutually understood at the sealing and delivering up of those instruments."[27]

Tucker's proposal to limit the authority of the national government to impose direct taxes was also decisively lost. Burke was silent, but Samuel Livermore of New Hampshire spoke out

24. *Annals*, 1: 757–59. The vote was 16 to 34. Burke, Sumter, and Tucker all voted for. Smith voted against.
25. *Annals*, 1: 761–63.
26. Ibid., 1: 751–52.
27. Ibid., 1: 768–73. The vote was closer, 23 to 28. The South Carolina delegation, except for the absent Huger, was unanimous in support of Burke's proposal.

in terms with which Burke would no doubt have agreed. This was an amendment strongly urged by the states, Livermore pointed out, and deserved serious consideration. "Unless something more effectual was done to improve the Constitution," he concluded, "he knew his constituents would be dissatisfied. As to the amendments already agreed to, they would not value them more than a pinch of snuff; they went to secure rights never in danger."[28] Tucker followed this defeat with a second series of amendments that were rejected without a division.[29]

In the end Madison's way proved acceptable. Seventeen proposed amendments, closely tracking those originally proposed by the select committee of the House, were sent to the Senate in late August. The Senate reduced the number to twelve by combining some and eliminating others. In addition to the prohibition on state interference with specific civil liberties, the Senate struck out one provision mandating exercise of the powers delegated to the national government strictly in accordance with the doctrine of the separation of powers and another limiting appeals to the Supreme Court. Finally, a clause requiring that crimes be tried before juries selected from the area in which the defendant resided was eliminated. In conference, the House insisted that the jury trial provision be restored but accepted the other Senate changes.[30] For Burke, the outcome of the debate on constitutional amendments was a frustrating disappointment. He was not thereafter silent, but his mood changed. He had no choice but to submit; but he was not reconciled.

Burke tried again when the bill to establish the judiciary came over from the Senate in September. Sumter and Tucker opposed the system of district courts, urging that the state courts could and should consider questions of federal law in the first instance. Smith held the dual system unavoidable. Burke supported Tucker and Sumter. The citizenry "never had an idea that by this revolution they were to be put in a worse situation than they were under the former government," he said. The dual system would be burdensome to persons called as witnesses and jurors to the new federal courts. Court sessions "might be made at a most inconvenient time of the year, and the place might be at

---

28. *Annals*, 1: 773–77. The vote was 9 to 39.
29. *Annals*, 1: 777–78.
30. *Documentary History of the First Congress*, Bickford and Veit, eds., 4: 45–48.

the most distant part of the State, where a man might be dragged three or four hundred miles from his home, and tried by men who knew nothing of him, or he of them." No doubt recalling the controversy concerning South Carolina's own judicial system, he was sure "the freemen of America could never submit to it." Madison again opposed him. The Constitution contemplated a separate federal judicial system, Madison said. Moreover, "a review of the constitution of the courts in many states will satisfy us that they cannot be trusted with the execution of Federal laws." In some states, "they are so dependent on State Legislatures, that to make the Federal laws dependent on them, would throw us back into all the embarrassments which characterized our former situation." Accordingly, "he did not see how it could be made compatible with the Constitution, or safe to the Federal interests, to make a transfer of the Federal jurisdiction to the State courts."[31]

Burke conceded defeat. "He had turned himself about," he said, "to find some way to extricate himself from this measure; but which ever way he turned, the Constitution still stared him in the face, and he confessed that he saw no way to avoid the evil." This confession was made "to let them know why he should be a silent spectator of the progress of the bill; and he had not the most distant hope that the opposition would succeed." But he was satisfied "that the people would feel its inconvenience, and express their dislike to a judicial system which rendered them insecure in their liberties and property; a system that must be regarded with jealousy and distrust." Gerry chided him on his withdrawal, because "gentlemen ought not to be tired out like a jury." Burke replied that he was not tired "but was satisfied that the opposition must be unsuccessful."[32]

Burke spoke to the issue only once more. Supporting Sumter, he insisted that the judiciary bill threatened serious consequences to the privileges of the people, particularly the long established right of trial by jury. In South Carolina, he said, a person accused of crime must be tried in the county where the crime occurred by a jury drawn from that county in order to assure the prisoner a fair and impartial trial. "But of this glo-

---

31. *Annals*, 1: 812–13. The legislative history of the judiciary act appears in the *Documentary History of the First Congress*, Bickford and Veit, eds., 5: 1150–1212.
32. *Annals*, 1: 813, 819–20.

rious and happy privilege the citizens of South Carolina are stripped. . . . If charged with committing a capital offense against the United States, at a place as far back as the Alleghany mountains, he is carried down to the city of Charleston, far from the aid of his friends, far from his witnesses; and if, in times of civil troubles, he be obnoxious to those in power, to be tried for his life in the fangs of his enemies."[33] It was all to no avail.

The judiciary bill was the last substantive measure debated in the first session and carried to conclusion. When it was completed, the governmental structure contemplated by the Constitution was in place and supported by a functioning system of national revenue. Amendments to the Constitution were ready for submission to the several states. By any objective standard, the first session was a session of solid accomplishment.

Completion of the judiciary bill marked a milestone in the history of the First Congress in another important respect. In late August, the issue of the permanent location of the national government emerged on the floor. That issue had been simmering in the background throughout the session and even before the session began, as the major states, particularly New York, Pennsylvania, and Virginia, maneuvered to obtain the benefits that all assumed would flow from possession of the national capital. Caucuses were held; alliances were made and broken. The issue would not be finally resolved until the second session, but as the first session drew to a close a new political orientation was introduced. Political goals centered on local interest, relegating the questions of great principle and the larger national interest debated during the first months of the session to the background. For practical purposes, this development marked the end of division on lines of distinction between Federalists and Antifederalists and the beginnings of an overt politics of interest that soon settled into divisions drawn to sectional lines.[34] The politics of nation building were not ended, but the nature of the process was significantly changed. To an increasing degree thereafter, the rhetoric of republican principle was adapted and employed for instrumental purposes.

33. Ibid., 1: 833–34.
34. Bowling, "Politics in the First Congress," 14–15, 152–70. The legislative history of the complex progress of the residence question in the first and second sessions appears in the *Documentary History of the First Congress*, Bickford and Veit, eds., 6: 1767–91.

Despite the accomplishments of the first session, for Burke and Tucker it ended on an almost spiteful note. Just prior to adjournment, Elias Boudinot of New Jersey proposed a resolution calling on the President to recommend to the people a day of public thanksgiving and prayer, "to be observed by acknowledging, with grateful hearts, the many signal favors of Almighty God, especially by affording them an opportunity peaceably to establish a Constitution of government for their safety and happiness." Burke objected. He "did not like this mimicking of European customs, where they made a mere mockery of thanksgivings," and where "parties at war frequently sang *Te Deum* for the same event, though to one it was a victory, and to the other defeat." Tucker thought the House had no business to act on such a matter. Moreover, the people "may not be inclined to return thanks for a Constitution until they have experienced that it promotes their safety and happiness." The resolution was nevertheless carried.[35] Soon thereafter, on September 29, the session adjourned.

Burke returned to South Carolina during the recess. There is no record of his activities or of discussions with constituents and others on political affairs. The proposed amendments were reported in the public press and officially transmitted to Governor Charles Pinckney. The governor also had in hand an earlier letter from Governor George Clinton of New York accompanied by resolutions of the New York legislature calling for a second constitutional convention.[36] No action in South Carolina was possible until the General Assembly convened in January 1790. It is beyond belief, however, that the subject was not a current topic of conversation.

Frustrated as he was by the failure of Congress to endorse any of the major structural amendments recommended by important states and urged by the Antifederalist minority in the House, Burke apparently planned his own history of the period in one last effort to arouse public opinion while the amendments proposed by Congress were before the states and some sentiment remained in support of a second convention. Samuel Bryan

---

35. *Annals*, 1: 914–15.
36. *JHR 1789–1790*, 301–302. Both the amendments and Clinton's letter, which was dated May 5, 1789, were submitted to the General Assembly in January 1790.

of Pennsylvania, author of the Antifederalist "Centinel" essays, was privy to the plan, and described it to John Nicholson, another committed Pennsylvania Antifederalist, in November 1789. "Judge Burke of South Carolina, a gentleman of distinguished patriotism and abilities is now engaged in writing a regular History of the late remarkable revolution in Government," Bryan told Nicholson, "a work I have every reason to believe will be highly advantageous to republicanism." A questionnaire attributed to Burke was enclosed.[37]

Like any experienced lawyer, Burke had a theory of the case he expected to make. His theory, clearly reflected in his questions, embodied the concerns of many Antifederalists. The new Constitution was a stage in the progress of a conspiracy by an aristocratic element in the populace to revive the tyranny of mixed monarchy. By manufactured crises, scare tactics, and illegal action, the conspirators had forced on the people a plan of government deliberately contrived to deprive them of their liberty. Thus, a revolution in government had been effected for the benefit of the few. Accordingly, Burke requested information on the background and proceedings of the Constitutional Convention in Philadelphia. Who proposed it and why? Was there in 1786 such a condition of anarchy, or spirit of licentiousness, or disregard of proper governmental authority sufficient to warrant fundamental change in the structure of government? What were the reasons for economic distress in 1786? Were there influential men unfavorable to a popular government and favorable to a "regal one?" Was there any party inclined to avail themselves of the popularity of a "certain personage" (presumably Washington) to bring about a revolution in government? Did that certain personage take any active part in framing the system? Were the Cincinnati in evidence? The questions clearly implied that the delegates exceeded their authority and that the people neither intended nor expected "that the republican system of government would be overturned or materially altered."

Consequently, Burke also sought to determine the response of the public. What was the reaction of merchants, mechanics,

---

37. Samuel Bryan to John Nicholson, November 21, 1789, John Nicholson Papers, General Correspondence, 1772–1819, Pennsylvania State Archives, Pennsylvania Historical and Museum Commission, Harrisburg. Burke's questions are numbered 1–30.

creditors, debtors, lawyers, Whigs, Tories, women, and other designated groups? Was opposition concerted and, if not, why not? Was support concerted and how was it done? Were there efforts to foreclose discussion on the merits? Was pressure applied against the opposition? Were letters intercepted or the distribution of communications prevented? Was the opposition coerced or threatened prior to and during the ratification convention? Did Federalists mislead or deceive the people or suppress publications of their opponents? How far was the press instrumental in effecting the revolution in government? Were printers and publishers coerced?

Only one response has been found, probably the work of Samuel Bryan.[38] It told Burke little he did not already know and, although not inconsistent with his theme, was hardly encouraging. There was consensus in support of a stronger central government, Bryan reported, particularly with regard to maritime affairs. Economic distress in the aftermath of the war was real. British goods flooded the market. Exclusion of American shipping from major segments of British trade was damaging. When the Constitution was presented to the people, the increased authority conferred on Congress was widely approved. The popularity of Washington and Franklin contributed to its support. The "Gentlemen of the Late Army," the Cincinnati in general, the Tory interest, and the "tools of Aristocracy" were also strongly in support. There was reason to believe that "some men among us had deeper views than they chose to declare and wished a Government even less popular than the one proposed," but no detail was provided. Some of the Cincinnati were indiscreet, again without detailed factual support. The public creditors were divided "according to their former predilections and attachments." The evidence of preconcerted "system" in the Federalist campaign for adoption "appears rather from the effect than from any

---

38. The document is in the George Bryan Papers, HSP. It clearly follows Burke's questions in numbered sequence and was probably prepared by Samuel Bryan. Elbridge Gerry also had a copy of the questionnaire but never read it. It was among papers in a trunk stolen from him while he was en route from New York to Marblehead after adjournment of the first session. Elbridge Gerry to Ann Gerry, November 15, 1789, Gerry Papers, MHS. Burke's questionnaire and Bryan's response are set out in Saul Cornell, "Reflections on 'The Late Revolution in Government': Aedanus Burke and Samuel Bryan's Unpublished History of the Ratification of the Federal Constitution," *Pennsylvania Magazine of History and Biography*, 117 (January 1988): 103–30.

certain knowledge beforehand." The press, largely dependent on the people of the towns, was generally favorable. There had been some interference with the mails. This was hardly the stuff required to support a polemic attacking the Constitution more than a year after it became effective and against the background of the recently approved amendments. The most divisive issues had not yet surfaced.

A broad attack on the goals of the framers and the processes by which the Constitution was ratified would have been out of phase with the realities of the political environment in 1790. On the theoretical level, Lance Banning has pointed out that the "classical republican foundations of American constitutional thought taught that a constitution, once established, changed only for the worse." Thus, the "accepted task for friends of liberty was neither counterrevolution nor reform. It was to guard against social and political degeneration, to force a strict adherence to the original principles of a government, to see that things became no worse."[39] On Burke's theory of the major events, his history would have constituted a direct attack on the legitimacy of the constitutional settlement, and might well have been perceived as a revolutionary act. The performance of the First Congress had been well received. The timing would not have been right to break from the tradition of watchful suspicion. Moreover, he would have found little support either at home or in Congress. The General Assembly in January readily accepted the twelve amendments submitted and rejected New York's call for a second convention as "inexpedient" because Congress had already acted on amendments, in each case without a division. The South Carolina congressional delegation was merely instructed to request that Congress take up the abandoned amendments again.[40] There was little interest in Congress. Early in the second session, the House appointed a committee to follow the progress of the pending amendments in the several states, but refused without a vote to direct that the committee report on "what other and further amendments . . . are necessary to be recommended by the House at present."[41]

---

39. Lance Banning, *The Jeffersonian Persuasion: Evolution of a Party Ideology* (Ithaca: Cornell University Press, 1978), 113.
40. *JHR 1789–1790*, 349–51, 374.
41. *Annals*, 2: 1621.

More importantly, the focus of national politics had shifted significantly. Controversy no longer centered on the issues debated by Federalists and Antifederalists during the ratification proceedings and in the early months of the First Congress. With the eruption of debate on the location of the seat of government in late August and September 1789, the old politics of constitutional principle became less important than a new politics of interest, and clear lines of sectional conflict emerged. The constitutional issues remained; but they were reflected principally in debate on other measures, tools employed in pursuit of goals other than constitutional revision.

Burke left Charleston in December to return to New York. Just prior to his departure, he attended the formal opening of the new United States District Court in South Carolina and administered the oath of office to William Drayton as judge of that court.[42] Personally, as his interest in a history of "the late remarkable revolution in Government" showed, he remained an unconvinced structural Antifederalist, fearful of centralized power and aristocratic pretensions. Although disappointed, he was perhaps not surprised. Early in the first session, before amendments to the Constitution were seriously debated, he had feared that no significant amendments could be effected. "Your high flying monarchical Gentry (and I am sorry to find they abound in New York as well as in Carolina) will oppose all amendments," he wrote Richard Hampton in May 1789. "The wealthy powerful families throughout the union, ridicule the notion, and will prevent it if possible."[43] Nothing had happened to change that view or to ease his suspicions of a monarchical faction.

Letters from Burke to Samuel Bryan in early 1790 suggest that Burke's contemplated history was still alive. Burke thanked Bryan "for the attention you have bestowed on the Commission of mine which you were so obliging as to engage in." Some "papers" were clearly delivered. And Burke was definitely in touch with Colonel Eleazer Oswald, publisher of the *Independent Gazetteer* in Philadelphia, a connection that Senator William Maclay would later note.[44] Burke may have been writing inci-

42. *Gazette of the United States,* December 30, 1789.
43. Burke to Richard Hampton, May 10, 1789, James T. Mitchell Autograph Collection, HSP.
44. Burke to Samuel Bryan, February 5 and 10, 1790, and Burke to Samuel Bryan, March 3, 1790, Miscellaneous Letters, R.G. 59, National Archives.

dental pieces for publication by Oswald, but no comprehensive articulation of Burke's fears in the aftermath of his disappointing experience in the first session of the First Congress has yet come to light.

In due course, ten of the twelve amendments submitted to the states were ratified, known to all thereafter as the Bill of Rights. Nine were "rights" or "protective" amendments and the tenth was declaratory of the proposition that powers not granted to the federal government were reserved to the states or the people. Two amendments, one designed to increase representation in the House of Representatives as population increased and another providing that no increase in congressional compensation could take effect until after the next election to the House, were rejected. But the reception was not wholly enthusiastic. Virginia ratified only in late 1791 and Massachusetts never did, until a symbolic ratification was recorded in 1941 to commemorate the sesquicentennial of the ratification of the Bill of Rights.[45] The ideologically oriented structural Antifederalists were not satisfied, but the public at large had long since turned its attention to other issues.

---

45. Robert A. Rutland, *The Birth of the Bill of Rights, 1776–1791* (Chapel Hill: University of North Carolina Press, 1955), 216–18. Connecticut and Georgia also symbolically ratified in 1941. Virginia's reluctant approval in 1791 and continuing efforts to stimulate interest in further amendments are described in Richard R. Beeman, *The Old Dominion and the New Nation, 1788–1801* (Lexington: University of Kentucky Press, 1972), 60–66.

VIII

Congressman Burke

1790–1791

Toward the end of its first session, the House of Representatives resolved to consider measures for support of the public credit and directed Alexander Hamilton, the new Secretary of the Treasury, to prepare an appropriate plan for submission at the next session. In response to that directive, Hamilton's famous Report on Public Credit was delivered to Congress in January 1790.[1] The ensuing debate dominated the business of the session. More importantly, with the emergence of controversy explicitly based on conflicting state interests, the intensity of proceedings on the floor of the House materially increased. Exacerbated by a disruptive interlude on the status of slavery and the slave trade, and by the byzantine maneuverings of various states to fix the permanent seat of government to their advantage, the relative restraint evident during the first session was shattered in the second.

Hamilton's financial plan, skillfully constructed to appeal to the broadest possible range of conservative constituencies, was clearly designed to strengthen the central government in relation to the states and to promote commercial capitalism. Congress held virtually unlimited power to tax under the new Constitution; and that power had been confirmed at the first session when Tucker's proposed limitation was decisively rejected. Hamilton's proposals completed the circle. War-related state debts would be assumed, thus becoming the direct obligations of the national government in parity with the existing national debt. The enlarged national debt would be rationalized and funded by the commitment of national revenues to the payment of principal and interest in specie. No distinction would be

---

1. *Annals*, 1: 1043–45, 1056. The resolution calling for the report was adopted September 21, 1789. *Annals*, 1: 904.

drawn between the original and subsequent holders of outstanding instruments adverse to the interests of the latter, whether speculators or not. A variety of alternatives were offered existing security holders, in the aggregate designed to reduce the interest payable on the existing national debt by an amount sufficient to assure that the additional burden of interest on the state debts to be assumed would be manageable. Possible alternative means less well suited to the larger end were rejected.[2]

Two major issues arose in the extended debate on Hamilton's program. The first involved the question whether subsequent assignees of outstanding securities, presumably speculators who purchased at a fraction of face amount, should be treated less favorably than the original holders. The second, more serious and more protracted, involved the proposed assumption of state debts, a matter of vital interest to South Carolina. Burke was engaged on both issues, and his performance was punctuated by two notable explosions.

Concerned South Carolinians had focused on the question of assumption long before Hamilton's report was presented to Congress. Indeed, at the Philadelphia convention John Rutledge had actively sought an explicit provision on assumption in the new Constitution.[3] The effort failed for reasons of expediency, but the South Carolinians were entitled to expect that the matter would be presented for consideration by the First Congress as soon as practicable. In late December 1789, before Hamilton's report was issued, Ralph Izard wrote from New York asking Edward Rutledge to obtain "as soon as possible the sentiments of the members of the Legislature upon the subject of the adoption of our state debt by Congress. If a vote in favor of the measure could be obtained, it would put it in my power to speak with greater confidence than by being possessed simply of the opinions of individuals." Assumption "would be of infinite advantage to our

---

2. E. James Ferguson, *The Power of the Purse: A History of American Public Finance, 1776–1790* (Chapel Hill: University of North Carolina Press, 1961), 289–305. The legislative history of the funding and assumption issues, including Hamilton's report, appears in the *Documentary History of the First Federal Congress of the United States of America, March 4, 1789-March 3, 1791*, Vols. 4–6, *Legislative Histories*, Charlene Bangs Bickford and Helen E. Veit, eds. (Baltimore: Johns Hopkins University Press, 1986), 5: 713–937.
3. Kenneth R. Bowling, "Politics in the First Congress, 1789–1791" (Ph.D. dissertation, University of Wisconsin, Madison, 1968), 201–202. Massachusetts, through Elbridge Gerry, had also pressed for assumption at the convention.

State if the measure should be adopted," he said. Butler disagreed, Izard continued, "and I am told some of our members in the House of Representatives are in sentiment with him." The General Assembly responded with a resolution adopted in January 1790, instructing the congressional delegation to press Congress for assumption, the state's debt "having been incurred in Consequence of the War between the United States and the Kingdom of Great Britain." In addition, the governor was directed to obtain a statement of the state's accumulated debt for use by the delegates in advancing her claims.[4]

This directive was undoubtedly transmitted promptly to New York. The precise date of its arrival is uncertain, but it must been been received by mid-February. It clearly influenced Butler to support assumption despite personal reservations. "Circumstanced as our State is, and instructed as our Legislature have thought fit to place me, I shall assuredly vote for and support the assumption," he wrote Edward Rutledge, "but I believe posterity in Carolina will not thank me for it, or approve the measure."[5] The evidence suggests that it influenced Burke as well.

A clear majority in Congress favored funding of the outstanding national obligations from the outset. The only significant issue was the question of discrimination, whether the original holders would be treated more favorably than subsequent assignees. The substance of the debate opposed sanctity of contract and the requirements of the public credit to the evils of speculation, which no one was quite prepared to deny. Smith and Burke, after a moment's hesitation, were with the opposition and against many of their southern colleagues. But however contentious, the debate was over before the end of February when Madison's motion in support of discrimination was beaten by a comfortable margin.[6]

Burke was quiet at the outset of the discussion on Hamilton's plan and entered the debate with some awkwardness. Tucker spoke up early for discrimination. At the end of the

---

4. Ralph Izard to Edward Rutledge, December 29, 1789, in Ulrich B. Phillips, ed., "South Carolina Federalist Correspondence, 1789–1797," *American Historical Review*, 14 (1908–1909): 776–90, at 777–78; Ralph Izard to Gabriel Manigault, December 19, 1789, Izard Papers, SCL; *JHR 1789–1790*, 357, 375.
5. Butler to Edward Rutledge, May 15, 1790, Letterbook of Pierce Butler, 1790–1794, Pierce Butler Papers, SCL.
6. *Annals*, 2: 1298. Madison's motion was defeated 13 to 36.

day on February 10, Burke joined in by formally proposing that "discrimination be made between the original holders and their assignees, and that a scale of depreciation be prepared accordingly." But the next day, he withdrew his proposal of the day before, saying that he had presented it "in consequence of a hasty promise given a member of this House" and that he did not mean to support it or vote for it.[7] Madison promptly took up the cause, probably to gather political capital in Virginia, and was thereafter its leading advocate.[8]

A week later, Burke explained his position. He had withdrawn his proposal, he said, because "on further consideration he deemed it altogether impracticable, and because he was not convinced that such a measure was honest and consistent with the public faith." Payment of a specific sum certain had been promised, he continued, and violation of the promise would be both unjust and impolitic, a "breach of honor" and "such a public calamity as no money can compensate." He regretted that speculators would profit, but their advantage "could not justify him, in his own mind, in giving a vote that would give a stab to the good faith and credit of a nation in whose councils he had the honor of a suffrage." A forfeiture of public faith, a loss of public credit, would be a national calamity. All other considerations were subordinate.[9]

Burke was similarly ambivalent when the debate first turned to assumption. South Carolina's large debt was contracted for the common cause, he observed, and a distinction between Continental and state debts so contracted was "a distinction without a difference." But "we ought to consider our ways and means, before we undertake a business of this enormous magnitude." He accordingly offered to support postponement of the matter, "because I wish not to be too precipitate. The political consequences which may arise to the State Governments give me some alarm, and that makes me still more desirous of the postponement."[10]

By the next day his doubts were set aside, and he withdrew his earlier reservations. The state governments might be weakened, but it was "too late to object as the Constitution is already

---

7. *Annals*, 2: 1182, 1191.
8. Ferguson, *Power of the Purse*, 298–99.
9. *Annals*, 2: 1292–95.
10. Ibid., 2: 1318–19.

established, and it is our duty to plant it in the soil as firmly and as favorably to the liberties of the people as possible." He was therefore ready to support assumption as based on "honest and just principles." Later, questioning whether South Carolina could carry the burden of her debt, he worried about her creditors. South Carolina, he said, "was no more able to grapple with her enormous debt, than a boy of twelve years of age is to grapple with a giant." His state had done all she could, he continued, "and if she is now suffered to fall, every thinking man must lay the blame on the United States. After wheedling us into the Union, and wheedling us out of the impost, we must consider ourselves wretchedly duped if we are now abandoned to our fate."[11]

By early March, the shape of the controversy was reasonably clear. South Carolina and Massachusetts were aligned as the primary adherents to the assumption plan. Most of the other states were either indifferent or hostile. In particular, Maryland, Virginia, North Carolina, and Georgia, which had paid or provided for most of their war-related debts, were strongly opposed. Moreover, a general settlement of the accounts of the states was already in progress. South Carolina and Massachusetts in effect sought relief in advance of the general settlement, confidently expecting that they would be creditor states and possibly seeking protection against the risk that a final settlement might never mature. The other states had little to gain, feared that assumption would prejudice their respective interests in any final settlement, and were reluctant to bear any part of the burden of the substantial liabilities of South Carolina and Massachusetts. In addition, some actively opposed federal interposition to settle state debts. In part, this view reflected belief that the debts could be readily settled at less than face amount and without commitment to specie payment. It also reflected concern with the thrust for centralization of authority in the national government.[12]

---

11. *Gazette of the United States*, March 13, 1790 (as to first and second quoted passages); *Annals*, 2: 1362 (as to the third and fourth quoted passages). *Annals*, 2: 1332, reports the statements quoted from the *Gazette of the United States* as follows: "I had some apprehensions it would injure the State Governments; but it is now too late to think of that; the evil is too firmly planted in the soil to be removed by anything we can do."

12. Ferguson, *Power of the Purse*, 306–13.

While the lines of state interest were hardening on the assumption issue, the House was suddenly diverted by the presentation of three memorials from Quaker groups demanding clarification of the ambiguities of the Constitution on the status of the slave trade in particular and slavery in general. In the first, presented on February 11 by Thomas Fitzsimons of Pennsylvania on behalf of Quakers from Pennsylvania, New Jersey, Delaware, Maryland, and Virginia, the memorialists complained of "the licentious wickedness of the African trade for slaves, and the inhuman tyranny and blood guiltiness inseparable from it," and called for "a sincere and impartial inquiry" to determine whether Congress was empowered to effect "the abolition of the slave trade." On the same day, John Lawrence presented a similar petition from Quakers in New York, expressing their desire "to cooperate with their Southern brethren in their protest against the slave trade." The next day, a memorial of the Pennsylvania Society for promoting the Abolition of Slavery, signed for the Society by Benjamin Franklin, was presented and read. This memorial was much broader than the first two. "Your memorialists," it said, "conceive themselves bound to use all justifiable endeavors to loosen the bands of slavery, and promote a general enjoyment of the blessings of freedom." To that end, "they earnestly entreat your serious attention to the subject of slavery; that you will be pleased to countenance the restoration of liberty to those unhappy men, who alone, in this land of freedom, are degraded into perpetual bondage, and who, amidst the general joy of surrounding freemen, are groaning in servile subjection; . . . and that you will step to the very verge of the power vested in you for discouraging every species of traffic in the persons of our fellow-men." These memorials were the product of a calculated and well-organized campaign; and nothing else could have served so well to arouse the outraged indignation of the representatives of the states in the deep South.[13]

When the first memorials were presented on February 11, Smith and Burke were immediately on their feet. Burke was particularly aggressive. "The rights of the Southern States ought not to be threatened," he said, "and their property endangered, to

---

13. *Annals*, 2: 1182–84, 1197–98. See Howard A. Ohline, "Slavery, Economics, and Congressional Politics, 1790," *Journal of Southern History*, 46 (1980): 335–60.

please people who would be unaffected by the consequences." He respected the Quakers, but "did not believe they had more virtue or religion than other people, nor perhaps so much, if they were examined to the bottom, notwithstanding their outward pretences." In this case, they were meddling "in business with which they had nothing to do; they were volunteering in the cause of others, who had neither expected nor desired it." Madison tried to calm the ruffled water. The matter was only important as opposition made it so, he suggested. Had the House permitted the memorial to be committed as a matter of course, "no notice would have been taken of it out of doors."[14]

The debate continued on February 12. Smith, Tucker, and Burke contended that the request was unconstitutional on its face and should therefore be dismissed. If committed, Burke said, "the commitment would sound an alarm, and blow the trumpet of sedition in the Southern States." Smith was also concerned that even debate on the subject would create alarm. "We have been told," he said, "that if this would be the case we ought to have avoided it, by saying nothing; but it was not for that purpose that we were sent here. We look upon this measure as an attack upon the palladium of the prosperity of our country; it is therefore our duty to oppose it by every means in our power." The memorials were nevertheless referred to a committee for consideration. Smith, Tucker, and Burke were all opposed. Huger joined them in one of his few recorded appearances. Sumter was not present. The vote was 43 to 14.[15]

The committee report was submitted on March 8 and consideration scheduled for the following week. The debate began late in the day on March 16 and was resumed the following morning. Burke took the floor early in the day and delivered a vitriolic attack on the substance of the memorials and the good faith of the Quakers. "I do not rise," he said, "to advocate the cause of slavery. I am on the contrary a friend to civil liberty, but I rise as an advocate for the protection of the property, the order, and the tranquility of the state to which I belong." The southern states were neither the authors of slavery nor guilty of the tyranny and despotism of which they had been accused. If slavery were a crime, which Burke denied, the British nation was answerable for

14. *Annals*, 2: 1186, 1189.
15. Ibid., 2: 1197–1205.

it. Slavery was a beneficent institution, he argued at length, under which the slaves were treated "with all the humanity and mildness consistent with the good order of the community and duties of industry." Emancipation would be "impolitic and mischievous to the public interest" and would be a disaster for the slaves.[16]

Who were these Quakers, Burke asked, "who would make us believe they came forward as volunteers in the cause of freedom?" Were they not, during the war, the avowed friends and supporters of the most abject slavery, "a slavery attempted on their countrymen from the disgraceful galling yoke of foreigners?" They acted as spies for the enemy, "for no other purpose but to rivet the shackles of slavery on their country." Now they have assumed another mask, that of enemies of slavery, offering one hand in friendship and wielding in the other "a torch to set flame to one part of the Union and sow discord through the whole of it," holding out the pretext of emancipation in the South and sowing the seeds of insurrection and public calamity in the North. "The Quakers, and the schemes they are now agitating," he continued, drawing again on his store of allusions from *Paradise Lost*, "put me in mind of Milton's Lucifer, who entered Paradise in the shape of a cormorant." Here Burke was called to order, as wandering from the point under debate and treating the Quakers with too much severity. He was in duty bound, he replied, "to paint the Quakers in their true colours; a sett of men, who, under the cloak of religion; with the pretenses of a religious society, are night and day carrying on the arts and management of a political faction." Interrupted again, Burke declared that "he would quit the Quakers, for the present," and surrendered the floor to Smith.[17]

Smith was calmer, more politic, but in substance little less critical of the Quakers. "When any class of men deviated from their own religious principles," he said, "and officially came forward in a business with which they had no concern, and attempted to dictate to Congress, he could not ascribe their conduct to any other cause but to an intolerant spirit of persecution. This application came with the worst grace possible from the Quakers, who professed never to intermeddle in politics, but

---

16. *New York Daily Advertiser*, March 19, 1790.
17. Ibid.

to submit quietly to the laws of the country." He then embarked on an extended justification and defense of the South's "peculiar institution," the first and possibly one of the most thoughtful of the genre. The North knew the South had its slaves, he suggested, and the South knew the North had its Quakers. "We therefore made a compromise on both sides—we took each other with our mutual bad habits and respective evils, for better or for worse; the Northern States adopted us with our slaves, and we adopted them with their Quakers."[18]

Burke returned the following day to defend himself against the charge of undue severity toward the Quakers. The memorials, he said, constituted "a solemn application to Congress to commit a public robbery of the southern inhabitants of a property vested in them under the laws, and guaranteed by a most solemn engagement of the Union." But the memorialists sought more. "They are seeking to strip us of the little strength and resources we have; and to weaken the southern states, weak and feeble enough already; they are eagerly striving to excite private conspiracies, and finally to raise the standard of insurrection in our country." And now the southern states were faced with a report that fully justified their apprehensions. The Quakers, Burke concluded, "came forward to the bar of this house and accuse the citizens of our state as being despots and tyrants, and as men steeped in *blood guiltiness*, as they call it." Surely the accused were entitled to show the true character of their accusers.[19]

On March 23, after nearly a week of continuous debate, the House amended and then approved the report of the special committee by the narrow margin of four votes, 29 to 25. The debate was over, and the southerners had won an important point. The third clause of the amended report explicitly acknowledged that Congress had no authority to legislate on the institution of slavery as it existed in any of the several states, "it remaining with the several States alone to provide any regulation therein, which humanity and true policy may require." The institution of slavery was thus explicitly acknowledged and legiti-

---

18. *Annals*, 2: 1453–64, quotes at 1453 and 1458. One reason the southerners were so upset was that, in their view, a bargain had been made at Philadelphia favoring northern interests in trade and southern landed interests in slaves. The South had kept its part of the bargain in the first session.
19. *New York Daily Advertiser*, March 20, 1790; CGDA, April 29, 1790.

mized as a matter of state concern, a step beyond the mere recognition of its existence reflected in the Constitution.[20]

With the disruptive debate on the Quaker memorials behind it, the House returned to the assumption issue. Already an element of rancor had appeared. James Jackson of Georgia, for example, had attacked the merits of South Carolina's claim. On March 1, he announced his opposition to the whole concept of assumption, "not only in its original form, but in every possible modification it might assume." He found no strong majority of states or individuals pressing the matter. Assumption was therefore not warranted on grounds of expediency. Nor did it constitute sound policy. Hamilton was able but not infallible. "Ambition," he argued, "laudable, perhaps, to do the utmost for the Union, might lead him too far." Assumption was proposed, he continued, for one of two purposes. First, it was "extended as an additional ligature to the Continent, by detaching the creditors from their dependence on the State Governments, and transferring that dependence to the nation, and thereby making it the interest of the remote parts of the Union to support its measures." Or, second, it was designed, "by this specious method of relieving the States, to remove every pretext for taxation from them, and thereby throw that power directly into the hands of Congress." Neither purpose would support assumption on policy grounds. Funded debt was a mortgage on the future of the new nation in the vigor of its youth. And assumption would create divisive jealousies among the people, "for will the citizen, who has already paid his proportion of the debt to his state, contentedly see a new burden imposed on himself and his posterity?" Georgia's citizens, Jackson concluded, had suffered in the war more than most but had nonetheless "cheerfully submitted to the payment of the State debt." They should not now be asked to share in the payment of debts of Massachusetts and South Carolina, particularly those related to such frolics as the Penobscot expedition mounted by the former and the naval pretensions of the latter in acquiring and fitting out the frigate *South Carolina*. "If those States have not done as they ought, if they have not extinguished their debts, they have only themselves to blame." In

---

20. *Annals*, 2: 1472–74; Ohline, "Slavery, Economics and Congressional Politics, 1790."

response to Smith's restrained defense of South Carolina's expenditures, Jackson was even sharper. South Carolina had no legal authority to fit out a ship of war, he insisted. Not content to be on equal terms with her sister states, she "aimed at a high sounding fame, of possessing vessels of war in her own employ."[21]

Burke joined the debate on March 24 with a detailed and somewhat overblown defense of the *South Carolina* enterprise and his friend, Commodore Gillon. In the course of it, he said something of himself and, indirectly, of his feeling for his adopted state. "I have not the honor of being a native of it," he observed, "so that I shall not be charged with vanity or ostentation. Such was the native generosity of that people, that they thought no expense too great; such their gallantry and spirit of enterprise, that though comparatively few in number, yet they deemed no danger or undertaking too arduous for them in the common cause." Burke described the enterprise as essential to protect the flow of supplies purchased abroad. Jackson laconically replied that he still opposed assumption.[22]

Burke's speech was unexceptionable in its substance on this occasion, but within a week he was in hot water once again. As the debate proceeded, criticisms became sharper and comparisons more invidious. Among other things, the contribution of the Southern militia was put in question. On March 31, Burke rose to respond, and, in the course of his address, he launched a personal attack on Alexander Hamilton that nearly precipitated a duel. The incident is not reflected in the pages of the *Annals*. But Senator Pierce Butler and William Loughton Smith were there and reported in full.

Butler was in attendance because the Senate had adjourned early. By his account, Burke took the occasion to praise the gallantry of the South Carolina militia "notwithstanding, said he, the affront given them by a Gentleman now high in office, in a place, and at a time when it could not be resented; he took an unfair advantage and I now embrace the opportunity to say in the presence of this house that it was a lye; and that Col. Hamil-

---

21. *Annals*, 2: 1378–84, quotes at 1378, 1379, 1380, 1381, and 1384.
22. Ibid., 2: 1484–86, quote at 1485. Jackson later analogized assumption to the case of an individual who would monopolize the debts of another to keep him in subjection. *Annals*, 2: 1507–508.

ton told a gross lye." Butler was "surprised and hurt," he continued. "How must it end? They are both men of spirit. I wish that neither of them had expressed themselves as they did. Hamilton has a large family depending much on his life I believe."[23] Butler knew Burke well. By implication, at least, he seemed to be suggesting that Burke was wholly capable of taking care of himself in a duel if need be.

Smith's account covered the same ground and more. "A gentleman now high in office," Burke charged, "in a public assembly called this militia, these brave men, the very mimickry of Soldiery—Sir in behalf of these brave men I give the lie to Colonel Hamilton, yes, in the face of this Assembly and in the presence of this gallery . . . I say I give the lie to Colonel Hamilton."[24] Here, according to Smith, Burke was called to order. When a friend of Hamilton's suggested that Burke was mistaken, that no aspersion had been cast on the South Carolina militia, Burke refused to retreat and proceeded to explain why he had not taken notice of the matter sooner.

> The observation, said he, was like a dagger in my breast, but it was impossible for me to notice it at the time; I was called an antifederalist, the people of this city were all federalists, Mr. Hamilton was the Hero of the day and the favorite of the people and had I hurt a hair of his head, I'm sure I should have been dragged thru the Kennels of New York and pitched headlong into the East River. But now I have an opportunity in as public a manner of retorting the lie which he gave to the character of the Militias.[25]

The occasion of Hamilton's remarks to which Burke took exception was a eulogy to General Greene delivered at St. Paul's Church in New York on July 4, 1789. Most of the Senate and the House of Representatives and many other dignitaries were present. The Cincinnati were present in full splendor, sitting in reserved seats and wearing their medals, a circumstance perhaps sufficient in itself to put Burke on edge. In the written version of his address, Hamilton criticized the Southern militia, if at all,

23. Pierce Butler to Alexander Gillon, March 31, 1790, Butler Letterbook, 1790–1794, SCL.

24. William Loughton Smith to Edward Rutledge, April 2, 1790, in "The Letters of William Loughton Smith to Edward Rutledge, June 8, 1789 to April 28, 1794," George C. Rogers, Jr., ed., *SCHM*, 69 (1968): 111–14.

25. Ibid.

only by implication, attributing most of Greene's success in the South to the Continental forces under his command. The words offensive to Burke related to an earlier engagement in the North. "From the heights of Monmouth I might lead you to the plains of Springfield," Hamilton said, "there to behold the Veteran Knyphaussen at the head of a veteran army baffled and almost beaten by a General without an army—aided or rather embarrassed by small fugitive bodies of volunteer militia, the mimicry of soldiership." That was all.[26]

Burke's outburst was followed by the elaborate ritual prescribed for affairs of honor. According to Smith, Hamilton was promptly informed of the insult and determined to proceed with deliberation. "He said he should at all times disregard any observations applied to his public station as Secretary of the Treasury," Smith continued, "but that *this* was not to be passed over."[27] On April 1, Hamilton wrote Burke, enclosing the portion of his address previously quoted, and suggesting that Burke had misunderstood his remarks. Having stated the matter in its true light, Hamilton said, "it remains for you to judge what conduct, in consequence of the explanation will be proper on your part."[28] Burke replied the same day, explaining his feelings and motives and believing that his conduct would stand inquiry by men of sensibility and honor.

> The attack which I conceived you made on the southern Militia, was, in my opinion a most unprovoked and cruel one. Whether the candour of your friends conveyed to you any intimation of it I know not: but the occasion will, I hope, excuse me if I assure you that Gentlemen from every quarter of the Union who were present deemed it a charge of a very extraordinary nature. As to myself, I have nothing to do respecting the feelings of others: I ever govern myself by my own. The insult, which I conceived was thrown at

---

26. Alexander Hamilton, "Eulogy on Nathanael Greene, July 4, 1789," in *Papers of Alexander Hamilton*, 26 vols., Harold C. Syrett and Jacob E. Cooke, eds. (New York: Columbia University Press, 1961–1977), 5: 345–59. The presence of the Cincinnati was noted by Senator William Maclay. *Journal of William Maclay, United States Senator from Pennsylvania, 1789–1791*, Edgar S. Maclay, ed. (New York: Albert & Charles Boni, 1927), 98.

27. William Loughton Smith to Edward Rutledge, April 2, 1790, in "Letters of William Loughton Smith," Rogers, ed.

28. Alexander Hamilton to Aedanus Burke, April 1, 1790, in *Papers of Alexander Hamilton*, Syrett and Cooke, eds., 6: 333–35.

me. The too keen misery I felt from it; the recollection I had of it until yesterday: together with the concurrent testimony of a number of public, and private men who understood you as I did must be with me, vouchers of equal authenticity with the extract you quote from your performance, which you will recollect you did not read in the delivery of it to the public. That you proclaimed aloud in the face of, I may say, thousands that the Militia were the mere Mimicry of Soldiery: That you spoke these words when you ran into the affairs of the War to the southward, and recounted the exploits of General Greene in that quarter, is not doubted and you will find it on inquiry in this City. You may have forgot it, but some of your Friends and all your acquaintances have not forgot it.[29]

The next move was Hamilton's.

The quarrel was ultimately resolved through the good offices of six members of Congress—Elbridge Gerry of Massachusetts, Senator Rufus King of New York, George Mathews and James Jackson of Georgia, Senator John Henry of Maryland, and Lambert Cadwalader of Pennsylvania. According to Burke, the accommodation was initiated by Hamilton through King and accepted by Burke through Gerry.[30] The report of the arbitrators concluded that nothing more was necessary to an accommodation between the parties than "a right understanding of each other." And they were satisfied that, although Burke had not taken Hamilton's letter of April 1 as "an explicit Disavowal of an intention in any part of the Eulogium delivered by him, to cast a reflection upon militia in general, or upon the militia of South Carolina in particular," Hamilton's intention had been to make such a disavowal. Accordingly, another exchange of letters was suggested—an explicit declaration of intention by Hamilton, and a full and satisfactory apology by Burke. And so it was done.[31] But the tension

---

29. Burke to Hamilton, April 1, 1790, in *Papers of Alexander Hamilton*, Syrett and Cooke, eds., 6: 335–37. This letter concluded with an explanation for the delay in Burke's response to Hamilton's original remarks similar in all material respects to Smith's account.
30. Burke comment noted on copy of Burke to Hamilton, April 1, 1790, in *Papers of Alexander Hamilton*, Syrett and Cooke, eds., 6: 335–37.
31. Elbridge Gerry, Rufus King, George Mathews, Lambert Cadwalader, James Jackson, and John Henry to Hamilton, April 6, 1790, and Burke to Hamilton, April 7, 1790, in *Papers of Alexander Hamilton*, Syrett and Cooke, eds., 6: 353–55, 357–58. The letter from Hamilton to Burke has been lost but is explicitly described in Burke's reply. Thus, Hamilton wrote first.

was high while it lasted. "The town is much agitated about a duel between Burke and Hamilton," Senator William Maclay of Pennsylvania noted in his journal on April 4. "So many people concerned in the business may really make the fools fight."[32]

Why did Burke explode against Hamilton as he did and when he did? From his personal perspective, he perhaps had ample reason to dislike and distrust Hamilton. Hamilton had been a leading figure in the Society of the Cincinnati and, indeed, had opposed Washington's attempt to mitigate the features of the Society most objectionable to its critics. Burke presumably knew of Hamilton's famous speech at the Philadelphia convention in support of executive power and aristocratic government. Despite the pledge of secrecy to which the delegates to the convention were committed, Hamilton's argument was in the public domain. And there may have been a more immediate and more personal basis for antipathy. Burke was "amazingly intimate" with Governor George Clinton of New York and was reportedly courting one of Clinton's daughters, according to Smith's initial account of Burke's outburst. "Clinton hates Hamilton mortally and has probably set on Burke," Smith said.[33]

These considerations seem hardly adequate. Hamilton's aspersions on the militia, if such they were, were all but forgotten except, perhaps, by the ultrasensitive. Sharper commentary than Hamilton's was common currency in the House of Representatives in March 1790. Moreover, according to an account of his speech published some two weeks after the fact, Burke "insisted that he had never been more guarded and cool in his life." Burke defended his action as related to the business before the House. "Not only the claim on the union for the services of the militia, but the substance and reality of those services, and the national military character of the people, was not only doubted, but denied, by a gentleman, whose assertion, from his high station and talents, must have had some weight."[34] Yet that same gentleman was the proponent of the plan, including particularly the imme-

---

32. *Journal of William Maclay*, Maclay, ed., 226.
33. William Loughton Smith to Edward Rutledge, April 2, 1790, "Letters of William Loughton Smith," Rogers, ed.
34. *Greenleaf's New York Journal & Patriotic Register*, April 15, 1790, quoted in *Papers of Alexander Hamilton*, Syrett and Cooke, eds., 6: 334–35. An original copy of this issue of the *Journal*, marked in Butler's hand "Bourkes speech," is in the Pierce Butler Papers, HSP.

diate assumption of state debts incurred in the nation's cause, that Burke and Smith were so vigorously supporting. If Burke was as guarded and cool as he claimed, he was at least impolitic.

There is another possible explanation, more complex and more speculative. Burke had been frustrated at the first session in the matter of amendments to the Constitution. Those he deemed most important were rejected. In the second session, he found himself actively supporting, for expedient reasons of state interest, and perhaps against his own best judgment, measures that supported and extended the centralization of governmental power that he professed to fear. Burke's private views were expressed in early March. Congress was daily involved in Hamilton's report, he wrote Samuel Bryan. "I know no man in either house who is not totally at a Loss on this important subject. Funding the debt, is the word at present, but no one can tell which way it will end. Funding the debt may, or may not be, a blessing or a Curse to the people of America for ought I can say, at present. But this I sincerely regret. It will add strength and power to that faction that brought about the late . . . revolution, and it will render them princely fortunes. You may judge that I stand in a particular situation not agreeable to me."[35] Burke could not have been unaware of the ambiguity of his position. In effect, he had compromised his principles and surrendered some part of his intellectual consistency. In conflict with himself, he finally lashed out at the most convenient target, a man he neither liked nor trusted, and the sponsor of the plan he was constrained by expediency and the directive of South Carolina's General Assembly to support.

The fracas with Hamilton apparently ended whatever prospects Burke may have had for a major presence in the House. For the balance of his term, he was an occasionally visible but never a leading figure. Apart from the casting of his vote, he played no significant role in the ultimate resolution of the assumption issue, concluded favorably to the hopes of South Carolina.[36] Routine appearances and committee assignments continued, but Burke was not again the vocal spokesman for South Carolina's interests that he had theretofore been.

---

35. Burke to Samuel Bryan, March 3, 1790, Miscellaneous Letters, R.G. 59, National Archives.
36. Ferguson, *Power of the Purse*, 319–25.

More importantly, Burke lost standing in his own delegation. Prior to his attack on Hamilton. Burke shared advocacy of South Carolina's cause with Smith. At the end of February, Smith complained to Edward Rutledge that Tucker had not stepped strongly forward on the assumption issue. The whole burden, he said, "has fallen on myself and Burke, who has behaved exceedingly well hitherto in this business: he has taken a decided part and came forward manfully." But on April 2, Smith reported that "Burke has been warmly with us but his mode of speaking and his roughness only excite Laughter." Moreover, by the violence of his attack on Hamilton, he had precipitated "a very disagreeable matter" and his conduct in that affair was "highly reprobated by everybody I have met with."[37]

Smith was also critical of Sumter, whom he considered "more a delegate from Virginia than of our state." When Jackson argued that the backcountry of South Carolina opposed assumption because it would deprive them of power in the state, Smith persuaded Sumter to abandon his opposition. An adverse vote by Sumter, Smith argued, would result in "evil consequences which would flow from an apparent disunion among the members of our State" and that Sumter's constituents "might sit uneasy under the measure" if he persisted in opposition to it. Of all his colleagues from South Carolina, Smith preferred Huger, who was unfortunately sick throughout the session, because "he votes right and behaves like a gentleman."[38]

The disruptive interlude of the Quaker memorials, coming as it did in the midst of the increasingly strident debate over assumption, left the House less disposed than ever toward conciliation and compromise. The vehemence of the proponents of assumption, and particularly Burke's attack on Hamilton, undoubtedly contributed. The impact of these diversions cannot be weighed, but on April 12 the House rejected assumption in a close vote. Thereafter, the House turned to other matters, including the equally divisive issue of the seat of government, and the contest over assumption was transferred to the Senate. There it remained through June, while the Senate also struggled with the

---

37. William Loughton Smith to Edward Rutledge, February 28, 1790, and April 2, 1790, in "Letters of William Loughton Smith," Rogers, ed., *SCHM*, 69 (1968): 107–10, 111–14.
38. William Loughton Smith to Edward Rutledge, July 4, July 25, and August 8, 1790, in "Letters of William Loughton Smith," Rogers, ed., *SCHM*, 69 (1968): 120–27, 130–38.

several interests contending for the advantages incident to location of the national capital. Finally, in late June, a deal was struck, negotiated at the highest level with the participation of Hamilton and Jefferson, to resolve both issues. Philadelphia would have the seat of government for ten years, during which a new capital city would be established on the Potomac River, representing a major benefit to Virginia long sought but theretofore beyond reach. The compromise was completed when enough Virginian and other votes previously cast against assumption were changed and assumption was finally carried in the House. Implementation took some time, however, and the debate proceeded in the interim.[39]

The Senate responded promptly to the compromise and forwarded its bill on the seat of government to the House on July 1. In the House, a motion was made to substitute Baltimore for the Potomac site, probably representing a tactical maneuver in opposition to transfer of the interim seat from New York to Philadelphia. Burke supported the motion and, in the process, managed one final scene confirming his volatile personality. A flourishing, trading, populous town was preferable to a wilderness, he said. The Potomac site was a "mere desert." The idea was chimerical, visionary, impracticable. Moreover, he opposed the interim move to Philadelphia. Once established there, the government would be all but impossible to move to another location "from the immense weight and influence of that wealthy power, state, and city." These advantages were the very "circumstance which give a serious jealousy—that if they have the government for ten years . . . they will have more weight and influence in the union than any three states in it." The Pennsylvanians maneuvered for that advantage from the beginning, raising "a tempest which has shaken not only these walls, and this city, but has agitated the continent." If the government located for ten years in Philadelphia, an even more strenuous effort to keep it would be made at the end of that time. "I will be bold to say," he proclaimed, "they would threaten to part from the union," and he believed that they would do it.[40]

The presence of the Quakers was another reason for opposing Philadelphia, a very bad neighborhood for South Carolin-

39. Bowling, "Politics in the First Congress," 176–86, 220–29.
40. *CGDA*, July 29, 1790 (extended account without attribution). A condensed account appears in *Annals*, 2: 1662–63.

ians. "I would as soon pitch my tent . . . beneath a tree in which was a hornet's nest," Burke said, "as I would as a delegate from South Carolina, vote for placing the government in a settlement of Quakers." He recalled their tactics in support of the memorials, "their hovering in the gallery during the debate; their incessant seizing and obtrusions on the members in their houses, in the streets, and in the lobby." Would they be less persevering, he asked, in their own city? At most, he concluded, the interim site should be split between New York and Philadelphia and the permanent site established in Baltimore.[41]

In the course of his remarks, Burke was called to order at least once. As before, his excitable temper apparently carried him away. Except that this time there was no point to it at all. He was either participating in a tactical exercise or had no notion that a bargain had been made. "The general government is not yet settled," he complained; "no decisive measures adopted for establishing public credit; the funding bill, the ways and means, arrested and slept," all laid by for this "inauspicious business."[42]

Despite Burke's concerns, the affairs of the session were concluded in short order; funding and assumption were approved in support of the Hamiltonian plan to establish the public credit; the seat of government was finally established. With the completion of this business the session promptly adjourned, no doubt with considerable relief. From the executive chair, Washington moved quickly to confirm the Potomac site and to scotch any incipient Pennsylvanian expectation that the eventual move from Philadelphia might be avoided.[43]

Burke again returned to South Carolina after the session ended, presumably no happier than he had been at the end of the first. In all events, he did not stand for reelection in November. "None of our members to Congress met with any opposition," John Rutledge, Jr. reported to Thomas Jefferson. But "Burke declined being continued, and the part of the state from which he came, will be represented by Mr. Barnwell, a very virtuous and good citizen."[44] No evidence has appeared to corroborate this report or to explain it. But if the hypothesis is sound that

41. *CGDA*, July 29, 1790.
42. Ibid.
43. Bowling, "Politics in the First Congress," 193–99.
44. John Rutledge, Jr. to Thomas Jefferson, November 20, 1790, in *The Papers of Thomas Jefferson*, Julian P. Boyd, et al., eds., 22 vols. to date (Princeton: Princeton University Press, 1950–1986), 18: 52–54.

Burke's major objective was to pursue the structural amendments to the Constitution advocated by the Antifederalists in 1789, the explanation seems clear enough. That course was run and lost. Moreover, Burke must have sensed, even then, that his capacity to influence events was limited, and he must have been uncomfortable as William Loughton Smith's prestige rose and Hamilton's influence expanded. Perhaps he concluded that he could accomplish more in his own country. Whatever his reasons, he was the only member of the South Carolina delegation to return for the third session of the First Congress as a lame duck.

The third session convened on December 6, 1790. Smith was the only member of the South Carolina delegation present. Traveling by sea, Burke was shipwrecked off the Virginia Capes and had to complete the journey overland by wagon.[45] Ironically, Burke had apparently planned to take passage on a different ship. Elbridge Gerry was sharing quarters with Huger and Burke in Philadelphia. When Gerry arrived, he was informed by a colleague "that Judge Burke was to have taken passage with him but dining with Governor Pinckney neglected to come on board" and would probably take the next vessel. "This is like the Judge," Gerry commented to his wife.[46]

Apart from the excitement of his journey, Burke's lame duck session was anticlimactic. There were no explosions; and there was very little fire. He did, however, regain some of his intellectual consistency. On December 13, the day of his arrival in Philadelphia, Hamilton's Report on a National Bank was presented. The bill to incorporate the Bank originated and was considered first in the Senate. It did not reach the House until January 21. Debate began on February 1, and the measure was carried 39 to 20 on February 8. In the final vote, Smith was for, Burke and Tucker were against, Huger was not present, and Sumter had not yet arrived in Philadelphia.[47]

The debate occupied most of the period February 1 to February 8. Jackson of Georgia was opposed in principle and on constitutional grounds. Creation of a national bank, he said, "will

45. William Loughton Smith to Gabriel Manigault, December 19, 1790, in Ulrich B. Phillips, ed., "South Carolina Federalist Correspondence," *American Historical Review*, 14 (1908–1909): 779.
46. Elbridge Gerry to Ann Gerry, December 2, 1790, and December 5, 1790, Elbridge Gerry Papers, MHS.
47. *Annals*, 2: 1800, 1875, 1960. Sumter finally arrived on February 15. *Annals*, 2: 1963.

essentially interfere with the rights of the separate States, for it is not denied that they possess the power of instituting banks." Madison was also opposed on constitutional grounds and, in effect, took command of the opposition. Ames, Gerry, and Sedgwick of Massachusetts, Boudinot of New Jersey, and ultimately Smith led the debate in support. Insofar as the *Annals* show, Burke was totally silent.[48]

On other issues he was somewhat more vocal. In the debate on a new revenue bill designed to support the enlarged national debt by imposing excise taxes on spirits and other specified items, for example, he objected that the compensation of governmental revenue agents was delegated to the discretion of the Executive. He was sorry, he said, "to see such a disposition in many of the members of this House to extend the powers of the Executive." The contemplated excise system of direct taxes was "universally odious; and gentlemen seem to be trying to render this more odious, by urging one exceptionable clause after another." The legislature should retain the power to dispose of their own money. His ideas on the subject of executive power had been called chimeras, he observed, "but this was a stale trick, which had been long practiced by those who are in favor of strengthening the arm of the Executive." Nothing "should deter him from placing every possible guard round the liberties of the people, and checking the undue extension of the Executive arm."[49] This sounded more like the Burke of 1788.

He also spoke to the militia bill, complaining of the number of exemptions and the imposition of monetary penalties on those declining to serve on grounds of conscience. We boast, he said, that in this land of liberty no one suffers "on account of his conscientious scruples, and yet we are going to make a respectable class of citizens pay for a right to a free exercise of their religious principles."[50] With respect to the proposed exemptions, he argued that the effect would be to divide the country into "two

---

48. The debate is reported in *Annals*, 2: 1890–1960. The Jackson quote is at *Annals*, 2: 1917.
49. *Annals*, 2: 1874. Burke's reference to "chimeras" is probably to a remark by Charles Pinckney in the debate in the South Carolina House of Representatives in January 1788 that preceded the decision to call a ratifying convention. Pinckney said "that he ever treated all fears of aristocracies or despotisms, in the federal head, as the most childish chimeras that could be conceived." Elliot, *Debates*, 4: 259.
50. *Annals*, 2: 1818.

tribes; and the rich, the governors and the rulers of the land would be relieved from the burden, while the mechanics, the farmers, the laborers, the hard working people of the community would be made to sustain the whole weight of the service in defending the country." He opposed exempting members of Congress, who could serve during the periods of recess, as he had done in South Carolina. But he was not opposed to all exemptions. "He would exempt the people called Quakers, and all persons religiously scrupulous of bearing arms, stage drivers, and instructors of youth; but their pupils, the students in colleges and seminaries of learning, should not be exempt; youth is the proper time to acquire military knowledge."[51]

There was nothing unusual, for Burke, in these positions. Even for the Quakers, he would insist on freedom from coercion against conscience. But he had worked his way into a position from which he could not easily extricate himself. The confidence of important South Carolina colleagues had been shaken without compensating enhancement of prestige elsewhere. On Monday, December 26, just a few days after his observations on the militia bill, he met Senator William Maclay at the home of Dr. George Logan in Philadelphia, good republicans both. "This was the very man who, while in New York, railed so tremendously against the Quakers, and against Pennsylvania for having Quakers," Maclay noted in his journal. "Behold a wonder! Now he rails against slavery, extols Quakers, and blazes against the attentions showed to General Washington, which he calls idolatry; and that a party wish as much to make him a king as ever the flatterers of Cromwell wished to raise him to that dignity." Burke "said many just things," Maclay continued, "but he is too new a convert to merit confidence. I find, however, on examination, that this is the same man who wrote against the Cincinnati."[52] As Maclay's observation suggests, Burke had failed to establish a place even among those with whom he was intellectually attuned. And his reputation, such as it was, still rested principally on the *Considerations*.

In retrospect, looking back over his term in national office as a whole, Burke was by no means an inconsequential figure in the First Congress. The House of Representatives was a small group,

---

51. Ibid., 2: 1822.
52. *Journal of William Maclay*, Maclay, ed., 356–57.

approximately one-third the size of the South Carolina House, and each member had many parts to play. Burke's vote was recorded ninety-eight times. He served on thirty-three committees, more than any other member of the South Carolina delegation, and reported to the House on behalf of nine. He reported, for example, for committees appointed to consider and present bills providing for the compensation of officials in the executive department, members of the legislature, and the federal judiciary. He reported copyright and patent bills. In addition to the major committee assignments previously mentioned, on departmental organization and constitutional amendments, he served on committees to consider bills on the collection of duties, Indian trade, compensation for certain invalid officers, and means to encourage the commerce and navigation of the United States. He was on conference committees to resolve differences with the Senate on the judiciary act and the act establishing the postal service. Finally, he joined Gerry and Alexander White of Virginia on a committee directed to prepare and report on the collection of books necessary for the use of Congress, an assignment that foreshadowed the establishment of the Library of Congress.[53]

Burke found occasion to describe his concept of the ideal republican society. The country should be filled with useful men, he said in the debate on the naturalization bill, "such as farmers, mechanics, and manufacturers." These should be encouraged. Others, "such as your European merchants, and factors of merchants," who come only so long as necessary to make their fortunes and then leave with all their property, he did not think useful. He compared them to leeches, who "stick to us until they get their fill of our best blood and then they fall off and leave us."[54] Thus, the sentiments of the *Salutary Hints* still lingered with him.

Nevertheless, he could always be diverted by his jealous concerns, on small matters as well as large. Toward the end of the second session, for example, a post office bill was pending, and the Senate proposed an amendment permitting the postmaster

---

53. *Documentary History of the First Congress*, Vol. 3, *House of Representatives Journal*, Linda Grant DePauw, ed., index and references. The recorded votes of Smith, Tucker, Sumter, and Huger were 100, 100, 90, and 29, respectively. Smith sat on 28 committees and reported for 12; Tucker sat on 27 and reported for 4; Sumter sat on 4 and reported for none; Huger sat on none.
54. *Annals*, 1: 1117.

general to make regulations with respect to the distribution of newspapers. Among other things, in order to promote the dissemination of news, an abatement of charges could be authorized. Burke and Gerry objected, construing the proposal to permit discrimination in favor of a preferred paper. The proposal carried "the plainest outlines of a system to establish a court press and court Gazette; to give this paper a currency and circulation through all parts of the Union in total discouragement, and exclusion, through the post office, of every other paper, if the administration thought proper to do so."[55]

Burke was not ideologically opposed to strengthening the central or national government in some respects. Concerned for the liberty of the people, he was suspicious of power, particularly power in the hands of the executive and a dominant aristocracy, and feared its abuse. His concerns were theoretically based. They addressed future possibilities and the assumed vagaries of human nature, not observable facts. Like those expressed in the famous pamphlets of 1783, they were the concerns of classical republicanism, of an old country party against a new court. But the pattern was not really a good fit. With the exception of Elbridge Gerry and a few others, including Tucker, there were few kindred spirits in the First Congress. Smith was more nearly representative. Burke's immediate audience was too sophisticated for his style of argument; and there was a new nation to manage. Its problems were operational and most in the First Congress were committed to more pragmatic concerns. They had to make the system work.

Thus, Burke failed to establish himself in a position of leadership or influence, even within his own delegation. After three sessions, he was an unpredictable, hot-tempered, sometimes rough Irishman from South Carolina who had once written a famous pamphlet attacking the Cincinnati. His relative isolation is confirmed by a mass of negative evidence. None of the contemporary records of his colleagues attached significance or weight to his presence. He was barely noticed by Washington, Jefferson, and Madison in their respective papers. He was noticed by Hamilton only on one highly dramatic occasion. William Maclay's view of him has been mentioned. Fisher Ames's published correspondence acknowledged his existence, nothing more; and

---

55. *CGDA*, August 14, 1790.

Theodore Sedgwick and Josiah Bartlett managed to ignore him. Thomas Tudor Tucker never mentioned him in an extensive correspondence with his brother in Virginia, the well-known St. George Tucker. Only William Loughton Smith acknowledged his presence in an affirmative way, and his regard evaporated with the Hamilton affair.

Burke's standing, and that of many other southerners, was prejudiced by the violence of their reaction to the Quaker memorials. Even in Charleston, a leading paper commented that the Quakers, as a Society, had been treated "with a degree of acrimony and invective, which ill becomes American Legislators, in particular, and must inevitably lessen that respect the ingenuity of their arguments might otherwise have inspired."[56] Many in the First Congress agreed.[57] Moreover, the exercise was counterproductive. Few if any votes were changed, either on the issue of the Quaker memorials or on the concurrent issues of funding and assumption. But sectional lines were reinforced and the relative harmony of the first session, already deteriorating over the residence issue, was further undermined.[58]

Burke's standing and effectiveness were also seriously damaged by the Hamilton affair. Solicited by Anthony Walton White to assist in pressing a claim on White's behalf, Burke professed a desire to be helpful. But he feared the Secretary of War would throw "cold water on the business." Knox and Burke were not on good terms since Burke's dispute with Hamilton, Burke said. "I found then," he continued, "that falling out with one of that Sett I made the whole administration my enemies for drawing all together, like Mules in a Team they make a common cause of any dispute with others—However, I care but little for any or all of them."[59] In substance, he was persona non grata to the administration and a lonely figure in the House of Representatives. "My countryman Burke is oftener heard than attended to," com-

56. *CGDA*, May 6, 1790.
57. James Madison to Benjamin Rush, March 20, 1790, James Madison Papers, Library of Congress; William Smith to Otho Howard Williams, March 21, 1790, Otho Howard Williams Papers, Maryland Historical Society; George Thacher to H. Roberts and A. Haven, March 21, 1790, George Thacher Papers, MHS; Benjamin Goodhue to Michael Hodge, Eben Stone Papers, Essex Institute.
58. Bowling, "Politics in the First Congress," 262.
59. Burke to Anthony Walton White, January 3, 1791, Anthony Walton White Papers, Rutgers University.

mented Thomas Fitzsimons of Pennsylvania in July 1790, after the Quaker debate and the Hamilton affair, "and never less than when he expresses himself by illiberal reflections."[60]

Burke tended to view his world in terms of absolutes, corruption opposed to virtue, power opposed to liberty. He had vision only for problems and his reactions were essentially defensive. He was thus ill-suited to the politics of overtly competing interests and unable to participate effectively in a system both justified and structured as one balanced and stabilized by such competition. In the practice of politics, at least, he lacked flexibility, adaptability, discretion, and control. On the larger scene of the national Congress, his volatile nature and the limited focus of his thought on major issues frustrated both his personal ambitions and his capacity to represent effectively the interests of his "country."

---

60. Thomas Fitzsimons to [Miers Fisher], July 15, 1790, Miers Fisher Papers, HSP.

IX

The Last Decade

1791–1801

Little dissatisfaction with the performance of the First Congress was evident in South Carolina as its third session drew to a close in March 1791. An enthusiastic tribute to its work appeared in the *State Gazette* in late March and, a month later, a correspondent referred to the federal Constitution as "a monument of human wisdom which will be the admiration of unborn ages."[1] More significant was the total lack of any critical commentary. Indeed, in contrast to the 1780s, relative calm prevailed in South Carolina throughout 1791 and 1792. A new period of turbulence began in 1793, however, and continued for the balance of the 1790s. The primary source of high tension was external to the state. War between monarchical Great Britain and republican France erupted in early 1793 and, despite professed American neutrality, forced individuals to take sides. A second source of conflict emerged in 1794 when a backcountry reform movement spearheaded by Robert Goodloe Harper challenged the apportionment of representation in the General Assembly favoring, excessively in the view of the reformers, lowcountry merchants and slaveholding planters over backcountry yeoman farmers. There were other domestic issues to be sure, but none generated the heat of the representation question. Burke was involved, but only indirectly. Barred by the new Constitution of 1790 from sitting both as legislator and judge, his public service in his last decade was on the bench.

Much had happened since Burke's departure for New York in early 1789. Most importantly, major constitutional revision was finally effected in South Carolina under a new state constitution, adopted by a convention of the people elected for that purpose.[2]

---

1. *SGSC*, March 24, 1791; *SGSC*, April 25, 1791.
2. Constitution of 1790, *Statutes at Large*, 1: 184–92.

Columbia was confirmed as the permanent seat of government. The troublesome problem of apportionment was addressed and a compromise adopted whereby the size of the House of Representatives was reduced to 124 and adjustments made to reflect relative sectional strength. The old parishes were retained as election districts, but the geographically bounded districts that had served as election districts under the Constitutions of 1776 and 1778 were replaced by the counties established in 1785. Relative to the whole, the representation apportioned to the Charleston District was somewhat reduced; that apportioned to the Georgetown and Beaufort Districts was modestly increased; and that apportioned to the rest of the state was more significantly increased. The concept that representation should reflect both property and numbers, introduced in the Constitution of 1778, was thus preserved in 1790. The lowcountry districts retained nominal control, and no provision was made for periodic reapportionment. Property and residence requirements for voters were retained without significant challenge, as were more extensive property requirements for legislative office in the House and Senate.

The legislature remained the dominant branch of government, electing the governor and all major state officials. The governor, as before, had no veto power and was ineligible to succeed himself for four years after completion of a term. Limited in power as it was, the governorship "was regarded as being, in addition to a position of public service, a sort of civil crown with which to honor exceptional public men." In substance, the governor was the state's first citizen.[3]

There was no explicit bill of rights in the Constitution of 1790, but civil rights were adequately protected. The free exercise of religious profession and worship was assured "forever hereafter." Bills of attainder, ex post facto laws, and laws impairing the obligation of contracts were proscribed. Excessive fines and cruel punishments were prohibited. Trial by jury and freedom of the press were guaranteed. And no freeman of the state "shall be taken or imprisoned, or disseized of his freehold, liberties, or privileges, or outlawed, or exiled, or in any manner destroyed, or deprived of his life, liberty, or property, but by the judgment of

---

3. David Duncan Wallace, *South Carolina: A Short History* (Columbia: University of South Carolina Press, 1951), 345.

his peers, or by the law of the land." In a related article, the legislature was directed to pass laws, "as soon as may be convenient," abolishing rights of primogeniture and providing for equitable distribution of the real estate of intestates.[4]

William Loughton Smith was initially critical when the text of the new constitution reached him in New York, but was increasingly satisfied as time progressed. "Your letter has reconciled me in a considerable degree to some parts which I thought highly objectionable; the Seat of government, the rotation in offices, the exclusion from the governor's chair, the size of the representation in both houses and some other points struck me as injudicious regulations," he wrote Edward Rutledge in June. "I am however satisfied on reflection that local considerations will always supercede strict political maxims and that you were obliged to pay due attention to those considerations." Shortly thereafter, Smith observed that he would have been highly satisfied had the seat of government not been fixed at Columbia. But "I am more and more pleased with it; the Census has thrown a new light on this subject and your reflections on the weight of population must make every low country citizen extremely thankful for your exertions." Reiterating the theme of general approval, he wrote in August that he was well satisfied and considered himself, as a citizen of South Carolina, "under very great obligations of gratitude to you and your friends, whose Labors obtained such advantages for the Low country and established a constitution which I believe will promote the Tranquility and welfare of the State in general."[5] Burke's views are not on record.

Even before the constitutional convention met, the General Assembly in 1789 responded to the report of the commission to digest and revise the laws and made the several circuit courts outside Charleston separate courts of record.[6] A major grievance of backcountry litigants was thus eliminated, as Burke and the other commissioners had recommended. In 1791, the judicial system was restructured to include two new backcountry districts,

---

4. Constitution of 1790, *Statutes at Large*, 1: 184–92, Articles VIII, IX (2), IX (3), IX (4), and X (5).
5. Smith to Edward Rutledge, June 28, July 4, and August 8, 1790, in "The Letters of William Loughton Smith to Edward Rutledge, June 8, 1789 to April 28, 1794," George C. Rogers, Jr., ed., *SCHM*, 69 (1968): 117–22, 130–38.
6. *Statutes at Large*, 7: 253–57.

Washington and Pinckney.[7] Despite the increase in volume of judicial business and the addition of two new districts, the number of judges was not increased in 1791. But the office of chief justice was retained and soon filled.

A dispute arose in the General Assembly between the House and the Senate as to the status of the circuit court judges previously elected to office. The House contended that all offices had become vacant on adoption of the new constitution. The Senate, however, insisted that incumbents elected to serve during good behavior should continue in office unless the constitution expressly provided to the contrary. In February 1791, the House tried to force the issue with a proposal to elect four assistant judges, thus implying that the incumbent Grimke, Waties, and Burke, who was still on leave but due to return shortly, no longer held the positions to which they had previously been elected. The Senate refused to concur. The House finally capitulated in a 50 to 39 vote, but only after a chief justice was chosen.[8]

This contretemps is difficult to evaluate. The issue was probably not one of principle but of politics. Surely, political intrigue was rampant and the opposing positions in the House were sectionally based. A substantial majority of those contending for a clean slate were backcountry members, and an equivalent majority of those opposing them spoke for the lowcountry. In late January, Jacob Read described the ongoing proceedings to Judge John F. Grimke. Complaining of the recalcitrance of the House on the issue, Read observed that "we are set afloat by a parcel of illiterate, inconsiderate fellows (for so they are generally speaking). . . . I hope the Senate will not concur. The Consequences are not to be foreseen by the wisest of us. . . . I think no good is intended to our present Judges."[9]

In February, Henry W. Desaussure delivered a further report to Grimke. "The Senate have not yet decided," Desaussure said,

---

7. *Statutes at Large*, 7: 260–65. A concurrent enactment established annual salaries for the judges in the amount of £800 for the chief justice and £600 for the assistant judges.

8. *JHR 1791*, 112–13, 257–59, 263–65. In the absence of a chief justice, such duties as inured to that office fell on the senior assistant judge, who thus became de facto chief justice. On Pendleton's death in late 1788, Burke became the senior sitting assistant judge and presumably would have retained his seniority when he returned from his leave of absence. He was de facto chief justice again when Rutledge resigned in 1795.

9. Read to Grimke, January 24, 1791, Grimke Papers, SCHS.

"but it is too well understood that they only postpone 'till we are ready to Elect, that there may be as Short an Interregnum as possible." The election would probably proceed when work on the fee bill was finished, he continued, and "we shall have a Chief Justice if the votes of the houses are to be relied on, which is not indeed saying that the Business is settled for the winds are not more fickle than we are." The problem apparently centered on the election of a chief justice. "I observed what you said about the office of Chief Justice," Desaussure continued, "and I should obey your directions in putting up your name, if Mr. John Rutledge had not consented to serve, if Elected—Your friends here conceive you would have excepted him as you did General P. and Mr. E. R. had you known of his determination—They therefore only offer you as a Candidate for your old place, and I take particular pleasure in telling you that after every investigation I can make I believe you will be handsomely reelected."[10] The next day Read wrote Grimke again. A chief justice would be elected, Read advised, and "Mr. Rutledge will be the man. Some idea was entertained of putting Mr. Justice Burke up in opposition but I find 'tis now extinguished and Rutledge will be the man."[11]

When the log jam was finally broken, Rutledge was elected chief justice on February 16, defeating Burke 70 to 51. The House then proceeded to fill the one remaining vacancy on the court by electing Elihu Hall Bay an assistant judge.[12] Rutledge's margin was clear but Burke had no reason to feel disgraced. His base of support was clearly substantial. Indeed, the evidence suggests a more dramatic tentative hypothesis, unsupported by direct evidence but circumstantially plausible. The backcountry had long been dissatisfied with the structure of the judicial system and with the way it functioned in practice. Determined to effect further changes, the backcountry representatives asserted themselves at the first session of the General Assembly convened under the Constitution of 1790. There had been no chief justice in office since Drayton's death in 1779, and the backcountry candidate was Burke. Only when Rutledge consented to resign from

---

10. Desaussure to Grimke, February 11, 1791, Grimke Papers, SCHS.
11. Read to Grimke, February 12, 1791, Grimke Papers, SCHS.
12. *JHR 1791*, 257 (election of Rutledge), 269 (election of Bay). The sequence confirms that the House held firm to its position on the status of the incumbent judges until the office of chief justice was filled. There is no evidence that Burke expected, or had reason to expect, that he might be elected chief justice on his return from Philadelphia.

the Supreme Court of the United States and to accept office as chief justice of South Carolina was there an alternative candidate of sufficient prestige in the state to prevail in the General Assembly.[13]

As a sitting judge on the state's superior court, Burke remained an important public figure in South Carolina. He was included, for example, among the dignitaries who greeted Washington when the President visited the state on his tour of the South in the spring of 1791.[14] But in the decade of the 1790s, Burke's interests were more wide-ranging than in the 1780s, when he was very much a man of his own "country" and largely stayed at home. After the "revolution in government" of 1787 and his experience in the First Congress, his horizon was considerably extended and his attention more closely focused on the larger scene beyond South Carolina's borders. Between 1791 and 1799, he made at least four extended trips to the North—in 1792, 1794, 1797, and 1799. His purposes are obscure, and were no doubt partly social. But he kept his eye on the larger political scene and found the devils abroad at least as threatening as the devils at home.

Burke's first trip to the North was in mid-1792. There he found certain Republican interests seeking to effect a change in the vice-presidency in the forthcoming national election and centering their attention on Aaron Burr of New York. After extended consultation between political leaders in New York and Virginia, that attention was shifted to New York's Governor Clinton.[15] Burke could hardly have been involved in these early manifestations of party activity. But on his return to Charleston, he delivered his view of the matter in a revealing letter to Monroe. When in New York, he said, he had earnestly begged the Republican interest there not to advance Burr as a candidate, "but they per-

---

13. Rutledge's letter of resignation from the Supreme Court was written after his election in South Carolina and asserted that "the peculiar Circumstances of the Appointment [were] such that I conceive I could not with any Propriety refuse it." Rutledge to Washington, March 5, 1791, in *The Documentary History of the Supreme Court of the United States, 1789–1800*, Maeva Marcus, et al., eds., 1 vol. to date (New York: Columbia University Press, 1985), 1 (Part I): 23.

14. Presuming upon the occasion, he later wrote Washington on behalf of a fellow Carolinian but was cooly rebuffed for his pains. Washington to Burke, July 19, 1791, in *The Writings of George Washington*, John C. Fitzpatrick, ed., 40 vols. (Washington: United States Government Printing Office, 1931–1944), 31: 314.

15. Noble E. Cunningham, Jr., *The Jeffersonian Republicans: The Formation of Party Organization, 1789–1801* (Chapel Hill: University of North Carolina Press, 1957), 46–49.

sisted and it ended like every effort made by that party." Burke was sympathetic to the Republican objective, "in spite of my judgment, which gives me to see them and their cause going down fast a powerful current, which to resist, is more vain than attempting to stem the Delaware with the wind and ebb tide against you." Everything was stacked against the Republican interest, Burke said, particularly "the fame and popularity, the weight and virtues of a certain great man." As for the incumbent vice president, John Adams, "I have long thought, that with principles like his, so hostile to a Republic, so bigoted to Royalty; that such a man should hold the second place in the Administration of our popular System, is a stain upon the System itself, and must give to its friends but a sad presage concerning its duration." The election of Adams "is a blow of suicide against the Republican system; the folly whereof strikes one more forceably when we recollect that under a Monarch or single Ruler, he would never dream of elevating to the summit of authority, a man who openly avowed himself a foe to Royalty. He would never commit an act of such supreme folly, as our Republicans have run into more than once or twice."[16]

This letter, isolated though it is in the larger stream of events, is revealing in several important respects. First, Burke was not telling Monroe anything he did not already know, since Monroe had been most intimately involved in the matter from the outset. Second, and related to the first, Burke could not have been dealing in New York with those intimately involved in the affair, because, if he had, he would have understood the course of it better than his letter suggests. He was, therefore, on the periphery and not at the center of the emergent Republican interest. Third, Burke's negative reaction was typically Burkean; the election of Adams to the second place in "our popular System" was "a stain on the System itself," but the forces arrayed against the Republican interest were too great to be overcome. Finally, Burke's characterization of Adams, although by no means unique to himself in 1792, revealed an oppositionist mind set firmly fixed at a time of relative calm in national politics months before the polarizing impact of the outbreak of war between Great Britain

---

16. Burke to James Monroe, December 16, 1792, James Monroe Papers, Department of Manuscripts and Rare Books, Swem Library, College of William and Mary.

and France in 1793. If nothing else, Burke was a consistent critic of all suspected friends of Britain and its constitutional structure.

Back in Charleston from his trip North, Burke was among those who greeted Edmond Genet when the first minister sent by the new French Republic to the United States landed in Charleston on April 8, 1793. Genet's arrival in Charleston was happenstance, the result of a stormy trans-Atlantic passage. But he was enthusiastically received and feted before beginning his overland journey to Philadelphia.[17]

The Genet mission was a failure, occasionally bordering on farce. Misled by popular enthusiasm, he did the French cause more harm than good.[18] But he struck a responsive chord in Burke. As Genet's enterprise came to an end in 1794 and he prepared to retire to private life in the United States rather than return to France, Burke wrote to commiserate. "We have in Charleston one thing in common with her sister cities of Philadelphia and New York," Burke said, "that is a ministerial party, tuned to perfect unison with a strong British party, both together celebrating at this moment, a sort of jubilee or triumph, for the victory supposed to be obtained over you, while the few Republicans in Town, and the mass of the Inhabitants of the Country, are seriously afflicted for it." In South Carolina, Burke continued, Genet had "the veneration and affection of that great body of men who, in our late conflict for overturning Royalty, have on many honorable and hard trials, given good proof how warm was their love for Republican Liberty. Nor have they, like some whom you and I know, changed their old tenets with their recent good fortune. They do not see, with the half-way Republican, Mr. Jefferson, the great criminality in your landing in South Carolina."[19] Genet's landing in South Carolina, of course, was not the real issue.

The initial response to the French Revolution in South Carolina was strongly supportive, and Burke would not have been in character unless he shared in it.[20] But Carolinian enthusiasm was

---

17. Paul Ammon, *The Genet Mission* (New York: W. W. Norton, 1973), 44–46.
18. Ammon, *Genet Mission*, 75–76, 99, 128–31, 142–45; Butler to Wade Hampton, December 10, 1793, Letterbook of Pierce Butler, 1790–1794, Pierce Butler Papers, SCL.
19. Burke to Genet, February 16, 1794, Genet Papers, Library of Congress.
20. Burke to James Loocock Cusack, December 10, 1794, reprinted in *CGDA*, May 22, 1795. Cusack was a young South Carolinian who enlisted in the French

beginning to wane in many circles by late 1794. And Burke has never been connected with the pro-French Republican Society of Charleston, although his friend O'Brien Smith was a member, or with support for the aborted military adventures against Spanish Florida that Genet committed to the charge of Michael Ange Mangourit, the French consul in Charleston. When the contemplated invasion of Florida collapsed under pressure from the General Assembly, the Society was reduced to the making of pronouncements. Resolutions were adopted in March 1794 complaining of British maritime policy and practice and expressing the opinion that war with Great Britain was inevitable. After Washington's presidential message in 1794 condemning the disruptive political activities of voluntary societies generally, the Society stirred itself to adopt resolutions justifying its conduct. "We will never relinquish the right of freemen to investigate the acts of any man or men who are or may be placed in power," the resolutions said.[21] Burke presumably would have concurred. But the Society's focus was limited, and it was never the force for political change in South Carolina that similar societies were in important states to the North.

Burke traveled north again in the latter part of 1794. "I have just arrived from a tour of four months thro' the state of New York," he wrote in December to James Monroe, then in Paris, and was exposed to "a great deal of court and country politics" that he hoped to discuss at another time. He did not elaborate, but he did have something to say about the Whiskey Rebellion in Pennsylvania.

> The insurrection in the four Western Counties of Pennsylvania against the Excise, is a most unfortunate business. To quell it by arms became necessary; and this has given at one stroke, to the administration more energy and decisive power, than any government of the old world obtained in a whole century. No one can form a judgment of this, any more than of other public matters, unless he can

---

army and was later killed in action. "Farewell, citizen!" Burke said, and expressed in hortatory terms his wish for the success of France against her enemies and the rewards of enterprise and gallantry for Cusack. Burke's letter was published after the report of Cusack's death reached Charleston.

21. Philip S. Foner, ed., *The Democratic Republican Societies, 1790–1800: A Documentary Sourcebook of Constitutions, Declarations, Addresses, Resolutions, and Toasts* (Westport, Ct.: Greenwood Press, 1976), 387–90.

survey them pretty closely. The consequences are important; but what did the silly, mischievous Yahoos think, or care, about consequences.[22]

Here Burke disclosed a typical Republican reaction to the Whiskey Rebellion and his own ideological orientation in the mid-1790s. The incident further strengthened the national administration, stimulating "energy" and conferring "decisive power" by encouraging those who advocated the creation of a standing army. The rebels were dismissed, almost with contempt, as "silly, mischievous Yahoos," thoughtless of consequences.

The precise period of Burke's absence in New York is uncertain, but he must have missed most of the last half of 1794 in South Carolina. If so, he missed the first phase of the heated controversy over the apportionment of representation. The campaign for reapportionment was precipitated in June 1794 by a self-styled and self-created Representative Reform Association speaking through Robert Goodloe Harper. Representative government, Harper argued, could not be free unless so constituted that every member of the community had an equal voice in public affairs. When a few thinly populated election districts, however wealthy, sent more representatives to the legislature than all others combined, though larger and more populous, the form of government was a perfect aristocracy. Such was the case, he said, in South Carolina, where approximately one-fifth of the white population in the lowcountry election districts elected a majority in both the House of Representatives and the Senate. He denied that property constituted an appropriate basis on which to apportion representation because, in such a case, the government could not be free. Some concessions had been granted, he conceded, but they were granted as a matter of favor, not of right. The backcountry districts were described as dependent provinces. The evil required immediate attention.[23]

The reaction from the low country was immediate and sustained. Timothy Ford and Henry W. Desaussure led the

---

22. Burke to Monroe, December 26, 1794, Gratz Collection, HSP.
23. "Appius" [Robert Goodloe Harper], *An Address to the People of South Carolina, by the General Committee of the Representative Reform Association* (Charleston: W. P. Young, 1794). Harper's pamphlet was subsequently published serially in the *CGDA*, August 1, 2, 4, 11, 12, 14, 15, and 16, 1794.

defense.[24] Arguing on theoretical and pragmatic grounds, both categorically rejected the Association's demand. Ford insisted that the issues had all been resolved in the making of the Constitution of 1790, when the matter was hotly contested. "After much debate," he wrote, "and when it was found the different parties could not agree in the house, a committee taken from all parts of the country, was at length chosen to adjust this knotty and difficult point." That committee reported unanimously in favor of the system adopted, and its report was unanimously adopted by the convention. Similarly, the completed constitution was unanimously approved. The agreed upon apportionment was therefore a compromise, agreed upon by all. In these circumstances, Ford asked, was it prudent "to awaken party prejudices, to call up into action the jarring interests, and drive the demon of civil discord over this fair and prosperous country?"[25]

Desaussure echoed Ford's theme, referring to the dissidents as a body of citizens who were "unfurling the standard of civil discord." He described the state as a divided country, with wealth concentrated in one section, and numbers concentrated in another. In such circumstances, wealth had no power to protect itself against a numerical majority centered in a separate part of the state with sharply dissimilar interests. A system of representation based on both property and population was therefore particularly appropriate. Any other division would expose one of the sections to legislative oppression. To Desaussure, the Association's demands "claim so peremptorily a representation based on numbers alone, and breathe so strongly the spirit of monastic intolerance, that they exclude the hope of negotiation and of amicable arrangement." Consequently, even compromise would be impossible, because new demands would follow; "and no wise

---

24. "Americanus" [Timothy Ford], *The Constitutionalist, or an Enquiry how far it is Expedient and Proper to Alter the Constitution of South Carolina* . . . (Charleston: Markland & McIver, 1794); "Phocion" [Henry W. Desaussure], *Letters on the Questions of the Justice and Expediency of Going into Alterations of the Representation in the Legislature of South Carolina* . . . (Charleston: Markland & McIver, 1795). The *Constitutionalist* was first published serially in the *CGDA* on September 30, October 4, 9, 11, 17, 24, 28, and 31, and November 4 and 18, 1794. The pamphlet was published shortly thereafter. The *Letters* were first published serially in the *CGDA* on November 26, 27, 28, and 29, 1794. The pamphlet was published early in 1795.
25. Ford, *Constitutionalist*, 50–55.

government, concerned with the interests of its people, could enter upon so hazardous a venture."[26]

One singular feature of the debate, as it developed in 1794 and as it continued through 1795 and 1796, was that both sides acknowledged the sectional division of the state and the existence of serious conflicts of interest separating them. A sense of unreality thus pervades the dispute. If the Representative Reform Association truly sought the reforms demanded, its spokesmen should have been arguing consensus and a commonality of interests, not differences. In the circumstances, reform could be achieved only by persuading the lowcountry parishes that their interests would not be adversely affected and that they could safely support it. The line of argument was precisely the opposite, emphasizing conflicts of interest and therefore serving to create apprehension rather than to ease tension. Moreover, as in 1783 and 1784, some of the language of the dissidents could be interpreted as threatening. Defenders of the status quo were thus offered a position of considerable tactical advantage from which to respond; and even those like Burke, who might have supported reform in principle, were offended.

The status quo prevailed in 1794. In December, a number of backcountry petitions were presented to the General Assembly. In more or less uniform terms, the backcountry men complained of "the great Inequality of the Representation in the Legislature of their respective election districts" and prayed for equalized apportionment in both House and Senate.[27] After extended debate in the House sitting as a committee of the whole, the prayers of the petitions were rejected on a close vote. It was inexpedient to grant the prayers, the resolution said, "inasmuch as the Representation established by the present Constitution was founded in a Spirit of Compromise and in an Equipoise of Interests between the different parts of the State; and has been proved by Experience well calculated to preserve the Tranquility and advance the prosperity thereof."[28]

---

26. Desaussure, *Letters*, 5, 17, 23.
27. Journal of the House of Representatives, December 10, 1794, SCA. The petitions are collected in Records of the House of Representatives, Petitions, 1794, SCA.
28. Journal of the House of Representatives, December 12, 1794, SCA. The resolution was carried 58 to 53.

The controversy over representation did not end with that determination, but it was soon overshadowed by the even more heated dispute on the Jay Treaty that began in mid-1795 and continued into 1796. Burke was extensively involved in this excitement and initially found himself aligned with a signficant segment of the lowcountry establishment. Before he was finished, he directly challenged the sincerity of Harper's stance as leader of the movement to reform legislative apportionment.

Nobody was satisfied with the terms of the Jay Treaty when they became known. The British interpretation of maritime rights was accepted. Discriminatory maritime restrictions, the means favored by Jefferson, Madison, and their followers to resist British maritime practices oppressive to American interests, were barred for ten years. No privateers could be fitted out in American ports. No limitations were imposed on British impressment of seamen. Trade with the British West Indies was permitted only under conditions so restrictive as to insult the American version of its sovereign rights. On one outstanding difference of particular importance to South Carolinians, no provision was made concerning compensation for slaves lost during the Revolutionary War.[29]

Public reaction to the Treaty in Charleston was spirited. Protesting crowds demonstrated in the streets and prominent figures, including John Jay and King George III, were burned in effigy. In contrast, the public proceedings were orderly and conducted in parliamentary fashion. Pursuant to notice published in the local papers, the Charleston citizenry gathered at the Exchange and then adjourned to St. Michael's church where John Rutledge delivered a resounding address in which he attacked the Treaty as "an humble acknowledgement of our dependence upon his majesty; a surrender of our rights and privileges, for so much of his gracious favour as he should be pleased to grant." Summarizing, the *State Gazette* observed that "to hear his abhor-

29. Jerald A. Combs, *The Jay Treaty: Political Battleground of the Founding Fathers* (Berkeley: University of California Press, 1970), 149–58; George C. Rogers, Jr., *Evolution of a Federalist: William Loughton Smith of Charleston (1758–1812)*, (Columbia: University of South Carolina Press, 1962), 276. Combs, *The Jay Treaty*, has been extensively relied upon in the text below for the general history of the Treaty and the political controversy it produced. The reaction to the Treaty in Charleston and the ensuing proceedings are described in some detail in William Read to Jacob Read, July 21 and July 27, 1795, Read Family Papers, SCHS.

rence of the whole instrument, unmoved, would argue a spirit which the union now finds necessary to her existence. When he declares he had rather the President should die, dearly as he loves him, than he should sign that treaty—when he pronounces for *war* rather than his country should approve the measures that will effect her annihilation, we are aroused into a sense of our danger."[30]

Notwithstanding the vehemence of his expressed views, Rutledge called for orderly proceedings, and orderly proceedings followed. A committee of fifteen was elected to study the Treaty and report to the citizenry. Over 800 voters turned out to cast their ballots, a larger number of votes, said the *City Gazette*, than had been taken at any other election in Charleston since the British evacuation in 1782.[31] One of those elected was Burke, joining an eminent group that included Christopher Gadsden, John Rutledge, David Ramsay, Edward Rutledge, Charles Cotesworth Pinckney, and Thomas Tudor Tucker.[32]

When the citizens assembled at St. Michael's to hear the committee's report, Governor Charles Pinckney opened the proceedings with an extended address more restrained than Rutledge's but no less critical. "Upon the whole of this business," he concluded, "it will be found that the treaty deserves the censure of every friend of this country, and of every man who wishes to see its commerce extensive and flourishing." It was injurious to the commercial rights of the country, degrading to its character, ungrateful to its allies, and should be rejected.[33] Gadsden then presented the committee's report criticizing the Treaty in detail, article by article, and concluding "that great evils would result to these states from this treaty, if ratified." The committee accordingly recommended an address to the President "praying that he will not ratify the said treaty."[34] The address was a disappointment after all the sound and fury. Authored by Thomas Tudor

---

30. *SCSG*, July 17, 1795; reprinted in *The Documentary History of the Supreme Court*, Marcus, et al., eds., 1 (Part 2): 765–70. An abbreviated account appeared in the *CGDA*, July 17, 1795.
31. *CGDA*, July 18, 1795.
32. *CGDA*, July 20, 1795. William Read later reported that Charles Cotesworth Pinckney declined to serve, "being very wary and prudent." William Read to Jacob Read, September 10, 1795, Read Family Papers, SCHS.
33. Charles Pinckney's address was summarized in the *CGDA*, July 23, 1795, and was published in full in the *CGDA*, August 4, 1795.
34. *CGDA*, July 23, 1795.

Tucker, it merely requested that ratification be suspended for a time so that the effect of the Treaty could be studied more carefully.[35] In the Carolinian style of the day, however, that suggestion was the functional equivalent of a direct negative. Whether Washington so understood it is, of course, another matter.

Beyond his membership on the committee, Burke was not in evidence during the progress of these events. Presumably he participated in the discussion, and his agreement with the conclusions of the committee may be safely assumed. Essentially analytical and legalistic, the report was a comparative model of restraint in contrast to the reported public temper. No part of it can be attributed to Burke, and his influence on the completed document, if any, is indeterminable.

The excitement in Charleston was duplicated elsewhere as anti-Treaty forces turned to the people after ratification in the Senate, hoping that popular disapproval would persuade Washington not to sign. Their efforts failed. After a violent debate in the press, Washington signed the Treaty in August 1795. The most prominent South Carolinian loser was John Rutledge, whose pending confirmation as Chief Justice of the United States later failed.[36]

Controversy over the Jay Treaty remained heated even after ratification and signature. It merely shifted to the national House of Representatives, raged there through April 1796, and spilled over into the domestic politics of South Carolina. William Loughton Smith initially led the pro-Treaty cause in South Carolina and published a pamphlet defending it in August 1795.[37] Pierce Butler

---

35. "Address of the Citizens of Charleston (South Carolina) to the President of the United States," *American Remembrancer* (Philadelphia, 1795), 2: 51–52; Thomas Tudor Tucker to St. George Tucker, August 31, 1795, Tucker-Coleman Papers, Department of Manuscripts and Rare Books, Swem Library, College of William and Mary.

36. Documents relating to Rutledge's address on the Treaty and the Senate's subsequent rejection of his appointment as Chief Justice are collected in *The Documentary History of the Supreme Court*, Marcus, et al., eds., 1 (Part 2): 765–831. George S. McCowen, Jr., "Chief Justice John Rutledge and the Jay Treaty," *SCHM*, 62 (1961): 10–23, calls the Rutledge speech a "political indiscretion." The high Federalists, McCowen says, made the Treaty a test of party loyalty and, for them, Rutledge had betrayed the administration. In the Senate, Rutledge fell one vote short of the vote required for confirmation.

37. William Loughton Smith, *A Candid Examination of the Objections to the Treaty of Amity, Commerce, and Navigation, between the United States and Great Britain, as*

was actively opposed, although from his seat in the Senate. At Butler's urging, and no doubt motivated by his own view of the matter, Burke was equally engaged at home.

Butler's continuing involvement on the Treaty issue, and indirectly Burke's, is disclosed in Butler's extensive correspondence with friends and supporters in South Carolina discussing the issue and encouraging the opposition.[38] One of his principal correspondents was Burke. Unhappily, Burke's letters to Butler, of which Butler specifically mentioned fifteen, have not been found. The exchange is therefore one-sided. Enough is said, however, to permit some reconstruction of Burke's views.

Burke had known Butler for years prior to 1795, but there is no evidence that they were particularly close. Indeed, some tension apparently arose between them during the years immediately following Burke's return to South Carolina from the First Congress. The circumstances are ambiguous and the only account is Butler's, written in September 1793 to Alexander Gillon. Apparently, Gillon reported that Burke had spoken disparagingly of Butler. Butler dismissed it, describing Burke as "a well meaning Man with striking particularities" whom Butler had consistently defended against criticism from others. "I am persuaded," Butler said, "at the time my four years in Senate expired, and an election was to take place, there were not wanting men who tried to instill into [Burke's] mind a jealousy of me, with a view to inducing him to take a part against a re-election; under a supposition, which I trust was a delusory one, that he alone could prevail in the Legislature not to re-elect Mr. Butler." Butler pointed to Izard as probably a leader of those attempting to influence Burke, and assured Gillon that he was fully prepared to stand on his reputation and his record.[39]

Whatever their differences in 1793, Burke and Butler were in close correspondence two years later.[40] In early October 1795,

---

stated in the Report of the Committee appointed by the Citizens of the United States, in Charleston, South Carolina (Charleston: W. P. Young, 1795; New York: J. Rivington, 1795); Rogers, *Evolution of a Federalist*, 279.

38. Letterbook of Pierce Butler, 1794–1822, Pierce Butler Papers, HSP. This letterbook is available on microfilm at SCL.

39. Butler to Gillon, September 26, 1793, Butler Letterbook, 1790–1794, SCL.

40. The apparent shift in the relationship between Butler and Burke raises an interesting, albeit highly speculative, question. The Butler Letterbook, 1790–1794, SCL covers the period indicated. Not one letter from Butler to Burke was recorded during that period, although Burke was no longer in Congress after

The Public Life of Aedanus Burke

Butler wrote Burke to report an extended trip through New England. The people were learning how they had been duped by "Mr. H," Butler said; "he and his faction have nearly ruined our Country and made a tool of our good President." The monied and commercial interests were working "to suppress and keep under the real voice of the Great body of Yeomanry throughout the Eastern and Middle States." More than seven-eights of the people in the eastern states opposed the Treaty. "In Jersey, New York, Rhode Island, Massachusetts and New Hampshire, the efforts of the monied interest and a part of the mercantile interest to keep under and suppress the general sentiments of disgust and dissatisfaction are as evident as the Sun at Noonday." Everything depended on the House, Butler concluded. Robert Goodloe Harper and William Loughton Smith would support the administration. Lemuel Benton and Richard Winn might. In that case, a majority of the South Carolina delegation would "oppose the sense of their country."[41]

The substantive part of Butler's letter shortly found its way into print, submitted by "A Friend to the People" for publication in the *State Gazette*. "The following extract throws a great light upon our political hemisphere," the people's friend said, "and cannot fail to be acceptable to that part of the community, who are by local and other circumstances, precluded an open view of governmental measures."[42] The people's friend could only have been Burke.

When Congress convened in December 1795, the House would have an opportunity to consider the Treaty because an appropriation was required to implement its terms. The administration delayed its request for the requisite appropriation, awaiting

March 1791. In contrast, there were a number of letters to Gillon. Gillon died in late 1794. If a reconciliation was needed between Butler and Burke, it was apparently effected in 1795, perhaps while Butler was in South Carolina between congressional sessions. In the aggregate, Butler's correspondence suggests a manipulative approach to his correspondents. Butler may have sought out Burke as a loyal lieutenant at home to replace Gillon. If so, he succeeded. As the discussion demonstrates, he made active use of Burke's services in 1795 and 1796.

41. Butler to Burke, October 10, 1795, Butler Letterbook, 1794–1822, HSP. This was the first letter in the series from Butler to Burke and acknowledged three letters from Burke to Butler. The record suggests that Butler had solicited Burke to keep him advised on events in South Carolina and that Burke was dutifully responding.

42. *SCSG*, October 27, 1795.

receipt of notice that Britain had ratified. For tactical reasons, the opposition was forced to wait.

Meanwhile, resolutions condemning the Treaty were presented to the General Assembly in South Carolina, specifically to the House of Representatives. On December 2, General Robert Anderson offered resolutions to the effect that the President and the Senate had mistaken their constitutional powers by ratifying the Treaty and that it would be "inimical and injurious to the commercial, agricultural and manufacturing interests of the United States of America." On December 6, Ephraim Ramsay offered a related resolution declaring that "in the opinion of this house, the honor of our country and interest of our citizens render it proper that the representatives of this state in the congress of the United States should be instructed to prevent, if possible, the appropriation of any money for the payment of debts due to the subjects of Great Britain, until Great Britain shall agree to make compensation for the Negroes and other property carried off by the British." The resolutions were taken up on December 10. After extended debate in the House, sitting as a committee of the whole, Edward Rutledge moved that consideration of the resolutions be postponed. That motion was defeated by a margin of eight votes.[43]

"Americanus" described the proceedings in the *City Gazette* some weeks later. In his view, the division had little to do with the merits of the Treaty, which both populace and House almost universally condemned. The issue was debated as one of propriety, whether the state legislature should interfere in the matter at all. Some argued that "*they* had no right, *in their representative capacity,* to vote an opinion concerning the acts of the general government" and that the state's representatives in Congress, "not having derived their powers from the [state] legislature, were independent of them." Moreover, adoption of the resolutions might impair popular confidence in the general government. The minority "damned the treaty, but deprecated the resolutions," Americanus said. "To pass them, they declared, would be like cutting the cable of a ship in a tempestuous moment."[44]

---

43. Journal of the House of Representatives, December 2, 6, and 10, 1795, SCA; *SCSG,* December 21, 1795.
44. "Americanus," *CGDA,* January 11, 1796. At least some of those who questioned the propriety of action on the Treaty were presumably supporters of it and therefore opposed to any action.

In these circumstances, a deal was struck. Anderson and Ramsay agreed to withdraw the original motions, and a general resolution was substituted to the effect that, in the opinion of the House, the Treaty was injurious to the interests of the United States. The resolution, Americanus said, "would go forth as the opinion of the house of representatives only." On the vote, it was carried 69 to 9. One member of the House missed the word and moved to have the resolution forwarded to the Senate for its concurrence. That motion had no support and was overwhelmingly defeated.[45]

Americanus was no friend to the Treaty. The sense of the people, he said, was confirmed by the vote on the substitute resolution, even though it was not the statement of the General Assembly. Four-fifths of the people, he believed, regarded the Treaty "as a damnable compact between the British government, and the American Anglomen, speculators, and poltroons." The American Anglomen "were anxious to strengthen the connexions between the two countries." The speculators "wished to preserve the value of stock." The poltroons "were horridly afraid of war, which their timidity made them suppose would be the consequence of not ratifying."[46] All this is difficult to evaluate with precision, but anti-Treaty sentiment was strong in South Carolina, and particularly in the backcountry.

At the end of 1795, Robert Goodloe Harper, representing Ninety Six in the national House of Representatives, released an address to his constituents announcing that he intended to support the Treaty in the forthcoming proceedings in the House. In a skillfully constructed argument, Harper claimed the right and duty to exercise his independent judgment and presented the issue as one of choice between war and peace. While he was at it, he directly challenged the accuracy of Butler's assertions to Burke in October and published in Charleston as previously described.[47] Not satisfied with that reply, he repeated it in a piece

---

45. "Americanus," *CGDA*, January 11, 1796; Journal of the House of Representatives, December 11 and 12, 1795, SCA; *CGDA*, December 21, 1795.
46. "Americanus," *CGDA*, January 11, 1796.
47. Robert Goodloe Harper, *An Address from Robert Goodloe Harper, of South Carolina, to His Constituents, Containing His Reasons for Approving the Treaty of Amity, Commerce, and Navigation, with Great Britain* (Philadelphia: Ormrod and Conrad, 1795; New York: J. Rivington, 1796).

signed "Caroliniensis" and published in Charleston in early January 1796. He had also traveled in New England, Harper said, and found the great majority of the people "perfectly well satisfied with the treaty and with the administration." Although not without defects, it was a wise and useful measure. In particular, he criticized the suggestion that scheming enemies of liberty were conspiring to foist it on the people.

> I should think it my duty in such circumstances to come
> forward in the most unequivocal manner, and denounce the
> traitors, whatever might be their station, who are contriving
> plots so mischievous and wicked. Let this writer and his
> friends pursue that plan. Let them deal no longer in dark
> hints, in anonymous paragraphs, in vague and general
> accusations. Let them give us facts and proof; develop this
> 'system of intrigue and wicked policy;' and tell us who
> compose Mr. Hamilton's faction, how it has nearly ruined
> our country, and in what instances it has 'made a tool of
> our good President.' 'Till this is done they will be justly
> liable to the suspicion of intending to promote sinister views
> of their own, views which they dare not avow, by diffusing
> jealousy and distrust into the public mind.[48]

It was an effective riposte.

Burke responded the next day in an open letter "To Caroliniensis, alias Mr. H———r, a delegate in Congress," subscribed "One of your Constituents, Mr. Caroliniensis." Burke charged Harper with blatant opportunism. He had condemned the President and the "new order of things for years past; the loud apostle of the party whom he then called republican, but now I suppose anarchists and jacobins." His obvious goal was political preferment and a place in the administration. "One thing the writer of this paragraph has to tell him freely," Burke concluded, "that whether he rises higher or rests where he is, without moral honor, candour, and sincerity, he will be an injury to his country, altho' he may succeed in his main object, that is helping himself."[49]

Butler identified the response to Harper as Burke's in a letter to Burke written in late January. Harper's motives were easily

---

48. *SCSG*, January 7, 1796.
49. *SCSG*, January 8, 1796.

seen through and well depicted in a "piece from Timothy's Paper of the 8th" just received, he said. "I see your strong, nervous stile, too forcibly to doubt the author. It will make Harper sore. . . . It shows the man in his true colors." He "is unworthy of our notice yet he ought to be placed in his true and proper character before his constituents."[50]

The Treaty was finally presented to the House of Representatives in Philadelphia on March 1. Before an appropriation was requested, Edward Livingston of New York, a Republican, precipitated the issue by introducing a resolution that called on the President to submit to the House all documents concerning it. "We shall," Livingston wrote, "after production of the papers submit resolutions declaratory of our rights to Sanction or refuse treaties which contain Stipulations affecting any of the powers vested in Congress—expressive of our opinion of this Treaty and containing a refusal to carry it into effect."[51]

The contest was joined when Washington declined to produce the documents. A House caucus indicated a majority opposed to the Treaty. The Federalists responded with a campaign of pressure supported by banks, mercantile houses, and insurance companies. In addition to economic pressure, they played on fear of war with Britain. The Republicans responded that acceptance of the Treaty would offend France and possibly precipitate a French war. Rejection, on the other hand, could not rationally create any danger of hostilities.

Burke had been alerted to these developments in part when Butler wrote in February to advise that Livingston, "a fine, manly, sensible Republican," would bring the Treaty issue before the House "notwithstanding the squeamishness of some Gentlemen on the grounds of Presidential feelings." He wrote again at the end of March. "Harper is low here," he said, "despised by the Republicans, and not likely to get anything from the other side." He reported that Washington had refused to comply with the House resolution calling for documents. If the House should yield, he predicted, "they may put the Constitution in the fire and the United States will have as little to boast of as Britain with all her treason bills surrounding her." An addendum the next

50. Butler to Burke, January 27, 1796, Butler Letterbook, 1794–1822, HSP.
51. Combs, *The Jay Treaty*, 174–77, Livingston quote at 176.

day acknowledged receipt of "your answer to Harper." Part of it was "in Bache of this day," he said. It "gives the highest satisfaction here and has completely humbled him."[52]

Burke's "answer to Harper," no doubt stimulated by Butler's earlier suggestion that Harper "ought to be placed in his true and proper character before his constituents," was a wide ranging and vitriolic attack published in early March.[53] Picking up the concluding remarks from Harper's "Caroliniensis" letter published in January, Burke charged that it was Harper who employed his rhetorical powers for the purpose of "diffusing jealousy and distrust in the public mind," pointing particularly to Harper's pamphlets calling for reform of legislative apportionment in South Carolina.[54] Harper took up the reform issue, Burke said, solely for revenge on leading lowcountry families unwilling to take notice of him. The manner of his attack on lowcountry political leaders created tension between backcountry and lowcountry and fostered such discord and distrust as to disrupt the public tranquility.[55]

Even "in a business wherein he should happen to be right," Burke continued, "Caroliniensis is totally incapable of conducting himself otherwise than as a disorganizer." His "itinerant habits of a country-court lawyer gave him a full range to inflame the public mind" against the compromise on legislative apportionment embodied in the Constitution of 1790. Instead of acting in "a cool, calm, dignified manner," Harper resorted to "virulence and acrimony, painting the people below in odious colors." Attempting "to rouse the passions of envy, distrust, hatred and vexation in the bosoms of those he calls the *poor*, he raises a sort

---

52. Butler to Burke, February 25, 1796, and Butler to Burke, March 31, 1796, with addendum dated April 1, 1796, Butler Letterbook, 1794–1822, HSP.

53. *SCSG*, March 5, 1796. Burke's piece purports to reply to a publication by Harper within the preceding few days. No such publication appears, but two numbers of the paper are missing from the available collection. The text takes as its point of departure Harper's January piece but does refer to later events. Harper's pamphlet on the Treaty, referred to in the text, was republished in the newspapers after March 5. *SCSG*, March 19 and 21, 1796.

54. Harper, *Address by the General Committee of the Representative Reform Association*; Robert Goodloe Harper, "An Address from the Representatives of the People in the Middle and Western Districts, met at Columbia, December 17, 1794, to their Fellow Citizens in the Eastern Parts of the State," *CGDA*, October 29, 1795.

55. *SCSG*, March 5, 1796. Quoted passages in the following three paragraphs are from this source.

of standard of hostility to those he called rich." Lowcountry residents were represented "as wallowing in wealth, as a faction of aristocrats determined to make of the upper country a sort of a land of Egypt, and house of Bondage." He portrayed the backcountry "as a province dependent upon and ruled by the lower country with an unfeeling despotism" and the lowcountry as a "ruling power" determined to impose on the backcountry "a system of government . . . replete with inequality, injustice and servitude." Then, "while he was setting the minds of the people on a blaze," he would occasionally pause to recommend that his readers be cool, calm, and moderate.

Harper's pamphlet "ran thro' the country like wildfire," Burke claimed, spreading discontent and resentment. Many who supported the principle, "which was never yet disputed in any part of the state," were distressed by the manner in which the campaign was launched and carried on. "What confounded the men of reflection below," Burke insisted, "was not that they disliked equal representation, but they dreaded the consequences to the welfare of the state, of calling a convention at a moment when the country was inflamed and with such a man as Caroliniensis at the head of it; a man just started up, unknown but by the flame he raised;" lacking both experience and connections, "without a *shilling* of property staked on the table; a man who had fevered the country by a hateful line of demarkation into upper and lower, rich and poor, democrat and aristocrat, and who had set the whole by the ears: I say what reflecting man but would stand in dread of the consequences, had he been able to give motion and impulse as he pleased, to public affairs!" Even backcountry leaders "beheld the ferment raised by Caroliniensis with dread and melancholy; *and were once persuaded that it would end in another Alleghany business.*"[56]

Caroliniensis "was only driving at his own elevation." Although now supporting the President in the matter of the Treaty, he had frequently abused him in the past and once declared him "far more dangerous to America, than Caesar was in Rome." As a defender of the Treaty, Harper was either misleading the people to whom he had professed love of liberty or misleading the President and his ministers by appearing to give them support. In either case he was entitled to no weight. Burke then arrived at his peroration.

---

56. The reference is to the Whiskey Rebellion in western Pennsylvania in 1794.

O! Ye Freemen of Ninety Six! Ye have made a pretty piece of business of it! Instead of sending some well-tried steady man among yourselves, you gave your votes to a man of yesterday, whom you knew not. Whose integrity and character you had never put to any other trial than his own insincere, hollow professions of democratic love for you. Who loved you no otherwise than as a step ladder to his promotion. . . . You sent to Philadelphia, a representative who made you believe that he was one of you, and exactly of your way of thinking: A man, however, that knew the way and bolted the moment he started from the post; for he did not go around the course even once.

No response attributable to Harper has been found. In April, however, "A Ninety Six Constituent" took Burke to task. With some asperity, he observed that "a profusion of wit, ridicule, and a singularity of language, characteristic of the author," had been employed "to humiliate his antagonist and degrade him in the estimation of his fellow citizens." It was wrong, he argued, to assume that the inhabitants of the backcountry had blindly tied themselves to an undeserving leader. The suggestion that the reform movement threatened "another Alleghany business" was the product of a "heated and perverted imagination." The upper country never entertained any such apprehension. The residents of the backcountry were not "those factious, turbulent and fiery spirits that a certain description of characters are disposed to pourtray." They were, rather, "a hardy, industrious race of men, friends to order, submissive to the laws, but conscious of their wrongs, and determined on a constitutional redress." It was ungenerous to cast aspersions on a respectable part of the state "merely to gratify [the writer's] spleen against an ambitious individual." It was illiberal to represent "the upper country as impatient to plunge into the horrors of anarchy, and for no other purpose than that the public indignation might be directed in an overflowing stream against his antagonist Caroliniensis." It exhibited "a disposition particularly malignant" by attributing "to a well disposed people the most horrid intentions."[57] There is no clear evidence that Burke pursued the matter in the press thereafter.

Meanwhile Burke's correspondence with Butler continued. "The President intends to retire if the friends of Monarchy will

---

57. *SCSG*, April 16, 1796.

let him," Butler advised on April 15. "Crowned Monsters" were to blame for all the misery in Europe. "European Systems" were abhorrent, "but our administrators have long been aping them." A few days later, he wrote again, beginning with a strong profession of lasting friendship for Burke and following with an extended review of the situation in Philadelphia. The House was against the Treaty, Butler said, and then continued:

> As the situation of the Faction grows more desperate, the baseness of their designs clearly develops. They lose temper, lay aside the thin veil that covered dark designs on the Constitution, and write and speak publicly of a separation of the Union. . . . Who, say they, will longer submit to a majority composed of a black representation, alluding to the allowance [for] the Representation of Negroes.

Even the Vice-President, at a recent dinner where Butler was present, "reiterated the Sentiment and civil war was spoken of with a sans froid that would shock the feelings of a . . . Caligula." Administration leaders were playing over again the part of the French nobility. "They are rapidly involving a certain character in difficulties they cannot extricate him from." All the weight of the money interest was being exerted in support of the Treaty.[58]

Shortly thereafter, on April 30, the issue was resolved in favor of the administration by three votes. Butler was bitter. Speaking of Harper, "the less we have to do with so unprincipled a man the better," he told Burke. But he would not be surprised if Harper were reelected. As for himself, Butler was determined to retire from the Senate at the end of the year. He expressed that same determination to Thomas Sumter. The Treaty matter was no longer of interest, he said. The maneuverings within the administration on the Treaty revealed the influence of Britain in American councils. "It requires a large portion of philosophy to reconcile you and other virtuous citizens to this new order of things, to this returning under the British Yoke." There was no alternative but to retire to private life.[59]

---

58. Butler to Burke, April 15, 1796, and Butler to Burke, April 20, 1796, Butler Letterbook, 1794–1822, HSP. The "certain character" referred to in the April 20 letter was surely Washington.
59. Butler to Burke, June 7, 1796, and Butler to Sumter, June 18, 1796, Butler Letterbook, 1794–1822, HSP. Butler was in the forefront of the opposition to the

He wrote in a similar vein to Burke. "It is, as you justly observe, useless to attempt to check the current, or to take the veil from the eyes of many," he wrote in late June. "Things must get worse before there is or can be any hope for change." Even so, the people surely could not be so inconsiderate as to reelect Harper. By August, it was "unthinkable" that Harper might be reelected. But the chances of the Republican candidates in the forthcoming presidential election were doubtful. "Till the republicans can get a Treasury and a Bank at their will and a number of fat places to give away they will I fear be always defeated."[60] Such factors did not operate for or against Harper, and he won reelection from Ninety Six by a substantial margin over General William Butler, although the vote was close in two of the four counties reported.[61] Pursuant to his plan to winter in the South and summer in Philadelphia, Butler returned to Charleston early in November, just in time to be greeted by the news.[62]

Even if Burke was led into the controversy by Butler, he must have endorsed Butler's opinion of the Treaty. Many shared the view that it was the work of designing "Anglomen." Burke's attack on Harper, however, said little for his perception or judgment. He may well have been right that Harper was following the path of opportunism, both in his campaign for office in South Carolina and his subsequent career in Philadelphia. Harper brought himself to the attention of his backcountry constituents by taking up the cause of legislative reapportionment and making it his own. In the House of Representatives, he took up the cause of the Treaty in support of the Federalist administration, arguing to his constituents that war was the probable alternative. His sincerity on these issues is irrelevant to evaluation of Burke's role in the matter. Harper embraced the issue of basic significance to the voters in his home district, and he must have concluded that his stand on the Treaty, presented as it was, would not turn them against him at the polls. At worst, he calculated the politi-

---

Treaty in Philadelphia. When the effort failed, he concluded that his influence was so impaired that he could no longer serve in the Senate in justice to the state or to himself.

60. Butler to Burke, June 27, 1796, and Butler to Burke, August 8, 1796, Butler Letterbook, 1794–1822, HSP.
61. *CGDA*, October 25, 1796. Harper's margin was 36 votes in Edgefield County, 55 votes in Laurens County, 331 votes in Abbeville County, and 422 votes in Newberry County.
62. *CGDA*, November 8, 1796.

cal odds, gambled on his judgment, and won. Such operational-
ism was foreign to Burke, who was never comfortable with the
politics of expediency. He challenged Harper on grounds of principle, consistency, and public virtue, wholly ignoring the merits
of the Treaty issue, but failed to move Harper's constituents. Indeed, Burke apparently offended at least some of them and may
have unwittingly contributed to Harper's winning margin in the
1796 election. Moreover, he endorsed the merits of legislative reapportionment at least implicitly, when he criticized Harper's tactics even "in a business wherein he should happen to be right"
and in support of a principle "which was never yet disputed in
any part of the state." And Butler had specifically endorsed that
principle in an earlier letter to Harper calling the existing apportionment "degrading to Freemen and dishonorable to the
country."[63] Thus, both Burke and Butler subordinated a domestic
political objective with which they were basically sympathetic to
their fear that the national leadership was surrendering republican independence to thinly disguised British dominion and
thereby sacrificing the hard earned benefits of the Revolution.

Burke and Butler continued to correspond intermittently after August 1796. Burke visited New York in 1797 and wrote Butler
to describe the scene there. Butler replied:

> Your observation on the mercantile men is correct—to them,
> with certain exceptions, we are to attribute the present state
> of things, as well political as pecuniary in America. Their
> increasing wealth has given them much influence in and
> over the Councils of the United States. To this class of men,
> backed by the intrigues of Hamilton and the unaccountable
> versatility of the late President, we are indebted for all the
> evils that are daily presenting themselves. If the British
> Treaty had no other bad effect than that of inflaming the
> minds of men, and causing distrust and party heat, that
> alone would have been in the eye of prudence and
> patriotism ground sufficient for rejecting it.

But the effect was even more serious. British ascendancy in
American councils might "lure" the United States into war on
the side of the monarchies against France. "No pains are spared,
no falsehood too great to overleap, for the purpose of poisoning

---

63. Butler to Harper, March 4, 1794, Butler Letterbook, 1790–1794, SCL.

the minds of the House of Representatives against the French—Falsehood on falsehood is propagated for the purpose of inflaming the public mind." In early 1798, he was writing to the same effect to Charles Pinckney.[64]

A few months later Butler was damning Harper again. "Had all the South Carolina members been republican, the republican side would have had a majority," he told Burke, "and war and all its mighty train of evils prevented. . . . I wish you would interest yourself in the next elections." He then launched on a long lament. The changes in the public mood were inexplicable. Was there no such thing as national gratitude? Sentiment was turning against the French, even in South Carolina. "Such a heresy" should not be countenanced.

> I think with you that [the French] have saved us more than
> once from despotism; yet our Government appears at this
> moment to be undergoing a great change. . . . I much fear
> the too apparent heat and animosity cannot be allayed by
> ordinary means. The evils that may grow out of the present
> jealousies are incalculable; and for all these are we, in my
> judgment, indebted to Mr. W———. Whenever a faithful
> historian gives a history of his time, he will say, that the
> evils he gave birth to in his civil capacity, more than
> outweigh the benefits derived to this country from any
> military service he may have rendered it. [Washington's
> actions] have caused such discord and distrust throughout
> all ranks of men, as no moderate efforts I fear can
> remove—That national character and internal harmony
> should be sacrificed by the wickedness of one man, Jay, and
> the imprudence of Washington, is to be lamented.[65]

In August, Butler wrote Sumter on the importance of electing real Republicans. In September, he dashed off a series of letters on the approaching congressional elections in South Carolina. If the Carolina delegation had been united, he argued, the Treaty would have been defeated. Because the delegation was divided, the state lacked the weight in the national House to which it was entitled. He urged his correspondents to use their influence in the elections, to call meetings of Republicans in ad-

---

64. Butler to Burke, December 22, 1797, and Butler to Charles Pinckney, January 10, 1798, Butler Letterbook, 1794–1822, HSP.
65. Butler to Burke, March 17, 1798, Butler Letterbook, 1794–1822, HSP. The reference is to the undeclared "quasi-war" with France.

vance of the vote, to agree on candidates, and to "let nothing divide the friends of republicanism." A "virtuous representation" from South Carolina, he said, was crucial to her influence and prestige.[66]

The correspondence between Burke and Butler concluded on that note. Whether Burke ever actively interested himself in the elections, as Butler suggested, cannot now be determined, but the rudimentary beginnings of organized political opposition in South Carolina seem clear enough. Suspicion of British intentions remained high, of course, even though enthusiasm for the French cause was signficantly diluted over time. As for the Treaty issue, it receded once it was resolved and as some of those most violently opposed had second thoughts. In December 1796, the governor calmly pointed out the wisdom of staying far removed from foreign turmoil and the expediency of union and efficient government.[67]

Moreover, despite all the attention given to the Treaty issue in 1795 and 1796, other political issues, approached more soberly, were of greater concern to most South Carolinians in the 1790s. Legislative reapportionment, agitated but thrust aside by the General Assembly in 1795, was agitated again in 1796. Reform of the judicial system was a rising issue. In November 1796, "a gentleman on the Western Circuit," possibly one of the judges, reported to a friend in Charleston that a "crisis" was approaching in the contest between the "nominal divisions" of lowcountry and backcountry. Backcountry leaders, he said, were planning "to bring their two favorite reforms, of the representation and of the judiciary, early before the legislature; and if they fail in the carrying of them through, to return instantly home, together with their phalanx, and thus put an end to the session, without passing a tax bill or any other."[68] No such eventuality occurred, but both matters were of serious concern to the people of South Carolina. Legislative reapportionment was defeated again by the General Assembly in 1796 on the same grounds given in 1794, and virtually in the same words. Judicial reform was approached

---

66. Butler to Sumter, August 6, 1798; Butler to Arthur Simkins, September 6, 1798; Butler to General Butler, September 7, 1798; and Butler to Thomas Fitzpatrick, September 8, 1798, Butler Letterbook, 1794–1822, HSP.

67. *CGDA*, December 8, 1796; Journal of the House of Representatives, November 29, 1796, SCA.

68. *CGDA*, November 10, 1796.

with traditional caution and was finally accomplished in 1799. The available record, however, does not suggest that Burke was significantly involved in either issue.

As an active Republican, Burke was unacceptable to conservative South Carolinian Federalists in the 1790s. When William Loughton Smith accepted appointment as minister to Portugal, John Rutledge, Jr. wrote home to urge the selection of a suitable replacement for Smith in the House of Representatives. "For God's sake," he said, "do not send us Charles Pinckney, Burke, Tucker or any of that low class."[69] Burke spoke for Jefferson in 1796, arguing that the defenders of Adams could not disprove the charges laid against him and therefore attacked Jefferson on ridiculous grounds.[70] In 1797, he decried the existing misunderstandings between the Americans and the French. The discontented, the worthless, and the wretched sought to provoke war with France, he suggested, but the citizenry was "too sensible to the just causes of offence which have lately been offered to the republic of France" to be misled and would be "watchful against the snares of the designing."[71]

He declined to be a candidate for the United States Senate in 1798.[72] And he was predictably offended by the alien and sedition laws. In his last surviving comment on public affairs, he wrote to Madison in 1801, hoping to save Edward Weyman's job as surveyor of the port of Charleston under the new Republican adminstration.

> During the reign of Terror in 1798 and 99 which struck into the minds of men such a dread and panic in this City, there were not ten men to whom I dared speak my mind; there were not, I declare before God, there were not half a dozen men, yet Weyman never quitted the ground; and I expected every week nothing less than his removal. I congratulate you Sir, that that Season of Tribulation is past. I have been a prisoner of war in the hands of the British for Sixteen

---

69. John Rutledge, Jr. to Edward Rutledge, July 7, 1797, Dreer Collection, HSP.
70. "A.B." in *CGDA*, November 11, 1796. Given the subject matter, "A.B." is assumed to be Burke.
71. "A.B." in *CGDA*, April 20, 1797. See comment in immediately preceding note.
72. *CGDA*, December 7, 1798. Edward Rutledge was elected governor and Charles Pinckney was elected senator. Pinckney defeated Pickens 79 to 63. *CGDA*, December 11, 1798. The senate seat was open because of the resignation of John Hunter, who succeeded Butler when Butler resigned in 1796.

months, captured with the Garrison in Charleston; and provided I had a good Guarantee of an Exchange, I would as lieve go to the Devil for Sixteen months more as be with the British again; and yet, it was not so excruciating to one's feelings, as the despotic insolence, with which one part of our fellow citizens hunted down those who differed from them in that day. I visited Philadelphia and New York during part of that time. No historical account will be able to give a good idea of it. I fear it is a national crime, and may God forgive the Guilty and Guard the innocent in future.[73]

Notwithstanding his unwilllingness to stand for the United States Senate in 1798, Burke surely yearned to return to national office after the Republican electoral victory in 1800. He had two opportunities. The first arose in December 1800, when Jacob Read's Senate term was about to expire. Read was defeated for reelection by John Ewing Colhoun in a close vote.[74] Colhoun was put up by the "antis because they could do no better," John Rutledge, Jr. told James A Bayard. "They wanted Colonel Hampton or Judge Burke, but, doubting their strength, they put up Mr. Colhoun, counting upon their party being joined by some yea and nay members who profess neutrality and to love *moderate men*, and they succeeded by a majority of *one*." Colhoun was not a man of "high powers," but he was "honest and from the western country" and should be conciliated. "I *know*," Rutledge said, "that with a little jockeying he may be whipped into the right course."[75]

Burke had his second chance in December 1801 when the vacancy created by Charles Pinckney's resignation to accept appointment as minister to Spain was filled. Pinckney resigned his Senate seat in early spring and was back in Charleston before the

---

73. Burke to Madison, December 13, 1801, in Gaillard Hunt, "Office Getting During Jefferson's Administration," *American Historical Review*, 3 (1897–1898): 278–79.
74. Journal of the House of Representatives, December 4, 1800, SCA. Neither candidate had a majority on the first vote, which was probably a tie. A motion to defer the election was defeated 59 to 49. On the second vote, Colhoun was the winner.
75. John Rutledge, Jr. to James A. Bayard, November 21, 1801, John Rutledge, Jr. Papers, Southern Historical Collection, Wilson Library, University of North Carolina. Rutledge was reporting on the South Carolina congressional delegation in the Congress scheduled to convene on December 1.

end of May.[76] In July, Peter Freneau delivered a wide-ranging report to Butler on the political scene in South Carolina. Some Republicans were grumbling that more changes had not been made by the new administration. As for himself, Freneau viewed Federalists, with but few exceptions, as men so soured by defeat that "they would make our government a monarchy, or even restore it to the stupid wretch who once was our Master, could they but bear down the present administration." He had no confidence, he said, "in federalists, every day exposing their cloven feet, and if our government does not act with a firm hand and make an example of all those who have trodden down the liberties of the people, and who ruled with a Robespierian sway in 98 and 99, they will rise into power again." In the forthcoming contest for Pinckney's Senate seat, the Federalists intended to support John Ward, "and their hopes of success rest as much on the prospect of a division amongst the republicans, as on their own strength, and, I fear, they do not calculate on false principles." Burke, he continued, "is privately determined to be a candidate," and Freneau would be glad to see him in any place he wished for and would go to all proper lengths to serve him. But he doubted that Burke would receive the unanimous support of the backcountry and without such support no Republican would succeed. Since Burke was planning another trip north, and would probably call on Butler, Freneau suggested to Butler that "a hint from you on the doubtfulness of his success and of the prospect it gives of distracting the administration" might be of weight with him.[77]

In early August, Freneau provided background to Burke's candidacy. Burke was being urged on, Freneau told Butler, by a colleague on the equity bench, presumably William Marshall, so that "a connection" of Marshall's could succeed to the vacancy. "I know the J——e," Freneau went on, "he is an honest man, and no person on earth would be more pleased than myself to have him whatever he would wish to be, but ought he not to consider well before he gives up an easy place of £500 a year, which he has for life—but the thing has been made very clear to the J——e, he is to sell his house for £3000 or £3500, put this in the funds and with the interest and the pay of a Senator, he is

76. Peter Freneau to Pierce Butler, May 26, 1801, Pierce Butler Papers, HSP.
77. Peter Freneau to Pierce Butler, July 24, 1801, Pierce Butler Papers, HSP.

to be more happy than he now is. Can you not put a stop to this business? Ought not his friends to prevent his being too precipitate?"[78] Quite clearly, Freneau questioned whether Burke's candidacy could succeed.

Later in the month Freneau reported further, advising that Burke's trip north was off and that Sumter had agreed to accept a gubernatorial appointment to the Senate if the governor would make it, which was not at all certain. "I think a line from you to the Governor on this head would have great weight," Freneau told Butler; "he will pay more attention to any thing you say than to what can be urged here."[79] No interim appointment was made, but in December Sumter was elected to fill the vacancy and took Pinckney's seat in the Senate in mid-December.[80]

Such maneuverings as may have occurred between August and December remain unclear, but Burke's position at the end of his public career seems plain enough. He was apparently unhappy on the equity bench. He would have welcomed an opportunity to return to the national political arena in the Senate, but he could not deliver the unanimous, or near unanimous, support of backcountry representatives in the General Assembly essential to that end. No doubt a variety of factors contributed to his relative isolation in the political environment of Jeffersonian South Carolina. But he had fallen out of phase, not for lack of principle, but for lack of capacity to adapt to the changing political scene. This was nowhere more apparent than in the form and substance of his attack on Robert Goodloe Harper in 1796. Burke perhaps sensed the change in his standing. When he sat in Ninety Six in April 1799, the grand jury submitted its presentments and pointedly acknowledged that the judge had not in his charge "troubled us nor himself with the subject of politics, foreign or domestic, confining himself to the business of the court."[81] Whether Burke simply passed the opportunity or consciously decided that the grand jurors were not receptive to a political lecture from him, the incident suggests awareness that even his judicial role as educator of the public had diminished as his public career neared its end.

---

78. Peter Freneau to Pierce Butler, August 7, 1801, Pierce Butler Papers, HSP.
79. Peter Freneau to Pierce Butler, August 21, 1801, Pierce Butler Papers, HSP.
80. Journel of the House of Representatives, December 3, 1801, SCA. Sumter was already a member of the national House of Representatives and in Philadelphia.
81. *CGDA*, June 4, 1799.

X

Judge Burke

1778–1801

The major part of Burke's public career was on the bench, where he served continually from 1778 until his death in 1802. His judicial service was broken only during the war years when the courts were not sitting and for the two years while he served in the First Congress. Indeed, he performed at least some judicial duties during periods when the First Congress was in recess and he was in Charleston, notwithstanding that he was officially on leave of absence.[1] Moreover, the judicial role was the role he fulfilled best. In contrast to the volatility and inconclusiveness of his performance in the role of legislator and the frequent stridency apparent in the performance of his self-assigned role as publicist and polemicist, his performance on the bench was decisive and effective. Operating within the formal framework of the law, following familiar precepts and established rules of judicial decision, he was both more comfortable and more confident. In essence, the requirements of the judicial role shaped his performance in it, while, in his other roles, the applicable parameters were more ambiguous in the new world of the young republic.

English common and statute law, together with the forms of English legal practice, were at the base of South Carolina's legal system in 1776. Many of the practitioners in Charleston were English trained. The circuit court system was new and relatively untried. And the political leaders of the transition from colonial status to sovereign independence were not inclined to be more adventurous than absolutely necessary. Accordingly, the existing legal and judicial systems were taken over virtually intact when independence was achieved. Nonetheless, although South Carolina was spared disruptive debate on the question whether continued deference to English law might be dangerous to the

---

1. *CGDA*, September 14, 1790.

republican integrity of the new state, she shared with her sister states the problems of adapting the body of received law to her indigenous circumstances, molding it to her needs as such circumstances changed, and administering it through an efficiently functioning judicial system. These were formidable problems, and part of the burden fell on the judges.

Prior to 1769, the common law courts of South Carolina sat only in Charleston. In response to long-standing demands of backcountry residents for a functioning system of courts within reasonable reach of their homes, the Circuit Court Act of 1769 divided the state into seven judicial districts: Charleston, Beaufort, Georgetown, Orangeburgh, Cheraw, Camden, and Ninety Six.[2] Through the 1780s, a court was convened seven times a year in Charleston; in three sessions, the court heard criminal cases, sitting as a Court of General Sessions; in the other four, it heard civil cases, sitting as a Court of Common Pleas. In the outlying districts, a court was convened twice a year in each of them and sat on both criminal and civil cases at each session. At these sessions, the court sat from day to day up to six days. Uncompleted business was carried over to the next session.[3]

Little enough time was allowed. In Beaufort and Georgetown, the court convened on April 5 and November 5 in each year; in Orangeburgh and Cheraw, on April 15 and November 15; and in Ninety Six and Camden, on April 26 and November 26. Normally, one judge covered Beaufort, Orangeburgh, and Ninety Six, while another covered Georgetown, Cheraw, and Camden.[4] Timothy Ford estimated that the usual circuit took approximately five weeks.[5] That period may have sufficed for the itinerant attorneys from Charleston, but it hardly seems adequate time for the judges.

---

2. An Act for establishing Courts, building Gaols and appointing Sheriffs and other officers for the more convenient Administration of Justice in this Province, July 29, 1769, Manuscript Acts, SCA, commonly referred to as the Circuit Court Act of 1769. The Act is reprinted in Richard Maxwell Brown, *The South Carolina Regulators* (Cambridge: Harvard University Press, 1963), 148–58. The text set forth in the *Statutes at Large* is an earlier version that never became effective.

3. In 1783, The General Assembly adopted "An Act for the Continuance of Process and Judicial Proceedings in this State," *Statutes at Large*, 7: 206–207, which reconfirmed the sittings provided for in the Circuit Court Act of 1769.

4. The dates precluded one judge from covering both circuits, and the applicable laws specifically authorized any one of the judges in office to convene a court.

5. "Diary of Timothy Ford, 1785–1786," Joseph W. Barnwell, ed., *SCHM*, 13 (1912): 199.

Two new districts, Washington and Pinckney, were created in 1791, increasing the number of country court districts from six to eight and the number of country court circuits from two to three. At the same time, one of the civil sessions in Charleston was eliminated. Accordingly, there were a total of twenty-two court sessions each year through the 1790s,[6] and three judges instead of two were required to cover the circuits. As court calendars became crowded, the General Assembly on occasion directed a second judge to sit in a particular district, but in general one judge covered each circuit alone.

The court was almost always undermanned. Between the death of William Henry Drayton in 1779 and the election of John Rutledge in 1791, there was no chief justice, and none was selected to replace Rutledge when he resigned in 1795. When the circuit court returned to its business in 1783, the sitting judges in addition to Burke were Henry Pendleton, the only carryover from the original panel of judges selected in 1776, and Thomas Heyward, Jr., elected in 1779. In early 1783, the General Assembly declined to elect a chief justice but did elect John F. Grimke an assistant judge.[7] Thus four judges were sitting when the court resumed its business after the Revolution. As the senior assistant judge, Pendleton was de facto chief justice.

In the aggregate, these judges constituted a capable bench. Pendleton, a native Virginian and a nephew of Virginia's famous Edmund Pendleton, studied law in Virginia before moving to South Carolina and was admitted to practice in Charleston in 1771. Heyward, member of a distinguished South Carolina family, studied law at the Middle Temple in England, was admitted to practice in England in 1770, and, like Pendleton, was admitted to practice in South Carolina in 1771. Grimke, like Heyward, studied law at the Middle Temple and was admitted to practice in England in 1769.[8] All four of the post-war judges had been delegates to the Jacksonborough Assembly; and the sitting judges

---

6. *Statutes at Large*, 7: 260–65. Courts convened in Beaufort, Georgetown, and Pinckney on April 1 and November 1; in Orangeburgh on April 10 and November 8; in Cheraw and Washington on April 10 and November 10; in Camden on April 19 and November 19; and in Ninety Six on April 18 and November 16.
7. *JHR 1783–1784*, 148, 261–62. Grimke was chosen after John Mathews was elected but declined to serve.
8. *Bio. Directory*, 2: 323–25 (Heyward); 3: 290–92 (Grimke); 3: 547 (Pendleton).

regularly served in the General Assembly until compelled to withdraw from the legislature by the Constitution of 1790.

Pendleton died in 1788 and was succeeded by Thomas Waties, who had studied law in Charleston under John Julius Pringle and was admitted to practice in 1785.[9] Heyward resigned in 1789, and was succeeded by William Drayton. Burke was by then on leave, and Drayton soon resigned to accept appointment to the federal bench as judge of the United States District Court in Charleston. Thus, during the 1780s, and until the election of Rutledge as chief justice and Elihu Hall Bay as an assistant judge in 1791, there were never more than four, and sometimes only three, sitting common law judges. The court was at full strength only from 1791 to 1795, when Rutledge resigned upon his nomination as Chief Justice of the United States. Thereafter, until the courts were again reorganized in 1799, there were only four sitting judges.

Travel on circuit was a burden. There were, of course, opportunities to socialize with friends or acquaintances in the course of travel from one court town to the next; and the sessions themselves were local social occasions. But there was always the pressure of time between sessions; and timely arrival for each scheduled session was a judicial duty, seriously regarded. Late arrival or failure to appear called for official inquiry and explanation.

Grimke has left a comprehensive calendar of his service for the period from his election until early 1793. He sat on the northern circuit (Georgetown, Cheraw, and Camden) in April and November 1783, April 1784, and April 1785. He was also on a circuit in April 1786, November 1787, November 1788, November 1789, April and November 1790, April and November 1791, April 1792, and April 1793. By his count, he rode 14 of the 45 circuits conducted between April 1783 and April 1793 and attended at 27 of 34 courts held in Charleston.[10] This was a full share of the load.

---

9. *Bio. Directory*, 3: 753–55.
10. In 1793, the grand jury in Ninety Six delivered a presentment complaining of delays in the disposition of cases and placing a large measure of the blame on Grimke. Presentment of the Grand Jury for District of Ninety Six, November 16, 1793, Grand Jury Presentments, SCA. Grimke submitted a long statement in reply, demonstrating that only one judge was required to attend unless the General Assembly directed otherwise, and summarizing his attendance at the several courts between 1783 and 1793. Records of the General Assembly, Miscellaneous Communications, SCA.

Burke probably did as much or more. The journal of the Court of Common Pleas in Camden, for example, covers eighteen sessions held in those years between November 1786 and November 1799 when Burke was active on the common law bench. He sat at six—in April 1788 for seven days, in November 1791 for eleven days, with Grimke in April 1793 for five days, in April 1794 for ten days, in November 1796 for seven days, and in November 1798 for four days.[11] On each of these occasions, he also sat in Georgetown and Cheraw, the other country courts on the same circuit with Camden.

The Camden journal provides considerable detail with regard to the practices of the court if not the substance of judicial performance. During the session at which Burke sat in April 1788, for example, forty-six civil causes were docketed as ready for trial. Twenty-five were disposed of by trial on the merits and several were withdrawn. But twenty-four were carried over to the next session. At the session in November 1796, fifty-nine cases were carried over from the prior session and sixty to the next, even though thirty cases were tried and five were dismissed. Much time was spent in disposing of individual motions and technical issues. [12]

Not all sessions were social occasions. In November 1796, a correspondent from Cheraw reported that the judge on circuit, who must have been Burke, had met with "a disagreeable accident." The judge was sleeping in an outside shed and while in court "a *general sweep* was made of his trunk and chair box." He was left only with his greatcoat and a bearskin "which were often his bed at night, and in the day a cover for his luggage." His clothes and all his money left in the trunk were taken. The judges were "no great favorites" in Cheraw District, the correspondent continued, "for the grand jury of the district absolutely libelled the late chief justice to his face, by way of presentment, for missing his way so that he did not arrive 'till the second day of the court." And Judge Waties, "as he was going to the court house one morning, was pelted with mud and cowdung."[13]

---

11. Camden District, Journal of the Court of Common Pleas, 1786–1799, SCA. The journal began with the November court in 1786. Burke also sat in Camden at the April term in that year.
12. Camden District, Journal of the Court of Common Pleas, 1786–1799, SCA.
13. *CGDA*, November 26, 1796. Burke rode the northern circuit in November 1796. Camden District, Journal of the Court of Common Pleas, 1786–1799, SCA.

The courts were often difficult to control. The notorious Camden riot, which shut down the court in April 1785, was the most notable instance.[14] The following year, Burke encountered problems of his own in Camden. The grand jury thanked him for calling to their attention an English law applicable to "all such as are guilty of the barbarous, savage, practice called GOUGING." It further expressed "in a particular manner our full sense of his decided conduct, and manly spirit, in bringing to immediate punishment the three gentlemen who were guilty of the riot the evening before last, and thus preventing any further violation of peace and order."[15] The details of the incident have been elusive. The grand jury asked that Burke's charge be published, but it never appeared and was presumably extemporaneous. Burke was surely forewarned by Grimke's experience the previous year, and the threat in 1786 was probably much less serious. Even so, Burke apparently handled it well.

In April 1795, the grand jury in Ninety Six directly challenged Burke's control of the business of the court. When the court met on April 23, the solicitor for the state announced that he had no further business to present but expected more in the course of the day. The grand jury, "with a certain peremptory and rude manner," demanded to be discharged as a matter of right. Burke announced that the business of the court was not completed, that disturbances had been threatened, and that riots had occurred at the courts on the western circuit, one at Pinckney and two at Washington. He then observed "that for a court, amidst such circumstances of turbulence, to discharge a grand jury would be highly improper; and that the claim of right set up by the grand jury, was setting up a liberty under which they may go home when they choose, and abandon the public service; a precedent that would lay the institution of jury trial in ruin."[16]

The grand jury denounced Burke by way of presentment, complaining that they were detained too long from their homes and families when there was no business for the solicitor, "as we have patiently done our duty until the indictments were ended." In less than half an hour, the solicitor advised the court that he

---

14. A similar event occurred at the Winton County Court in 1790.
15. *CMP*, May 20, 1786.
16. *CGDA*, May 20, 1795. Quoted passages in the following paragraph are from this source.

had a bill of indictment ready to present against a man charged with murder. The grand jury returned an appropriate bill, and the man was tried the next day, found guilty of manslaughter, and punished accordingly. "This circumstance alone opened the eyes of the grand jury, to see that their demand and denunciation were alike unreasonable," Burke reported in a statement read in court before the grand jury and the audience present. "Heaven knows," he concluded, "there were sources enough already for undermining the authority of the laws, and creating disorder in our infant republic, without a grand jury's lending a hand, by spreading a slanderous misrepresentation against a magistrate under the shape of a presentment."

The backcountry was generally unruly, and crime was rampant, particularly in the mid-1780s. In December 1783, following his return from the November session in Ninety Six, Burke informed Governor Guerard that the people of the district were "exposed to great distress, and perpetual alarms, by a few outlyers or banditti, who infest that part of the Country." The outlaws, he continued, "now carry on their villainies without molestation, being well mounted, and the Inhabitants plundered of good horses to pursue." Since the local magistrates were unable to maintain order, Burke recommended that a company of militia be dispatched to Ninety Six.[17]

A year later the situation in Ninety Six was even worse. "It is not in my power," Burke reported to Guerard, to describe "how much the poor people of this District are worried and harassed by a set of horse thieves and an outlying Banditti that constantly beset the roads, rob the inhabitants and plunder their dwellings. No man has security for even a worthless plow horse. . . . As to Trade and commerce it is at an end in that District unless Government take some measures for extirpating the outlyers," such as the militia unit on duty in Orangeburgh. Intercourse with the lowcountry was only possible, he said, when travelers banded together for mutual protection. Lacking security for life or property, the people were precluded from improving their estates and would be without funds for the payment of their taxes. "Except when the Judges go the Circuit," he continued, "the influence of

---

17. Burke to Guerard, December 10, 1783, Records of the General Assembly, Governors' Messages, SCA.

Government is felt but feebly nor can I see that [the people] would be worsted if they had not the name of it." In the criminal cases tried at Ninety Six, five defendants were convicted of capital crimes and in two the jury recommended mercy. No recommendation of mercy came from the court, Burke concluded. "For however averse I ever was to the taking away of life, I have seen so much of distress in the country on my circuit that I am resolved never again to recommend a horse thief for mercy 'til the Crime be less frequent." If you pardon, you must banish, he told the governor.[18]

Burke's most dramatic realization of his post-Jacksonborough fears occurred at the Ninety Six court in 1784. During the war, a party of loyalist partisans under the command of William Cunningham took prisoner a patriot force serving with Colonel Hayes and, in violation of the terms of capitulation, hung Hayes and massacred a number of his men. A prominent member of Cunningham's force was a man named Matthew Love. After the war, Love returned to the vicinity of Ninety Six and was taken into custody by a justice of the peace, "who committed him to jail," Burke said in his report of the incident, "thinking so barbarous a man did not come under the treaty of peace, so as to be sheltered from prosecution." When Love came before the court, Burke "overruled the prosecution; I being of opinion That under the Treaty, his Conscience and his feelings alone stood responsible for what was alleged." Love was accordingly discharged on the motion of his counsel. The Love matter was the last item of business on the criminal docket, and the court adjourned immediately after his discharge. Burke returned to his lodgings. Shortly thereafter, a number of the local citizenry, "without tumult or noise," took Love prisoner, marched him into the woods, and hung him. Burke made no apology for his own action in the affair. The people of Ninety Six wished ardently to forget the injuries of the war, he observed. "Many plunderers and other mischievous people now set down among them without molestation; nor can I learn that there exists resentment against any man who acted like a Soldier and fought them in fair open action." But he regretted that a man such as Love would be "so infatuated as to

---

18. Burke to Guerard, December 14, 1784, Records of the General Assembly, Governors' Messages, SCA.

return among the Citizens, and thus prevent the restoration of the public tranquillity."[19]

The hanging of Matthew Love became over the years an important item in the anecdotal record of Burke's life. His report was published in mid-1785 with minor changes designed to emphasize that the lynching was conducted by respectable citizens without tumult or disorder, even adding a sentence to the effect that through the whole affair the persons involved "studiously affected to preserve every appearance of respect toward the judge."[20] Subsequent versions contributed to Burke's reputation as an unpredictable and eccentric Irishman, suggesting that he was unable to control the mob and fled the scene for his own safety.[21]

Burke was a caring judge when the circumstances warranted. On the same circuit in 1784, at the court in Orangeburgh, a boy of sixteen was convicted of horse stealing and sentenced to be hanged. The jury recommended mercy, but the boy had no reliable friend to intercede for him in Charleston. Burke, fearing that he might not return in time, set up an automatic reprieve with the local sheriff to assure that the sentence would not be executed before the case could be properly reviewed. The boy was so young and the family so impoverished that he was "easily debauched into his present unhappy condition," Burke told Governor Guerard, and earnestly supported the jury's recommendation.[22]

Burke could be stern when his court was defied, and he was jealous of its prerogatives. In late 1784, the celebrated Colonel Hezekiah Maham forced a sheriff's deputy to eat the writ of the Court of Common Pleas that the hapless deputy was trying to serve on him in a proceeding to collect an unpaid debt. The Court of General Sessions thereupon issued a series of bench warrants for Maham's arrest until he finally appeared to stand trial. The court, with Burke sitting as one of the judges, sen-

19. Burke to Guerard, December 14, 1784, Records of the General Assembly, Governors' Messages, SCA; reprinted in Michael E. Stevens, "The Hanging of Matthew Love," *SCHM*, 88 (1987): 55–61.

20. *CH*, July 4, 1785.

21. Stevens, "The Hanging of Matthew Love."

22. Burke to Guerard, November 17, 1784, Records of the General Assembly, Governors' Messages, SCA.

tenced Maham to three months imprisonment, fined him, and bound him to good behavior for seven years under a £2000 bond. The governor commuted the prison term, but referred him to the General Assembly for further relief. Maham then submitted a petition to the General Assembly, claiming that the punishment was excessive and charging the judges with "great cruelty and oppression." Burke responded for the court. "As he was a Citizen of Character and repute," Burke said, "the Court of Sessions saw there was a necessity of bringing him to justice, and lest other offenders should under his example, from hopes of impunity, trample on the laws." His accusations against the judges, Burke continued, "looks as if he thought himself too big for a Court and Jury to deal with." His attempt to censure the judges was "calculated to terrify present and future magistrates, from executing Justice on other Citizens, who might violate the laws, on the confidence that wealth, influence or powerful connections would shelter them from punishment." If Maham were excused, the courts would be embarrassed for lack of consistency in any proceeding to enforce judicial process against persons of lesser rank. And his conduct "has laid a mischievous precedent in this country, that its Laws and Government may be set at defiance by powerful Citizens, provided he has but the assurance to defy it."[23]

Maham's petition was submitted in February 1786. In March the House approved a committee report recommending that his fine be refunded and his bond released. Although his conduct was "very reprehensible for an Opposition to the Civil Authority," the committee found that Maham "was carried Away by a Sudden gust of passion and not Actuated by any motives of condemning the Judicial authority."[24] The Senate, however, refused to concur until a second resolution was included expressly announcing the General Assembly's approval of the action taken by the judges.[25]

At least one citizen was upset. The release of Maham, he wrote in a letter to the *Charleston Morning Post*, was a case in which "declamation and regard to private interests prevailed over reason and attachment to the Commonwealth" and "was

---

23. Aedanus Burke, Memorial to the General Assembly, March 1, 1786, Records of the General Assembly, SCA. See Michael E. Stevens, "Influence or Powerful Connections: Aedanus Burke and the Case of Hezekiah Maham," *SCHM*, 81 (1980): 163–68. Maham's petition is in *JHR 1785–1786*, 455–58.
24. *JHR 1785–1786*, 486.
25. Ibid., 498.

pregnant with more evils than issued from Pandora's box." Already, "at a few miles from the capital, have a few men resisted the execution of legal process. . . . The laws will become contemptible. The officers of justice will be insulted, and government exist only in name." Such conduct, the writer concluded, tended to throw the country into anarchy, to destroy civil liberty, and to encourage the "curse" of aristocracy.[26] The writer is unknown, but the words have a Burkean ring.

While the Maham matter was pending in the General Assembly, the Court of General Sessions was sitting in Charleston with Burke and Heyward presiding. On February 18, Major William Clay Snipes appeared for trial, charged with the murder of Colonel Maurice Simons in a duel fought in November 1785.[27] Snipes and Simons were both prominent Charlestonians with distinguished records of service in the war. The duel was precipitated when Snipes complained of testimony given by Simons in a civil action between Snipes and Rawlins Lowndes.[28] It was not entirely clear which of the two had demanded satisfaction, whether Snipes challenged Simons on the basis of his testimony at the trial, or Simons challenged Snipes for questioning the integrity of his evidence. There was, however, testimony to the effect that Snipes had demanded satisfaction of Simons or would post him as a "perjured coward."[29]

Charging the jury at the conclusion of the evidence, Burke observed that, "although duelling was in point of law a capital offense, yet such was the prevalence of custom . . . that duelling might be considered as the law of some countries; schoolmen might employ themselves in writing books against it—divines execrate this practice from their pulpits—and lawyers harangue against it with all the powers of eloquence, yet so long as mankind continued to consider the fighting of duels as the only manner in which points of honor could be adjusted it was improbable that duelling would fall into disuse." The evidence "pressed

---

26. *CMP*, March 28, 1786.
27. The duel was reported in the *SCGDA*, November 15, 1785, and the *CEG*, November 17, 1785.
28. Snipes criticized Lowndes's conduct during the British occupation of Charleston. Lowndes sued for slander and won. Henry Laurens and Simons testified for Lowndes. Carl J. Vipperman, *The Rise of Rawlins Lowndes, 1721–1800* (Columbia: University of South Carolina Press, 1978), 236. The proceeding was reported in the *CEG*, October 27 and 28, 1785.
29. *CMP*, February 21, 1786.

hard" on the defendant, Burke said. He "had challenged the unfortunate deceased gentlemen for giving his evidence in a court of justice—a most unwarrantable aggression, because it had a tendency to destroy the foundation of justice." The Attorney General had argued that, once publicly affronted by Snipes, Simons had no alternative but to send a challenge and that Snipes was therefore the aggressor. Burke described the affair from a somewhat different perspective. Once Snipes had given the unjustifiable affront, "he had put it out of his power to recede; after declaring that he would post Col. Simons for a coward because he refused to give satisfaction, when this called for satisfaction was offered, to have refused it—to have in any respect appeared unwilling to meet in the field or forward to make advances towards a reconciliation, would have laid his character open to such imputations as no man of spirit could bear to live under." In effect, angered and perhaps "still flushed a little with liquor," Snipes had "plunged into a dilemma from which he could not extricate himself." Nonetheless, in Burke's opinion, no verdict could be found short of manslaughter, for which the punishment was burning in the hand and loss of property, "a heavy punishment, but yet necessary to expiate so high an offense."[30]

Heyward was less favorably disposed. The duel had been precipitated by "the violent affront given by the prisoner—and from a cause that was itself an offense—being on account of evidence given in a court of justice." He could find no extenuating circumstances. He concluded that "he considered this crime as amounting to murder." The verdict, however, was manslaughter.[31] A week later, Snipes appeared for sentencing and pleaded a full pardon.[32] He was accordingly released.

Burke is not on record as actively supporting major overhaul of the judicial system in the 1790s. Perhaps he was deterred by the legislature's initially negative response to the scope of the report submitted by the commission to digest and revise the laws in 1789. Nor did he adopt the cause of penal code reform projected by the Constitution of 1778, also recommended in 1789, and agitated in the press during the 1790s.[33] He did, however,

---

30. Ibid.
31. Ibid.
32. *CMP*, February 27, 1786.
33. Burke generally endorsed harsh criminal penalties and did not hesitate to apply them when sentencing those convicted of crime. This attitude was con-

address some of the more glaring defects in the day to day administration of justice. One was the atrocious condition of the jails. Another was the extreme burden imposed by the established jury system on many of those required, on penalty of substantial fines, to serve as jurors.

After the Circuit Court Act of 1769 was approved, court houses and jails were built at the several locations where the courts were scheduled to sit. The court houses were small but adequate. Small, spare, and indifferently maintained, the jails steadily deteriorated in the ensuing years and were totally inadequate in the 1790s. Jail breaking was common. The newspapers regularly reported escapes and printed proclamations promising rewards for recapture.

In April 1795, Burke reported from the Pinckney District that three men accused of horse stealing had made their escape by breaking a hole through the wall. This was the third such incident, he said, "an enterprise of so easy execution that there is in it no sort of difficulty or risk." Thus, "as far as the want of a jail to confine malefactors renders a Country lawless, this District may be said so far to be without law." Burke had examined the jail. It was thirteen feet long and twelve feet wide, "with only one small grated window, ten inches high and nine inches wide, and upwards of five feet above the floor. The miserable wretch whose destiny it is to lodge there, is without light enough to read, chilled and suffocated with cold, and with damp and foul air in winter, and dissolved with scorching heat in the warm weather. As to the execution and finish of the work, it is the most faithless, unworkmanlike and bungling: an excellent example it is, how a very good republican people, will sometimes spend the public money."[34]

---

firmed during Burke's term in the First Congress. When a bill dealing with punishment for crimes was under consideration, Smith and Burke together successfully opposed an amendment permitting a lesser punishment than hanging for counterfeiting and forgery. "They severally dilated on the injuries that society was liable to from the ingenuity of these unprincipled persons," and "the extreme difficulty of guarding against their depredations, rendered it highly expedient they should be cut off." *Annals*, 2: 1521. Counterfeiting and forgery were also capital crimes in South Carolina.

34. Burke to Vanderhorst, April 1, 1795, Records of the General Assembly, Letters relating to Public Improvements, SCA. On jail conditions generally, see John A. Hall, "A Rigour of Confinement that Violates Humanity: Jail Conditions in South Carolina during the 1790s," *Southern Studies: An Interdisciplinary Journal of the South*, 24 (1985): 284–305.

Again in December 1795, Burke complained of the condition of the jails throughout the state. They were so flimsy that sheriffs were obliged to take extreme measures to prevent escape. Some prisoners were chained to each other or to the walls. One man, on learning that his trial had been put over and that he would have to remain in jail through the summer, obtained poison from a friend and committed suicide. A year later, conditions were no better. Prisoners were without blankets or warm clothing in the cold of winter, and some had died. Some bedding, at least, should be provided.[35] Except for modest repairs to enhance security, nothing was done. Improvement of the jails was not a matter of high priority, and the harsh conditions under which prisoners were held evoked little public sympathy.

As the business of the courts increased, the burden of jury service increased with it. Sessions were extended by delays in the disposition of pending cases, to the distress not only of jurors but of litigants, witnesses, and counsel. Jurors away from their homes were detained, sometime without any immediate work to be done. Their resentment occasionally impaired the efficient disposition of the court's work. Burke's experience with the grand jury at the Ninety Six court in 1796 was just one example.

Nearly every court session was followed by a published list of defaulting grand and petit jurors fined for nonappearance. Despite the recommendations made by Burke, Pendleton, and Grimke in their report to the General Assembly in 1789, no provision was made to compensate jurors for the time and trouble of attending court sessions. Those who could afford the fines were the most frequent absentees. Those who could not attended under protest. As a result, many who petitioned the General Assembly for more convenient courts in the early 1780s changed their position after adoption of the County Court Act in 1785.[36]

Hardship was perhaps more severe for jurors who appeared to serve than for those who did not. Lodgings were scarce and expensive. "The hardships that these poor jurors suffer," Burke reported to the governor in 1796, "are such that men who enjoy plentiful meals and warm beds can form no idea of." Denied the

---

35. Burke to Vanderhorst, December 4, 1795, and Burke to Vanderhorst, December 8, 1796, Records of the General Assembly, Governors' Messages, SCA.
36. John A. Hall, "That Onerous Task: Jury Service in South Carolina During the Early 1790s," *SCHM*, 87 (1986): 1–13.

comforts of the town where the court was sitting, they were "obliged to quit it, and retiring into the woods to the brink of some spring or water course, draw forth out of their wallet a bit of cold victuals if they have it, and whether the weather freezes or pours down rain or not they pass the night under the open sky on the cold earth." The poor had no alternative but to accept such hardships, because "if the juror fails to attend, he is subject to a fine which in many instances all that he has in the world would be insufficient to pay." Adequate compensation should be provided for serving jurors.[37]

Burke's report was duly transmitted to the committee on grievances in the House of Representatives. The committee conceded that some redress was desirable but concluded that the state could not afford to compensate jurors out of the public treasury. Since jurors summoned to serve in civil cases were most affected, because they had to remain on hand for the whole session, the committee suggested that compensation be taxed as a court cost against the successful party in each civil action brought to trial.[38] The problem remained unsolved.

The records of cases decided by the courts in early South Carolina are fragmentary. For many, perhaps most, of the identifiable cases no more than the result is known, entered on a surviving journal or judgment roll, which commonly identifies the parties but not the sitting judge. In the trial courts, instructions and decisions were delivered orally from the bench. Only in cases of great public interest, such as the trial of William Clay Snipes, were contemporaneous accounts published.

Appellate proceedings, the modern source of data for evaluation of judicial craftsmanship, were rudimentary. Decisions in the county courts could be appealed to the circuit courts, and were disposed of in the latter in the same manner as other matters presented for decision. Prior to 1790, the judges convened an "adjourned court" in Charleston after the completion of each circuit to hear and determine motions for new trials, motions in arrest of judgment, and other points of law related to the cases tried on the circuits. The Constitution of 1790 required that an

37. Burke to Vanderhorst, December 8, 1796, Records of the General Assembly, Governors' Messages, SCA.
38. Records of the General Assembly, Committee on Grievances, Report on petitions dealing with various matters, December 15, 1796, SCA.

adjourned court also be convened in Columbia.[39] Accordingly, over time the old adjourned court came to be called the constitutional court, but there was no change of function and the so-called constitutional court was not established by or under the Constitution of 1790. There were no other provisions for review of judicial decisions. In the circumstances, the court of final resort was usually the General Assembly.

Unless decisions were reported in the press, and few were, knowledge of them was buried in the notes of the judges and counsel. No compilation of statute law was available prior to publication in 1790 of Grimke's *Public Laws of the State of South Carolina*. And a usable guide to the existing statute law was not available until Joseph Brevard, one of the judges, published an alphabetical index to the statutes in 1814.[40]

The first collection of cases was published between 1809 and 1811 by Judge Elihu Hall Bay, Burke's colleague on the court after 1791. Bay's work was designed to cover the cases decided by the state's superior courts after the Revolution, but the collection was by no means complete. Working virtually without help, Bay collected what he could. Some reports are mere summaries, derived from lawyer's notes. Others are more extensive. They are more complete after 1791, when Bay joined the court. For the period 1783 to 1795, the collection includes decisions from both the trial courts and the so-called adjourned or constitutional court. For the period from 1796 through 1799, the collection includes only constitutional court decisions. In all, some 220 cases are reported for the period 1783 to 1799.[41]

Burke was manifestly not an enthusiastic creator of extended legal opinions. Neither were his brethren. A majority of the

39. Constitution of 1790, *Statutes at Large*, 1: 184–92, Article X (3).
40. John F. Grimke, *Public Laws of the State of South Carolina* (Philadelphia: R. Aitken & Son, 1790); Joseph Brevard, *An Alphabetical Index to the Public Law of South Carolina*, 3 vols. (Charleston: John Hoff, 1814).
41. Elihu Hall Bay, *Reports of Cases Argued and Decided in the Superior Courts of Law of the State of South Carolina Since the Revolution*, 2 vols. (New York: I. Riley, 1809–1811). M. Leigh Harrison, "A Study of the Earliest Reported Decisions of the South Carolina Courts of Law," *American Journal of Legal History*, 16 (1972): 51–70, surveys the work of the courts on the basis of the cases reported in Bay's first volume. More than half the 161 cases reported were actions on contracts, principally debt interests. Only 22 were criminal cases. Given the circumstances under which Bay collected his materials, these numbers may mean only that, in Bay's opinion, civil cases were of greater interest as precedent than criminal cases.

court's decisions were reported per curiam, for the court as a whole, the author unidentified. In many others a single judge spoke for the entire court. In all such cases, Burke's concurrence must be assumed. Unanimity was the general rule. Occasionally dissents were noted, but extended written dissents were rare. So were occasions on which the judges elected to express concurring views in individual opinions separately delivered.

There are, however, a few cases in which glimpses of Burke's judicial personality may be seen. In one, decided in 1793, the defendant was charged with counterfeiting a note of the paper medium, a capital offense. The jury found him guilty. Before the constitutional court, the defendant's counsel pointed out that the note in question carried only two official signatures where the law required three. He accordingly argued that the note would have been void even if officially issued. The defendant thus could not have been guilty of forgery, since the creation of a void instrument was no crime. Rutledge, Grimke, and Bay concurred and held the conviction "insufficient." Burke and Waties disagreed. Burke argued that the defendant intended to defraud by passing the bad note as good and that the technical character of the note was therefore immaterial, citing in support of his argument a series of English cases on the point. He concluded his opinion with typical Burkean whimsey. "In giving this decision," he said, "there is one circumstance that gives me pleasure, which is, that the opinion I give is not likely to affect the life of the prisoner."[42]

Zylstra v. The Corporation of Charleston, decided in 1794, provided Burke his best opportunity to speak out on his republican principles. Zylstra was charged with violating a city ordinance of Charleston, and the court of wardens assessed the specified fine against him. The amount of the fine, however, exceeded the statutory maximum limiting the jurisdiction of the court of wardens. The city argued that the limitation on its general jurisdiction did not apply to fines for violation of city ordinances, claiming the right to exercise discretion in fixing the amount of such fines. The city's action was struck down unanimously, but Burke seized on the occasion to deliver an address. The city's defense, Burke asserted, "is a pretension so extravagant, that it seems to me to be paying a very sorry compliment to law and common sense, to

---

42. State v. Gutridge, Bay, *Reports of Cases*, 1: 285–91.

dwell upon arguments to the contrary. The claiming of such authority, by a body too of very inferior jurisdiction, not equal perhaps to our county courts, and publicly supporting this claim as they do, shows clearly, that our laws, and the decisions of our courts, are in a state of uncertainty that men of sense and reflection very little think of." The city's attempt to assert such a right despite its limited authority confirmed an important principle, he concluded. "It serves to illustrate upon a small scale, the intruding, usurping, nature of power; and with how much greater than the energy of a wedge, it is essentially at work to force open for itself, more elbowroom and free license, than foresight itself or reason ever intended." Since the defendant was denied his right to trial by jury, the ordinance was unconstitutional and void. His conviction was therefore "nugatory."[43]

State v. Gaillard, et al., decided by the constitutional court sitting in Charleston in January 1796, is perhaps the most interesting and is the most extended of Burke's written opinions. The cause was for debt on a bond. The plaintiff was the state. The defendants were the maker of the bond and his sureties. The bond was given in payment for a tract of timberland purchased from the commissioners of confiscated estates on which the purchaser intended to erect a sawmill. The jury found for the defendants, in effect rescinding the original transaction. The state moved for a new trial before the constitutional court.[44]

Timothy Ford appeared for the state. His strongest ground, Burke said, was that only a court of equity could rescind or set aside a sale of land and that the jury had therefore exceeded its jurisdiction and authority. The court held that the action of the jury was proper. There was no difference between sales of real and personal property when the issue was whether the transaction was just and reasonable. And there could be no objection to the exercise of such authority by the jury under the supervision of the court. If "a speculator should sell a bargain to some forlorn French or Dutch emigrant just escaped out of the conflagrations of Europe, and singed of every thing but life; what must his

---

43. Zylstra v. The Corporation of Charleston, Bay, *Reports of Cases*, 1: 382–98. The issue was not new. Earlier cases of lesser import reached the same result.
44. State v. Gaillard, et al., Bay, *Reports of Cases*, 2: 11–20. Bay's report of the case is condensed. A more complete report appeared in the *CGDA*, April 4, 1796, and is the basis of the discussion in the text. Quoted passages in the following five paragraphs are from the latter source.

feelings and opinion be of us, and the public justice of the country, were a doctrine like this to be held out to him; that the court have ample authority to make him pay the bond which he gave for the land, but none to enquire what the bond was given for, or whether it is land or water, earth or rock, or good or bad, or exists at all? And that he must be turned over to the court of chancery to get the bargain rescinded, and his money how he can. This court, however, will not send him for justice such a round about way; whether the man so imposed on be citizen or foreigner, he will find shelter in this court from certain practices which for three years past have been spreading through the continent like a pestilence."

Burke had reason to be annoyed. The evidence established that the plat delivered to the purchaser by the commissioners clearly showed a running stream through the property, whereas in fact there was a mere trace and that usually dry. There was no affirmative representation made by the commissioners, but *"the mill-stream on paper* misled the buyer to believe there was an abundance of water, which would have made the tract of great value, when in reality it was only a small run which rendered the tract of no value; if this was not a misrepresentation, a *suggestis falsi,* I know not what is." There was also a deficiency in the size of the tract to the extent of at least 500 acres. Such a deficiency in a tract of timberland, Burke said, might so depreciate the value of the tract that no abatement in the price could compensate for the reduced acreage, "and the court is to presume that the jury thought so."

Thus the purchaser, "having given a sound price, and been betrayed into mistakes by the wrong suggestions of the public agents," was entitled to relief, and the jury could properly dissolve the contract. "Justice and sound discretion," Burke concluded, "seem to us to have governed their decision." There was nonetheless a larger message to be delivered.

This verdict, and the law henceforth to be settled upon it, so far from loosening, as is apprehended, will draw tighter those obligations and duties which secure honesty and fair dealing among men. It will shelter the foreigner from imposition, and be the means of encouraging the sale of the immense bodies of fertile good land, which abound in our interior country; . . . this decision will give a death warrant to the practice of selling as good land and for sound prices, such as nobody that knows it would take as a gift; and finally it will convince the world, that although some citizens may have permitted themselves to be drawn into the vortex of buying and selling sand-hills, rocks and mountains, yet that the justice of the country is clean; and possesses the inclination and authority to give such speculations every proper discouragement.

The decision is interesting in another respect. "Our state legislature," Burke said, "too long have been in the habit of holding out fine bargains of confiscated and other property to our citizens; golden delusive prospects that ended in the ruin of many of them; and if some have escaped that ruin, it is owing to one circumstance, that the judges, shaking off the trammels of old law prejudices, have engrafted on the administration of public justice, the honest equitable doctrine of *civil law*, respecting the recision of sales, or abatement of price according to circumstances." The court, he said, had seen justice done between the state and her citizens in several instances, "and in so doing has been instrumental in making her to act towards her children, the part of a natural parent, instead of an unfeeling stepmother."

There was nothing revolutionary about the legal doctrine Burke announced. The decision was unanimous. The prevailing legal doctrine required a fair exchange to support a contractual obligation, a mutuality of benefits as well as promises. The doctrine of caveat emptor was a later legal development. "The jury could not do otherwise than consider the sale of the land and the execution of the bond as one entire transaction," Burke said, connected as cause and effect. The transaction could not be broken down into separate parts "without doing injustice; nor could the jury form a sound judgment on the justice of recovery on the bond, without considering at the same time what the bond was given for."

Burke's eloquent elaboration of his underlying rationale, however, was distinctive. His concern for the individual dealing with the state, his concern for the unwary dealing with the sophisticated, his contempt for landgrabbers and speculators, all addressed issues of relative power and spoke to the interests of the less powerful. They were of a piece with his views on seditious libel, for example, and with his more general views on individual rights requiring the protection of law. In the circumstances, it made no difference that Gaillard was a man of substance in

Charleston, a well-known merchant, even associated with a suspected loyalist family, and not "some forlorn French or Dutch emigrant just escaped out of the conflagrations of Europe."

Burke had another opportunity to declaim in *Lindsay v. Commissioners*, decided by the Court of Common Pleas in the Charleston District in 1796.[45] He let it pass but his decision and the decision of the court illustrate as definitively as any of the cases decided during the 1790s the ambiguity of the court's role in the political system as a whole.

Early in 1796, the General Assembly authorized a Board of Commissioners in Charleston to connect the commercial area on East Bay with the developed residential area on South Bay by extending East Bay Street through undeveloped property. The cost of the road was to be assessed to the property owners who would benefit from the extension. Lindsay and others, administrators of a decedent's estate holding part of the property involved, petitioned the Board for adjustment of the assessment and for compensation in the amount of the value of the property taken. The assessments were adjusted, but compensation was denied. The petitioners then moved in the Court of Common Pleas, contending that they were entitled to compensation before the road could be built and invoking the provision of the Constitution of 1790 protecting the freemen of the state against any taking of life, liberty, or property except by the judgment of their peers or by the law of the land. The case was argued before all four sitting judges. The court was evenly divided on the issue presented, and the motion was accordingly denied.

Grimke and Bay found that the right to appropriate land for public roads and highways was an essential element of sovereignty and all private rights were held and enjoyed subject to the condition that it might be exercised. Arteries of communication, they said, were of such importance that the power to establish them should forever by invested in the supreme legislative body, and the legislature of South Carolina had exercised that power from its very beginning. The power was thus part of the law of the land. Because the cited provision of the Constitution was not declaratory of new law, it confirmed the principle and did not interfere with or contradict the long established authority of the

---

45. Lindsay, et al. v. Commissioners, Bay, *Reports of Cases*, 2: 38–62. Quoted passages in the following five paragraphs are from this source.

legislature. The act was therefore constitutional and binding, and the City Council was fully justified in directing the Board of Commissioners to proceed.

Burke dissented. In a short statement of a single paragraph, he admitted the power of the state, "on great and necessary occasions, to appropriate a portion of the soil of the country, for public uses and national purposes, but was of opinion that there should be a *fair compensation made to the private individual, for the loss he might sustain by it*, to be ascertained by a jury of the country."

Waties agreed with Burke and spelled out his reasons in greater detail. He conceded the authority of the legislature to take property for public purposes but insisted that "*a full compensation should be provided at the time* for every injury that the individual might suffer." In the absence of provision for such compensation, he argued, the taking was invalid. Since the act before the court did not provide for compensation, the requirements of law had not been complied with. Responding to the argument that no compensation was warranted because, in the circumstances, no injury would result, he denied its relevance. The fact may be so, he said, but it would make no difference. The legislature was not empowered to make the decision. "This would be attributing to it a power which belongs only to despots."

Waties concluded with a rousing declaration on judicial independence and the constitutional role of the courts. He was pained, he said, to question the exercise of any legislative power. But that was the most important of all the duties incumbent on the judges. "If the legislature is permitted to exercise other rules than those ordained by the constitution, and if innovations are suffered to acquire the sanction of time and practice, the rights of the people will soon become dependent on legislative will, and the constitution have no more obligation than an absolute law." But if the court did its duty by "giving the constitution an overruling operation over every act of the legislature which is inconsistent with it, the people will then have an independent security for their rights, which may render them perpetual."

Subsequent developments in the East Bay Street affair are illuminating. Following the adverse decision of the court, Lindsay and his co-administrators petitioned the General Assembly for relief in December 1796.[46] The matter was referred to a committee of the House of Representatives, which reported favorably.[47] Since the question was presented late in the session, no action was taken in 1796. A second committee reported favorably in 1797.[48] Thereupon a bill was enacted directing the judges of the Court of Common Pleas to summon a jury in the usual manner to determine whether any damages had been sustained. If damages were assessed, they would be entered in the books of the City Council and paid within eighteen months.[49] The ultimate outcome is unknown. But the effect of the decision was to reserve to the legislature a power that the general trend of the law, as Burke and Waties argued, was vesting in courts and juries.

These scattered materials permit only the most tentative of conclusions. The quality of the court was generally high, and Burke was by no means out of place on it. His style was different, and his Irishness was surely evident. His reputation for personal eccentricity was undiminished by his judicial performance.[50] There is no evidence of any close personal or social relationships between Burke and his brethren. He probably moved in a wholly different social circle. But neither is there evidence that he was a disruptive or abrasive presence in the court's councils.

The court had difficulty reestablishing its authority after the war, evidenced principally by the incident of Love's lynching and the Camden revolt against its authority. But these incidents were not really the fault of the court. Lawlessness in the backcountry was perhaps partially a product of the "disruptions of war" but, as Burke observed from Orangeburgh and Ninety Six in 1783 and 1784, it was controllable when the area was adequately policed.

---

46. Records of the General Assembly, Petitions, 1796, Petition of Robert Lindsay, et al., SCA.
47. Records of the General Assembly, Committee Reports, 1796, Report on Petition of Robert Lindsay, et al., SCA.
48. Records of the General Assembly, Committee Reports, 1797, Report on Petition of Robert Lindsay, et al., SCA.
49. Act to ascertain what damages Robert Lindsay, et al. have sustained by East Bay Street being continued through their land, Acts and Resolutions of the General Assembly, 1797, SCA.
50. A surviving writ of discharge in a habeas corpus proceeding bears the following directive: "Let Mr. Neuville be discharged from this most cruel arrest. A. Burke. March 18, 1796." On the face of the writ, the following words were written by an unknown author: "Judge Burke our eccentric Irishman." Etting Papers, HSP.

The jurisdiction of the courts could have been protected had there been the will to do it.

The South Carolinian legal culture may have been a stabilizing force in the country. At least a disruptive debate on the proper source of its law was avoided. But the more singular features of the period point in a different direction. The record suggests that the legislature, for reasons of its own, never gave the judicial system adequate support. For most of the period, there was no chief justice to provide affirmative leadership, although men of prestige were abundantly available, and the office was eliminated when the judicial system was reorganized in 1799. The court was almost always undermanned. Obvious reforms were delayed. Means to enforce judicial process were not provided. More importantly, throughout the period, the citizenry was encouraged to look to the legislature for relief and not to the law or its agencies. Such was the case under the confiscation and amercement acts, during the critical period of economic distress of the 1780s, and even on questions of constitutional interpretation, as in the *Lindsay* case.

In 1796, after Rutledge had resigned, the remaining four judges were constrained to complain of the burdens they were required to bear, and particularly of additional responsibilities imposed on them by the legislature. Their principal objections were constitutionally based. But they also raised more practical objections.

> The business of the Charleston District alone occupies more than one half the year, and the remainder of it is almost wholly taken up in the Courts of the other Districts. The imposition therefore of other labours would be not only unwise and impolitic, but personally unjust; and if the safety of the community was not opposed to it, yet we should expect that a just and considerate Legislature would not augment our duties, when those already appointed us are with difficulty performed, and when we might urge besides that the progressive dearness of every article of living has operated, and will continue to operate, as a diminution of our salaries.[51]

Any deviations from constitutional principles, they concluded, should be corrected "before they have been legitimated

51. Burke, Grimke, Waties, and Bay to Vanderhorst, October 24, 1796, Records of the General Assembly, Governors' Messages, SCA.

by time and practice, and when this will not damage the general system." Moreover, it was incumbent on the judges to watch over the constitution and defend it from any violation. "In resisting therefore these encroachments on it, we are performing a sacred and indispensible duty, and we hope that the subject will receive from the Legislature that careful and candid consideration which the serious nature of it requires."[52]

Notwithstanding the judges' claim to preeminence for the judicial power in the protection of public freedom, the overall record suggests that the prevailing political culture did not assign so high a value to a strong and independent judiciary. Charles Pinckney admitted as much in his message to the legislature in 1798 dealing with reform of the judicial system. The power of the judges should be limited, he argued, and the authority of juries enlarged. Following the Jeffersonian view of proper constitutional practice, the legislature, not the courts, should determine constitutional issues.[53] The judges were independent enough in theory, but the judicial system was subordinated in fact. Burke recognized this condition of affairs. But he never challenged it directly, nor did any of his brethren.

In 1799, the judicial system was completely reorganized. The county court system of 1785, which had never worked well because it was never established throughout the state, was abolished. Twenty-five new districts were created, and the new districts were divided into four circuits. Writs of error were authorized to facilitate judicial review. No separate appellate court was established, but the appellate function of the established courts was enlarged. The Court of Chancery, which had languished for years, was reinvigorated, and Burke was elected one of the three chancellors. Three new assistant judges were elected to sit in the common law courts: William Johnson, later a justice of the United States Supreme Court, Ephraim Ramsay, and Theodore Trezevant. The number of common law judges was increased from five to six; but the office of chief justice was eliminated.[54]

Burke thus spent the final years of his public career in the court of equity after more than twenty years of service in the

52. Ibid.
53. Records of the General Assembly, Governors' Messages, Message of Governor Charles Pinckney, November 28, 1798, SCA.
54. *Statutes at Large*, 7: 283–300.

courts of common law.[55] There he joined Hugh Rutledge, the only sitting chancellor in 1799, and was joined by William Marshall, elected to the court with Burke. Theoretically, the chancellors held significant power and the court served an important function in the administration of justice. Even so, it is by no means clear that Burke regarded his accession to the office a promotion, and his election was possibly evidence of some loss of standing in the political community. Once before he had declined the honor, commenting that he would "walk in the dirty water 'till he came to the clean."[56] His meaning is suggested by his language in the *Gaillard* case, where he said that the court's decision would serve "to convince the world . . . that the justice of the country is clean." In Burke's legal world, "clean justice" was the sine qua non of a free society; and this simple statement perhaps reflects the highest ideal to which the famous Judge Burke aspired.

The Court of Chancery was dominated by Hugh Rutledge, the senior sitting chancellor, who wrote most of the published decisions rendered in 1800 and 1801. Burke was in regular attendance throughout 1800 and for most of 1801, and the burden was surely less onerous than the burden of service on the common law courts. Nothing in the record suggests that he made any significant contribution to the court's work or that his distinctive personality colored its proceedings. Perhaps, for him, the position was less one of honor than a sinecure, lacking in the stimulating human drama continually played out in the common law courts. His interest in election to the national Senate suggests, at least, that he was restless and seeking more active involvement in public affairs.

Burke died a few months after the senatorial election in December 1801. Although nothing is known of his last illness, his health may have impaired or foreclosed his prospects for selection to that office. He made his will in January 1802, and died on

---

55. The reports of equity decisions during these years appear in Henry W. Desaussure, *Reports of Cases Argued and Determined in the Court of Chancery of South Carolina from the Revolution to December, 1817, Inclusive* (Columbia: Cline and Hines, 1817). The reports show Burke in attendance for decision making purposes through most of 1801. Chancellor Hugh Rutledge was clearly in charge. The record suggests that Burke's role was essentially passive.

56. John Belton O'Neall, *Biographical Sketches of the Bench and Bar of South Carolina*, 2 vols. (Charleston: S. G. Courtenay & Co., 1859), 1: 38.

March 30. He was then fifty-nine years old. He was a robust man, with no record of poor health. And there is no reason to believe that he suffered any significant decline of intellectual capacity during his last decade. He remained true to character to the last, at least on the anecdotal record. Shortly prior to his death he was tapped for dropsy. He asked the doctor whether the medical verdict would be for life or death. "Life, my good fellow," the doctor replied. "Then, by Jasus," Burke announced, "I shall be the first thing that ever lasted long in this house, after once being put on tap."[57]

There is no epilogue. Burke died still a bachelor. After a funeral service in St. Michael's Church, he was buried on the plantation of his friend O'Brien Smith in St. Bartholomew's Parish, near Jacksonborough, and his grave lies there today next to Smith's. Ruth Savage remains an obscure figure. Isabella Murphy disappeared from the New York City Directory in 1807. "The boy George Burke" is forever lost.

---

57. Benjamin F. Perry, "Aedanus Burke," in U. R. Brooks, *South Carolina Bench and Bar*, (Columbia: The State Company, 1908), 8; Alexander Garden, *Anecdotes of the Revolutionary War in America* (Charleston: A. E. Miller, 1822; reprint ed., Spartanburg: The Reprint Company, 1972), 196–97.

Conclusion

Burke could reasonably have been satisfied with his position in South Carolina as the Revolution approached its end. Within a few years of his arrival he was a judge and a member of the General Assembly. His tenure on the bench was secure during good behavior. He had survived the war and sixteen months of incarceration in Charleston without discredit. Shipped out for exchange in mid-1781, he had visited Philadelphia and returned to South Carolina as an aide to General St. Clair in time to serve in the Jacksonborough Assembly in early 1782. En route he watched the British surrender at Yorktown. He was at least on terms of speaking acquaintance with many notable figures of the Revolutionary era and was in regular correspondence with the distinguished Arthur Middleton. He had been offered high judicial office in Georgia. He had not been returned to the General Assembly in the general election of late 1782, to be sure, but he could regard that failure as mere happenstance in the confusion of the days immediately preceding the British evacuation of Charleston, a freak of fortune that was soon rectified. The Burke of 1783, the Burke of the *Address*, the *Considerations*, and the charges to the grand juries in June and November, was a confident man, apparently established in the public life of South Carolina and secure in his own self-esteem. He was hardly a representative South Carolinian of the late eighteenth century, but he was a loyal and devoted adopted son.

In the ensuing years, however, Burke increasingly appeared almost as two men. In one manifestation of character and personality, he reflected his basic orientation to the law. In the various roles he occupied from time to time, one of them was always that of lawyer and judge. In that role, he was comfortable although occasionally eccentric as the anecdotal record suggests. He had a

Conclusion

body of rules to guide him that he understood and generally endorsed. His judicial role required him to act in accordance with those rules. In his court, there was always one spot of neutral ground, in which he sat, as he observed to Arthur Middleton in 1782. In the context of his judicial role and the known or discernible rules applicable to it, Burke knew exactly how to act and acted effectively. In the service of "clean justice," from his position on the bench, he was in control. In his reported charges to grand juries, he was eloquent, persuasive, and restrained. He was firm but respected for his conduct of the proceedings in his court. There is no evidence that he was ever at serious odds with his brethren concerning matters of judicial administration. He carried more than a fair share of the burdens of riding the circuits. And his work on the report of the commissioners appointed to digest and revise the laws of the state submitted to the General Assembly in 1789 was a thoughtful, comprehensive, and responsible contribution to the public interest.

In his alternative manifestations of character and personality, Burke was quite different. In the roles of legislator and publicist, he was sometimes uncertain, sometimes overbearing, generally either directly oppositionist or merely reactive. His appearances were intermittent and unpredictable. He rarely demonstrated the inclination or the capacity to mount a sustained effort toward a defined objective. In South Carolina, his legislative career was undistinguished, particularly when compared to that of Henry Pendleton, his colleague on the bench and in the General Assembly during the 1780s. In the First Congress, he did sustain an effort to gain support for substantive amendments to the Constitution; but the cause was lost, and he soon knew it. As a member of the committee on the executive departments in the first session, he was characteristically ambivalent. In the second session, he consistently and actively supported the assumption of state debts after an uncertain start; but he was never a key figure in the proceedings and lost standing as a result of his visible demonstrations of intemperance, particularly his attack on Hamilton. The record confirms that, as his term drew to a close, he was impotent and all but ignored.

Throughout his public career, Burke consistently adhered to the fundamental principles of the republican creed. The proper source of power rested with the people, but the people's hold on liberty was always exposed and often at risk from hidden threats. Their security lay with the law and timely warnings of danger. In his judicial role, the constraints of his judicial office limited the expression of ideologically oriented perceptions, although they appeared on occasion, as in the language of his opinion in the *Zylstra* case and in his commitment to "clean justice." They appeared also in his defense of individual legal rights, and in his labors on the commission to revise and digest the laws of the state, a task undertaken to clarify and simplify for the people at large the laws to which they were subject.

In the realm of politics, however, Burke was much more volatile and much less flexible. In the idiom of the time, freedom and independence were nearly equivalent concepts, both encompassing the precept that free men were not subservient, or threatened with subservience, to a superior order of authority based on force or to a higher order of men claiming superiority as a matter of right or privilege. In his eyes, men who pursued power by subtle manipulation of the citizenry were prospective despots, and despotism once established, as he told the South Carolina convention debating the Constitution in May 1788, "was a monster very hard to get rid of." When liberty confronted power, threats to liberty were everywhere. History told him so and justified his fears.

Since despotism was the natural object of encroaching power, Burke tended to be most watchful of men in power and measures designed to confirm or enhance the authority of men in power. Consequently, like many of his ideologically driven contemporaries, he was poorly prepared to respond to the demands of nation-building, in which new institutions of governmental authority had perforce to be established to replace those cast off by the Revolution. As a man of the law, Burke stood for order when order was threatened and, as history also taught, recognized disorder as a fertile seedbed for the would-be despot. He was distrustful of "Yahoos" and "Yahooism;" and his faith in the capacity of the people to respond to timely warnings hardly implied faith in the capacity of the people to govern. The republican creed was not incompatible with a governmental structure in which men of demonstrated worth would lead. He was as sharply critical of those who appeared to promote civil discord for personal advantage, such as Fallon and Harper, as he was of those who appeared to threaten the integrity of republi-

Conclusion

can institutions, such as John Rutledge in 1783, the Cincinnati, the domestic friends of Britain, and the "Anglomen" of the 1790s. Thus, after the "revolution in government" of 1787, he was more closely watchful of national affairs than affairs in his own country.

Freedom and equality were essentially negative concepts. No man could be both subservient and free. But the free man could accept authority based on intellect, reason, and civic virtue as the natural product of differences among men, so long as there were no artificial barriers blocking his participation in the political process. For Burke and his contemporaries, the prevailing concept of equality had little to do with the modern concept of egalitarianism. Even the most vocal dissidents of 1784 proclaimed a limited and legal understanding of equality and incorporated into it a reciprocal concept of obligation. When the Secret Committee of the Whig Club of Six Hundred charged "the wealthy families of the Commonwealth" with monopolizing power and the offices of the state to themselves by "destroying the *republican equality* of citizenship" so as to confirm "family influence" in government and establish an "odious aristocracy," the term was carefully defined. "When we speak of equality," that ephemeral committee wrote, "we do not mean an extreme, absolute, and consequently chimerical equality: we mean that happy equilibrium which renders all the Citizens equally subject to the laws, and equally interested to observe them."[1] Thomas Tudor Tucker spoke to generally the same effect more than a decade later.

> By equality is to be understood, equality of civil rights, and not of condition, for, the latter could never be produced, but by the total destruction of the former, and could only have place in a state of barbarism and wretchedness. Equality of rights necessarily produces inequality of possessions; because, by the laws of nature and of equality, every man has a right to use his faculties, in an honest way, and the fruits of his labour are his own. . . . And thus inequality, so far from being an evil, is absolutely necessary to the well being of society; it is the cement that binds together the various employments of life, and forms the whole into a beautiful system of dependencies.—The rights of property must be sacred, and must be protected; otherwise there

---

1. "Address of the Secret Committee of the Whig Club of Six Hundred," *SCGGA*, September 16, 1784.

could be no exertion of either ingenuity or industry, and, consequently, nothing but extreme poverty, misery and brutal ignorance. No man can be a friend of equality, in its true and proper sense, who has not the most sacred regard to the rights of property.[2]

Another important element lay embedded in Burke's cognitive structure. Although seldom mentioned in his surviving writings, Burke knew Irish history as well as the history of ancient times and the more modern history of England. And the Irish understood oppression in a very particular way, subjected to it as they were for years at the hands of both Anglo-Irish and emigrant British aristocracies. Burke's intellectual equipment, therefore, included a major component of Anglophobia, naturally acquired and reinforced by the experience of the Revolution in South Carolina, which colored the standard republican obsession against elitist aristocratic pretensions in general and monarchist tendencies in particular. This element was most evident in Burke's thought when he attacked the British and their trade policy in the *Salutary Hints*, aimed not at corruption from within but at corruption from without and the threat that the new republic would be reduced to neocolonial subservience to the dominant economic power of Britain. It was evident also in his stance against the "Anglomen" in the 1790s, when public opinion polarized on foreign policy issues in general and the Jay Treaty in particular. Frustrated by the course of events since adoption of the Constitution, foreseeing the risk that the noble republican experiment might collapse, urged on by the eminent Pierce Butler, Burke lashed out at Robert Goodloe Harper with an attack so extreme as to suggest that he had lost all touch with political reality. Thereafter, in the late 1790s, he was ideologically isolated in the political spectrum of his country for all practical purposes.

Burke was not an organizer or mobilizer of the people against Britain in the years leading to the Revolution. But his ideas on government and the social order were shaped during that period and were never cluttered with the regard for British institutions, in the abstract uncorrupted form perceived, for example, by John Adams and shared by many Americans. In the

---

2. Thomas Tudor Tucker, *An Oration delivered in . . . Charleston, South Carolina, on the 4th of July, 1795; in Commemoration of American Independence . . .* (Charleston: Timothy and Mason, 1795), 20–21.

Conclusion

post-Revolutionary years, he purveyed a few simple principles derived from the republican creed and from historical precedent teaching by example. Liberty was exposed to corruption by power because liberty depended on virtue, and history taught, in case after case, that avarice was a fundamental element of human character leading men in power to aggrandize themselves at the expense of liberty. Thus, it was the responsibility of good republicans to point out the danger of tyranny, and call the people back to virtue and reason whenever their rights were threatened.[3] This was Burke's fundamental rationale in both the *Address* and the *Considerations*. With the passage of time, his faith in virtue evidently waned; and, as the moral underpinning was diluted, his warnings became more strident and less relevant. Burke was by no means alone in his stridency. But in the final analysis, his career demonstrated the fundamental weakness of a political stance based principally on jealousy.

Burke was not of an age with Pauline Maier's "Old Revolutionaries,"[4] but he was closer to them in spirit than he was to those whose political thought was shaped by participation in the institutions established to implement the Revolution after it occurred. Like the Old Revolutionaries, he was more obsessively concerned with the dangers inherent in centralized power than were the new leaders such as Madison and Charles Pinckney. Like the Old Revolutionaries, he was a nationalist who acknowledged the need to reform the institutions of the Confederation but balked at the terms of the new Constitution when it was submitted. Like the Old Revolutionaries, he responded instinctively to the charge of corruption and castigated the proponents of the Constitution as "partisans of monarchy."[5] The revolution of 1787, Maier says, "lay beyond the Old Revolutionaries' capacity for innovation and very often for understanding. They had moved forward, but were also held back by their beginnings."[6] So it was with Burke. Limited by his beginnings, he was not well attuned

---

3. The same duty fell on the contemporary historians of the Revolution, practitioners of "exemplary history." Lester H. Cohen, *The Revolutionary Histories: Contemporary Narratives of the American Revolution* (Ithaca: Cornell University Press, 1980), 185–211.
4. Pauline Maier, *The Old Revolutionaries: Political Lives in the Age of Samuel Adams* (New York: Alfred A. Knopf, 1980), 269–94.
5. Ibid., 288.
6. Ibid., 294.

to deal with the uncertainties and ambiguities of an experimental exercise in nation building. Apart from his contributions as lawyer and judge, by no means inconsequential, that business proceeded without much help from him.

The introduction promised that this would not be a study of Burke's life and times and, despite some necessary digressions, that promise has been generally honored. Yet one cannot follow Burke's career without formulating some tentative hypotheses about his times, and it is perhaps permissible to mention them at the end.

The political leaders of South Carolina in the last quarter of the eighteenth century were eminently practical men. Planters, merchants, and professional men for the most part, they were men of business, commercially oriented cosmopolitans fully capable of balancing risks and rewards. Committed to the common cause against England in 1774, they bargained to except rice from the embargo proposed by the Continental Congress. Among the first to adopt their own constitution of government in 1776, they were among the last to surrender the prospect of ultimate reconciliation. The enthusiasm of such firebrands as Christopher Gadsden and William Henry Drayton was carefully contained. Individually, they were proud and fiercely independent. But collectively, they were cautious men who took their time when confronted with pressure for change.

Even while the war was on, the South Carolinian pattern of politics was gradualist and adaptive in all matters of fundamental importance. The evolution of the Constitution of 1778 illustrates the process. Studied by a select committee and debated in late 1776, principles were established for consideration by the next General Assembly. A draft prepared in early 1777 lay on the table nearly a year for study and comment. The political crisis of March 1778 was not so much a confrontation between conservatives and radicals as a difference of opinion among conservatives, centered on the extent to which concessions to the people at large were necessary or desirable to achieve unity in the face of danger.

The Constitution of 1778 limited the power of the executive and expanded the authority of the legislature, to be sure, but it did not change the locus of ultimate control. Moreover, many of its concessions were no more than promises for the future. The apportionment of representation would be taken up within seven years. Counties would be laid out and county courts established.

Conclusion

The harsh penal code would be revised. After 1783, each of these subjects, and a number of others, was approached in the same gradualist style.

The creation of counties and county courts was taken up in 1783. Thanks principally to the determination of Henry Pendleton, it was completed in two years. Nonetheless, it was completed with a reservation that would be typical of South Carolina politics into and through most of the nineteenth century. The county court system was controversial in some sections of the state. Accordingly, those counties that did not want them were not required to have them. Over the ensuing fifteen years, until the county courts were abolished in 1799, the county court act was subjected to a number of amendments. Some counties that had them wanted to abolish them. Some that did not have them wanted to establish them. When sufficient unanimity was evident, the General Assembly complied. Local wishes were accommodated but only at the expense of a uniform system for the administration of justice throughout the state.

Further constitutional revision was under discussion as early as 1783. It failed in 1784, when the House of Representatives voted to call a constitutional convention over strong opposition but the Senate rejected the proposal by a substantial margin. According to Thomas Tudor Tucker, the opposition in the House centered on concern that total dissolution of the existing constitution would produce a state of anarchy and confusion, that return to a state of nature in which all would have an equal right to be party to a new compact could have consequences fatal to republican freedom, and that a convention subject to no control might "fasten on monarchy."[7] In the circumstances of 1784, these reasons may be freely interpreted to reflect a sense that the prevailing turmoil throughout the state would preclude the thoughtful deliberation requisite for so important an enterprise.

The result was the same in 1786 and 1787, with one important difference. The sixth General Assembly in 1786 finally responded to backcountry pressure and agreed to transfer the capital to a more central location, choosing the site of the present capital in Columbia for that purpose and establishing a commission to lay out a new capital city and begin construction of the necessary public facilities. Following this concession, constitu-

---

7. "Philodemus" [Thomas Tudor Tucker], *Conciliatory Hints* (Charleston: A. Timothy, 1784), 23–27.

275

tional revision was successfully deferred until 1790, when conditions in the state were somewhat more tranquil. By the time the state constitutional convention met in Columbia in May 1790, a new national Constitution had been ratified, the structure of a more energetic national government had been established, a bill of rights for inclusion in the federal Constitution was before the states and already approved by the General Assembly, backcountry violence was under better control, acceptable debtor relief measures were in place, an improving economy was confirming the viability of such measures as a solution to the problems to which they were addressed, and differences between Whig and Tory were fading. New issues would shortly arise, to be sure, but the timing was good.

This pattern evidenced astute political management at work. It was at work throughout the 1780s, both as a general proposition and in specific micropolitical situations. Two of the best examples of the latter may be observed in the skillful maneuverings through which the initial debtor relief measures evolved in 1785 and the careful orchestration of proceedings in the General Assembly and at the ensuing state convention where the new national Constitution was ratified in 1788. In the first, Edward Rutledge changed his position and swung behind Henry Pendleton to change the course of debate from an indecisive exchange of individual views to directed progress toward an acknowledged goal. In the second, John Rutledge, Edward Rutledge, Charles Cotesworth Pinckney, and Thomas Pinckney combined their talents to direct the proceedings toward the desired end, leading with Charles Pinckney's acknowledged powers of persuasion and holding the heavyweights in strategic reserve. In both, practical men were at work to achieve defined goals, just as they had been in the Provincial Congresses of 1775 and 1776, in the preparation of the Constitutions of 1776 and 1778, in the administration of the confiscation and amercement acts of 1782, and in representing the interests of their state at the Philadelphia convention in 1787.

The habits of cautious advance, tactical delay, and careful management were equally evident in the 1790s, most particularly in the handling of the divisive domestic dispute over the apportionment of representation that raged from 1794 to 1796. The Constitution of 1790 reflected a compromise negotiated in committee when agreement could not be reached in debate on the floor of the convention. The controversy erupted again in 1794

Conclusion

with Robert Goodloe Harper in the lead as "Appius," and was resolved when the General Assembly determined to adhere to the compromise of 1790.[8] Ralph Izard explained the position of the political leadership, and incidentally one salient element of its political style.

> The attack on the Constitution of the State, has for the present been repelled. It will however be renewed, and I have no doubt that in a few years a considerable change will take place in the representation. If Appius's plan were adopted immediately, the lower Country would be considerably injured, and the whole State disgraced. Taxes would be partially laid, and the Offices of Government would not be filled by the most respectable Characters. I hope, and believe that the evil will in a great measure be removed by the inland navigation, when carried farther than is at present contemplated. When men of property and education are distributed through all parts of the State, an exact apportionment of the representation, whatever may be the standard, will be of much less importance than it is at present.[9]

Where tactical delay featured the response to the pressure for reapportionment, careful inquiry and a cautious balancing of interests featured other approaches to reform in the 1790s. For reasons mentioned above, the county court system had never functioned up to the expectations of its sponsors and the superior common law courts could not fulfill their responsibilities to the satisfaction of the people at large. In addition, the Court of Chancery was all but defunct, with only one judge in office and two required to hold a court. Pressure for reform was building at least as early as 1795, and the issue of judicial reform was before every session of the General Assembly in the late 1790s. In 1799, the county courts were finally abolished, the common law courts restructured, and the Court of Chancery reconstituted, but only after exhaustive study and several false starts. As the eighteenth century ended, the subject of penal code reform, promised in the Constitution of 1778, was under similarly cautious and methodical consideration but with no prospect of early action.

---

8. The issue is discussed at greater length in Chapter IX. The compromise of 1790 held against further attack in 1795 and 1796. The issue was finally resolved in 1808 by another compromise which remained in effect until 1868.
9. Ralph Izard to C. C. Pinckney, January 18, 1795, Izard Papers, SCL.

Impressionistic as it may be, this portrait is not one of an ideologically driven political or social system. With recovery of the economy in the 1790s men turned to pursuit of individual interests. Like the leaders of most business oriented societies, they valued stability more than the ephemeral elements of a highly intellectualized republican creed. Like the men of New England, they could marshal the language of republicanism as needed. But their primary attention was directed to practical matters.

This does not mean that the ideology of republicanism was unimportant in Revolutionary and post-Revolutionary South Carolina. A special version of "country" ideology clearly informed South Carolinian resistance to British demands during the pre-Revolutionary and Revolutionary years. The established leadership accepted and even encouraged an extension of popular participation in the political system and endorsed the principles of public virtue and responsibility. But neither in South Carolina nor elsewhere in Revolutionary America did the commitment to virtuous republicanism imply rejection of a hierarchical political structure in which men of demonstrated merit would hold the requisite authority to govern. With independence won, the patriot rebels in the lowcountry became, overnight, the metropolitan establishment responsible for the management of political affairs and the preservation of both liberty and order. While Burke was critical in the *Address* and the *Considerations*, his ideological stance remained within bounds and he never spoke in support of the ideological pretensions and extralegal tactics of the rambunctious Marine Anti-Britannic Society and its allies.

The residue of "country" ideology in post-Revolutionary South Carolina was reflected, first, in the fierce independence of all South Carolinians, second, in the brief attack of the Charleston crowd on establishment policy toward former loyalists and British merchants in 1783 and 1784, and, third, in the language and style of backcountry demands against lowcountry assumption of the right to rule. During the balance of the 1780s and throughout the 1790s, backcountry demands on the metropolis for constitutional revision, reapportionment, judicial reform, and other measures were presented in the standard language of oppositionist republicanism. While Burke was quietly supportive, he never assumed the lead.

Conclusion

Burke was more ideologically oriented than most South Carolinians in public office during the 1780s and 1790s. But, after publication of the *Salutary Hints* in 1785, he held his tongue, by and large, until his vitriolic attack on Harper in 1796. Then, apparently perceiving the "Anglomen" in Philadelphia more dangerous to the republic as a whole than the resistance of the metropolis to the ideologically structured demands of backcountry South Carolina, he turned on Harper and forfeited at least some of the backcountry support that had once been his.[10] He was consistent, perhaps even foolishly constant. But he was simply left behind in the course of events.

South Carolinians turned away from the party of Washington, Adams, and Hamilton when they concluded that it no longer served their interests. Adams was shut out by Jefferson in the state's electoral vote in 1796. After a Federalist revival in 1798, the rejection became permanent when the Federalists fell into disarray in 1799, and the Republicans carried the state's electoral vote again in 1800. The shift was important, both short term and long term; but it was more anti-Federalist than consciously Jeffersonian. The "revolution of 1800" in South Carolina hardly seems to have been an ideological revolution. Wade Hampton, a good South Carolina republican in 1800, made this clear to Edward Hooker a few years later. "He appears to set very little value on names," Hooker reported, "and to discover very little of that prejudiced feeling, which, nowadays, is so apt to accompany the mention of any denomination of parties. He is called a republican; yet he certainly has many notions and sentiments which are more characteristic of federalism. And he does not hesitate to condemn, openly and unequivocally, some measures of the republican party." Similarly, he did not hesitate to express his indignation "at the prevailing practice of blending every interest in society with party politics, and forcing everything to bend to what is called 'republicanism' or 'federalism' according as these or those political opinions happen to predominate in any section of the country."[11] South Carolinians in the early Jeffersonian era

---

10. Harper's sin, for which he was castigated by Butler and Burke, was apostasy. Neither of them ever spoke or wrote against William Loughton Smith for his support of the Treaty. Smith acted as he was expected to act.

11. "Diary of Edward Hooker, 1805–1808," J. Franklin Jameson, ed., *Annual Report, American Historical Association, 1896* (Washington: United States Government Printing Office, 1897), 847.

were not disinterested in politics, but most of them had other things on their minds.

Several historians have examined the early politics of South Carolina in recent years. The more conventional view, represented by Raymond Starr and Jerome Nadelhaft, depicts a society in conflict. Thus, the revolution against Britain was a conservative revolt designed to consolidate and confirm the political power of a tightly knit group of powerful men and to preserve the social position of an established elite. The conflict continued through the 1780s as the governing elite fought off challenges from radical mechanics and artisans in Charleston and underrepresented yeoman farmers in the backcountry. These challenges were repulsed, but only at the price of continuing political conflict.[12]

S. R. Matchett offers an alternative model of South Carolina politics in the late eighteenth century, arguing that the conventional view "is based on a fundamental misunderstanding of the eighteenth century Carolinian conception of politics." Matchett found the very idea of class conflict incomprehensible to the Carolinian mind. Carolinians believed a politically divided society was a weak society. Public life was in fact dominated "by a belief in the necessity of maintaining social unity and political consensus." The political culture emphasized property rights and their protection. "In a society where slaves and land were relatively inexpensive, this ideological assumption was not likely to divide society between rich and poor." The elite leadership held power because it reflected community values and interests. Political life was not dominated by conflict between an entrenched, obscurantist aristocracy and a less affluent egalitarian opposition. Rather, the Carolinian commitment to social unity enabled differences to be resolved within the established political framework. In contrast to the conflict model, Matchett thus offers a model of conti-

---

12. Raymond Starr, "The Conservative Revolution: South Carolina Public Affairs, 1775–1790" (Ph.D. dissertation, University of Texas, 1964); Jerome J. Nadelhaft, *The Disorders of War: The Revolution in South Carolina* (Orono: The University of Maine at Orono Press, 1981); Jerome J. Nadelhaft, " 'The Snarls of Invidious Animals': The Democratization of Revolutionary South Carolina," in Ronald Hoffman and Peter J. Albert, *Sovereign States in an Age of Uncertainty* (Charlottesville: University Press of Virginia, 1981).

Conclusion

nuity and stability.[13] And his interpretation of the prevailing political culture is reinforced by the prevailing legal culture, which reflected the values of leaders of the bench and bar trained at the English Inns of Court and likewise emphasized stability and continuity.[14]

Neither of these models is wholly satisfactory. There were forces for change which created tension. There were also forces strongly supporting stability and moderation. Similar forces were at work in all the states; and social conflict is not necessarily dysfunctional. A more useful model would assume a polity seeking adjustment, accommodation, common ground, and ultimate consensus in a process basically dialectical in nature,[15] would give more weight to the interplay of ideological differences within the state, and would extend the period of inquiry at least through the 1790s. In essence, this is the sort of model suggested by Thomas P. Slaughter in his recent study of the Whiskey Rebellion.[16]

Many of the issues dividing South Carolinians in the 1780s and 1790s had their origins in the pre-Revolutionary years. As to those issues, the Revolution was not a great divide. Only the terms of reference changed, as one source of authority was lopped off and another substituted in its place. As Slaughter found in the case of the Whiskey Rebellion, there was a remarkable degree of continuity from the crises of the 1760s through the crises of the 1790s. Differences between localists and cosmopolitans remained long after ratification of the Constitution, and were debated in much the same terms that they had always been. Throughout, the basic tension was between liberty on the one hand and order on the other. "When eighteenth century Americans discussed politics," Slaughter said, "they generally spoke in

---

13. S. R. Matchett, "Unanimity, Order and Regularity: The Political Culture of South Carolina in the Era of the Revolution" (Ph.D. dissertation, University of Sydney, Australia, 1980), quotes at 14 and 55.
14. James W. Ely, "American Independence and the Law: A Study of Post-Revolutionary South Carolina Legislation," *Vanderbilt Law Review*, 26 (1973): 939–71.
15. Samuel P. Huntington, *American Politics: The Promise of Disharmony* (Cambridge: Belknap Press of Harvard University Press, 1981), 1–12.
16. Thomas P. Slaughter, *The Whiskey Rebellion: Frontier Epilogue to the American Revolution* (New York: Oxford University Press, 1986), 222–28.

a shared political language" and "conceived of governance as something of a balancing act between the few and the many, the rich and the poor, the powerful and the weak." Their model was a scale "with liberty on one side and order on the other," in delicate balance between anarchy and tyranny.[17] This was the model of the Appius who addressed his fellow South Carolinians in 1787 and warned that in unsettled times following the institution of a new "machine of government" the political system would often be in tension between the extremes of anarchy and despotism. "Improper measures" would suffer it to fall into one or the other. "Skillful management" would permit it to achieve balance "at the proper point."[18]

Burke should have his place in any analysis of South Carolina's post-Revolutionary history based on tension between the concept of liberty and the requirements of public peace and order. That tension was evident throughout his public career, and his responses to it both shaped his career and helped to identify and circumscribe the areas of public controversy as the republican experiment evolved. South Carolina was by no means ideologically sterile during the post-Revolutionary period, and conflicts of interest and opinion were frequently debated in ideological terms instrumentally adapted to the issue at hand. But Burke should not be cast as an ideological type in post-Revolutionary South Carolina or as the ideological spokesman for any special interest or group. Neither reformer nor innovator, his intellectual approach to public affairs was essentially negative. He understood the tension in ideological terms but had few of the talents required for "skillful management." Singularly limited by his oppositionist orientation, he was close to the mark when he said, as he was often constrained to do, that nobody saw things as he did.

17. Ibid., 225.
18. "Appius," *SGSC*, February 22, 1787.

Note on Sources

The primary and secondary sources relied upon in this study are all cited in the notes. Accordingly, no useful purpose would be served by mere recapitulation here.

Most of the surviving Burke manuscripts have been known to historians of Revolutionary and post-Revolutionary South Carolina for many years. Burke's letters to Arthur Middleton in 1781 and 1782, for example, were published in the *South Carolina Historical Magazine* in 1925 and 1926. His famous letter to John Lamb on South Carolina's ratifying convention in 1788 is equally well known and was quoted at length in George C. Rogers, Jr., *Evolution of a Federalist: William Loughton Smith of Charleston (1758–1812)* (Columbia: University of South Carolina Press, 1962). Burke's letters in the Nathanael Greene papers and the Anthony Wayne papers at the William L. Clements Library, University of Michigan, were used and cited by Rogers in his "Aedanus Burke, Nathanael Greene, Anthony Wayne, and the British Merchants of Charleston," *South Carolina Historical Magazine*, 67 (1966): 75–83, in which Rogers for the first time identified Burke as the author of *A Few Salutary Hints*.

Burke's authorship of the *Address to the Freeman* and the *Considerations on the Society or Order of the Cincinnati*, both published in 1783, was known to his contemporaries and has been known to historians ever since. Copies of these two pamphlets are available in a number of repositories, but the only known copy of the *Salutary Hints* is that held by the American Antiquarian Society, Worcester, Massachusetts. All three are listed in Clifford K. Shipton and James E. Mooney, *National Index of American Imprints through 1800* (Worcester: American Antiquarian Society, 1969) and are reproduced in the Early American Imprint series issued by the Society and Readex Microprint Corporation, a Philadelphia reprint of the *Address* as Evans number 17861, the Charleston imprint and various reprints of the *Considerations* as Evans numbers 17863–67, and a New York reprint of the *Salutary Hints* as Evans number 19645. For general information on these and other South Carolina imprints, see Christopher Gould and Richard Parker Morgan, *South Carolina Imprints, 1731–1800: A Descriptive Bibliography* (Santa Barbara, Calif.: ABC-Clio Information Services, 1985).

The Pierce Butler papers at the Historical Society of Pennsylvania proved a fruitful source of new materials. Butler letterbooks covering the years after 1794 included a series of letters from Butler to Burke relating primarily to the controversy over the Jay Treaty in 1795–1796 and its aftermath; and letters from Peter Freneau to Butler in 1801 established Burke's unrealized desire to return to the national legislature after the Jeffersonian triumph in 1800. These letters, all cited in Chapter IX, gave substance to the otherwise fragmentary documentation dealing with the last decade of Burke's public life; and Butler's letters to Burke permitted identification of one important newspaper piece never previously attributed to Burke. In contrast, despite the affinity of their interests in the First Congress, the Elbridge Gerry papers at the Massachusetts Historical Society yielded only a few detailed references. The Theodore Sedgewick papers at the Massachusetts Historical Society and the Josiah Bartlett papers at the Dartmouth College Library were barren. So were the numerous letters of Thomas Tudor Tucker, Burke's contemporary in South Carolina politics in the 1780s and 1790s and his colleague in the First Congress, to his brother, St. George Tucker, included in the Tucker-Coleman papers, Department of Manuscripts and Rare Books, Earl Gregg Swem Library, College of William and Mary.

The sweep of the search conducted by the Documentary History of the Ratification of the Constitution Project at the University of Wisconsin and the Documentary History of the First Congress Project at George Washington University produced relevant manuscript materials, collected but not yet published, that might otherwise have been missed. However, the small number of such documents tends to confirm the overall scarcity of Burke's personal manuscripts. Only a few others were found, and those at widely scattered locations.

Given the relative scarcity of Burke manuscripts, public records, published and unpublished, and the newspapers of the period, provided the data which made reconstruction of his public life possible. For South Carolina, the records of the General

Note on Sources

Assembly collected in the South Carolina Department of Archives and History at Columbia include legislative journals, committee assignment books, committee reports, governors' messages and accompanying documents, memorials and petitions, grand jury presentments, and a variety of miscellaneous papers and records. There are, of course, many gaps, but a remarkable quantity of relevant records supplementing the journals has been preserved and indexed for the use of scholars. In addition, the surviving journals of the Provincial Congresses of 1775 and 1776, the early journals of the General Assembly and the House of Representatives to 1780, and the journals of the relevant constitutional proceedings in South Carolina have been published, as have the journals of the Privy Council for the years 1783–1789. The journal of the House of Representatives in the Jacksonborough Assembly of 1782 was published in 1916. Since 1977, the journals of the House of Representatives for the years 1783 through 1794 have been published in a modern edition, consisting of six volumes to date, each containing a useful introduction and substantial supplemental material from the records of the General Assembly. These volumes were invaluable to the present study. Full citations to the published journals to date may be found in the list of abbreviations.

The operation of the legal system in South Carolina during the years of Burke's public career is less well documented. Elihu Hall Bay, *Reports of Cases Argued and Decided in the Superior Courts of Law of the State of South Carolina Since the Revolution*, 2 vols. (New York: I. Riley, 1809–1811), selectively collects common law cases gathered from a variety of sources and is manifestly incomplete, particularly for the years prior to 1791. Henry William Desaussure, *Reports of Cases Argued and Determined in the Court of Chancery of the State of South Carolina from the Revolution to December 1813, Inclusive*, 4 vols. (Columbia: Cline and Hines, 1817) is similarly thin on the early years. Statute law is collected in Thomas Cooper and David McCord, comps., *The Statutes at Large of South Carolina*, 10 vols. (Columbia: A. S. Johnston, 1836–1841), and John F. Grimke, *Public Laws of the State of South Carolina* (Philadelphia: R. Aitken & Son, 1790). Cooper and McCord is the standard work.

Few working records of the courts have survived. The most useful are the judgment rolls of the Court of Common Pleas, 1783–1790, and the journal of the Court of Common Pleas of the

Note on Sources

Camden District, 1786–1799, both in the South Carolina Department of Archives and History. There is no institutional and political history of the post-Revolutionary development of the judicial system in South Carolina, and one is badly needed.

The debates and proceedings of the United States House of Representatives, of which Burke was a member from March 1789 to March 1791, are reported, albeit imperfectly, in Joseph Gales, comp., *The Debates and Proceedings in the Congress of the United States*, 42 vols. (Washington: Gales & Seaton, 1834–1856). The first two volumes, published in 1834, cover the proceedings of the First Congress. The *Documentary History of the First Federal Congress of the United States of America, March 4, 1789–March 3, 1791*, 6 vols. to date (Baltimore: Johns Hopkins University Press, 1972–1986), includes *The Journals of the House of Representatives*, Vol. III, Linda Grant DePauw, ed., and *Legislative Histories*, Vols. IV–VI, edited by Charlene Bangs Bickford and Helen E. Veit. In addition, the files of the project contain an extensive collection of newspaper accounts of proceedings in the First Congress and relevant manuscripts of its members. These sources, supplemented by the newspapers published in South Carolina, permitted Burke's career in the First Congress to be reconstructed in some detail.

The four volumes of *Commentaries on the Constitution: Public and Private*, John P. Kaminski, et al., eds., included in the ongoing publication of the *Documentary History of the Ratification of the Constitution*, 7 vols. to date (Madison: State Historical Society of Wisconsin, 1976–1986), contain a wealth of relevant materials. So does the *Documentary History of the First Federal Elections, 1788–1790*, Merrill Jensen and Gordon DenBoer, et al., eds., 3 vols to date (Madison: University of Wisconsin Press, 1976–1987). Vol. I, Merrill Jensen, ed., includes the materials on the elections in South Carolina.

The early history of South Carolina's newspapers is described in Clarence S. Brigham, *History and Bibliography of American Newspapers, 1690–1820*, 2 vols. (Worcester: American Antiquarian Society, 1947), II: 1023–54. Two papers, albeit under changing names, published continuously from 1783 through 1802. The *South Carolina Weekly Gazette* commenced publication in February 1783, and continued to publish thereafter as the *South Carolina Gazette and Public Advertiser*, then as the *Charleston Morning Post*, and, after 1787, as the *City Gazette and Daily Advertiser*. The *Gazette of the State of South Carolina*, which published under

Note on Sources

that name from 1777 to 1780, resumed publication in early 1783 and continued as the *State Gazette of South Carolina* and the *South Carolina State Gazette* until 1802. In addition, the *Columbian Herald* published from 1784 to 1796, the *Charleston Evening Gazette* in 1785 and 1786, and the *South Carolina Gazette and General Advertiser* (later *South Carolina Gazette and Daily Advertiser*) from 1783 to 1785. As in the case of public records, there are gaps in the coverage, but, taken together, the collection of the Charleston Library Society, supplemented by microfilm copies of issues at the State Historical Society of Wisconsin and other repositories, is reasonably complete. The Charleston Library Society collection of original papers, which is in the process of being duplicated on microfilm, is by far the most comprehensive and represents an invaluable resource for all students of early South Carolina history. As the notes reveal, these newspapers yielded a substantial amount of information bearing on Burke's public life without which the reconstruction of it would have been much less complete than it is.

For the most part, research was focused specifically on Burke. The principal exception was precipitated by the lack of data concerning his entry into the public life of South Carolina in 1778 and the initially apparent incongruity of his attack on John Rutledge in the *Address* in early 1783, later generalized and extended in the *Considerations*. These uncertainties led to research on the circumstances of the adoption of the Constitution of 1778 and subsequent developments reflected in Chapter II. Such research drew heavily on the papers of Henry Laurens collected by the Laurens Papers Project at the University of South Carolina but not yet published. Burke was not mentioned in any of those papers, but the hypotheses derived from them seem rational and persuasive.

Numerous secondary sources were consulted in the course of this study and served a variety of purposes. Some served to give context to the evidence derived from primary sources. Some suggested paths of approach to the period. Others were valuable principally as guides to relevant primary material. Those relied upon for substantive purposes are cited in the notes.

Two works merit special mention because they suggested approaches to an understanding of Burke that gave coherence to an otherwise ambiguous record. Stephen R. Boyd, *The Politics of Opposition: Antifederalists and the Acceptance of the Constitution* (Millwood, N.Y.: KTO Press, 1979), influenced the structure of the discussion of Burke as Antifederalist in Chapter VI. Kenneth R.

Note on Sources

Bowling, "Politics in the First Congress, 1789–1791" (Ph.D. dissertation, University of Wisconsin, 1968), similarly influenced the structure of the discussion of Burke as congressman in Chapters VII and VIII. In addition, Gordon S. Wood, "Conspiracy and the Paranoid Style: Causality and Deceit in the Eighteenth Century," *William and Mary Quarterly*, 39 (1982): 401–41, and James H. Hutson, "The Origins of 'The Paranoid Style in American Politics:' Public Jealousy from the Age of Walpole to the Age of Jackson," in David D. Hall, John M. Murrin, and Thad W. Tate, eds., *Saints and Revolutionaries: Essays on Early American History* (New York: W. W. Norton, 1984), 332–72, provided the basis for my understanding of the patterns and processes by which Burke evaluated current events.

Finally, something must be said of the expanding corpus of scholarly literature on republicans and republicanism. The roots of republican ideology lie deep, as Robert Shalhope pointed out in "Toward a Republican Synthesis: The Emergence of an Understanding of Republicanism in American Historiography," *William and Mary Quarterly*, 29 (1972): 49–80. The major scholarly works are Caroline Robbins, *The Eighteenth-Century Commonwealthmen: Studies in the Transmission, Development, and Circumstances of English Liberal Thought from the Restoration of Charles II until the War with the Thirteen Colonies* (Cambridge: Harvard University Press, 1959); Isaac Kramnick, *Bolingbroke and His Circle: The Politics of Nostalgia in the Age of Walpole* (Cambridge: Harvard University Press, 1968); Bernard Bailyn, *The Ideological Origins of the American Revolution* (Cambridge: Harvard University Press, 1967); Gordon S. Wood, *The Creation of the American Republic, 1776–1787* (Chapel Hill: University of North Carolina Press, 1969); and J. G. A. Pocock, *The Machiavellian Moment: Florentine Political Thought and the Atlantic Republican Tradition* (Princeton: Princeton University Press, 1975). In addition, Forrest McDonald, *Novus Ordo Seclorum: The Intellectual Origins of the Constitution* (Lawrence: University Press of Kansas, 1985), is a more recent and more eclectic treatment of the ground covered by Wood and deserves equally careful consideration by all students of its subject.

Building on the base constructed by Robbins, Bailyn, Wood, and Pocock, other scholars have sought to demonstrate the centrality of republicanism and classical republican patterns of thought during the early national period of American history. Where Wood concluded that the adoption of the Constitution marked the end of a period in which classical republicanism was transformed into a concept of government "recognizably modern," Lance Banning, *The Jeffersonian Persuasion: Evolution of a Party Ideology* (Ithaca: Cornell University Press, 1978), argued that the heritage of British oppositionist thought fundamentally shaped the Jeffersonian response to Federalist government in the 1790s and supplied the intellectual frame of reference that bound together the Republican party and justified its existence. Drew R. McCoy, *The Elusive Republic: Political Economy in Jeffersonian America* (Chapel Hill: University of North Carolina Press, 1980), accepted the republican paradigm, extended its scope to include eighteenth-century concepts of political economy, and examined the significance of such concepts for political thought in early America.

In recent years, the republican synthesis has been the subject of intensive reexamination and some criticism. In particular, its significance in the post-Revolutionary era as the core of Jeffersonian thought has been strongly questioned. Joyce Appleby, *Capitalism and a New Social Order: The Republican Vision of the 1790s* (New York: New York University Press, 1984), is illustrative. The historiographic debate is summarized in Lance Banning, "Jeffersonian Ideology Revisited: Liberal and Classical Ideas in the New American Republic," *William and Mary Quarterly*, 43 (1986): 3–19, and Joyce Appleby, "Republicanism in Old and New Contexts," *William and Mary Quarterly*, 43 (1986): 20–34. In "The Creation of the American Republic, 1776–1787: A Symposium of Views and Reviews," *William and Mary Quarterly*, 44 (1987): 549–640, twelve well-known contemporary historians commented retrospectively on Wood's *Creation of the American Republic* and Professor Wood responded. Taken together, the essays of Banning, Appleby, and the contributors to the symposium indicate the areas of disagreement among scholars and offer a reasonably complete current bibliography on the subject. Robert Shalhope, "Republicanism and Early American Historiography," *William and Mary Quarterly*, 39 (1982): 334–56, is an earlier reexamination. In general, recent work has significantly refined the republican paradigm as initially postulated by Bailyn and elaborated by Wood, Banning, and McCoy and has insisted on the continuing relevance of other strands of thought as well as the socio-economic factors previously emphasized by historians. The question is primarily one of balance, however, and the importance of republicanism and re-

Note on Sources

publican ideology to analysis and understanding of the Revolutionary and post-Revolutionary eras remains clear.

To some extent, the study of republicans and republicanism has suffered from overemphasis on the thought of a few preeminent personalities, particularly Jefferson, Madison, and Hamilton. Such emphasis is understandable but leaves a blurred picture of republican ideology in action at lower levels of political life during the post-Revolutionary years. There are few good studies following individual Revolutionary republicans through the post-Revolutionary years that assess the impact of events on their ideology and their contribution to the course of such events. Pauline Maier, *The Old Revolutionaries: Political Lives in the Age of Samuel Adams* (New York: Alfred A. Knopf, 1980), is one notable exception. George A. Billias, *Elbridge Gerry: Founding Father and Republican Statesman* (New York: McGraw-Hill Book Co., 1976), and Robert E. Shalhope, *John Taylor of Caroline: Pastoral Statesman* (Columbia: University of South Carolina Press, 1980), are the best of the individual studies. South Carolinians have been all but ignored. Previously published biographies of William Henry Drayton and Christopher Gadsden are less than satisfactory as studies of ideological orientation. Such key figures as Henry Pendleton, Thomas Tudor Tucker, and Thomas Sumter remain in the shadows.

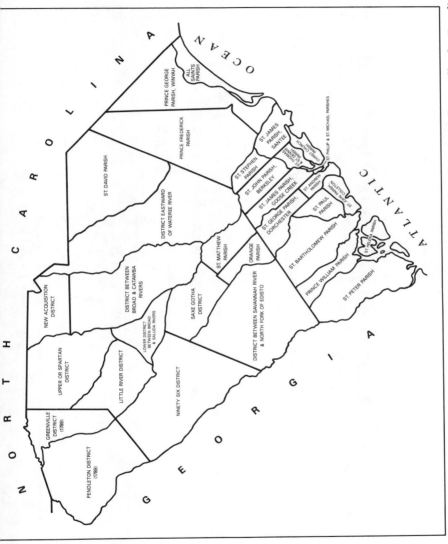

Map 1. South Carolina Election Districts, 1778–1789. In 1789, the Pendleton and Greenville election districts were created in lands ceded by the Cherokee Indians in 1777. All the other election districts were established by the Constitution of 1778, which duplicated in all material respects those established by the Constitution of 1776.

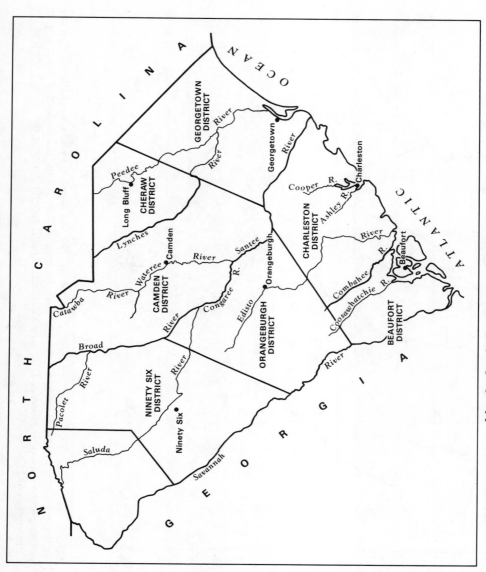

Map 2. South Carolina Judicial Districts, 1769–1790.

NORTH CAROLINA

OCEAN

ATLANTIC

GEORGETOWN DISTRICT

Peedee
Long Bluff
CHERAW DISTRICT

River

River

Georgetown
River

Cooper R.
Ashley R.
Charleston
Charleston

Lynches

Wateree

Camden
Camden
River
Santee
River

Orangeburgh
Orangeburgh

CHARLESTON DISTRICT

River

R.

Beaufort

Catawba
River

CAMDEN DISTRICT

Congaree R.

Edisto

Combahee R.

Coosawhatchie R.

River

Broad

ORANGEBURGH DISTRICT

BEAUFORT DISTRICT

Pacolet
River

River

NINETY SIX DISTRICT

River

A

Saluda

Ninety Six
Ninety Six

Savannah
River

GEORGIA

N

292

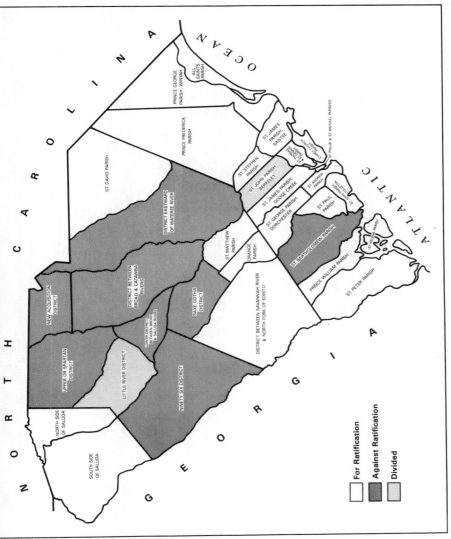

Map 3. Distribution of vote by Election Districts on ratification of the United States Constitution, May 1788. The District North of the Saluda River and the District South of the Saluda River were special districts created by the General Assembly to send delegates to the ratifying convention. Regular election districts were not established in the former Cherokee Indian Lands until 1789.

293

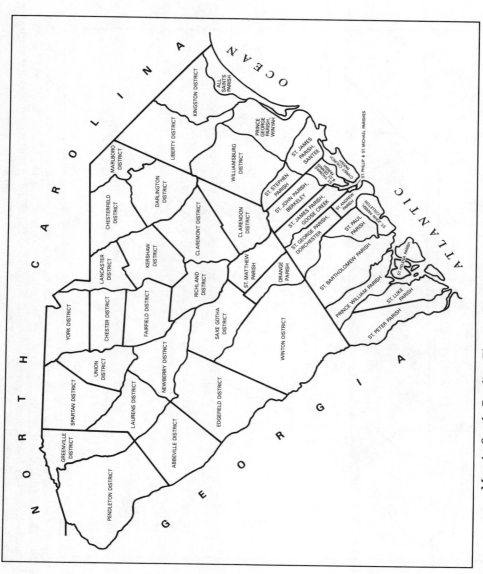

Map 4. South Carolina Election Districts under the Constitution of 1790.

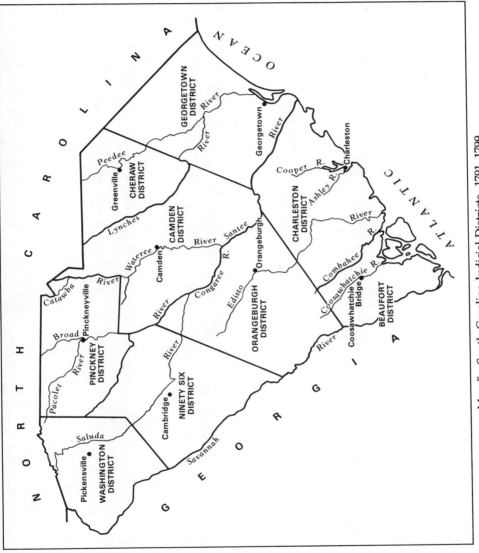

Map 5. South Carolina Judicial Districts, 1791–1799.

NORTH CAROLINA

OCEAN

ATLANTIC

GEORGIA

GEORGETOWN DISTRICT

CHERAW DISTRICT

CAMDEN DISTRICT

CHARLESTON DISTRICT

ORANGEBURGH DISTRICT

BEAUFORT DISTRICT

PINCKNEY DISTRICT

NINETY SIX DISTRICT

WASHINGTON DISTRICT

Peedee River

Greenville

Lynches River

Wateree River

Camden

Catawba River

Pinckneyville

Broad River

Pacolet River

Saluda

Pickensville

Cambridge

Savannah

River

River

Congaree R.

Santee River

Edisto

Orangeburgh

Georgetown

Cooper R.

Ashley R.

Charleston

River

Combahee R.

Coosawhatchie Bridge

Coosawhatchie River

295

Index

Index

Index

Index

Gadsden, Christopher, 37, 40, 42, 43, 48, 51, 76, 97, 110, 113, 274
Garden, Alexander, 26, 68, 149
General Assembly, S.C.
    1776, 39
    1778, 59
    1782, 63–67
    1783, 77, 101, 104–105, 107, 112–114
    1786, 124
    1787, 135, 136–138
    1788, 151
Genet, Edmond, 29, 215
Gerry, Eldridge, 88, 138–139, 169, 171
Gervais, John Lewis, 47, 52, 104n, 144
Gillon, Alexander, 105, 107, 108, 109, 110, 128
    and debtor relief, 151
    on debtors, 137
Goodhue, Benjamin, 168
Greene, Nathanael, 76, 117, 130, 193
Grimke, John Foucheraux, 25, 29, 113, 128, 154, 158
    as judge, 115, 243, 244
Grotius, Hugo, 93
Guerard, Governor, 88, 107

Hamilton, Alexander, 28, 92
    financial plan of, 182–183
    on assumption, 191
    quarrel with AB, 192–197
Hampton, Wade, 279
Harper, Robert Goodloe, 208, 217, 277, 279
    quarrel with AB, 226–227, 228–231, 233–234, 272
Hazard, Ebenzer, 46n
Heyward, Thomas, 27, 43n, 59n, 243, 244, 252
Hibernian Society, 31
History of England (Rapin), 22
History of Ireland (Keating), 22
Hobbes, Thomas, 93
Hooker, Edward, 17, 26
Hooper, George, 82
"Horatio," 121
Hornby, William, 111n
Huger, Daniel, 85, 164
Hume, David, 94
Hutson, Richard, 108

Independent Gazetteer (Philadelphia), 180
Indians, 52
Intellectual paranoia, 96
Intolerable Acts, 35
Isaac, Rhys, 15
Ithuriel, 123
Izard, Ralph, 128n, 154n, 183–184

Jackson, James, 168, 191–192
Jacksonborough Assembly, 64–67, 76, 113n, 114
Jails, 253–254
Jay, John, 88
Jay Treaty, 220–223, 224–228, 228, 232
Jefferson, Thomas, 89, 92
Jeffersonians, 10n
Johnson, Joseph, 26
Johnson, William, 128, 265
Judicial system, S.C., 24n, 29, 156–158, 264–265
    admission to practice, 24n
    character of the circuit courts, 245–246
    county courts, 275
    court opinons, 256–257
    court records, 255–256
    districts, 242, 243
    juries, 65–66, 127n, 254–255
    justices, 243–244
    sessions, 242
Judiciary Act, U.S., 173–175

Kalteisen, Michael, 128
Kean, John, 154
Keating, Geoffrey, 21
Klein, Rachel, 38

Lamb, John, 145–146
Laurens, Henry, 40, 41, 54n, 56, 57, 128, 135, 251n
Lawrence, John, 187
Law reports, 256
Lee, Richard Henry, 139
Legislative Council, 39
Liberty, 150n, 162, 273
Lincoln, James, 150
Lindsay vs. Commissioners, 261
Livermore, Samuel, 172
"Localists," 136, 150, 281

300

Index

Index

Index

Whiskey Rebellion, 216–217, 281
Winnsboro Academy, 114n
Wood, Gordon, 4
Writ of Election, 64n

"Yahoos," 12, 165, 217, 270

Zylstra vs. The Corporation of Charleston, 257–258

DATE DUE

MAY 0 7 2007			